Creative
Salesmanship:
Understanding Essentials
WITH PHENOMENOLOGICAL PROJECTS

Creative
Salesmanship:
Understanding Essentials
WITH PHENOMENOLOGICAL PROJECTS

Kenneth B. Haas

Emeritus Professor of Marketing
University of Washington

John W. Ernest

Professor of Business Administration
Los Angeles City College

GLENCOE PRESS
A Division of The Macmillan Company
Beverly Hills, California
Collier-Macmillan Ltd., London

First printing, 1969.

Library of Congress catalog card number: 75-86251

GLENCOE PRESS
A Division of The Macmillan Company
Collier-Macmillan Canada, Ltd., Toronto, Canada

Printed in the United States of America

Preface

When we decided to pool our knowledge and experience in personal selling, we found that — together and individually — we have been involved in a broad range of selling activities. While both of us have concentrated on personal selling, we have also taught salesmanship in junior and senior colleges and in high schools. We have both been responsible for guiding the sales policies of many American companies. In talking together about our work in the selling field, we found that our combined experience amounts to seventy-five years and covers a span in time of almost forty years.

Over these years, we have watched the salesman's work change radically. The old-time wheeler-dealer — who depended primarily on his personality to get by — is at a disadvantage in today's sophisticated, competitive selling market. Now, the successful salesman not only uses the traditional selling skills, but also puts to work the lessons of modern psychology, soci-

ology, economics, business research and oral communication. He learns to bring together selling skills, diverse knowledge, and an ability to watch the selling process as it happens. From this basis, he develops an intuitive understanding of how to proceed with each prospective customer.

Throughout our book, we have provided experiences and information that, we have found, help both beginning and experienced salesmen to think creatively. At the end of each chapter we have placed problems, questions, exercises and, most important, phenomenological projects which involve the students in the selling process. In short, we believe that the person who uses the suggestions in this book will be able to think creatively, pick his way through complicated human behavior patterns and return to his office with many more successful sales.

BEVERLY HILLS   KENNETH B. HAAS
1969   JOHN W. ERNEST

Acknowledgments

We are happy to acknowledge the contributions of the organizations and individuals who have supplied materials for

this book. Special thanks are extended to Prentice-Hall, Inc., for permission to use certain cases in *Case Problems in*

Creative Salesmanship and to Holt, Rinehart & Winston, Inc., for permission to use certain topics in *Professional Salesmanship.*

Donald P. Horton and Gilbert J. Black, of Sales-Marketing Executives, International, are thanked for permission to use materials written by one of the authors. We also thank Murray Shelby of Universal Publishing and Distributing Corporation for giving us permission to adapt materials from *Opportunities in Sales Careers.*

We also wish to thank the following organizations for allowing us to use their materials: the U.S. Department of Commerce, the U.S. Department of Labor, the National Association of Wholesalers, the National Auto Dealers Association, the College Placement Council and the Council on Opportunities in Selling.

About this Book

Throughout this book, the student is exposed to a variety of selling techniques; the more possibilities for enticing customers that a salesman has at hand, the more likely he is to find the technique that fits his prospective customer. In making his choice of available techniques, the salesman of today calls on many fields of knowledge. From psychology, sociology, economics, business research and oral communications, we have selected information that gives insight into the selling process. The student learns to understand *why* people buy and *how* to guide their thinking and emotional processes; further, he becomes aware of the factors that can change the situation in which he and his customer function.

The phenomenological projects are designed to enable the student to participate in the kind of selling situations that he will be facing as a salesman. We use the word "phenomenological" because, in these projects, the student examines the specific phenomena of salesmanship. We provide two kinds of phenomenological projects: role playing and case studies.

In role playing, one student pretends he is the salesperson and another pretends he is the prospective buyer. A script is provided that includes a problem to be solved and a resolution of the problem. But rigid adherence to the script is not a necessity; there are times when students delight in improvising.

After the roles have been played, the members of the class comment and offer suggestions for improvement. Interest revolves around these questions: How well did the behavior fit the role? How often and how well did the participant alter his behavior to fit the reactions of his partner? How much and in what ways did his behavior change from one part of the selling situation to another? Answers to such questions may often be obtained best from discussion of natural conflict situations, rather than from the script.

Sometimes, participants in these "plays" feel threatened and become defensive. Therefore, to be fully effective, an atmosphere of security and cooperation should be created in the classroom.

In role playing, students and teachers together can analyze and carefully examine sales situations. This technique sharpens empathy, perception, awareness and insight as related to personal marketing activities and concepts. Role playing is the only classroom technique that offers the student an opportunity to learn *how to act* in applying what he has learned.

Case studies, or reports of real-life episodes, provide situations in which facts, opinions and judgments are in conflict. The conflict leads the student to analyze, decide and act which, in turn, trains him to think critically, a habit that he will eventually need, not only in selling but in any other kind of business activity.

The object of the case-study method is to present the student with a series of problems for consideration. There often is no "correct" solution to the cases because nothing can be learned definitely until the solution is tried out in practice.

In casework the student, first, must learn what is going on within the limits of the case according to the facts on the printed page. Second, he must ask himself questions about what he has read. He learns to recognize that, before a question can be answered, it must be asked.

A student's analysis of a case in salesmanship is like a doctor's analysis of a patient's disease. The medical doctor usually has discernible facts on which to begin his diagnosis; for example, pain, discoloration or temperature. He sees the symptoms; his task is to discover the cause of the symptoms and then reach a decision that will lead to a cure. Students, too, discover facts in a case that are symptomatic of some problems. On the basis of the facts, the student can reach a decision about a course of action that, for a particular case or situation, may affect a "cure."

A doctor's diagnosis must relate specifically to his patient and not to patients or cures in general. Students, too, must proceed on the same basis. They must decide on a course of action appropriate to the specific facts in the particular situation, problem or company and not to facts, situations or problems in general. They cannot decide, for example, that "the salesman used the wrong closing method." They must state decisions in terms of why, how, what, when, where and who.

Specific steps to follow when attempting to solve a case are:

1. Read the case.

2. Discover and recognize the factors to be solved.

3. Arrange the facts in the order of their importance.

4. Set up alternatives that would possibly solve the problem or situation.

5. Make a decision based on the alternatives that may solve the problem or situation.

6. State the decision.

The questions that accompany each role and each case will help guide the student toward possible solutions.

Role playing and case studies are probably the most dynamic, practical techniques of learning ever devised for classroom use. The student analyzes and makes decisions through participating in an important experience. He is encouraged to raise significant questions. He learns to think them through on his own.

Contents

Part One

Getting Ready to Sell

Chapter One

The Role of Selling in Our Economy

The salesman is the personal spokesman for business, industry and commerce. Salesmanship is a means of communication between business and potential buyers. It is a tool used by management and field representatives of an organization to create buyer acceptance of a product, service or idea.

In this book we will emphasize the personal selling process. We will view this process as people communicating with each other about products or services provided by one group to satisfy the needs and desires of another group. The techniques of personal salesmanship create communication between seller and buyer, between maker and user, and between the person who originated an idea and the person who can be influenced to receive the idea.

Salesmanship principles are also appreciated and used by the people responsible for advertising and display. Television, newspaper and radio advertising, and marketing research techniques involving person-to-person interviews are more effective when the researchers use salesmanship principles for the purpose of motivating and persuading other people to do something about the seller's products, services and ideas.

Advertising has been described as "salesmanship in print." Display has often been referred to as the "silent salesman that moves merchandise at the point of purchase."

THE TRANSFORMING IDEA

The salesman uses the features of a product or service to influence the potential customer to buy. In other words, the salesman changes or transforms the features into a reason for purchase. This is known as the transforming idea. Nothing can bring about this transformation as effectively as the sales representative of a business organization. All modern salespeople are transformers of ideas and they all have a genuine understanding of the need for a particular product or service plus an effective technique for presenting its benefits. This kind of salesman approaches professional status because he understands why he uses transforming ideas for motivating and guiding the minds and emotions of people.

The salesman's success comes from offering a better value in a product than has been offered elsewhere, and from an imaginative idea that raises the humdrum proposition into something desirable to a prospective purchaser. The idea begins with the product, continues through its production, and reaches the prospective buyer through the way it is distributed.

SALESMANSHIP DEFINED

"A sale," according to one dictionary, "is the transfer of title in goods, property, or a service from one person to another for a consideration."

A *salesperson* is the individual who brings about the transfer. This individual is also known as a company representative, sales engineer, account executive, commercial traveler, promotion man, contact man, missionary, detailer, commission man, rack man, broker, and by many other designations. Depending on the situation and functional need, all of these titles will be used in this text.

A salesperson has also been defined as an individual so adept at understanding and handling people that he is able to persuade them to buy what he has to offer at a profit to himself, to his company and to the buyer.

The salesman is the ambassador of goodwill for his company. In this capacity, he has been described as the custodian of the firm's customers.

Salesmanship is the ability to interpret product and service features in terms of benefits and advantages to the buyer and to persuade and motivate him to buy the right kind and quality of product or service.

Consider the case example that follows; try to apply our definition of salesmanship as you read it through.

A customer enters the housewares department of a large department store and walks up to the nearest salesperson.

SALESPERSON: Good morning. May I help you?

CUSTOMER: Yes, I'm looking for something in outdoor barbecue equipment. Something to heat the coals.

SALESPERSON: Yes, ma'am, you mean a charcoal automatic heat starter. Here they are right on this table. We have several kinds. (Salesman stands by while customer makes a selection.)

CUSTOMER: Oh dear. I guess it doesn't make much difference which one I take. Barbecuing outdoors is such an ordeal. I wish I could get my husband and children to accept more of my regular recipes.

SALESPERSON: It doesn't make any difference which one you take. All charcoal lighters work the same way.

CUSTOMER: O.K. I'll take this one. (Hands the salesperson a charcoal lighter and a five dollar bill.)

SALESPERSON: That will be $3.15 out of five. I'll have your change for you in just a minute.

In this case would you say that a sale was made? Yes, we certainly can say that a sale was made. There was a transfer of title in the goods from one person (the store) to another person (the buyer) for a consideration. Can we say that salesmanship was used by the salesperson? It would seem doubtful when the definition for salesmanship is applied. No attempt was made by the salesman to interpret the product features in terms of benefits or to persuade or motivate the customer to buy. In fact, the customer appeared to be pre-sold when she entered the store. If any persuading or motivating took place, it originated with the customer herself and not with the salesman.

Incidents such as the above occur every day in our retail stores. We even find such situations in the industrial and wholesale fields. In such cases the salesperson is merely an order-taker. He is doing nothing that an advertisement or a display could not accomplish. In order to qualify as a professional salesman applying the principles of creative salesmanship, the salesman must:

1. Determine the needs or wants of the customer.
2. Present the product features to the customer in terms of benefits.
3. Help the customer find the solution to his or her problem.
4. Persuade·or motivate the customer to take action.

A professional salesman would have handled this transaction differently. Suppose the customer has chosen the charcoal lighter she wants and is handing a five dollar bill to the salesperson:

SALESPERSON: I was interested in your mentioning that outdoor barbecuing is an ordeal for you. Would you mind telling me why?

CUSTOMER: Well, you see, we don't have a nice patio so we barbecue our steaks, chicken and hamburger patties outside, and then we bring them inside to the dining room. It's a lot of work. And then I have to clean the messy grill afterward.

SALESPERSON: Those barbecue grills are rather hard to clean, aren't they?

CUSTOMER: Yes, I have to clean it in the laundry sink in the garage.

SALESPERSON: I suppose your husband and children like that barbecue flavor you get by using a grill?

CUSTOMER: Oh yes, that is the problem.

SALESPERSON: Let me show you something that might solve that problem for you. (Takes customer over to an appliance display.) Here is Farberware's open-hearth broiler that gives you an outdoor barbecue system right inside, on your kitchen drain board or dining room table.

CUSTOMER: But won't it spatter and make the air greasy and smelly?

SALESPERSON: Not a bit. There is no smoking, no spattering, no steaming with the Farberware open-hearth broiler. We can promise you that, because this stainless steel chassis is designed so that you get a perfect draft just as in a well-built fireplace.

CUSTOMER: It seems like a good idea. But I just can't believe you won't get grease or odors inside the house with the cooking out in the open.

SALESPERSON: That's exactly why you don't get grease or odors. The top of the broiler is made out of thin air. No walls, door or roof. The air can circulate freely as well as quickly. So the air you cook in doesn't have time to get greasy or smelly.

CUSTOMER: But what about steaming or smoking?

SALESPERSON: Since the air isn't boxed in, it can't get steamy. Food fats drip down through the heating element, past a zone of cool clean air, into the drip pan where they can't spatter, flame up, or smoke. And the beauty of it is, all the natural meat juices stay in.

CUSTOMER: It certainly sounds like the answer to my problem. But I imagine it's just as hard to keep clean as outdoor equipment.

SALESPERSON: That's the nicest part of it. It's very easy to clean. Everything comes apart into four pieces, like this. (Demonstrates by disassembling each part and laying the parts out in front of the customer.)

Did you notice how easy that was? Now all you do is just put the parts into sudsy water and you wash them clean in minutes. And you don't have to wash the heating element. It's self-cleaning.

CUSTOMER: How much is it?

SALESPERSON: You can have the large size with the rotisserie for $49.00, and one of the nicest things about the broiler is that it is so easy to use. The children can cook their own hamburgers themselves right in the kitchen and have that barbecue flavor without making you do all of that work which you hate. I would suggest the large size with the rotisserie. It's very light so you could take it with you right now.

CUSTOMER: I'll take the large size.

Would you say that this salesperson practiced the art of salesmanship? She certainly did. And that's what salesmanship really is — an art, not a science. Every customer must be handled as an individual. Every customer feels that his, or her, problem is a special one. Consequently, the salesman must learn to treat each customer as if he or she is a very special person. The process of determining customers' wants and needs requires techniques that can be learned only through understanding and constant practice. Did you notice how the professional picked up the remark about outdoor barbecuing being an ordeal? The salesperson recognized this remark as the root of a problem and, with a question, got the customer to talk about her prob-lem. After pinpointing the problem, the salesperson provided the answer and completed the sale.

The salesperson here used an intuitive approach to selling. This approach views the sales process as a series of separate and distinct situations in which the salesman is working with and trying to understand people and why they behave as they do. Another name for this point of view is *phenomenological*. It is the approach to be presented throughout this book.

THE MARKETING ENVIRONMENT IN WHICH THE SALESMAN SELLS

The total production of goods and services in the United States was about $840 billion in 1968. This figure is known as the gross national product, and is extremely important to everyone since it serves as a barometer for the level of prosperity in our nation. It not only measures the amount of goods and services that will be made available, but also provides a measure of the total personal income and personal consumption expenditures that will be enjoyed by approximately 205 million people. By the early 1970s we may attain a gross national product of one trillion dollars and it is estimated that our population will reach 220 million.

This rapidly expanding economy of ours points to a tremendous number of new products and services that will be pouring out of our business firms in the next decade. The U.S. consumer has exhibited a receptive attitude toward these new goods and services. Perhaps the chief reason for this receptivity is the abundant earning and spending capacity of the family. Prosperity has created for the typical American family new kinds of wants and new standards of taste and quality. There is a rising level of confidence among our customers. Indeed, ours has been described as an economy of abundance with wants that are insatiable.

The years ahead promise exciting developments for the man in marketing. Since the salesman performs his duties and responsibilities in both the consumer-goods and industrial-goods markets, he will be certain to share in the excitement.

THE MARKETING CONCEPT

Today, the big idea behind modern selling is the "marketing concept." Like many other big ideas, it is simple. Formerly, a manufacturer might have said, "This is what we make, now hit the road and sell it." Now, he says, "What does our prospective customer need and how can we help him?" Instead of being product oriented, industry is becoming customer oriented. "We don't sell equipment," says William Bader of IBM, "we sell solutions to problems."

The marketing concept is a philosophy or attitude that permeates the firm's entire organization. The company's objectives are formulated in terms of what the market needs or wants.

The production, engineering, research and development and finance divisions of the firm are all organized so that they will be broadly customer and market oriented. While engaged in carrying on their day-to-day operations, these departments do not lose sight of the consumer. When decisions are made regarding the company's products and markets, these decisions are the results of the joint efforts of all the various divisions of the company. Each of these parts of the company, having played such a role, will exercise concern over the success of the company's marketing program.

The marketing division, rather than the production division, becomes the all-important aspect of the company's operations. The sales department becomes a part of the marketing division, sharing

in the promotional mix along with advertising, display and sales promotion. The person in charge of marketing is assigned a broad range of duties and responsibilities including sales, advertising, display, product planning, marketing research, pricing and dealer relations. This person may be named vice-president in charge of marketing or director of marketing. If the product manager plan is used, this person will be the product manager, himself.

In a market-oriented company, the marketing executive will deal with the following factors:

1. The product
2. The price of the product
3. The places in which the product will be offered for sale
4. The promotion of the firm's products

These factors are called the *marketing mix* and, as the name implies, are mixed in many different ways to help the firm achieve a marketing program. If the marketing executive mixes them in the right way the firm will enjoy a successful marketing program. The product must be designed for the company's target market and constantly improved to maintain the share of the total industry sales that should go to the particular company. The price must be right for both the market and the seller. The product must be placed where it can be sold most effectively. The channels of distribution must be chosen carefully and dealers and distributors must be carefully selected and trained.

Finally, a strong and effective promotional program must be developed using all the forces of the promotional mix that will be most suited to the firm's marketing objectives and budgetary aims. Some firms will place excessive emphasis on advertising, using very little personal salesmanship. Other firms will base their marketing program on a strong sales organization. Still other firms will attempt to mix both advertising and personal salesmanship in equal proportions. Although the salesman's role is most important in those firms that concentrate on personal selling and sales promotion, the salesman will always be considered a big factor in helping the market-oriented firm achieve marketing success.

THE VARIED ROLES OF SELLING
Creative Selling

Creative selling is a term used to describe an activity which creates both discontent and buying satisfaction. It does not sell the product itself, but what the product will do.

Creative selling anticipates customer problems and the selling opportunities those problems present. It adds value to what a salesperson has for sale. It is subtle selling that finds the seller "worried about the other fellow's business." For example, this is the way an insurance salesman employs creative selling.

SALESMAN: Mr. Gavin, would you say that your present income is a pretty important factor in maintaining your family's present standard of living?

PROSPECT: Why yes, I would.

SALESMAN: And would you say that if that income was suddenly cut off that your wife and children would have to make an immediate adjustment to a lower standard of living?

PROSPECT: Yes, I guess they would. I hadn't thought of it.

SALESMAN: Your problem, Mr. Gavin, is no different than that of thousands of young businessmen like yourself. I'm here to help you solve that problem.

By your giving me the answers to a few simple questions, I can build an insurance program for you. If this program is what you want for your family and is well within your ability to pay I should get the business, otherwise I should not. O.K.?

PROSPECT: That sounds fair.

Could you see the creative selling aspects in this sales situation? Did you notice how the salesman established the general problem thus creating discontent in the prospect's mind? Did you notice how the salesman then went on to indicate that he had a solution for this problem?

The creative individual is intimately acquainted with his company's long-range sales objectives. He couples a belief in his product or service with a feeling that he is making a worthwhile contribution every time he sees a prospective buyer. Creative selling adds another dimension to selling known as *added value*. Added value is something which the perceptive, imaginative sales representative never fails to consider in a sales presentation.

Team Selling

Modern selling often requires teamwork. For example, salesmen do not try to sell a rolling mill or steam turbine or an airplane with a sales talk on a single call. It may take months of homework before the approach is made and often it is not simply a question of one person selling to another. Whole teams may be involved, and sometimes even the presidents of the companies concerned.

The Boeing Company, for example, has worked for years on some of its jet airplane sales. Before trying to sell, Boeing studies an airline's routes to determine whether it can use jets profitably. Then it tries to sell the prospect on the need for jets, and later on the need for Boeing jets. A typical presentation often involves a pile of specifications twelve inches high. The company has sixty representatives, all with good engineering experience, selling to airlines all over the world. They can call on another fifty home office experts to support their efforts.

Guided Selling

Sales are made in much the same systematic way that a house is built, an automobile is manufactured or a television set is assembled. As with any of these products, a sale is the result of certain basic steps that have been guided and controlled to assure the desired result. In selling, the salesperson can supply the guiding and control. He need not let nature take its course in hopes that a sale will be the happy outcome. Instead, he knows what must be done and can control the situation so that a sale will result.

As a salesperson, then, you should understand just what makes a sale. You should know what makes people buy and how they are guided toward favorable buying decisions. Once these basic ideas are understood, you will be able to build your selling skill upon them and obtain greater success from your selling efforts.

Selling as a Service

The extent to which the individual salesperson profits from his activities is in direct ratio to the number of people he serves and the quality of his service to them. Authorities agree, in fact, that the chief difference between the professional salesperson and the average salesperson is in the degree of service rendered.

The professional salesperson is motivated by what he can do for his prospects or customers; he carefully considers his prospect's needs and offers benefits that justify the cost involved. Since he serves his prospects well, he has many satisfied customers.

The Modern Salesmen

Modern salesmen deal with prospective buyers who are better educated and more skeptical than those in the past. Also, today's buyers dislike too much talk and too many weak claims. They want salesmen to cut out the cackle, employ controlled selling techniques and, above all, be able to prove what they claim.

Today's salesmen must be problem-solvers, motivators, and marketing experts, all in one. They must be able to cope with all kinds of people and be thoroughly conditioned and oriented toward persuading and motivating them. They should understand enough psychology to be able to thread their way through a prospect's skepticism and come away with an order.

Modern salesmanship includes procedures for orderly, planned and purposeful ways of finding new customers, new markets, and retaining the goodwill of established customers.

Through the use of marketing research and advertising, modern salesmanship aims to create among users and consumers a maximum awareness of, and a desire for, old, new and improved products and services. It also strives to provide efficient facilities through which these products and services can flow to users and consumers.

The technical age has caused a selling revolution, and a new kind of salesmanship is required. The Du Pont Company describes the new kind of salesman: "A salesman of today must offer more than a good product, he must offer, as well, the technology to go with it. Unless he shows customers how to use the product profitably, he often makes no sales ... [He] must be part scientist and sometimes part economist, sometimes part market or product-development specialist."

In addition, according to the Du Pont company, this new kind of salesman must have a broad educational background, the ability to handle people and be liked, and a knowledge of the product and its application.

A modern salesman's occupation is also distinct in other ways. First, there is little supervision over his work activities. While he is studying his prospects, his competition and his market, and especially when he is talking to a prospective buyer, he works independently. Details of what happens, what he says and does, or what the prospect says usually remain unknown to his manager.

The salesman also operates alone, without the benefit of an audience. He does not work with other employees nor is his manager in evidence. He must sell by himself, he usually travels and lives by himself when away from home, and he must often direct his own efforts. Therefore, a salesman has to provide much of his own motivation and morale, since he is often unable to obtain either from fellow salesmen.

REWARDS OF A SELLING CAREER

Successful salespeople have jobs that are secure, full of opportunity for advancement, interesting, challenging, vitally useful and well paid.

Security

Selling is one of the craft-professions that can never be replaced by machines. Good salespeople have been, are now and always will be in great demand. In our country the salesperson is important, for his efforts are necessary to sell our surplus and keep the wheels of industry turning.

The salesperson is our front line of defense against a depression. He helps industrial expansion and helps raise the standard of living for all of us. So long as our nation exists, the salesperson will have work and security because the de-

mand for good salespeople is always greater than the supply. For example, it has been stated that soon there will be a shortage of one million salespeople in the United States.

Employment Trends

For the past thirty years the number of workers in sales occupations has increased fairly rapidly. In some kinds of sales work, however, the rate of increase has been far greater than in others.

Among the large occupations which have had relatively rapid increases are real estate salesman, insurance agent, manufacturers' salesman and wholesale salesman. The smaller sales occupations of demonstrator, stock and bond salesman and house-to-house salesman have also increased rapidly. Among the slowest growing of all sales occupations during this same period has been retail sales worker, an occupation which nevertheless employs more people than all other sales occupations combined.

The main reason for the anticipated rise in employment is the prospect of increased sales resulting from rapid population growth, business expansion and rising income levels. Within retail stores, however, special circumstances have restricted employment growth in the recent past and will probably continue to do so.

Automation

According to sales authorities, it hardly seems possible that automation will greatly affect the number of employed salesmen. This fact confirms the statement that in the 1970s we shall need one million more outside salesmen, or a total of five and a half million.

However, some major companies have some form of automatic inventory control, either punch cards or computer systems. In these companies, orders are placed automatically. Consolidated Industries, for example, reports that it has tied its sales computer to its customers purchasing computer to handle the selling of industrial staples and shelf items.

Computers in the retail field maintain inventories, calculate turnover and determine order sizes. In some instances they report items that should be dropped. Routine orders are printed, and often mailed, automatically. Buyers see salesmen only when there is a change in the products, when a new product is being introduced, or on promotion deals.

The use of computers limits the salesman's ability to increase sales through his selling skills; computers do not react to persuasion and motivation. Even greater limitations to salesmanship may be on the horizon. One major food chain has experimented with the idea of eliminating salesmen altogether. After a salesman has recorded his presentation on tape, the tape and sales materials are left for an unseen buyer to consider at leisure.

In some cases, according to a Dartnell survey, "The salesman will become more of a local manager in charge of administering marketing programs, locating new customers, service and credit."

Note that automation does not affect all industries; in many, its role is small. Automation by no means eliminates salesmen. It is still true that at least 10 percent of the nation's employed will be salespeople.

Opportunities for Advancement

Most people want their future jobs to grow. In addition to paying well along the way, selling offers one of the most rapid means of reaching the top. No job provides a more well-rounded experience with a company than selling.

Dartnell Corporation has reported that approximately 55 percent of the presidents of American corporations rose from the rank of salesman. The Sales-Marketing Executives Club of Chicago has reported that, of the 250 presidents of member companies, 38 percent came directly from sales, 6 percent came from

sales and manufacturing, and 4 percent came from sales and finance. In other words, a total of 48 percent of the 250 company presidents came from the selling divisions of their businesses.

Normally, a salesperson may be promoted to a branch, district or territorial managership. Advancement opportunities for salesmen, however, are not limited to the sales field. Work areas that often need the experience of a salesperson are these: sales training, advertising, sales promotion, market research, credits and collections, and merchandising. Also, departments not related to selling, such as personnel, public and industrial relations and the like, often need workers who are good at dealing with people.

Although certain types of firms are not usually classified as sales organizations, many require that new employees have sales training because, in their jobs, such workers meet the public. Among such firms are banks, public utilities, brokerage businesses, hotels, transportation companies and certain types of restaurants.

Selling opportunities are continually arising. The experienced salespeople in a firm may be transferred to other departments or territories, may be promoted or may retire; expanding business requires additional salespeople; new businesses demand sales forces.

Ten percent of all the positions in the United States are selling jobs. The countless related positions in which sales training plays an important role raise the total to a high number. Basic training in salesmanship can be a steppingstone to a field of endeavor other than the one in which a man begins his sales career.

Former salesmen who have become topflight executives include A. N. Seares, vice-president of Sperry Rand Corporation; John A. Hoban, former president of The B. F. Goodrich Company; Charles H. Percy, former chairman of Bell and

Howell Company; James J. Nance, former president of Studebaker Corporation and later vice-president and general manager of the Lincoln-Mercury Division of the Ford Motor Company. These men have inspired many young people to choose selling as a career.

For those who are suited to it, selling offers an opportunity limited only by the individual's own ability and ambition. Selling can be an open door to a lifework that can produce all that a person may reasonably ask, both in personal satisfaction and in an assured, substantial, ever-rising income.

Interesting, Challenging Work

Do you like the excitement of travel? Do you want to see new places, meet various kinds of people, inspect new markets — or would you rather work close to home? Do you want to be your own boss, or do you prefer direction and support? Are you fascinated by dealing directly with people — watching their mental and emotional processes, their buying habits, their behavior in the marketplace? Or would you rather work behind the scenes, preparing catalogues and brochures, answering correspondence, planning advertising campaigns? All this variety and more is offered by the selling field — variety in prices, products, prospects, services, dealers, competitors, forecasting, research, promotion.

If you want a job that is interesting, challenging, exciting — a job that promises personal satisfaction — selling is the job for you.

Usefulness

Everyone in the modern community is served and benefited by salespeople, because everyone regularly uses much of the great variety of merchandise and services that are sold. Consider any item in daily use — for instance, a new and improved form of food. A salesman sold it to the grocer, who in turn sold it to the consumer. Today the automobile is commonplace, for it has been widely sold by salesmen. The electric refrigerator, the television set, the vacuum cleaner — these and thousands of other items have been sold by salesmen, who have played an important part in our American way of life.

Economists tell us that, to maintain our present economy, we must sell $300 billion worth of merchandise each year at present price levels. This would require from ten to twelve million salespeople. The salesperson is indeed indispensable in our economic system. To stimulate purchases for more and better things, greatly stepped-up sales are required to balance the supply of and the demand for merchandise.

Financial Rewards

Salesmen are well paid. A great many are so well paid that their company treasurers and their sales managers have good reason to resent the size of the checks some of their salesmen receive.

Earnings of salesmen depend almost entirely on personal effort. Pull, influence, nepotism, knowing the right people have little or no effect on his income. Successful salesmen clearly recognize that to earn more, they simply have to sell more. And there is rarely a ceiling on their income. The salesman is sure to be paid according to his effort and skill because his contribution to his company's operations can be measured and he is usually paid according to his personal production.

Highest paid salesmen for most companies receive between $10,000 and $20,000. Surprisingly, 15 percent of the companies included in one study paid their salesmen over $25,000. When compared with salaries in other fields, it is quite obvious that selling is a well-paid vocation.

The following are examples of earnings paid to salesmen:

Type of Salesman	Sells to	Annual Salary
Retail	Customers inside stores	$3,000-$ 8,000
Retail	Customers inside and outside stores	5,000- 10,000
Wholesale	Retailers	6,000- 10,000
Manufacturer's	Consumers	6,000- 12,000
Manufacturer's	Other factories	6,000- 25,000
Real estate	Property buyers	6,000- 15,000
Insurance	Buyers of insurance	6,000- 28,000

Some salesmen earn $100,000 a year, and $25,000 a year is fairly common. Many are paid as much as $50,000 yearly. College graduates entering the sales field are often paid $475 to $650 a month as initial salary, plus the cost of their training.

In addition to providing a means for advancement to a position in company management, a selling job is well compensated during the period of progress to an executive position. Although starting salaries are currently reported to be somewhat lower than those offered engineers and scientists, financial rewards in selling move ahead faster than those in other fields. At the end of ten years, outside salesmen usually are paid more than engineers and scientists.

Salesmen work hard and often under difficult conditions, but there is financial reward to compensate for the hard work. The highest-paid man in his company, reports James R. Bingay, of Mutual Life Insurance Company, is not the president, but a salesman. How much commission does a salesman earn from selling $1 million worth of insurance? "It depends on the mix, or kinds of policies, but probably over $30,000 minimum."

IMPORTANCE OF SALESMANSHIP

It is unfortunate that the average consumer forms his opinions and beliefs about salesmanship from only a limited number of selling activities: namely, order-taking in retail stores and door-to-door selling. Few people are aware of the highest level of selling; that is, the ac-tivity of selling to the industrial buyer, the wholesaler and the retailer. Few college salesmanship classes even teach about the many unseen kinds of selling, but concentrate on the kind with which students are already acquainted.

Another reason for misunderstanding the nature of salesmanship is the failure of management to match the man with the specific job or the failure of the salesperson to choose the job that matches his qualifications. When either failure occurs in job selection, no amount of training, or compensation or supervisory attention will make the person really effective, for he must possess by nature the qualifications the position demands. Unfortunately, very few sales administrators, job applicants or educators actually know the kind of person required for specific selling jobs, and they are not often aware of the importance of matching the man and the job.

Do not blindly believe that salesmanship is all good or that it is a science with laws, rules and solutions. Salesmanship is not a panacea for curing all the ills of distribution and all the errors of business judgment, nor is it a management device that can alleviate production errors. Salesmanship is not yet a profession in the sense that engineering, law, medicine and education are professions, but many people are anticipating its eventual elevation to that rank. But selling has been called "the heart of the marketing task." And we should never forget that "nothing happens until something is sold." Finally, salespeople are the keys that wind up the economy and make it tick.

The Duncan Study

A study among chief executives of important American corporations reveals that they consider personal selling the most important element in attaining marketing goals.

For many years, Charles K. Rudman, president of the Klein Institute for Aptitude Testing, had been investigating articles and books critical of the salesman, his future and his role in society. In order to get at the truth, the institute conceived the idea of a survey of those top management executives who approve the budgets and who are responsible for the direction of important enterprises.

The project was proposed to Dr. Delbert J. Duncan, a member of the institute's marketing advisory board, and professor emeritus of marketing, the University of California at Berkeley. He agreed to conduct the survey, made possible by a Ford Foundation grant for research in marketing to the Graduate School of Business Administration at Berkeley.[1]

Chief executives of 960 corporations, each with a net worth of a million dollars or more, were sent a four-page questionnaire. Some 389 of these busy men, or 40 percent, replied in depth.

They stated generally that the *salesman is becoming more important than ever*, and they supported this conclusion with facts about their own companies' operations. Let's examine the findings.

The salesman's job is becoming more important. Some 79 percent of the respondents stated that the job in their companies is becoming more important. Another 18 percent stated that no change is evident. A mere 3 percent said that the job is becoming less important than it has been before.

Most companies now employ more salesmen than in 1960. Some 74 percent of the companies are employing more salespeople than in 1960, and 18.6 percent reported "about the same number." Only 7.4 percent reported "fewer salesmen."

Most companies have increased that part of the budget allocated to personal selling. Compared to 1960, 63.2 percent have increased the proportion of their marketing budget allocated to personal selling with 29.6 percent reporting "about the same." Only 7.2 percent indicated that the portion spent for personal selling has decreased.

Chief executives anticipated larger budgets for personal selling by 1970. Almost half the presidents anticipate increases in the proportion of total marketing budget allocated to personal selling by 1970. Some 48.1 percent expect to allocate a greater percentage of net sales to personal selling by 1970; 36.4 percent, about the same; 13.2 percent, less; and 2.3 percent do not feel they are able to anticipate the situation at this time.

Personal selling is the most important element in attaining marketing goals. When asked to rank the seven most important factors in the marketing mix [reaching marketing goals, by this text's definitions], personal selling received 34.3 percent of the mentions; product research and development, 23 percent; and the five other elements, less than 15 percent each. . . .

Here is how the respondents felt about the following critical statements:

Statements	Percent Disagreed
Well-informed buyers require fewer salesmen	66.7
Salesmen have low professional standards	87.3
Advertising makes salesmen less necessary	89.1
Salesmen have low social status	92.8

---

1. Quoted by permission from the Klein Institute Survey, "What Management Thinks About Selling," *Sales/Marketing Today*, April 1, 1966, pp. 13–14.

Salesmen have	
questionable ethics	90.2
Computers will tend to	
replace salesmen	96.1
Salesmanship holds few opportunities	
for college students	98.7

The Elite Population

The consensus points to the fact that young people would do well to have selling experience, provided they are heading for managerial spots in the business world. The study relates to outside salesmen: the salesmen for firms selling to industry and to wholesale and retail channels of distribution. The outside salesperson represents what is psychologically known as an "elite population." He stands head and shoulders above the so-called man in the street.

Although significant differences exist among manufacturers of industrial goods and consumer goods, and even among those in each of these categories, note that each salesman in a sense provides jobs for about nineteen people.

Executives favor selling experience for those seeking a business career. The overwhelming response was "Yes" to the question: "Assuming your son, or other close relative, wants to become a successful businessman, would you like him to have selling experience?"

Profit from Selling

Slightly more than 76 percent of the companies report that current criticisms of salesmen and salesmanship have little or no effect on recruiting. Some 87 percent report the same about the performance or attitude of present sales forces.

What is the attitude of business executives toward salesmanship and salesmen? Obviously, management is well aware of the importance of the salesperson's function, as evidenced by these quotes from respondents to the Duncan survey:

"The salesman's role in our present economy is one of extreme importance.

I believe the entire matter can be summarized with a comment I recently read: 'Business profits do not come from making things, but from selling the things that business makes.'

"Salesmen are a company's most valuable contacts with customers and a good one cannot only get business, but can save business in many cases when problems develop with customers, as they always do. I believe that nothing can ever replace the personal touch of a good salesman.

"It takes sales and profits to build anything. When sales can be made, you can build plants, machinery, borrow money from banks, hire all the experts that it takes to run a business. But you must have sales and they must be profitable."

Because this study was made among men who manage important business enterprises — the men who know the facts and who have reported them frankly — its findings should do much to clear the air of the many misconceptions about the selling profession.

This report, it is hoped, will contribute to a better understanding of the salesman and help build his image as a potent contributor to the success of the American economy. The Duncan survey shows that, far from dying or vanishing, the salesman can look forward to greater personal opportunities than he ever could in the past.

POWER POINTS

When successful salespeople are asked why they like to sell, they invariably give these replies: freedom to manage themselves, challenging work, financial reward, job security, importance of selling, liking for people and belonging to an elite fraternity.

Freedom to manage themselves is considered something precious by these people. There is little or no supervision over their activities. They work at their own pace. What happens, what is said and done by the salesperson and the buyer, usually remains unknown to others. They consider the opportunity to be themselves, to express themselves, a very important factor in their lives.

Challenging work is considered an opportunity by successful salesmen. They welcome the opportunity to solve problems for others, to suggest new applications of their product or service, to cope with the vagaries of customer behavior and to meet new and difficult situations.

Financial reward is important to these people not only because it is an indication of their success, but also because high salaries enable them to buy the things they want. Salespeople are well paid. A great many are so well paid that they earn more than their managers.

Job Security. Selling is an occupation which can never be automated or replaced by machines. Good salespeople need never be out of work for they are now, have been and always will be in great demand. The demand for salespeople has always exceeded the supply and this alone provides great opportunity, as well as security.

Importance of selling. Everyone wants to feel that his job is important and selling satisfies that desire. No item is profit-able until it is sold and very little is sold without the help of personal salesmanship. To maintain our present economy we must sell more than $500 billion worth of merchandise each year. This would require more than 12 million retail and outside salespeople. Furthermore, each salesperson is said to keep nineteen other people employed.

Liking for people. Selling provides a wonderful opportunity for watching the mental and emotional processes of people, their buying habits, their behavior in the marketplace. In addition, salespeople have the unique personal opportunity to persuade, guide and control the behavior of others. This provides tremendous self-satisfaction for those people who like to deal with people.

Belonging to an elite fraternity. Professional salespeople consider themselves members of an elite fraternity. Salesmanship offers the greatest area of learning and experience for people on the way to top management. Approximately 50 percent of top managers in American business rose from the rank of salesman. The opportunity for advancement, the importance to our national economy, the ability to prosper personally places salespeople head and shoulders above the average man in the street.

DISCUSSION QUESTIONS AND PROBLEMS

1. How is salesmanship defined?

2. Is this statement true? "Salesmanship is the key that winds up the economy, for nothing happens until a sale is made."

3. "The salesperson is a prime factor in our economic system." Why?

4. What is the meaning of marketing concept?

5. What is meant by marketing mix?

6. What is team selling, creative selling, guided selling?

7. What will be the general trend of employment for the next ten years?

8. What is your opinion of the social and economic status of salespeople? How do salaries of salespeople compare with those of other occupations?

9. What do top management executives think about the importance of salesmanship?

10. "Personal salesmanship is the area of greatest learning and experience for executives on the way to the top." What does this statement mean? What is the source for the statement?

11. Would you advise a young person to become a salesman? What would you say to him about the advantages and disadvantages?

12. What are the chief factors revealed in the research report made by Professor Duncan?

13. Explain how the following individuals use selling and tell what they sell:

    (a) physician   (d) lawyer

    (b) carpenter   (e) store manager

    (c) teacher   (f) army captain

PHENOMENOLOGICAL PROJECTS

Henry Weber Case

Henry Weber has been a successful field representative for thirty years. The other day he said to me:

    "Do you know why I like to sell? First of all I like security. The most secure job in the world is the job of the man who can sell. There never have been enough good salespeople.

    "Second, I like to sell because of the money angle. Money: That's what everybody wants. There is no better-paid job in the world than selling.

    "The next thing I like about selling is the chance for promotion. Do you know, Ken, that 50 percent or more of the presidents of American business concerns rose from the selling end of the business?

    "I also like interesting, varied work with people. I like people and there is no job more interesting, more varied, more human, than selling.

    "Finally, I like the feeling that I am doing something for my fellow men. There is no group in America doing more to keep factory workers in jobs, raise the scale of living, and promote the general welfare than the salesperson."

Obviously, Henry Weber is "sold" on this job and he is undoubtedly a success. However, you have been reading books, pamphlets, magazines and reports about this topic, "Selling as a Career," and have certain ideas, opinions, attitudes and facts of your own.

Questions:

1. What are the key points in this case that indicate why Henry Weber is successful?

2. Are there other claims about selling that Henry could have introduced in addition to the ones mentioned?

3. What are your conclusions about the statements in this narration?

Salesmanship — An Art, Not a Science

A customer enters the furniture department of a large department store with a newspaper in her hand and walks directly to the nearest salesperson.

SALESMAN: Good morning. May I help you?

CUSTOMER: I would like to see these coffee tables you have advertised in the morning paper for $19.95. (Shows the salesman the ad.)

SALESMAN: Yes, ma'am, they are right over here. (Leads customer over to a display where he stands nearby while she examines the tables. Finally, she picks one out.)

CUSTOMER: I'll take this one.

SALESMAN: Yes ma'am. Will that be charge or cash?

Problems:

1. How would you rate this salesman? (a) above average, (b) average, (c) poor? State the reasons for your evaluation.
2. Since there is always room for improvement, rewrite this sales situation as you think a selling champion would handle it. Refer back to the section in this chapter dealing with the definition of salesmanship in order to get a good start.

Chapter Two

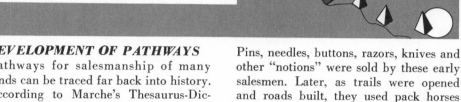

Pathways to Successful Selling

DEVELOPMENT OF PATHWAYS

Pathways for salesmanship of many kinds can be traced far back into history. According to Marche's Thesaurus-Dictionary, a person who sold was variously distinguished in early days by these designations:

> Trader, dealer, cadger (traveling or itinerant huckster), chandler (sells and makes candles, other commodities, too), chapman (a dealer in small wares), colporteur (sells or gives away Bibles and religious literature), costerman (sells fruit, vegetables), hawker (sells goods in streets by crying), higgler (peddles provisions), monger (a dealer or trader), regrader (sells and buys corn and provisions), sutler (a person who follows an army and sells goods to soldiers), vivandiere (French for a female sutler). He was also named a commercial traveler, clerk, counterjumper, packman, tallyman, duffer (English slang), canvasser, solicitor, go-between, middleman, negotiator . . . ad infinitum.

In early America, there grew up four new types of salesmen: the Yankee peddler, the credit investigator, the greeter and the drummer.

The Yankee peddler carried a pack and sold largely to back-country settlers.

Pins, needles, buttons, razors, knives and other "notions" were sold by these early salesmen. Later, as trails were opened and roads built, they used pack horses and specially built wagons.

The credit investigator traveled to make financial inspections of customers, to call on old customers, to collect past due accounts and to iron out difficulties. His goodwill-building activities gradually made him a full-time salesman who sold from samples.

The greeter was sent by wholesalers and manufacturers to hotels to greet newly arrived buyers from small-town and crossroad stores, and to invite them to visit the wholesale house or the factory represented by the greeter.

The drummer went a step further than the greeter. The drummer went to the railroad station to meet customers, and arranged for entertainment and a trip to the wholesaler's warehouse or factory. They were named "drummers" because they tried to "drum up" trade for their companies. Little by little drummers began to board trains before they reached the city; later they went all the way to the buyers' home towns.

John H. Patterson, founder of the National Cash Register Company, was the first man to recognize the need of sales training for "outside" salesmen, as well as for stimulation and supervision, sales quotas, high salaries, use of visuals, dramatizations and standardized sales talks.

Later, retail selling made great progress, too. John Wanamaker, the innovator, was the first to work for large sales volume and rapid turnover, liberal use of advertising, handsome fixtures and equipment, window displays, customer services, strict honesty, one price, and training of personnel.

From these beginnings, there developed our modern types of salesmen who may be classified by the customers to whom they sell and the services offered. These salesmen include retail, wholesale, specialty, service and several other classifications.

In the United States there are more than eight million people engaged in retail selling and approximately four and a half million engaged in "outside selling."

All kinds of selling are going on right now, all around us: the insurance man is selling ideas; a job applicant is trying to sell his personal services; the retail store owner is selling merchandise; and the instructor is trying to sell his course. Everyone who deals with people uses salesmanship: doctors, lawyers, clergymen, accountants, elevator operators and practically any other person who works for a living.

TANGIBLE AND INTANGIBLE SELLING

The first broad division of salesmanship is between tangible and intangible selling. Examples of tangibles and intangibles are:

Tangible	Intangible
coal	stocks
lumber	bonds
typewriters	advertising
autos	travel
groceries	insurance

In general, tangibles are products; intangibles are services. Some people like to sell products, or tangibles; some like to sell services, or intangibles. Some people like vanilla and some like chocolate ice cream, no one knows exactly why he makes this choice. Both are good and both are worthy.

Specialty Selling of Tangibles

A specialty has been defined as "any article of relatively high price, of fairly durable nature, nonconsumable in use, irregular in time of purchase, and in practically every case, calling for the exercise of personal selection upon the part of the buyer."

This form of selling requires considerable creativity and presents many challenges because it is admittedly not easy to take a new product, whether it is an air conditioner, a vacuum cleaner, or a new computing machine and sell it to people who are sometimes only barely aware of the need for it. When selling is so difficult, however, it also is generally associated with a higher salary, commission, bonus or other reward. In the following sections we shall present some typical examples of specialty selling.

Specialty Selling of Accounting Machines
Specialty selling of accounting machines involves a wide range of duties and responsibilities. Here is an example

Interviews. The first phase in this kind of selling is securing and conducting interviews. Prospective buyers must be selected carefully so that time will not be wasted on those who are unlikely to need accounting machines in the near future.

Conducting Surveys. Unless the prospective buyer knows what he needs as a result of the advice of a consultant or a specialist, it is necessary for the salesperson to study and survey his operations in order to recommend suitable equipment. This may be done by the salesperson himself or by a specialist employed by his company.

Presenting and Selling the Proposition. After the needs are evaluated, the salesperson can make a proposal. In guiding the prospective customer, the salesperson has an opportunity to perform creative work. Explanation and demonstration are needed to aid in the solution of the prospective customer's problems.

Closing the Sale. This is facilitated by special closing techniques explained in detail in Chapter Thirteen.

Servicing Customers. This is undoubtedly one of the most vital facets of the seller's job. Accounting machines are so technical and complicated that it is not possible to operate them without instruction and practice. The salesman is expected to educate the customer's personnel or refer them to his company's training department. As work is turned out on the machine, the salesperson will review it with appropriate company executives until everybody is satisfied that personnel is capable of operating the equipment so that it produces the desired results. Sometimes the salesperson must aid in recruiting and selecting the necessary personnel to operate the machine. He will always tell his customers about the latest equipment and methods, the users of this type of equipment in competitive industries, company publications which may be of help to him and accessory services which are available.

Handling Executive Duties. The accounting machine salesperson needs to utilize his time and talents in the most productive manner. He must (1) schedule his work and use his time efficiently; (2) get acquainted with several key men in each business; (3) analyze territory opportunities; (4) learn manufacturing methods, products, and problems of prospects; (5) maintain a list of active prospects; (6) prepare call reports and other reports as needed; (7) keep in touch with former and competitive product users; (8) constantly study competitive products, the claims made for them and the limitations of their equipment.

It will be noted that persuading and convincing prospects requires only a relatively small part of this person's time as well as skill. The bulk of this work involves preparing the survey, analyzing the prospect's needs and, after the sale is made, making certain that the customer is satisfied with his purchase and is adequately serviced to get the most out of his machine.

Specialty Selling of Automobiles

In contrast to the sale of accounting machines, selling automobiles involves devoting a great proportion of time to persuading and convincing prospects. The automobile salesman's varied duties have been listed as follows:[1]

Locating Prospects. Obviously, the first task is to locate prospective customers who either are or may be interested in buying a new car. Some prospects will appear at a showroom; others will have to be discovered by diverse methods.

Evaluating the Needs of Prospects. Since the needs, tastes and purchasing power of families vary, it is necessary to learn something of the needs of prospects. Such matters as how many in the family drive and how extensively the car is used are some of the factors used to discover and evaluate needs.

Recommending the Model. Since manufacturers make many models, the salesman can recommend the one best suited. He can show the prospect the actual car, if he has it in stock, or he can use illustrations.

Explaining the Recommendation. This

---

1. Eugene J. Kelley and William Lazar, *Managerial Marketing: Perspective and Viewpoints.* (Homewood, Ill.: Richard D. Irwin, Inc., 1958), p. 392.

is done by careful explanation and a skillful demonstration planned to show how the recommended model fits the customer's needs.

Handling Objections. Knowing the common objections made by prospects and devising effective ways of handling them is especially important in dealing with problems relating to competitive makes of cars.

Asking for the Order. At every interview the salesman must try to close a successful sale and he must take the first opportunity to ask for the order.

Handling the Trade-in. Before making an offer for a trade-in it is important to sell the new car thoroughly or else the emphasis in the sale will shift quickly from the customer buying a new car to selling his old one.

Selling Accessories. Suitable accessories should be presented and sold.

Routine Duties. These refer to the data cards which are the heart of a salesman's operations. They record information to be transmitted to the sales manager, and they must be filed properly to facilitate the follow-up of prospects. There are separate cards for (1) new prospects, (2) calls on prospects, (3) summary of sales efforts.

Executive Duties. A salesman is expected to manage his time and effort so as to facilitate and assure future business. To fill his job successfuly he must (1) mail advertising to prospects before he calls on them; (2) build his prospect list from customers, friends, canvassing and other sources; (3) set a daily objective of calls, demonstrations and appraisals; (4) read company literature, industry trade papers and competitive literature to obtain a broad knowledge of the field; (5) make a daily work plan each night for the next day's work; (6) attend sales meetings.

Building Good Will. When the salesman takes a sincere interest in seeing to it that the customer obtains the fullest measure of service that the dealer is capable of giving, he is not only doing a favor for the customer, but for himself and his employers as well. It is desirable that the salesman be present when the service manager delivers and explains the service policy to the customer. He is also expected to remind the customer to get the service provided in the policy. By calling on the customer once a month, the salesman can assure himself that the customer will be satisfied with his purchase and will, therefore, recommend him to others.

Specialty Selling of Intangibles

When a prospective customer can touch, smell, taste, or test the article he contemplates buying, there is a greater possibility of the customer imagining himself as the owner and, of course, purchasing the item.

A different approach to selling is demanded of the salesman who sells such intangibles as advertising, life insurance and investment securities. In this case, the salesman asks the prospect to exchange his money for a sheet of paper, such as a stock certificate, which may represent a share of ownership in a company a thousand miles away, making products used only in heavy industry. If the prospect could see the plant or the machines turning out the product or the orders flowing in from two hundred salesmen, it would seem more real to him. Without this opportunity, the prospective buyer of securities must depend on his imagination, and often his imagination is not sufficiently developed for him to visualize an intangible. Imaginative selling, therefore, requires the ability on the part of the salesman to paint a picture that will portray clearly to the prospect what he is buying. The salesman knows the prospect is buying not only a share in the company but also an opportunity to share in its profits and its growth. It is in making the intangible seem real and tangible that a salesman in this field performs his greatest service.

Continuity and Nonrepeat Selling

Continuity selling means calling on a steady list of customers and offering a product or a service to them. A route milkman is an illustration of this kind of selling. A wholesaler's salesman who calls on the same accounts week after week is another example.

Nonrepeat salesmen sell such items as heavy machinery, building materials and other products which ordinarily will not be purchased again, or at least not for many years. Some salesmen sell autos, appliances and other specialty items on a single-shot basis, while hoping that their selling will be on a continuity basis, at least in part.

TYPES OF SELLING
Classification of Salespeople

Classifying sales activities can be quite difficult since we must deal with so many variables which form the basis of classification. If we base our classification on the salesman's employer, we will recognize that some salesmen work for manufacturers, some for wholesalers, some for retailers. Other bases for classification are:

1. Type of product: Some salespeople sell tangible products such as stoves and refrigerators, while others sell intangibles such as life insurance and advertising.
2. Degree of prospecting: There are inside salesmen who serve customers who come to the business premises, and there are outside salesmen who call on prospects and customers in the field.
3. Complexity of the sales job: Some sales jobs are extremely simple requiring little or no training, while others

are extremely technical requiring a great amount of training and education.
4. Method of compensation: Salesmen may be paid on straight salary, or a commission basis or on a combination of both.
5. Type of market: The salesman's job may require selling to wholesalers and retailers for resale purposes, selling to industrial buyers for processing and fabricating purposes, selling to purchasing agents, selling to professional people, selling to personal consumers or selling to government agencies.

For the purposes of this discussion we shall analyze selling in terms of three broad markets and classify the various types of sales activities within each market as follows:

Consumer Selling
1. Retail store selling
2. Personal direct selling (house-to-house, specialty selling)
3. Telepurchasing (catalogue and mail-order selling, telephone and television selling)
4. Detail salesman

Wholesale Selling
1. Wholesaler's representative
2. Merchandising man
3. Promotion man

Industrial Selling
—Manufacturer's representative

Consumer Selling
The largest of these three markets is of course, the consumer market composed of approximately 200 million persons and estimated to rise to 275 million by 1985, an increase of 41 percent over 1965. Salesmen who work in this market see many prospects and customers, regardless of whether they work in a retail store or in the field. As we noted in Chapter I, consumers have many wants and needs and

the purchasing power to back them up. They have a great deal of leisure time and varied buying habit patterns which must be studied and recognized if the salesman is to enjoy above-average success. The woman is the predominant customer in this market. She owns or controls two-thirds of the personal wealth in this country. She spends over five billion dollars on her personal needs every year and is the decision-maker on the expenditure of more than $350 billion for family purposes. Of course, other important submarkets that are recognized within the consumer goods market are the leisure market, the youth market and the senior citizen market, each of which has its own peculiar characteristics.

Salesmen in the consumer market may represent manufacturers who sell direct to personal consumers, manufacturers or retailers who sell to consumers by using the mails or the telephone as the vehicle to carry their message, and retail store salespeople. We shall discuss the latter type of selling first.

Retail Store Salespeople

The professional retail salesperson considers himself both a problem-solver and a creative salesperson. He knows his stock and how to analyze the customer's needs. He knows how to introduce the right merchandise to fit those needs.

The chief characteristic of retail selling is that the customer contacts the salesman instead of the salesman going to the customer. Since many customers already know what they need or want when visiting the store, the salesman must be alert to recognize as well as to help satisfy, the customer's needs and wants. The duties of the retail salesperson will vary, of course, according to the size and type of store and its policies. In general, however, the retail salesperson must:

1. Approach and serve customers
2. Write up the sale in a salesbook or operate a cash register

3. Wrap the merchandise (where clerk wrap policies are followed)
4. Make change
5. Arrange and replenish stock
6. Keep the stock clean and neat
7. Handle complaints and adjustments

In some retail store situations, salespeople will be required to engage in outside selling, in calling on customers in their homes or places of business. Appliances and furniture stores fall into this category. Automobile dealers require their salesmen to spend a definite proportion of their time outside the showroom. Sears Roebuck salesmen selling in the building materials, roofing, fencing, plumbing and kitchen-modernization departments spend a great deal of their time in contacting prospects in their homes or offices.

Such retail salesmen are much like the direct-selling, specialty salesmen described in the next section. They have the opportunity to use creative sales ability and earn a larger income than the typical inside retail salesperson. They follow leads, solicit new business and persuade prospects to visit the store for demonstrations. This type of selling requires an amount of aggressiveness and hard work equal to that of the typical house-to-house salesman. Besides being interested in and liking people, this type of retail salesperson must possess a good imagination and lots of drive. In addition he must be able to manage his working day, since he is responsible for his own time and amount of business produced.

Personal Direct Selling

House-to-house selling accounts for approximately one percent of the total retail sales in the United States every year. Many persons think of house-to-house or door-to-door as the most typical form of selling. Actually this method of selling is relatively unimportant, as can be determined from the sales volume mentioned above.

This channel of distribution is extremely expensive to use because it involves intensive training and selling effort which must be backed up by an abundance of sales promotion and costly sales branch organizations throughout the country. Since this type of selling requires a great deal of prospecting and sales effort, it must command an income commensurate with this selling effort. Commissions for house-to-house salesmen selling such goods as cooking utensils, cosmetics, brushes and vacuum cleaners will range from 20 to 40 percent of sales. Some companies have built sizeable businesses on the basis of this method of selling. The Fuller Brush Company, for example, has more than 7,000 full-time dealers. Avon Products Inc., with more than 100,000 part-time saleswomen, has the largest sales volume of any cosmetics manufacturing firm in the United States.

Personal direct selling is also exemplified in the specialty salesman who may sell real estate, insurance or stocks and bonds. He usually works on a commission basis and attempts to build his own clientele.

The retail routeman sells and delivers to individual customers. Most retail route selling is house-to-house, as with laundry, cleaning and milk. The retail routeman has many prospective buyers, but each account is small. His chief job is to retain his established clientele, find new accounts and sell more to all accounts.

This type of salesman is usually thought of as being in business for himself, since he works on a commission and is responsible for managing his selling time. He must possess an extroverted personality and be self-assertive and persuasive. He must be a quick thinker and a good talker in order to handle customer objections quickly and easily. He should possess a constructive imagination and initiative in order to demonstrate his

product effectively and to enable the prospect to picture the benefits of his sales presentation. Because he is required to make many calls each day, he must be a hard worker with plenty of energy and enthusiasm. Often, he must convince his customers to sell for him by recommending his product or service to others.

Telepurchasing

A resurgence of an old method of selling, which has been described as telepurchasing[2] (from the Greek *tel* for far off), is emerging again in retailing. It may be thought of as "long-distance buying" in which the product is brought to the customer instead of the customer to the product. A large part of this new trend is simply a stepped-up use of the old methods of catalogue, mail order selling and telephone selling. House-to-house sales work itself may be thought of as a form of telepurchasing.

Some forms of this long-distance buying are entirely new, such as the touch-tone telephone which is hooked up to a central computer enabling shoppers to order a variety of items from their own homes. Another electronics development being considered for future use in selling is the picture phone which, when integrated into a closed circuit television, will bring this type of transaction closer to a direct selling situation.

Probably the biggest area of telepurchasing today is catalogue and direct mail sales which in 1967 amounted to approximately $44 billion in the United States. These sales were generated by the expenditure of $2.5 billion for direct mail advertising, exceeding the amount spent on either television or magazine advertising.

In its earlier forms, catalogue selling meant using the mails to promote goods displayed throughout the pages of large and elaborately-printed catalogues to rural consumers. The present trend is the mod-

2. "Telepurchasing: Major Trend in Retailing," *Forbes* (October 15, 1967), pp. 56-69.

ern catalogue store, maybe only a desk in a retail store where the customer can order from a catalogue goods that the store itself does not carry. Often this store is a separate retail outlet located in a town or small city where the company has not established a complete store.

Catalogue selling accounts for a significant share of the total sales of many old and established retailers. Sears has increased its catalogue and telephone sales offices from 984 in 1960 to a 1967 total of 1,653 and is contemplating an even greater increase in these outlets in the years ahead. The J. C. Penney Company launched its catalogue sales operations in 1962, and in 1967 had approximately 640 catalogue desks in existing stores. Catalogue sales increases have also taken place among the thousands of small, independent mail order retail firms that offer the consumer everything from food to housewares.

From this description of the various forms of telepurchasing, one might easily assume that we are dealing with an automated, non-personal type of selling that has little or no use for the art of salesmanship. But this is far from true, since the people who are responsible for planning these activities must constantly pay attention to the needs and wants of the consumers in the market. The people who prepare the sales promotion literature in the catalogue and mail order field appreciate and understand the principles of persuasion that salesmen everywhere must learn if they are to be successful. The success of a catalogue, a direct mail brochure or advertisement is based upon the effective use of selling principles. These sales promotion devices must be designed to attract attention and create interest and desire. In addition, they must win the confidence of the customer and, indeed, close the sale by inducing buying action. Although catalogues and electronic picture phones cannot close a sale,

a salesman present at the time can accomplish this goal if he or she is skilled in using salesmanship principles.

Wholesale Selling

This field of selling involves the sale of goods and services to middlemen who, in turn, resell the goods to others for a profit. Examples are selling to retailers, to wholesalers, and to industrial and commercial firms. The goods sold to these latter firms become a part of a finished product or facilitate the production of finished goods, for example, electronic condensers sold to a potentiometer manufacturing firm or the sale of soaps to an industrial firm.

The Wholesaler's Representative

The person who sells to retailers works for a wholesaler, jobber or distributor of products and may handle from 500 to 50,000 items. He literally sells from a catalogue, since he has too many items to memorize and he usually represents more than one manufacturer. He may work for two or more competitive companies that sell the same kind and class of products.

The wholesaler's representative makes regular calls and becomes well known to his customers. Often he goes directly to his customer's "want" book, checks off the items that his company supplies, writes up the order and asks for approval. At other times, he may spend hours with a customer, turning over page after page of his catalogue and price book. When the buyer sees something he needs, the wholesaler's representative enters the quantity, stock number and price in his sales book on the appropriate order form.

For many years, wholesalers' representatives were considered order-takers because it was necessary for them to write as much business as possible in their short working days. These men would frequently see one or two hundred customers a week. It was hard work but it provided a good, stable income. Substantial changes, however, have taken place in this kind of selling and today the man really sells a merchandising program. Whether it is a new drug or a different kind of cigarette, the salesman stresses the sales promotion plan his company will employ to popularize the new product and gain consumer acceptance for it. Actually he sells the sales promotion as well as the merits of the product itself.

The objective of this kind of selling is to communicate enthusiasm to the retailer and to make him feel the thrill and excitement of handling a new or improved product. The representative often gets a department store to stock his product and advertise it. Then he takes the advertisement to other stores as evidence that the product is everything he claims it to be. Salesmen who sold the first cash registers, refrigerators, television sets, vacuum cleaners or typewriters often pioneered sales in this manner. Such men and their activities are a vital force in their industries. They are action minded — they plant new ideas and they stir retailers to do something about the "marvels" that they sell.

Very few wholesale salesmen are the pressure kind. They are usually steady, reliable, friendly, always available. They must be well schooled in their field and in the needs of their customers, because an important part of their job is to keep customers posted on changes in prices, merchandising, new or special products or special sales that the company is offering.

This is well-paid, secure selling, but it takes time to master its intricacies because the salesman has to learn about so many items. Many wholesale salesmen have worked in the warehouse, stockroom, shipping room, order room and other departments of the company before

going on the road and most have also had previous selling experience.

Generally, wholesale representatives do not travel extensively. Many of them, in fact, never leave their own city or, at most, county limits although occasionally they may cover a state, especially in the West and Midwest.

The Merchandising Man

The merchandising man sells to retailers. His main responsibility is to develop a territory so that it produces the maximum volume of business for a product. Not all companies that employ merchandising men follow the same policy in fulfilling this objective. For example, one company may insist that the representative be held responsible for maximum sales volume. When he calls on retail accounts in his territory, he is directed to follow a program designed to get the dealer to buy and sell as large a volume as possible. A good example of such a program is the following procedure developed by a large food manufacturer:

1. Check stock. It is hardly possible to discuss buying without knowing what is needed; therefore, this first step is important. Food merchants are usually too busy to do this thoroughly. They welcome the salesman who checks their stock for them.

2. Discuss and take regular orders. Recommend and discuss the amount needed of the merchandise regularly carried.

3. Show the monthly special. Obtain the order for it.

4. Show other varieties. Try for an order for a product that the dealer is not carrying at the present time.

5. Discuss special sales. Make a determined effort to get company's goods on display or in dealer's advertising.

6. Service stock. Keep it clean and well organized. While this may be handled in connection with checking inventory, it may be best to defer this job to the

end of the visit while following through the seventh step.

7. Build displays. Put up signs, promotional displays and displays of merchandise.

To carry out their duties, these men may purchase stock from wholesalers. when necessary, at the regular wholesale price. They may also work with printers in preparing advertising for retailers. Besides performing sales promotion duties, these men adjust complaints and credit or replace damaged merchandise. They keep the company informed about competitive activities in their territory, new products being tested, price changes, new or changed packages and other merchandising activities. Merchandising men must also report their activities regularly and prepare expense reports and a schedule of planned calls for the next week.

Comparison of the selling operations of a variety of companies shows that success can be achieved through the use of widely differing approaches to the selling task. Generally, it is the role of sales management to determine these policies, while the job of the field men is to operate within the framework of his company's requirements.

The Promotion Man

Also called a missionary or a pioneer, the promotional man usually sells for a company that is establishing its product for the first time in a new market. Promotional men work in every field, but most commonly in those which sell to department, variety and specialty stores, as well as to drug and grocery stores. They make first calls on jobbers, wholesalers, distributors and dealers to familiarize them with the product. When a promotional man has established his product or service in one area, he moves on to another.

This man may also work the retail trade, selling and promoting the product by performing merchandising and display work much in the manner of the merchandising salesman. Since in addition to selling he offers advice on prices, problems and services to distributors and dealers, he must be well-informed about company policies and products. The promotional man needs to have teaching ability, as well as selling and promotional skills, because jobbers, dealers, distributors and other salesmen must learn from him how to sell the products. He must have initiative and imagination, and he must be able to make an appeal so attractive and convincing that buyers take his product.

So that he may coordinate his own promotion with magazine and newspaper advertising, the promotional salesman usually works closely with the company's advertising agency. Sometimes he works for the advertising agency directly, either for special campaigns or on a permanent basis.

Detail Salesman

There are two general kinds of detail salesmen: the straight detailer and the combination detailer and missionary.

Straight detailing is a routine kind of selling. The straight detailer will go into a grocery or drug store which already stocks his merchandise and proceed to check the inventory. If, for example, custom calls for six bottles of Lydia Pinkham's Compound and he finds only three on the shelf, the detailer proceeds to the stockroom, brings up three more and arranges them. He checks advertising displays and rearranges them when necessary. He also checks the amount of stock on hand to be sure it is adequate until his next visit.

He then reports to the buyer or manager and tells him of his findings. He tells the buyer what merchandise the store needs, what should be increased, what should be ordered, and finally he writes the order.

Both the drug and grocery detailer

may also show the manager or buyer how the store can increase its sales by better displays, better advertising, where and when shelf space could be used to better advantage and other operating suggestions.

The medical detailer is in a class by himself. He must be fully and accurately informed about his company's products and its claims. He must be able to talk the language of doctors, dentists, pharmacists, veterinarians, stockmen, cattlemen and other specialists. He must know his company's background, policies and services thoroughly so that he can make concise, informative presentations.

The medical detailer usually receives thorough training before he tries to sell and is closely supervised and observed during his initial selling period. After that experience, ordinarily he is responsible for his own time, his own calls and his own success.

The combination detailer and missionary salesman is usually found in the drug field. His work pattern is to call on from four to eight doctors each day with samples of his products and literature. This detailer must represent an ethical house with known ethical products, since doctors are skeptical about new products, new companies and new developments.

Instead of selling to the doctor, this salesman "details": he introduces his company's products, and describes their properties and ingredients, capability and usage. He provides documentation from authorities and information on research, tells who has used the products with what results, how long their products have been on the market and how they have been accepted by other physicians. The drug detailer usually leaves free samples and asks the doctor if he would prescribe or recommend the product to his patients.

The drug detailer then visits three to six drug stores during the same day, again introducing himself, his company and his products. He suggests that it will benefit the druggists to be able to supply the new products he has introduced to local physicians.

This kind of detail salesman may establish a new product in a store that is already a customer of his company, a new product with a new account or an established product with a new account. He may also turn the account over to a straight detailer when he has established it.

Industrial Selling

Manufacturer's Representative

This man works directly for the manufacturer and is an employee of the company. He calls on wholesalers, dealers and distributors who in turn resell to the consumer.

The manufacturer's representative is in reality an industrial salesman. He is not only a salesman, but also a contact and promotion man, advertising supervisor, sales manager, complaint handler, adjuster and goodwill ambassador. In short, he *is* the company more than any other type of salesman.

He must be a top-flight man of considerable selling experience. He must be imaginative, aggressive, emotionally well adjusted, able to manage his time and capable of making fast decisions. He must know all about his products, their use and acceptance; company policies and prices; and the benefits his products will bring to prospects. He must be able to make intelligent presentations to a buyer about a new product, a dealership or a franchise.

He must be well educated and know business operations so that he can offer advice and counsel to his buyers. He sometimes calls on established businesses, or he may develop his own outlets by setting up new distributorships and dealerships in new areas. If the product is already established, the manufacturer's representative will enlarge and increase the number of products handled, as well as the sales volume.

This man must travel. He may cover an area with a 500-mile radius, or a region or the nation. He lives out of his suitcase more than other salesmen. The person who wants to be home with his family every night will not fit into his kind of selling.

He must be able to train others to sell his product on the retail level, hold meetings, give lectures and teach salespeople how to overcome customer objections and how to close profitable sales. He must be able to inspire others to sell more.

Sometimes this salesman turns over his sales to the wholesaler, jobber or distributor, since he receives credit at any level. He must keep his manufacturer informed at all times about every aspect of the product and territory, refer back customer complaints, offer suggestions related to advertising and sales promotion in general. He actually conducts his activities as though he owned the company in his territory.

A great many top-tier salesmen prefer this kind of selling, since it offers them an opportunity to earn bigger salaries as well as to be their own boss. Compensation may be on a base salary and commission basis, but more often will be a straight commission.

This kind of selling is for the man who wants to be his own boss, has the ability and willingness to perform the tasks required and who wants to be paid in full for his planning, time and effort.

THE PROMOTIONAL LADDER

The various positions in the selling area are not always easy to classify and catalogue. The following descriptions and explanations of the more common steps up the promotional ladder may, however, be of help to the individual who is not familiar with them.

Retail Selling

Many young people are interested not only in money but also in obtaining a challenging job. Retailing offers this kind of compensation to many people; if an individual "loves" retailing, he will be well rewarded.

So far as salary is concerned in retail operations, the beginner must resign himself to starting at a rather low wage. Retail management, however, has stated that bright people can move up fast from a beginner's salary in the large stores and retail chains. The beginner can be earning from $10,000 to $20,000 in ten years. In short, if he is intelligent, loves retailing and is willing to chance advancement, he can enter a field that is challenging and worthwhile.

Actual Route to Top

From the position of salesman, the line of advancement is to head of stock, department manager, assistant buyer and buyer. The buyer in a large department store carries an important responsibility and may earn an income of from $6,000 to $30,000 a year depending upon the type of merchandise and whether the firm practices unit buying (single department buying) or centralized buying (buying a single merchandise line for all the departments).

The position above buyer is the division merchandise manager, who is in charge of a group of buyers. He must coordinate their activities and transmit policies to them from top management.

Above the division man is the merchandise manager, who is in complete charge of all merchandising activities. Finally, there is the general manager who is considered the top-ranking administrative officer of the firm.

Wholesale and Industrial Selling

The usual sales trainee in the industrial or wholesale firm has had little or no selling experience or related education; he is not familiar with the product or service. The training period may start in a company division or department connected with sales activities: receiving dock, shipping room, sales order desk or telephone sales.

These beginning jobs are provided to familiarize the novice with the company products or services, its mode of operation, its policies and other details of value to a salesman. While they are learning on the job, beginners may take correspondence courses, receive on-the-job instruction or attend formal sales-instruction classes. The training period may also include a minimum of selling under supervision. Training may extend over a period of one month to four years, depending on the needs of the company.

Junior Salesman

Junior salesmen include those who have completed their training program. Also included are salesmen who have had from one to three years of selling experience in another line or for another company. The junior is an active salesman; he starts selling immediately after his initial training. Such selling may be alone or under supervision. If he starts as a junior salesman with considerable experience, he may receive shorter initial training and move ahead much faster than the raw beginner.

Senior Salesman

This class of salesman may have had from two to twenty years of selling experience. He has come up from trainee and junior status and has obviously had much practical experience. He thoroughly knows his product, service, field and industry. He knows how to handle obstacles, manage his time, use visuals and give demonstrations. He is a qualified, able craftsman in his occupational group.

Sales Supervisor

This individual is a salesman who has been promoted to the supervision of a small number of other salespeople. In most companies he also continues to sell. He may be responsible for the field training of trainees and junior salesmen in his territory, as well as for supervision of senior salesmen. He is one of the middle-management group who stand between top sales management and the sales force. He maintains company policies; sustains and increases sales volume; travels the routes with his salesmen; turns in various sales reports; coaches, boosts morale and appraises the men who work for him.

Assistant to Sales Manager

This position is often the same as that of sales supervisor. The assistant's duties, however, may include much more than supervision, since they often entail handling paper work, statistics, chart making, study and analysis of sales reports and many other details. He may also help the sales manager organize sales meetings and prepare material for them; recruit and screen prospective salesmen; handle complaints and claims of both salesmen and customers.

Product Sales Managers

Companies with many products find it profitable to place specific responsibility for a product or group of products on the shoulders of specialists in selling them. Usually these persons do not exercise authority over the field sales force but deal only with product policy, pricing and promotion of their particular products. Some companies segregate their sales force on a product basis. At the head of each product division is a product-operating executive who is responsible for managing the men who sell one line of the company's products.

Territorial Sales Managers

There can be a great many territorial sales managers in a large company and as many as three kinds of job levels. Each one has responsibility for a certain geographical area that may be called region, division, area, district or territory; each is headed by a territorial sales manager.

In the case of the regional operation, for example, a large company may divide the nation into five big regions with a regional sales manager in charge of each. Each region may have been divided into from five to twelve territories, depending on the importance of the areas, with a territorial sales manager in charge of each. Under each territorial head, several districts would be in operation, each with a district sales manager.

The territorial sales managers have direct authority over their sales forces. In modern sales organizations they do most of the recruiting and selection of personnel. They are also directly concerned with the supervision, motivation, training and education of the salespeople.

Sales Manager

The sales manager can be a supersalesman or a top-management director of marketing.

Usually the sales manager is in charge of the administration or management of an outside sales force and its activities. With larger companies, he may be in charge of a branch, district, territory, area or region. In smaller companies, he may be in charge of the entire selling program. His duties are not the same in all organizations, but usually they include the recruiting, selection, hiring and training of salesmen. The sales manager is also in charge of organizing them into a work force and appraising the results of their work. His responsibilities include the operation of the entire sales force under his jurisdiction and all duties assigned to him by his management.

General Sales Manager

Another type of sales executive is the general sales manager. He is the adminis-

trator who is in complete charge of the sales force. His role varies among companies, but he is usually given some responsibility for price and distribution policies of his company's product. This executive is often a company vice-president and is in charge of other kinds of sales managers and supervisors. His duties are to transmit company information to his sales managers and to see that policies are carried out. He assigns and delegates responsibilities and orders throughout the sales organization.

In addition to his selling functions, the general sales manager is in charge of all company service operations. He assigns territories, branches, areas or regions; assigns quotas for each; and often establishes selling prices. He conducts market studies, anticipates trends and plans adjustments to changes. He keeps abreast of new developments in operation, organization and distribution methods. The position demands much paper work, interdepartmental conferences, sales meetings, field inspections and morale building.

Chief Sales Executive

Usually called marketing manager, director of marketing or vice-president of marketing, this individual focuses attention on the total marketing concept rather than on selling alone. In brief, the chief marketing executive's activities include all responsibilities connected with the administration of the following four major areas: product policies, pricing policies, channels-of-distribution policies and promotional policies. He is in charge of the entire marketing program for his company.

Sources For Sales Managers

A recent American Management Association survey reveals that 95 percent of all first-line sales managers are selected from within their own company. It is estimated that replacement and expansion of sales forces will require 75 percent more first-line sales managers within the next few years. Moreover, a recent Dartnell Corporation survey reveals that approximately 50 percent of company presidents and board chairmen rose from the rank of salesman.

With only a few exceptions, the practice prevails of filling sales-management positions with salesmen who have the highest sales records, regardless of their leadership or executive ability.

The rate of turnover of top management personnel is greater than popularly supposed. The American Management Association survey says, "The average corporation president's job lasts five years. In the past, companies picked lawyers, bankers, engineers or accountants to head up businesses. Men with their backgrounds are finding it difficult to cope with current business conditions. . . . You have to be a marketing man with selling experience to compete in today's opportunities for advancement."

A survey conducted by Victor Lazo of New York University, reveals that more than 60 percent of the directors added since 1950 have had marketing backgrounds. Furthermore, according to the magazine, *Industrial Marketing*, corporation presidents reported that, if a vacancy were to occur on their present boards, 19.5 percent of the vacancies definitely would be filled by men who rose from the rank of salesman.

Preparation For Selling

Marketing men view the modern salesperson as a problem-solver. He has replaced the earlier concept of the salesperson as an order-taker, and the still earlier concept of the seller as a spellbinder who was able to influence people to buy things they did not need or want.

The modern salesperson must know something about his own behavior and thinking; he must also understand the emotions, perceptions, attitudes and behavior patterns of the people with whom

he transacts business. With this psychological insight, he is able to advance from the older concept of making people buy to the newer concept of helping people buy. As a result of this new approach, the modern salesperson finds that his activities are less a matter of personal persuasion than of intelligent, planned explanation.

In today's market the person who sells is responsible for possessing complete knowledge of the economic and social significance of the product or service he sells. He must study every feature of the item, in relation to its usefulness, from the buyer's point of view.

POWER POINTS

All kinds of salesmanship are going on all around us: the insurance man sells an idea; a person applying for work tries to sell himself; the retailer sells merchandise; people try to sell others on the idea of doing what they want done.

Salespeople may be classified according to the customers they sell and the services offered. First, there is the familiar *behind-the-counter* selling, the kind done in retail stores. Then, there is *specialty* selling: the kind used in selling autos, insurance, office equipment and manufactured products of a special nature.

Specialty selling of intangibles is done by those who sell insurance, securities and similar items which cannot be touched, smelled, tasted or seen by the prospect. This kind of selling requires salesmen who can portray clearly, through words and visual aids, the benefits which will accrue to the one who buys. In other words, making the intangible seem tangible is the chief job of this kind of salesman.

Industrial salesmanship includes selling to industrial concerns, fabricators and processors who buy machinery, raw materials, equipment, professional supplies and miscellaneous items. This kind of selling requires technically trained experts and its nature varies with the kind of goods sold.

Salesmen who sell to *retailers* work for wholesalers, jobbers or distributors. These salesmen make regular calls, check stocks, communicate enthusiasm and avoid pressure. Others who sell to retailers are known as merchandising men, promoters, missionaries or pioneers.

The *selling agent* and the *manufacturer's agent* sell manufactured consumer products to middlemen. These salesmen are the ultimate in selling.

Selling to chains and wholesalers for resale is big business. Buyers for these organizations are experts who buy in accordance with carefully laid plans and detailed specifications.

Detail salesmen are of two kinds: the *straight detailer* and the *combination* detailer and *missionary*. Straight detailing is a routine kind of selling in which the salesman checks the inventory in a grocery or drugstore, suggests the purchase of whatever he believes is needed and writes up the order. The combination detailer and missionary is found in the drug field. He calls on medical doctors, drugstores, wholesalers and hospitals, leaving samples with each. He does little or no selling; he presents his name, his company name, his products and tells what his products will do.

The *contact salesman's* chief duty is to like people and cause them to like him. His main product is a likable personality. He is a public relations man, a counselor, a troubleshooter and an adviser.

Door-to-door salesmanship is another form of selling. Great skill is required to approach customers at their homes and in presenting such items as Tupperware, Easterling silver, Fuller brushes, Avon cosmetics and Watkin's products.

Wholesale selling is another form which is limited to the sale of merchandise in wholesale lots to dealers, jobbers, brokers and other bulk distributors.

Service salesmanship consists of retailing such items as cleaning and dyeing, laundry, beauty treatments, auto and jewelry repairs.

Self-service selling is exemplified by food markets where the customer chooses items displayed on counters and shelves. There is also *semi-self-service* selling, a kind of merchandising in which displays do the biggest part of selling, but with the aid of salespeople.

In addition to the normal requirements for salesmen, some companies train their men to *sell to buying groups*. These men often sell programs of continuous supply and must not only know how to do this, but also be adept in speaking before groups made up of expert buyers.

The art of persuasion enters into all selling activities. Persuasion is employed by those who sell to manufacturers, wholesalers, dealers, jobbers, door-to-door prospects and retail customers. Moreover, many businesses such as banks and public utilities, usually not thought of as selling organizations, are insisting that new employees who meet the public shall have salesmanship training. Also doctors, dentists, lawyers, teachers and other professional personnel are realizing more and more that selling skills may mean the difference between success and failure in their professions.

Each kind of salesmanship requires emphasis on different things. The industrial salesman is often an engineer who is able to offer technical advice and help solve production problems. Salespeople who sell to wholesalers and other dealers must understand the problems of these business people. Those who sell door-to-door and behind the counter must know how to deal with the vagaries of the retail customer. Basically, all salesmanship aims at convincing the prospective buyer that he will benefit if he buys the product or service offered to him.

DISCUSSION QUESTIONS AND PROBLEMS

1. Briefly describe the following types of early salesmen:
     (a) Yankee peddler   (c) the greeter
     (b) credit investigator   (d) the drummer

2. How do the selling methods for tangibles differ from those used in selling intangibles?

3. What are the differences in the techniques employed to sell automobiles and accounting machines?

4. What are the chief differences in the techniques of selling continuity and non-repeat items?

5. House-to-house selling is doomed to extinction as a selling method. Do you agree or disagree? State your arguments, both pro and con.

6. Salespeople are classified according to the nature of their jobs. Please describe the nature of, or activities involved in, the following jobs:

wholesaler's representative	industrial selling
merchandising man	detail man
promotion man	contact salesman
	manufacturer's representative

7. What basic, common requirements are necessary to succeed in all types of selling?

8. What makes a professional salesperson?

9. What kind of selling, as described in this chapter, would be used to sell each of the following products:

foreign autos	furniture
counseling service	hard water softener
industrial air conditioning	Diesel locomotives

10. From your own viewpoint, what do you believe are the advantages and disadvantages of being a salesperson? Why?

11. Do large manufacturing or industrial firms have any right to expect salespeople who call on them to give technical advice to company engineers, research men and production experts? Why?

12. After you have studied the job descriptions in this chapter, evaluate your personal assets. Do you believe that you could fulfill the requirements for any of the jobs described? Why?

13. In addition to financial rewards, what are the "psychic rewards" which salespeople enjoy?

PHENOMENOLOGICAL PROJECTS

The Wilshore Company (Case) by Victor Holmberg

"Do you need a teacher? Then I'm your man! Call me a marketing specialist if you will, or just a plain salesman. In any case, I like to specialize in solving problems and in educating customers. The more problems I can solve, the more orders come my way. The more customers I can educate, the more customers like me. In a nutshell that's how I, Tom Byrnes, sell paper. And I claim that this kind of selling depends on one factor: You've got to be able to get inside whatever company you're dealing with and analyze its operation.

"Finding a problem is not difficult, however, and once you've found one it means you're already on second base. To get on first base and into the place of business where you can see the problem, you must gain the prospect's confidence in you as a salesman and in your company as a reliable concern. The customer must be completely convinced that he is talking to an expert from a reliable house. You can do this only by making his lot easier for him by taking over his problem in which you are an expert.

"After all, the buyer's job is purchasing, not solving problems. Let me give you an example of what I mean. One firm that we do business with had been oversold by another manufacturer. I happened to observe that the product he was using was twice as heavy as it needed to be and was costing him nearly twice as much money. It wasn't the buyer's job to question the product for it was working fine, but when I showed him that he was purchasing more than double the protection he needed at more than the price of my product, he gave us his company's business. You see, I'm a trouble-shooter and a teacher. It's surprising how many mistakes a buyer can make. Sometimes they're not really mistakes, because a buyer cannot keep informed of all the new developments. Again, that's where teaching enters the picture. That's my job: finding problems, solving problems and educating the buyer.

"It takes only one or two examples of helpfulness to win the buyer's confidence completely, and I guess winning his confidence is the whole philosophy on which I operate. It sometimes takes years to develop this confidence and gain an account, but then it's our account."

Questions:

1. Does this man sell dealers, retailers, wholesalers or manufacturers?
2. How does the sales technique of this man differ from that used in other kinds of selling?
3. Is it actually possible for a salesman to know more about the uses of a product than a well-informed purchaser?
4. How do the activities of this kind of salesman differ from those of an instructor or teacher? Do you believe a salesman is an educator, instructor or teacher?
5. What other ways for winning confidence can you suggest in addition to the one mentioned in this case?

Albert Goodman: Role

Albert Goodman had been having a rugged time selling a purchasing agent. The agent was noncommittal and would not even give Al's products a tryout. The account was big and important enough to mean a great deal to Al if he could land it, but call after call produced no results. Naturally, Al gave considerable thought to possible approaches he might use.

One day during an interview with Al, the purchasing agent was called out of his office. While idly gazing around the room, Al saw a cartoon and some drawing materials on a bookshelf near the purchasing agent's desk. An idea was born!

When the prospect returned, Al resumed his presentation and managed to slip in a word about his interest in art. The prospect's mouth widened into a smile.

PROSPECT: Do you like to draw?

SALESMAN: Well, I've done some cartooning and some woodcarving . . . not much good at it . . . but it's wonderfully relaxing after a day on the road. Do you do any sketching or cartooning?

PROSPECT: I surely do. Every day I return early from lunch and amuse myself sketching some of the "characters" around here. It's the only humor I get on this job.

From this point on, the conversation became more and more friendly, while before it had been strictly a formal contest of wits. Both men discovered common interests. These common interests ripened into respect and friendship and Al Goodman walked out of the office with a warm friend and a big fat order.

Questions:

1. What psychological factors are revealed in this transaction?
2. What insights into human behavior may be acquired from studying this transaction?
3. How many ways can you name in which these insights may be used to help salespeople?
4. How would you go about improving your knowledge of psychology in the light of Al Goodman's experience?

Chapter Three

Facts Make Sales

Seven-eighths of an iceberg is under water and invisible. Seventh-eighths of a salesperson's work may also be invisible because it consists of preparation for meeting the prospective buyer. The preparatory activities are numerous, but among the more important are learning to know the product or service from A to Z, and using facts to build the salesperson's oral presentation.

There are four good reasons for knowing the facts about your product or service thoroughly: (1) to enjoy your work, (2) to overcome sales obstacles, (3) to develop self-confidence in selling and (4) to make effective sales presentations.

HOW TO ENJOY SELLING

No more impossible task exists than trying to explain to a prospective customer what you yourself do not understand. Salespeople without sufficient knowledge tend to talk in generalities, hoping to make a sale without preparation.

A salesperson who knows his product or service from A to Z is confident. If the opening remarks do not convince the customer that he will benefit from the sale, the informed salesperson is ready to elaborate, introducing new ideas. He can be patient and unhurried because he knows that he can eventually demonstrate the values and benefits of what he sells.

Knowledge is power. If a salesperson lacks knowledge, he may worry, and he may unintentionally convey his worry to the customer. The salesperson may fear that the customer will not buy; he may anticipate that difficult objections will be raised; he may fear making a mistake; or he may dread competition. Most of his tensions are the result of insufficient preparation for the sale.

Facts Overcome Obstacles

A salesperson should know his product or service thoroughly so that he will be equipped to overcome obstacles. Questions are continually arising in the minds of customers about the merits of numerous articles and services. Although many of these questions are never voiced, their answer should be anticipated and included in every sales talk.

Self-confidence is like money in the bank. A sale is based largely on confidence. The salesperson's confidence in himself is an important factor, and the customer's confidence in the product, the company or the salesperson is equally important. Confidence produces confidence, and the natural result is a sale.

Complete knowledge of your products or services and of the advantages for the

customer, develops the personal quality
of self-confidence which you yourself
feel and others readily perceive.

As soon as the customer meets you, he
can tell whether you have self-confidence.
Self-confidence is a quality you can acquire by study or training. It can come
to you as the result of your knowing all
about your products or services and what
they will do for the customer.

Facts and the Customer
All through your presentation keep clearly in mind that your facts are for customers who are really interested only in
themselves. Your customer wants to hear
facts about things that will contribute
to him, his wants, his interests, his desires and his gain.

If your facts do not appeal to your
customer's basic interest in himself, you
will not be a successful salesperson. Every
customer you meet has this question he
wants answered clearly and loudly:
"What's in it for me?"

Usually your prospect or customer will
be interested in a money gain, which
means added profits, or savings, or both.
Some prospects are also motivated by
safety, pride, competition, increased efficiency, dependability, outclassing competition, employee satisfaction. There are
other buying motives, but chances are
that the preceding are among the most
important. This you can depend on: The
success of all your endeavor will depend
on the direct benefit facts you have for
your prospect. When your proposition
appeals to *his* interests, *his* desires, *show
him a gain,* the chances are that he will
buy.

KINDS OF BENEFITS
Today, no matter what is sold or to whom
it is sold, the salesperson must have a
complete awareness of such benefits as
exclusives, values, advantages and gains.

In general, benefits are of three kinds:

(1) apparent benefits, (2) exclusive benefits, and (3) hidden benefits.

Apparent benefits are attributes anyone can see, such as the beauty of the
product or the purpose for which it was
made. These are the qualities that any
salesperson can easily recognize and that
require little explanation to the customer,
yet they play an important part in closing
successful sales.

Exclusive benefits are attributes that
competitors do not possess; therefore, they
give the fortunate salesperson a clear advantage. Many products and services owe
their popularity to the discovery of only
one exclusive benefit.

Hidden benefits, in contrast to apparent benefits, are values not recognizable
without explanation. Finding hidden
benefits requires the kind of thinking that
raises a salesperson above the mediocre
and denotes creative status. It also lifts
selling out of the humdrum and makes
it a joy instead of a chore.

Hidden benefits add strength, character and glamor to a sales talk. For example, when creative salespeople sell clothes,
they really sell personal appearance and
attractiveness. When they sell shoes, they
sell foot comfort and the enjoyment of
a brisk walk in the open air. When they
sell television sets, they really sell happiness and the pleasure of entertainment,
knowledge and good living. When they
sell furniture, they really sell a home
that has comfort and refinement. When
they sell tires, they really sell the joy of
safe driving. When they sell toys, they
really sell gifts that make children happy.
When they sell books, they really sell
education ideas, emotions, self-respect,
home life and happiness.

Facts about products, merchandise or
services must be stated in terms of what
appeals to, or benefits, customers. Customers are rarely interested in bare facts
or technical information unless such facts

furnish solutions to their buying problems or needs.

Benefits Create Interest

Professional salespeople sell benefits;
average salespeople usually concentrate
on features. People do not ordinarily buy
features!

A feature is any marked peculiarity,
anything especially prominent. Features
include such things as quality, delivery,
design, workmanship and construction.
A feature tells the prospect what the product is.

A benefit on the other hand, is whatever promotes welfare, advantage or gain.
A benefit explains why the proposition
is important to the buyer and states the
advantages of owning the product or
using the service. A benefit tells the prospect what the product will do for him.
Which would most often persuade and
motivate you to buy — benefits or features? The answer is easy: you would
buy benefits. Since your customers respond to the same influences as you, they
would also buy benefits rather than features.

THE HAMMER STORY[1]

To learn the importance of selling
benefits and knowing your merchandise
thoroughly, read the famous Hammer
Story as told by Dr. Paul W. Ivey. Doctor Ivey has effectively illustrated the necessity for knowing the facts about your
proposition in the story which follows:

The first principle of salesmanship is
to know your merchandise from A to Z,
so that you can take the value out of
your merchandise and paint a picture of
it on the customer's mind.

Many salesmen use glittering generalities instead of specific points of

1. Material from *Sales Horizons* — 2nd Edition, by Kenneth Brooks Haas and Enos C.
Perry © 1963 by Prentice-Hall, Inc., Englewood Cliffs, N.J. Reprinted with permission.

value, and then wonder why the customer does not buy.

I will illustrate this principle by an
experience I had in buying a hammer.
No matter what you are selling — hats,
shoes, automobiles, refrigerators, real
estate, insurance or what not — this
hammer story will help you to sell more
of your merchandise, provided you apply
it. Think of your merchandise as I talk
about this hammer.

One day some years ago I wanted a
hammer. I went into a hardware store,
and this is about the way the salesman
handled me:

He put a hammer in my hand, and as
I looked at it he said, "That is a mighty
fine hammer. That is a real hammer. We
sell a good many of those."

I shook it up and down as though I
were going to drive a nail, wondering
whether I should buy it or one of some
others displayed in the case.

He looked at me; I looked at him;
then we looked at each other.

After awhile he spruced up a little,
thought he had better say something
more, and said, "That is a mighty fine
hammer. That's a real hammer. You can't
go wrong on that hammer."

Nothing registered in my mind — no
value. But I absentmindedly shook the
hammer, balancing it a little, and wondered if I had better ask to look at some
of the others in the case.

He looked at me, I looked at him,
then we looked at each other.

After a while he brought in his final,
closing sales talk. He brought in his
heavy artillery, the heaviest he had. Do
you know what he said? He said, "That's
a mighty fine hammer. That's a real hammer. You can't go wrong on that hammer."

I said to myself, "Ye Gods! Is that the
way they are trying to sell merchandise
in the United States of America, the
greatest commercial nation in the
world?"

I decided I would find out. So on my
next business trip, I went into more
than one hundred hardware stores in
ten different states asking to look at
hammers, and not one salesman told me

much more about a hammer than was told to me in the first store.

If any of you want to have a little fun even now, just drop into half a dozen hardware stores and ask to look at hammers.

A short time after this experience, I went through a large mail order house in Chicago. In those days they had no retail stores and did strictly a mail-order business.

The guide took a crowd of us around, showed us many interesting things and told us many illuminating facts. He also told us the gross sales. I marveled that a company could reach out with a long arm and pull in all those millions of dollars through a mail order catalogue. Finally, a bright idea came to me and I said, "By the way, my friend, you have interested me very much; but at this particular time I am interested in one line of merchandise. What were your gross sales of hammers last year?"

"Hammers?"

"Yes, hammers."

I could see by the way he looked at me that he thought I was crazy. Now it is always a hard thing for me to know just what to do when a person thinks I am crazy; so I said, "I can see by the way you look at me that you think this ridiculous. Of course, I have never had the pleasure of meeting you before, and you have never met me, but, if you only knew it, you are looking at the greatest hammer expert in the United States."

Then he was sure that I was crazy.

Well, he did not know what to do with me, so he turned me over to another man. When you don't know what to do with anybody, turn him over to somebody else.

This other man, when he saw that I was a very inquisitive individual and wanted to know how the wheels ran in business, treated me in a wonderful way. He told me more interesting facts, showed me some more interesting things, and finally told me the gross sales of hammers.

"Do you sell all that of just hammers?" I asked.

"Yes," he replied.

"Would you mind letting me look at them?"

"Certainly not."

He brought out four. Ugh! They looked like old friends of mine.

I said, "You will pardon me, but they look like ordinary hammers. How in the world do you ever sell so many of them?" And he replied, "Maybe you will find the reason if you look in our catalogue."

I went to their catalogue, and the sales talk that I am now going to give you about a simple thing called a hammer, I read in that catalogue; and if you happen to have the latest edition of their catalogue, you will find an enlightening sales talk embodying several changes which they have made in recent editions:

First, "This hammer is full nickel-plated."

I said to myself, "I am sure some of those hammers I looked at must have been full nickel-plated."

You say, "Mr. Ivey, when you had those hammers in your hand, and looked at them, couldn't you tell whether they were full nickel-plated?"

To tell you the truth, that fact never once impressed itself upon me. All I knew was that they were "mighty fine hammers; real hammers; I couldn't go wrong on them," whatever that means.

Second, "The handles are mahogany-finished."

"Oh," I said to myself, "some of those handles I looked at must have been mahogany-finished."

You say, "Mr. Ivey, when you had the handles in your hand, couldn't you see whether they were mahogany-finished?"

I suppose I knew it in a general sort of way, but here is a company that does not believe in glittering generalities. They believe in a bull's-eye hit. Take the value out of the merchandise and paint a picture of it on the customer's mind, so the latter will want it and pay the price for it.

Third, "This hammer is made of crucible cast steel!" Now an ordinary customer might not know what crucible cast steel is, but he feels it must be some steel. It is.

Fourth, "The faces and claws are tempered just right."

What comes into your mind as a practical person? That is a test of any salesmanship. I know what comes into your mind. You say, "If the faces and claws are tempered just right, I can pull a big spike with that hammer and the claws won't break." Certainly!

Have any of you ever owned a one-claw hammer? Why, as I recall it, I was nearly twelve years old before I knew that a hammer was supposed to have more than one claw. Ours was always broken off.

Fifth, "The claws are split to a fine point."

What comes into your mind?

I know. You say, "I can pull a very fine nail with that hammer." You bet you can. Have any of you ever tried to pull a very fine nail with the hammer at your home and had the nail slip right through the claws? Then you tried again and the same thing happened; then you tried once more and it happened again? (Then you paid your respects to the hammer!)

Here is a company that says, "You can pull the finest nails with our hammers." They don't say it in so many words; they leave it to your imagination.

Sixth, "The handles are made of selected, second-growth hickory."

Not one salesman told me that. Some salesmen did say to me, "That is a mighty fine hickory handle." How fine? Mighty fine. Ugh! I can't grasp that, quite. Mighty fine!

Another salesman said, "This is a real hickory handle." I thought it might be artificial hickory.

Here is a company that says "selected, second-growth." The customer feels that this is not an ordinary handle. They have been selecting the hickory for these hammers.

Second-growth! Now what goes through your mind? People who do not know what it is may say to themselves, "Well, I guess it must be very good or they wouldn't say so"; or they may even think, "They couldn't grow it good enough the first time so they grew it the second time."

Seventh, and final, "The handles are put in with iron wedges so that they will not come loose." Does that ring the bell?

Have any of you ever had the head of a hammer fly off? At one time I used to think it was one of the functions of a hammer for the head to fly off.

Do you see this hammer?

Full nickel-plated, mahogany-finished handle, made of crucible cast steel, faces and claws tempered just right, claws split to a fine point, handles made of selected second-growth hickory, put in with iron wedges so they will not come loose.

Do you see it?

Do you know what I have done? I have gone into a retail store and had a flesh-and-blood salesman put a real hammer in my hand, and I have looked at that hammer with my own eyes; yet I have seen less value in that real hammer when I held it in my hand than when I read about a hammer in a mail order catalogue.

I take my hat off to any company a thousand or five hundred miles away that can make me see more value in a hammer when they put a cut of it on cheap paper with a description underneath than I can see when I actually have a real hammer in my hand in a retail store.

And that brings me to one of the most remarkable principles of merchandising and selling: nine people out of ten do not see what they look at. They cannot even see a hammer by looking at it. They only see what they are educated to see. Are you educating your customers to see the full value in your merchandise?

Do you think a person could come into a salesroom and look at an automobile and immediately see the style lines, the speed lines, the luxurious comfort, the staunch and reliable bumpers, the artistic instrument panel, the performance of the motor? Do you think customers can see anything by looking at it? Let us not deceive ourselves.

Take the dark glasses off the customer's eyes. Make the picture clear in the customer's mind by talking about specific, definite points of value.

Did you ever wonder why your competitor, with an inferior product, sometimes takes business away from you?

You may have better merchandise for the money than a competitor, but you lose out because your competitor makes the customer see more value in his merchandise.

This is proved by my study of hammers. Do you think that this mail order house has more value in their hammers for the money than all the hammers I saw in a hundred different stores? Do you think they have? Not on your life. I know. I am an expert on hammers.

They have excellent value for the money, but there were hammers I saw in retail stores that had drop-forged steel, instead of crucible cast steel. I have seen better hammers for the money. Did they sell as well as the mail order hammer? No. Why? They did not look as good in the customer's mind.

I have seen many a merchant put out of business, not because he did not have better goods, but because he did not know merchandise value himself and he could not make a customer see what he did not see himself. He was not a salesman.

Do you ever take it for granted that the customer sees the full value in your proposition?

When value is lower than the price, the customer loses interest.

When value is equal to the price, the customer feels that he is getting a fair deal.

But, when the salesman builds up value until it is higher than the price, then the customer feels that he is getting extra value — a bargain.

Be a creator of value.

Leave generalities for the order-taker.

Make the picture clear with specific facts.

In short, apply the "Hammer Story" to your merchandise, and you will increase your sales.

SELLING BENEFITS

It is wrong to sell only features, because they leave too much thinking to the customer and he will not or cannot think about them. You have to translate your product, service and merchandise features into benefits if you want people to appreciate whatever you are selling. Benefits do not speak for themselves; you must sell them! Imagine yourself trying to sell a proposition on the basis of features such as these:

performance	price
reputation	design
components	availability
colors	method of
taste	installation
smell	packaging
sizes	promotion
exclusives	laboratory
uses	tests
applications	terms
ruggedness	workmanship
delivery	
service	

Personal Benefits. Read the following list carefully and note how personal benefits do most of the thinking for the prospect, chiefly because they are not generalizations. They are specific and they have personal appeal.

time saved	preservation of
reduced costs	beauty
prestige	ease of operation
better health	reduced inventory
maximum comfort	low operating cost
bigger savings	simplicity
greater profits	reduced upkeep
pride of possession	increased safety
greater convenience	satisfied ambitions
uniform production	added protection
uniform accuracy	reduced waste
continuous output	self-improvement
leadership	ease and comfort
increased sales	long life
pride of	greater production
accomplishment	mental ease
economy in use	

Whenever you mention benefits as something personal, you have an added advantage. Some personal benefits can be used even in selling to a professional buyer or businessman. For example:

"This is something that will speed up your work."

"This will reduce the number of complaints you have to handle."

"The workers who use this product will appreciate your giving them a better tool."

"This is a chance for your company to get out in front of competition."

"This gives you more of the advantages enjoyed by your competitors."

Dealer Benefits. Benefits for dealers always arouse the buying interest of this group. For example:

more consumer business
more retail business
more repeat business
ease in selling
faster turnover
higher markup
lower inventory
community leadership

Old Selling Habits

When selling benefits, one should guard against a natural tendency to continue to sell features because of the natural pull of old habits of selling. Most salespeople were probably trained to appreciate their product features. The more they know about the features, the more likely they are to sell them rather than benefits. The moral is: "Sell benefits, not features!"

Feature selling has other pitfalls. For example, features imply more for the money. They suggest advanced service. That is the trouble — they only imply and suggest. They leave too much thinking to the buyer. You must translate your product, service and merchandise features into benefits to the buyer. How about you? On thinking it over, would you actually sell benefits? Or would you

really sell features while telling yourself that "benefits speak for themselves." Do they? You cannot prove that benefits speak for themselves. You must speak for them.

Side Effects of Selling Benefits

A valuable side effect accrues to the salesman who deliberately and consciously sells benefits rather than mere product features. First, when benefits are sold the salesman make a more enthusiastic, interesting and natural presentation. He will have a buoyant quality that can rarely be acquired in any other way.

Second, the salesman who sells benefits will no longer regard himself as a seeker of favors, but as one who offers them. Furthermore, with this viewpoint he will not call on prospects because he is directed to do so, but because he wants to do it. His mind will be so full of the giving attitude, rather than getting, that he will be eager to tell his good news to prospects.

Benefits Analysis

Before they try to sell a new product or service, creative salespeople get the facts about each of its features. Then they make a list of the benefits offered by those features. Since all customers want benefits for their money, you should find out the benefits your merchandise or service possesses and sell them.

The usual method of determining the benefit points of a product or a service is to list the important features. On the basis of the features, the salesman can easily determine the product benefits for the buyer.

Many salesmen prepare benefits-analysis forms that assist them in listing not only the features and exclusives of the product but also the benefits and advantages the prospect will enjoy if he purchases it. These salesmen draw up a form like Table 1.

Table 1. PROSPECT BENEFIT ANALYSIS
PRODUCT: LONG-HANDLED SHOVEL

*Product features
and exclusives*

1. Perfectly balanced handle and blade.	*Benefits, advantages and values provided by the features and exclusives*
2. Rigid lock-socket design.	Means less strain on your back. Feels comfortable to handle.
3. Steel blade and straps are forged high-carbon steel.	Prevents the blade from coming loose. Prevents the blade from breaking off when and if you happen to catch the blade on a root or other object.
4. Back strap and all seams electrically welded.	Assures a longer life for your shovel. Assures greater strength because it has uniform welding throughout, rather than common spot-welding.
5. Handles are made of selected northern ash.	Provides a strong, hard-to-break handle selected of the very best second-growth ash by men trained to choose the best wood.
6. Handles are sanded, polished and shaped.	For a comfortable grip. Splinter-proof.

How would the previous benefit analysis help a salesman make a sale? Let us study the following situation which shows how hardware salesman, Harry Green, closes a sale on shovels to a concrete building contractor. The benefit statements are in italics.

The Harry Green Success Story
The scene takes place in the builders' hardware department of a retail hardware store. The customer has removed a shovel from a display and is carefully examining it. Harry Green, a salesman who sells benefits rather than features, approaches.

SALESMAN: Good afternoon, sir. How does that feel?

CUSTOMER: Pretty good.

SALESMAN: We consider this one of our best shovels. The reason it's *so comfortable to handle* is because handle and blade are perfectly balanced. This means *less strain on the back* to the person who is using it. A pretty important point, wouldn't you say?

CUSTOMER: Yes, it would seem to. I'm a building contractor. I'll be needing a few of these for my men.

SALESMAN: Then it's pretty important to you that they have a shovel they can use *easily and comfortably in order to put out more work*. Of course you are entitled to our *contractor's discount*. How many shovels would you want, sir?

CUSTOMER: I'll be needing six right now, but I'm not sure this is the one I want yet. It seems a little high-priced (looking at the price sticker on the handle).

SALESMAN: I'm sure you're interested in *buying something that costs less* over the long run, isn't that true? Lower-priced shovels often break or splinter, causing you to discard them sooner than a shovel of this type. This means you are buying shovels more often.

For instance, sir, consider the rigid lock-socket design in this shovel. This prevents the blade from coming loose.

This should be especially important to you when working in hard ground. This shovel *will stand up and talk back to hard use.* Also notice the steel blade and the straps holding it. They are both forged with high-carbon steel. This *will prevent the blade from breaking off* when and if you happen to catch the blade on a root or hit a rock. All of this means *a longer life for your shovel.*

And notice the back straps and seams, sir. They're constructed for *greater strength and longer life* because they are electrically welded instead of just being spot-welded.

CUSTOMER: Those are good points. But our men have broken a lot of shovels, even some that have had extra strong blades and straps. They break in the handle.

SALESMAN: I'm glad you brought that up. You are wise to be concerned about the handle. The handle on this shovel is made of selected northern ash. The company that makes this shovel has skilled buyers who are trained to select only the best wood for the handles. This means *you get a strong handle.* I won't say you can't break it, but it will be *extremely hard to break.* Here, let me show you.

(Salesman places shovel on top of two tool chests, then stands on the handle. Next he sits down on the handle and lifts his feet off the ground for a second. Customer is visibly impressed.)

CUSTOMER: You sure made your point, mister.

SALESMAN: But don't forget that even though this shovel is built for heavy duty work it is *still comfortable to use,* and it's *splinter proof.* That's because the handles are sanded, polished and *especially shaped for the kind of heavy duty work you and your crew will give them.* Did you say you needed six? We have about ten in stock right now, sir.

CUSTOMER: I'll take the ten. Also, I want to look at your axes and hammers.

Motivation Analysis
Many salesmen use a motivation-analysis form to learn more about the prospect's basic reasons for buying their products or service. In the left-hand column, they list the benefits and values that they believe their proposition possesses. In the right-hand column, opposite each benefit, they explain why and how the benefit should assist in motivating people to buy. The form often used appears like Table 2.

Table 2. PROSPECT MOTIVATION ANALYSIS
PRODUCT: BENTAG WASHING MACHINE

Product Features	Buying Motives
1. Gyrofoam water action, sediment trap, roller water remover — all mean quick, easy and thorough cleaning.	Physical comfort
2. Square, one-piece cast aluminum tub.	Utility-economy gain
3. Each part skillfully made, carefully fitted. This guarantees perfect performance throughout the life of the washer.	Happiness-utility gain
4. Saves on current. Uses less soap.	Economy gain
5. Bentag means quality in washers. More than three million owners enjoy satisfied use.	To imitate, to gain pride-of-ownership

Simple analysis of the product can reveal many ways in which it satisfies the buying motives of the prospect. The preceding breakdown shows how the salient features of a washing machine may be attuned to the buying motives of a qualified prospect.

Sources for Benefit Facts

The most obvious and practical source of product facts is the product or the service itself. The salesman should study it and, if possible, use it himself to become thoroughly familiar with it.

Second, in every sales organization there is a collection of product bulletins, advertising materials, catalogues, manuals and information booklets that contain much of value to a salesman. It should be clear, however, that the salesman must study these publications thoroughly to receive anything from them, and he must then put his facts to productive use.

Other good sources are (1) fellow salesmen, (2) sales managers, (3) customers, (4) company executives, (5) library books, and (6) dealer publications.

What to look for. Several road signs serve to help the salesman who is seeking benefit facts. For example, he can examine his source materials with the following considerations in mind:

1. Concept of the product or service. What led to its creation? What is the history of its development?
2. What the product is made of. Are the materials new and different? Where are the materials obtained? How are they selected?
3. The finished product. Its appearance, quality, novelty; special or individual features, appeal, style, suitability or intrinsic value.
4. Product uses. What will it do? How can it be used? Does it have convenience, ease and speed of operation, patent features, a good service record and durability?

5. Price in relation to quality and competition.
6. Service and replacements.
7. How to care for the product.
8. Consumer recognition by consumer agencies.

Comparing with competition. To obtain a complete representation of a product or service, every aspect of it should be balanced point-by-point against competitive products or services. If a product has special benefits, values or advantages, the alert salesman gauges these in advance against competition. He gains this information through attention to competitive advertising, trade papers, personal examination of competing products and continual alertness and watchfulness as he makes his rounds.

Full-Line Knowledge

Salesmen who work for wholesalers and other distributors, as well as many who sell for manufacturers, may handle so many lines that a thorough knowledge of each one is impossible. However, they should at least be able to explain why each one has been included in their list and why the buyer will benefit from its purchase.

It is natural for a salesman to try to boost his sales volume with the easy sellers and neglect to push the slow items, even when the latter are the most profitable. But a professional salesman has enough pride to do a well-balanced job. He has considerable knowledge about his best-selling items and sufficient familiarity with the others to enable him to discuss them intelligently with buyers.

PLANNED ORAL PRESENTATIONS

One of the chief complaints of industrial buyers, as well as consumers, is that too many salespeople do not carefully prepare their sales presentations. Buyers like the kind of planned sales presentation which was made recently by a young salesman of industrial specialties who believed in organizing himself. For example, he knew the name of the buyer, the average production of the factory, the type of product that was manufactured, the approximate amount of supplies that were used and other facts about the business.

When this salesman entered the buying office and introduced himself, there was a businesslike air about him which instantly appealed to the buyer. His sales presentation was complete, brief and well-constructed. He did not force himself upon the buyer, but let his benefit facts speak for themselves. He asked the buyer to test the product before he asked for the order.

Of course, it required considerable time to prepare a sales talk of this kind, but it paid well to do so. And it is so different from the presentation of the salesman who has that "happen-to-be-near-and-just-thought-I'd-drop-in" attitude that makes it so easy to turn him down.

Even George Jessel, known as one of the greatest extemporaneous speakers, admits that the most successful of the extemporaneous speeches he has made were very carefully prepared in advance. But Mr. Jessel's art is so perfect that he makes his speeches appear extemporaneous, because he is able to give them an apparent freshness and spontaneity, even when they have been rigidly planned before he speaks.

The best trial lawyers carefully prepare each presentation in advance. Every point they expect to make is worked out, placed in its logical position and rehearsed. Just like a professional salesman, the lawyer concludes by summarizing the points he has proved. Every outstanding lawyer is actually a professional sales engineer who tries to influence the judge

and jury by proceeding through every step of the selling process.

A professional salesman emulates the professional speaker, the actor or the lawyer by leaving nothing to chance. What can the ambitious salesman do to remove the chance of errors from his oral presentation? What is the best way of presenting a proposition? What words and phrases should be used? To what motives should he appeal and in what order should he appeal to them? How can he prove that the prospect will benefit if he buys? How can he avoid making "off-the-cuff" sales talks? He can perform all of these things by preparing a well constructed, interesting sales presentation.

Planning Procedure

A prepared sales presentation requires a definite plan of procedure or action. However, it should not be inferred that a sales presentation should always be learned word for word. The ideas and the order of presentation should be learned, memorizing only a few distinctive words and phrases which are particularly descriptive or striking. These words and phrases may then serve as "memory hooks" on which to hang the entire sales presentation.

A *planned* sales presentation is the useful kind to attempt. Many salesmen write their own presentations, occasionally reviewing their manuscripts so that they can express their benefit points in the best manner and in the most effective idea sequence. They do not memorize their presentations and repeat them verbatim, but they do constantly review and strengthen them. Turn back and read the Harry Green example on page 46 again, and notice how Harry memorized and used specific points from his benefit analysis.

Outlining the Presentation

A prepared, planned sales presentation is not canned, it is not wholly memorized, and it certainly is not impromptu. It should first be outlined in complete statements rather than in words or phrases. This forces the salesman to organize and clarify his ideas and eliminate useless, meaningless words.

When the outline is complete, it should be transferred to small note cards. The salesman rehearses the talk, referring to his notes when necessary. He should rehearse at least ten times, varying the wording each time. The value of this method is to train the salesman to think on his feet and to prevent him from giving a routine presentation.

Once the salesman is familiar with the material and has practiced it many times in varying ways, he replaces the complete statement outline with an outline of key words or phrases on a single card. After more speaking practice, he throws this card away. Thereafter, he develops and refines his technique, analyzing and judging the suitability of his examples and supporting materials.

A professional salesman gives to his sales talk the same amount of interest and practice that he gives to a sport he likes. He knows that good form is the test here, the same as it is in a sport, and that good form only seems effortless — it is achieved through hard work, planning and practice.

Standardized Sales Talks

Many successful sales managers insist that their salesmen be able to recite their presentations before they are permitted to sell.

These companies claim that through the combined experience of their best salesmen they have developed the most effective sales presentations. They insist that, unless other salesmen can develop something better, they should be willing, for their own good as well as for that of the company, to use the tested methods that obtain results.

There are three possible ways to use standardized sales talks. The first way is to give the salesman complete sales information and allow him to organize and develop his own sales presentation. Second, specific sales presentations are given to the salesperson but he is instructed to give them in his own way. Third, the salesman is given specific sales talks with instructions to memorize them completely and to deliver them verbatim.

The first method is effective when the salesman is exceptional and has the ability to organize facts and translate them into usable material. For certain salesmen, the second method is more desirable, provided they acquire the substance of the complete information.

For inexperienced salesmen, the third method may be the best. It concentrates the salesman's attention on what he is going to do and not on how he is going to do it. It gives him something definite to say. It keeps him away from generalities and ambiguous statements which might create confusion rather than a clear picture of values, advantages and benefits.

The chief criticism of the memorized sales talk is that it creates a mechanical presentation. If this happens, it should be discarded, since there is nothing more ineffective than a salesman who parrots information. However, does memorizing a sales talk make the salesman mechanical? Many sales trainees and sales managers say, "No."

Some sales managers argue that although every word uttered by an actor is memorized, it does not necessarily make his performance mechanical. Why? Because the actor thinks out every idea as he goes along. He lives his part. He becomes, for the time being, the person he is portraying. Memorizing by an actor has one purpose: it acts as a guide to his thinking.

This is probably the best answer to the critic who says that memorizing anything produces a parrot-like delivery. Mechanical sales talks are not produced by memorizing, but by lack of thinking. There are many mechanical salesmen who have never memorized anything. They have merely developed through numerous repetitions a sales talk of their own with no planning or logical development.

Every professional salesman has a prepared sales talk whether he develops it himself or someone develops it for him. What is needed is to produce the most effective sales talk possible, and it can be developed only when based on sound planning and organization.

Preparing for Buying Committees

More and more often salesmen are finding it necessary to sell to a purchasing committee instead of to one buyer. This is particularly true in the food field, where committee buying now accounts for as much as 80 percent of sales volume and is soon expected to increase another 15 percent.

The growth of large business units and the decline of small ones has caused this shift from traditional buying methods. The supermarket, stocking more than 4,000 different items of merchandise, is an example. The purchase of such a great variety and volume of merchandise could not be performed through a simple salesman-to-buyer relationship. The movement away from person-to-person selling has caused the men who sell big accounts to employ a more formal group-audience approach.

As in all good salesmanship, the group-audience approach requires adequate preparation by the sales representative. Before the meeting, the salesman may try to talk to each committee member to introduce his proposition, as well as to learn something about each individual's interests, attitudes, behavior pattern, experience and education. He may attempt to discover their opinions of his product or service. If he cannot meet everyone on the committee, he may try to discover the strongest personality in the group and talk to him. He may also find it advantageous, when possible, to have an advance talk with the member who usually raises the most objections. This kind of salesman also studies a prospect's current purchases or use of competitive products or services. He tries to discover the strong and weak points of his competition and what complaints the prospect may have about the competing product or service.

An important part of the salesman's preparation should be to plan an agenda of the major points to be presented. This might be in the form of a schedule, showing the time limits for each part of the presentation.

Next, the salesman should prepare a specification sheet stating briefly the chief advantages, benefits, values, services, conditions and other facts of interest to the committee. A copy of the specification sheet should be given to each member of the buying group at the start of the meeting.

Finally, a rehearsal is needed. This should be somewhat like a theatrical production, and it demands practice on the part of the salesman. If a mechanical product is being presented, a cast of characters may be needed in the presentation, corresponding to the makeup of the buying committee: engineers, finance men, accountants and researchers. The sales representative's purpose is to have enough specialists on his team to satisfy the needs of the buying group and to make an effective presentation.

POWER POINTS

Sales of any consequence are said to be more *the result of preparation* than of selling techniques. The battlefield is no place to plan, and by the same rule, preparatory planning of the presentation cannot be delayed until the salesman is facing the prospect. It must be done long in advance of the interview.

Product knowledge, features, characteristics, specifications, performance, advantages, benefits and competitive differences are things the salesman must know perfectly and in detail. These things are his tools, and he must have them stored in his mind for use *in toto* or by single items.

To paraphrase Peter F. Drucker, the salesman has a specific tool: *Information*. He does not "handle" people; he motivates, guides and organizes people to do their own thinking. His chief tool for all this is oral communication.

DISCUSSION QUESTIONS AND PROBLEMS

1. Briefly explain the iceberg principle and why it is important to the salesman.
2. What are four good reasons for knowing the facts about your product?
3. How can a complete knowledge of his product increase a salesman's income?
4. If you were selling in a hardware store and a customer asked you if the mixing valve needed a volume regulator and you did not know, what would you say?
5. Can a salesman know too much about his product?
6. What is the right way to use facts in a sales presentation?
7. What information would you need about women's shoes before going on the selling floor? About men's shoes?
8. Should a salesman listen to people who find fault with his product? Explain.
9. What are the three types of benefits? Describe each briefly.
10. What is a feature? A benefit?
11. What is a benefits analysis? How can it help the salesman?
12. What is a motivation analysis? How does it differ from a benefits analysis?
13. Where does the salesman get facts and product knowledge about the product he sells and the company he works for?
14. Bring an item to class that you have purchased recently. Prepare a benefits analysis on it. Be prepared to talk about its selling features and benefits before the entire class.
15. What is a standardized sales talk?

PHENOMENOLOGICAL PROJECTS

Swift and Company
Assume that you are selling for Swift and Company and that 90 percent of your effort is expended in selling to buying committees. Prepare a sales presentation and situation plan for yourself. Give the complete details to your group about how you would proceed to sell a one month's supply of beef to a committee representing a large chain of supermarkets. In addition to this chapter, you may wish to reread material in Chapters I and II.

Hotel Corporation
Assume that you are a salesman for the manufacturer and distributor of a very fine cleaning compound and disinfectant used by restaurants, hotels and institutions.
1. Outline and be prepared to give the sales presentation that you would use to sell

your product to a hotel buyer who is not now a customer. What sales points would you emphasize? How would you start your presentation? What would you say to attract his attention and stimulate his interest?

2. Would your presentation be different if you were selling to the owner of a small restaurant?

3. Would you use a *planned* or a *standard* sales talk?

4. If you found yourself becoming stale, how would you correct the condition?

Preparing a Benefit Analysis

Assume that you are selling kitchen appliances. Prepare a benefit analysis form from the following factual information about a built-in double oven.

1. Oven-control for self-cleaning. Allows you to clean the oven automatically by electrically burning out spillings, dripping and particles at extremely high temperatures. All you do is (1) move the door latch to clean (2) set oven control to clean, and (3) set oven timer to desired length of cleaning cycle. The self-cleaning oven takes over, using the same electricity you use to cook your food.

2. Meat thermometer which can be inserted in a roast or steak and set by dial for degree of cooking desired (rare, medium, well). A buzzer sounds when meat is ready.

3. Easy-set oven timer. Turns either oven on or off automatically. Just set start and stop times. Separate minute timer signals one to 60 minutes. No manual reset necessary after automatic operation.

4. Automatic rotisserie. Spit and rack turns automatically for spit roasting. Spit and rack can be removed in seconds for storage.

5. Radiant heat broiler. Charcoal-type broiler with a curved reflector directing intense, radiant heat right on the food with searchlight concentration has a safe, fully enclosed calrod broil unit for electric heating.

6. Automatic oven light in both ovens which shows when oven has reached correct temperature.

7. Maximum width for each oven is 24¾ inches.

8. Doors finished in acid-resistant porcelain enamel or brushed chrome, with bright trim.

The Biff Small Case

Biff Small sold television sets for the Monarch Manufacturing Company. His territory included Western Kentucky and Tennessee. We begin with Biff showing a retailer his newest model, which has been set up in the retailer's store.

Biff points to guarantee and Underwriter's Laboratory Approval plate as he begins his demonstration.

BIFF: This set is designed to give your customers reliable, picture-perfect television. No fuzzy, out-of-focus pictures. (After he has made the device ready, he points to the twenty tubes, including three rectifiers and a 12½-inch television tube.)

BIFF: Notice those tubes and rectifiers that come with this television set. No skimping there. The cabinet is available in gum and walnut finish and can be moved all over the room without having to change the wire and plug.

PROSPECT: What about the operating controls and the speaker? Many of these television sets give fuzzy, jumpy pictures.

BIFF: The operating controls in this set provide fine tuning, channel selector, contrast, sound volume, on-off, picture horizontal hold, and brightness and vertical hold, all conveniently located for fast, simple station location.

PROSPECT: What is the retail selling price?

BIFF: You'll be surprised. You can sell it for only $199. You get a 33⅓ percent markup on it, too.

PROSPECT: I wonder if television sets will sell in this area. We're rather far from . . .

BIFF: These sets will pick up video casts from as far away as seventy-five miles. Your customers can get both Cincinnati and Louisville. We guarantee excellent reception.

PROSPECT: How about service?

BIFF: We will provide service for you until you have learned to do it yourself, or until your business grows sufficiently for you to hire a service man. We will drop-ship for you, connect, make necessary adjustments and service each set for ninety days — until you are ready to install and service your own work.

PROSPECT: It is a good-looking job, but . . .

BIFF: Here, you try it out for yourself. Notice how simple it is to operate. Notice the clear image, the tone. This set will be in heavy demand when your customers hear about it.

Questions:

1. Did this salesman appear to know his merchandise?
2. How did this salesman emphasize benefits to the dealer?
3. Why did this salesman ask the prospect to try out the set?
4. What suggestions can you offer to improve his presentation?

Chapter Four

Finding and Qualifying Buyers

Because of the inevitable mortality in buyer lists, it is constantly necessary for the salesman to discover and analyze new buyers who will benefit by purchasing his product, service or idea. Therefore, each salesman must recognize the need for a healthy ratio between active buyers and non-buyers, as well as between prospects and *suspects*.

Successful salesmen never lose sight of the fact that their customers are their competitors' best prospects. They never assume that an account is their personal property or that they have an account tied up.

Salesmen exercise constant vigilance about this point because they realize not only that their competitors are trying to dislodge their customers, but also that there is frequent turnover in key buyers because of promotions, resignations and so forth.

Despite the old rule that "customers are the best prospects," the salesman who merely tries to keep his established accounts is overlooking the mortality of customers. In many lines of business, customers leave at the rate of 20 percent each year, so that a man who takes over a terri-

tory with 600 customers and finds no new ones will be down to 307 at the end of three years.

EXTENSIVE-INTENSIVE SELLING

The successful salesman leaves nothing to chance. Like a lawyer, he realizes that the better he prepares his case, the greater his chance to win it. In selling, too, he can win by systematically planning his sales. To increase his sales, the salesman must sell to *more* prospects and more to each customer.

Extensive selling increases sales by selling to more prospects. *Intensive selling* increases the unit of the sale; that is, instead of selling one or more items, the full line is sold.

In extensive selling you will need to have imagination, information and ideas. You will have to use both ingenuity and initiative to get new customers.

Finding hidden prospects requires skill and patience on the part of the salesperson. When model homes are shown in a new subdivision, only an alert salesperson can locate the real buyers. The beginning salesman may waste valuable time until he learns to distinguish the lookers from the real customers, but this experience develops his skill in identifying *suspects* and prospects.

In selling, one should never overlook any bets. Many gas-station attendants become annoyed when rush-hour customers casually add, "Oh yes, and check the battery, too." One salesman noticed that all his associates disliked this service and he determined to make it a selling device. Whenever a car drove into his station, he asked the driver if he could check the battery. Most of them were happy to have it done. He would show them the hydrometer reading whenever the cells were low and the battery down. He would then explain the unpleasant situation of a dead battery on an expressway; the trade-in value of the old battery, the guarantee on the new; and the security of a quick start on a cold day. As a result he sold many batteries that would not otherwise have been sold, and won a battery sales contest. His ingenuity and initiative increased his sales.

PLANNED SALES STRATEGY

When seeking new customers, make sure you have fully explored your own territory. Have you tackled the big accounts? They are the real challenge, calling for persistence, perseverance and self-confidence, plus *planned sales strategy*. The extra preparations, presentations and planning required to sell a really big account will give you better organization of your selling preliminaries, plus the confidence that comes from being thoroughly familiar with every phase of it.

If you do land the account of a big user, your forethought has paved the way to a greater selling opportunity. Even if you do not sell the account, if your presentation didn't carry enough weight, remember that a baseball batter always swings two bats before he is up. Then when he is at the plate, his single bat seems light in comparison, yet has plenty of weight to make a hit if properly aimed.

STANDARD SOURCES FOR NEW PROSPECTS

Suppose a friend of yours gave you a list of 100 names and said: "Jim, these prospects need what you sell. They'll buy from you if you can prove yours is best." What would you do? You would hit the road and you would not stop until you had seen every single prospect. In this chapter we are going to be that mythical friend and tell you where 100 or more prospects can be found.

First, however, you should make a complete study of the benefits that your product or service offers. When you know what your product will do for the people who might benefit if they bought it, you will be able to determine *who* might buy it.

The young salesperson should understand at the start that a steadily maintained and up-to-date list of prospects is as important to his success as a steadily increasing volume of orders. This is true whether he is sent into new territory where his company has few or no customers, or works in a field where there are many. He must be prospect minded as well as sales minded.

Prospect hunting has other advantages in addition to plugging holes caused by lost customers. In the first place, a salesperson must not only be able to present a convincing sales presentation, he must learn to find new buyers by using his own initiative and imagination.

In the second place, nothing boosts a salesperson's morale and self-confidence more than finding a prospect and turning him into a customer. A large order from an old buyer is always a thrilling experience, but to open a new account, even if it is only a sample order, gives a still bigger thrill.

One authority on salesmanship has written that "prospecting is the salesperson's search for those who are *needers* who can be changed into *wanters* and then into *buyers.*" This may appear to be difficult but it is really a very simple process if you work systematically and with patience.

Another preliminary step is to make oneself familiar with prospect sources, which vary in number and kind according to the nature of the product or service. Who are *needers* who can be changed into *wanters* and then into *buyers* who are likely prospects?

Prospect Lists

Before setting out on his first trip, the salesperson is usually given a list of customers, unless the territory is new to his company, in which case he gets a list of *prospects.* He may be given a list of *both,* but he will be wise to build up his own prospect list, or add to the customer names given him. He will naturally be more interested in potential buyers he finds himself; his own list will be screened and more apt to be *alive* than a list prepared for him. Here are a variety of methods used by successful salesmen to build a prospect list:

Cold Canvass

This is also called "cold turkey prospecting." Victor Adding Machines' house magazine is named *Walk and Talk.* This title aptly describes much of the daily activity of the salesmen in the Victor organization.

When a Victor salesman walks and talks the line of products, he does just that. He covers his territory block by block. He goes into every store, office or factory in search of prospects who can and may buy. Having found them, he talks with them, educates them on the value of a Victor and persuades them to own one. Since the law of averages is working for the salesman in such cases, a certain number of sales will likely result.

Not only must the cold canvasser have the courage and the willingness to put

forth the effort required for this type of prospecting, but he also needs a systematic approach. One of the most difficult and discouraging types of selling is house-to-house. Consider the example of a stainless-steel cookware salesman using a systematic approach in cold canvass prospecting:

SALESMAN: (at the door) Good morning. I'm Jack Cramer with Kitchen Kraft. Kitchen Kraft has just opened a new branch office in your area and we want to acquaint you with our location. May I present you with this booklet? It's filled with ideas.

HOUSEWIFE: Thank you.

SALESMAN: Do you have a set of waterless cookware?

HOUSEWIFE: No, I don't. I'm not sure I know what it is.

SALESMAN: We love to show off our new cookware. May I make an appointment for twenty minutes to show it to you tomorrow morning?

Observation in the field will provide the best leads for a canvasser. A salesman for lubricants says that much of his success came from following smokestacks when he visited a new area. Smoke meant machinery and machinery needs lubricating. A salesman for a domestic oil burner outstripped all other members of the sales force. He toured residential districts and noted the ash cans outside large houses and apartments. Coal ashes gave him his leads. One young fellow who sold office supplies built up a good clientele by systematically working the big office buildings in his city, beginning at the top and working down.

Endless Chain

The endless chain method of prospecting is based upon the idea that everybody on whom the salesman calls is a source for prospects. For example, the insurance salesman calls upon Mr. Williams who purchased a basic home protection policy. Just as he is getting ready to leave, the salesman presents the new policyholders with a handsome little address book saying, "I'm sure that you may have some friends, neighbors or business associates who would be interested in the same service I have rendered for you, Mr. Williams." Professional salesmen attempt to get prospect names whether they succeed or not in selling their product or service. If they use this technique with finesse, it results in an endless array of prospects to keep the salesman busy. In fact the salesman may never run out of people to see as may be seen from the illustration of the endless chain.

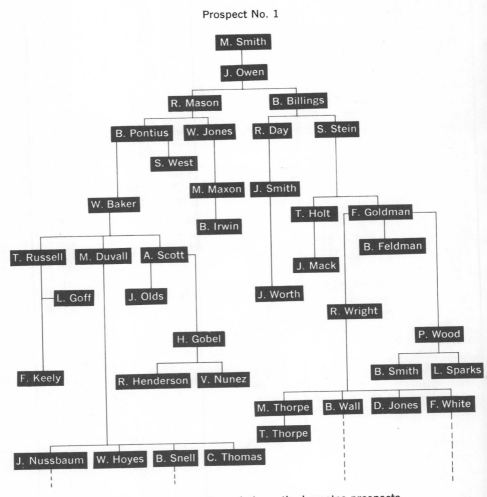

Figure 1. How the endless chain method creates prospects.

Users of a product or service are often the most valuable sources of prospects that a salesman can have. In some lines, more than 50 percent of new sales are influenced by present users who furnish names and addresses of prospective buyers. A salesman's customers, who form an endless chain, can be the lifeblood of his business.

Referral

The endless chain technique supplies names and addresses. The referral method goes a step further. Users can pave the way for an interview with friends, acquaintances or relatives by telephoning, writing a letter of introduction or by a personal introduction.

Centers of Influence

Often the salesman is blessed with the friendship of influential persons in the community who are willing to refer prospects to their salesman friend. Such people may be prominent business leaders, clergymen, educators, union officials or attorneys. They may supply all the information a salesperson needs. They may even make appointments and recommend the salesperson and his proposition to the prospect. Salesmen offering genuine benefits should not be timid about asking customers or friends for the names of new prospects.

Social Contacts

A successful salesman not only obtains names from satisfied users, or customers, he also develops his ears like radar antennae to detect sounds. His ears are always open to listen for hints from people he meets: gas station attendants, secretaries, store employees, plant workers, conversations during social contacts and tips from friends and acquaintances.

Other Sources

Company files and records are usually replete with information about customers and prospects. Company officers and older salespeople possess great funds of information.

List houses, or organizations that make a business of selling assorted lists of all descriptions, are useful sources for prospects.

Organization membership lists may be obtained from chambers of commerce, service clubs, alumni associations, country clubs and many other similar organizations. Such lists are valuable not only for the names they contain, but also because they reveal many things about the prospect's interests.

Lists of professional people such as doctors, lawyers and other groups are of value when selling to the members of the professions. Local tax lists are also valuable not only for the names and addresses they offer but also for their indication of the prospect's ability to buy.

Newspapers, trade journals and house organs provide some of the best sources for new business with the information they offer on new products, new equipment, new applications, personnel changes and other vital facts useful to the alert salesman. Many men make a practice of filing away such items on the principle that something of little value today may later supply a lead for new business.

Telephone directories in every city contain a classified section from which salesmen can select prospects engaged in the various lines of business that could benefit from their product or service.

Sales associates or bird dogs — also referred to as hostesses or spotters — do preliminary prospecting for certain salespeople. Autos, major appliances and brushes are only three of hundreds of products suitable for sales associates. While some of these junior salespeople may be employed full or part time, most of them may be meter readers, milk routemen, moving men, real estate agents,

GETTING READY TO SELL

laundry men and others who meet the public. They are paid a commission or a flat rate for each prospect who is sold.

Dinner plans and party plans used by direct-selling companies are a good source of prospects. In this kind of prospecting the salesperson finds a housewife who, in return for a small gift or the prestige involved, will lend her home for a demonstration of the products offered.

Advertising leads from the salesperson's home office, classified advertisements for customers, sales letters and direct mail advertisements are also valuable prospect finders.

News items in local papers are rich sources of prospect information. Every day, there are news stories or incidents which reveal the needs of potential customers. For example:

An incident in a local factory reveals the need for accident insurance or safety shoes.

Wedding announcements indicate an opportunity to sell everything that is used in a home.

The arrival of a new baby is always an occasion for selling new merchandise.

The organization of a new bowling league provides prospects for athletic supplies, uniforms, shoes and other items.

The opening of a new factory gives opportunity to sell many things.

A falling tree may damage the roof of a house and the home owner is a prospect for new roofing materials and insurance.

News of a church picnic might mean the sale of paper plates, tableware, food and supplies.

The opening of a new restaurant provides a prospect for tableware, glassware, waitress uniforms, food and supplies.

Sponsors of contests and exhibitions may want prizes which a novelty retailer may supply.

Consider the business in any community. What are the needs of their employees which you can supply? Ways can be found for contacting the workers, as well as management and owners, through their unions or by direct canvassing. When a salesperson makes his proposition known to any organization or person, he helps to increase sales volume.

Calling on the Prospect

How often should calls be made on a prospective buyer? A prospect's time is worth money, and so is the salesman's. If the prospect knows little or nothing of the salesperson's firm it might be argued that he cannot make too many calls; but calling for the sake of calling rarely gets the salesperson anywhere. This is particularly true of the salesperson who says, "I happened to be passing and just dropped in."

Numerous tales are told of aggressive salesmen who have tried to take dramatic advantage of the prospect who does not want to see a salesman. "My time is worth ten dollars a minute," was the message relayed to a salesman by a certain prospect. The salesman promptly produced a twenty dollar bill and asked for two minutes of the prospect's time. The stories usually have a happy ending, with the salesman obtaining the interview, closing the deal and having his money reimbursed.

Persistent Effort

A recent survey reveals that 80 percent of all sales are made after the fifth call. It also revealed that 48 percent of salespeople calling on unsold prospects make one call and quit; 25 percent make two calls and quit; 10 percent keep calling and make 80 percent of the sales. These figures indicate the value of systematic, methodical, purposeful and patient follow-up of prospects.

Creeping Vine Prospecting

Creeping vine prospecting has also been described as *back-door* prospecting and *progressive prospecting*. It is not a mysterious kind of prospecting, because it simply means that the salesman (1) places himself in his customer's shoes concerning general problems and attitudes; (2) estimates the kind or class of business and marshals answers to problems likely to be related to it; (3) prepares the sales talk and plans its presentation in a way that will interest the prospect.

Creeping vine prospecting also means starting on a fact-finding tour before seeing the person with authority to buy. It is natural for the salesman to seek facts and related information from people who work for or with the prospective buyer. These people can tell the salesman what the problems are, what future purchasing plans may be, whether a change of supply sources is contemplated and which other personnel might influence the buyer's decisions.

If a salesman were selling an industrial product he might start his creeping vine prospecting with the engineer. He could ask questions of anyone and everyone he sees, including the custodian or elevator operator. If the engineer is out, the salesman could see a mechanic, a service man, the doorman, the manager's secretary, the buyer's assistant, the plant superintendent, foreman, workmen, clerks or receptionist.

Creeping vine prospecting should not be used to undermine the authority or prestige of the buyer or purchasing agent. The salesman should not sneak around or prowl the premises to gather his facts. If he finds that his fact-finding activities may cause ill-feeling in a certain situation he should not use the creeping vine method.

Questions to Ask

Through asking questions and listening to these people, the salesman may gain a complete picture of the buying situation and at the same time deliver a short sales talk to each one. He can arouse their interest by assuring them that they are the real buyers, regardless of their actual titles, because they are the people who will be directly concerned with his product or service.

When the real buyer is not available, the salesman must not withdraw from action. That is the time to ask the assistant buyer a few questions, to give a demonstration, to offer solutions to problems, and to mention benefits and exclusives to be gained if the product or service is purchased.

When preparing a creeping vine approach, the salesman should plan to solve problems by digging up answers beforehand. A buyer does not order if he feels that he will have to justify his decision later by explaining and selling it to others.

The questions to ask when making this type of sales approach will vary according to the type of business, but the salesman should find out if the firm has a product similar to the one he is recommending, what condition it is in, who bought it and why. He should learn who the buyer is and whether others also have authority in this area. He should obtain as much specific information as possible in order to make a sales presentation designed to appeal to the specific firm.

After obtaining this information, the salesman is ready to ask the buyer for an interview. He knows what benefits, values and advantages will interest his prospect. Because of his questioning and back-door selling he has acquired allies and well-wishers and should be on his way to a successful sale.

Specialty Prospecting

The Toledo Scale Company defines and describes its ideas of what constitutes good prospecting or canvassing. Canvassing, states the Toledo Scale Company, "is the systematic coverage of territories to find the most likely customers in each community, and pre-selling them on our products and service whenever possible."

The Toledo Scale Company trains its salesmen to pursue the following course when seeking new business through canvassing for new prospects:[1]

1. *Spend some time canvassing each day.* Usually the more good prospects you have, the more business you'll get.
2. *Make your friends prospect-conscious.* Keep them on the alert for new business.
3. *Keep records of your good prospects.* List their names and addresses, type and size of business, kinds of present equipment, names of buyers, dates and results of your contacts with them.
4. *Call back on satisfied customers.* A happy customer usually is so proud of his new machine that he shows it off to his business friends, neighbors, and customers. He's your assistant salesman and pre-sells other people. A friendly call-back is a good way to get the names of these new prospects, and to pyramid the sale of another machine to the already satisfied customer. Add these names to your mailing list, too.
5. *Watch for new building, moves, remodeling.* Canvassing the territory, items in the newspapers, and tips from your friends will help.
6. *Get route lists for your territory* from the local newspaper. Such lists give store names by streets, the addresses, and frequently show the managers' names. Sometimes the lists are free; otherwise, the cost is small.
7. *Get reverse telephone lists* from the local telephone company. These can be rented at relatively low cost and show stores and industries by streets, the addresses and types of business, and often include the managers' names. The Yellow Pages of the telephone directory are a good source of prospects by type of business.
8. Get acquainted and attend local meat, grocery, and other dealer associations.
9. *Pre-sell by mailing appropriate literature* a day or two before you plan to call.
10. *And—once you get a prospect, keep him active.*

Prospect Cards

Prospect cards may contain a record of all sales and calls, particular problems, names of individuals the salesman contacts, names for a mailing list and many other details. A prospect file should be made from these cards, so they can be shifted about.

Here is the information for a prospect card: company name, address, telephone number; name of buyer and his position; names and positions of others who might influence the sale; credit clearance; competitors' products bought by prospects; data of special interest about the buyer; space for listing calls and progress notes.

BLUEPRINTING THE BUYER IN ADVANCE

Topflight salespeople often accumulate more information about their prospective customers than an FBI file. It might not be important to the FBI, but the knowledge that Mr. Abbott, purchasing agent for the Steel Corporation of America, likes baseball, has a son on the Washington crew, is allergic to onions, dislikes cigarette smokers and collects wood carvings is invaluable to the salesperson. He will be careful not to offend Mr. Abbott by smoking, otherwise he might be ruled out before he is in, and he will never know why! As an icebreaker, the salesperson might inquire about the son in college, mention a wood carving he has seen written up in a magazine or comment on a recent ball game.

Knowledge of these personality facets

---

1. Sales Training Manual, Toledo Scale Company.

indicates to Mr. Abbott that the salesperson is alert, friendly and considerate. He is then inclined to be more receptive to the salesperson's sales talk. If no order is possible on that particular call, the way is paved for a return visit when the salesperson will be cordially received and a sale may be made.

Specific Facts

Salesmen should really appreciate the advantage of understanding the buyer and knowing his needs *before* the interview. Too often it is only at the end of a presentation that the salesman has a good grasp of the buyer's needs, and then it may be too late. Salesmen have often been heard to complain, "If I could have another crack at Brown, I'm positive I could sell him."

The solution to this problem is to blueprint the buyer before coming face-to-face with him, to do the planning before, not after, the presentation. Furthermore, the salesman should reveal to the prospect early in his presentation that he knows something about his problems and needs and that a solution will be offered. This approach will provide hope and arouse interest in the prospect's mind early in the interview.

Business Data

To complete an adequate blueprint the salesperson should know at least some of the following business data about his prospect:

1. His specific need for the product or service.
2. The territory and his customer if he is a retailer or wholesaler.
3. His personality, including temperament.
4. The reasons he should buy, including any peculiar motives he may have.
5. The approximate volume of his business, including the kind and class of merchandise he handles.
6. His merchandising methods, including the peculiarities of his clientele.
7. His financial standing and credit rating.
8. His present suppliers, including the reason he is or is not buying from the salesman.
9. His typical objections, including possible tricks to shunt the salesman aside.
10. His family relationships.

Personal Data

A professional salesman might like to have even more information about a prospect. He might, for example, like to have answers to the following rather personal questions in addition to those above:

1. What is the prospect's general attitude toward the salesman, his product and his company?
2. Does he buy on the basis of impulse, logic or reason, friendship or reciprocity?
3. What are his hobbies? Does he play golf, bridge, checkers, chess, tennis, croquet, cribbage, pinochle or poker? Is he interested in boating, swimming, bowling, motoring, gardening, painting, boxing, wrestling or the like?
4. What kind of a home does he have? Does he have a wife and does she help or hinder him? Does he have children? How many and what sexes? What are they interested in? Are they in grade, high school or college?
5. Where did he go to school? What is the state in which he was born? What are his fraternal organizations and clubs?

The possession of this kind of detailed information places the salesman in a better position to understand the prospect. Much of it may never be used, but the salesman has the facts if he needs them to close a successful sale. It has been said that if a salesman can base the first five minutes of his presentation on the above knowledge of the buyer, he will have advanced at least half way through the job of closing a successful sale.

You cannot expect to obtain all this information before your initial interview, but by keeping tab from call to call, you will always discover more interesting details about your prospect.

Keep a Record Sheet. Though it is possible for a salesman to recall many details about each customer, it is wise for him to make a memorandum of the individual characteristics of buyers with whom he deals regularly or hopes to deal. In this way he will not become confused with trivia and can avoid making mistakes. For instance, he will not ask Mr. Abbott about his daughter at Vassar, and compliment Mr. Klein on the fact that his alma mater, Michigan State, seems destined for the Rose Bowl, when in fact Mr. Abbott has a son at Penn State and Mr. Klein attended Ohio State, not Michigan State.

Credit Facts. When special information is needed about the finances of a customer for specialty items, such as life insurance, automobiles, stocks and bonds or real estate, it is possible to obtain credit ratings from credit associations and banks. Large firms usually have departments that obtain such information and it is available for their salespeople.

QUALIFYING PROSPECTS
Value of Qualifying

One of the keys to successful selling is carefully qualifying the prospect. Failure to qualify prospects is reported to be the chief reason why salesmen make 65 percent of their sales calls on the wrong person.

Qualifying means that the salesman determines whether or not the prospect has certain attributes, qualities or bona fide interests which indicate that he may benefit if he buys the proposition. To determine if the prospect has the qualities

necessary to make him worthy of a salesman's effort, answers to these questions are required:

Does the prospect *need* the product or service?
Has he the ability to *pay*?
Has he the *authority* to buy?
Is he readily *accessible*?
Does he have a sympathetic *attitude*?
What is his business *history*?
What is his *reputation* as a buyer?
Is he a *one source* buyer?

In addition to saving otherwise wasted effort and increasing sales, the salesmen who qualify prospects have a fund of information which enables them to visualize how their propositions can be of *maximum benefit* to the prospect. While qualifying entails considerable preparation, it is an infinitely better method than the drop-in call when the salesman merely hopes the law of averages will bring him a sale.

The salesman who fortifies himself in these ways receives the kind of welcome never accorded to the salesman who drops in to pass the time of day. The prospect recognizes that the professional salesman is there to serve him, not simply to meet him.

Basis for Qualifying

To turn a prospect into a customer, the salesman must have in mind seven criteria about each prospect. If a prospect rates high in relation to these criteria, the salesman can actively pursue the account, knowing that he will probably get a customer.

The most important of these qualifying factors is the customer's *need* for the product. A need may be known or unknown, latent or felt, realized or unrealized. It is the job of the salesman to discover the need, and if it is not yet a realized need, to call the need to the prospect's attention.

Ability to pay for the product or service is the second qualification. It may be necessary to eliminate customers who do not possess sufficient income, purchasing power or credit standing. This does not mean that some people should be eliminated because they appear to lack buying power. It does mean that people who cannot pay under any conditions, or who are slow payers, do not ordinarily qualify as prospects. It is an obvious waste of time to seek business from someone who will be refused by the credit office.

Authority to buy is the third qualification. Salesmen can afford to deal only with those responsible for purchasing — for example, husband and wife, minors with parents, business partners, or proper company officials. We mentioned before that a salesman can sometimes influence those who influence the individuals with authority to buy.

Accessibility is the fourth qualification and it means: Can the prospect be readily interviewed? Is he within easy or economical travel distance? Is he located in a convenient place for a sales call? Is he usually available for an interview. Obviously, unless the prospect is accessible, he cannot qualify.

A *sympathetic attitude* on the part of the buyer is the fifth qualification. When a buyer is favorably inclined toward the salesman, his company and his product, he will frequently qualify regardless of his need. Similarity in background, education and temperament is helpful in establishing a cordial relationship between salesman and prospect.

An investigation of the *business history* of a prospect to determine if he is a progressive businessman is the sixth qualification. It is valuable for a salesman to know if a buyer is interested in increasing his business and whether or not he is a good merchandiser.

Qualifying prospects according to their *reputations as price* or *quality buyers* is the seventh criteria. Neither should be taken for granted, for the salesman may make the mistake of emphasizing price to a quality buyer and quality to a price buyer.

Occasionally, the salesman qualifies a prospect by determining in advance if the prospect is accustomed to purchase from *one source of supply*. If so, he may not attempt to sell the prospect. On the other hand, the salesman may feel he is justified in making a much greater effort to obtain the account because of its probable permanence.

Every salesman will find it necessary to work out his own system for gathering prospect information. What will be effective for one salesman may be ineffective for another. However, every salesman should have a systematic method of finding and cataloguing information on the buyer and on his business needs.

PREPARATION OF SURVEYS
The sale of some products is helped greatly by the use of a survey. The word "survey" means "to look over." In other words, instead of merely trying to sell a product, the salesman looks over the prospect's needs so that he may recommend the best product to satisfy those needs. The survey is a part of the problem-solving approach.

The survey offers the following advantages to the salesman:

1. Since the prospect is getting professional advice without charge, the product is lifted out of the price-commodity class. This very often eliminates competition.
2. The salesman can ask for help and advice from his manager, his fellow salesmen or his home office, before he makes his final recommendation.
3. He can make an attractive, graphic or political presentation as a result of his survey.

4. Such tailor-made presentations offer the smoothest, easiest possible kind of presentation.
5. Prospects and customers often like the survey idea and generally appreciate the efforts of the salesmen who use them.

The survey may sometimes consist of only a few minutes' conversation to ascertain a few simple things. At the other extreme, it might consist of a long study of the needs in many different departments over a period of time.

The results of a short and simple survey might be communicated verbally or explained by a simple design or sketch. The results of a long detailed survey should be given to the prospect as a neatly typed and prepared presentation folio. Such a presentation folio, complete with all the necessary supporting data and illustrations, serves not only to impress the prospect with the thoroughness with which the survey was prepared, but also carries a fairly complete sales story in cases where the prospect must convince other members of his own organization of the desirability of the proposition.

Naturally, the amount of time and effort spent by the salesman on a survey should be governed by the sales potential of the prospect.

Obviously, it would not pay a salesman to spend several days of his valuable time on a prospect whose orders could never amount to more than fifty dollars each year. However, a salesman can afford to spend considerable time on a very small order if this order could lead to a great many other orders in a sizable account.

When selling the survey idea, the salesman should avoid the danger of overselling. He should not promise more than he can deliver by claiming to be more of an expert than he really is. He can safely claim to know his own business; however, if he claims to know more about the

prospect's business than the prospect does, he is treading on dangerous ground.

Preparation for Selling to Professional Buyers

Selling to professional buyers requires salesmen who possess poise, urbanity, technical information and great selling skill. Therefore, this kind of selling requires such skillful preparation that it is said to result in the ideal sales call.

Professional buyers have their own ideas of how salesmen should sell and they have suggested the ingredients that should be used in the creation of an ideal sales call, as well as the order in which they should be mixed. For example, Harry T. Flynn describes the ideal sales call in the following words:[2]

1. Whenever feasible the salesman should telephone in advance to make an appointment.
2. When the salesman arrives at the buyer's office, he should be able, briefly but thoroughly, to describe his product and its purpose. If possible, a sample of his product should be shown at this time.
3. The salesman should state briefly the need his new product is going to fill for the consumer.
4. The salesman should be prepared to tell the buyer what the new product might replace in the buyer's present inventory.
5. The salesman should be able to give the buyer a price comparison between his own product and that of competitors. While pricing is not always a determining factor in completing a sale, it helps if the price is a realistic one.
6. The salesman should be prepared to give a brief description of his company's promotion plans for the product. He should be ready to sketch the upcoming advertising campaign

2. Harry T. Flynn. Adapted from *McCall's* Supermarket Buyer's Pocket Letter, McCall's, 230 Park Avenue, New York 17, N.Y.

and have samples of art work or proofs of ads which will be used in the promotion effort.

All the information the salesman expects a buyer to utilize should be briefly stated in writing so the buyer can digest it after the sales call.

Purchaser's Value Analysis

The content of the sales presentation could also be based on the value analysis used by many industrial purchasing agents.

The purchasing value analysis involves a careful analysis of each purchased item in search of the answers to the following questions:

1. Does the item's use contribute value to the end product?
2. Is its cost proportionate to its usefulness?
3. Does it need all its features?
4. Is there anything better for the intended use?
5. Can a usable substitute be made by a lower-cost method?
6. Can a standard item be found to do the job?
7. Is it made with the use of proper tooling?
8. Do material, labor, overhead and profit charges total the purchase price or reasonably approximate it?
9. Will another dependable supplier provide it for a lower price?
10. Is anyone else buying it for a lower price?

Value analysis assures purchasing agents that they buy on the basis of the cost-in-use of products. Salesmen of industrial products in particular would be wise to mesh their thinking, research and development and selling techniques with the purchasing value analysis.

The questions in the *purchaser's value analysis* could be studied and analyzed and specific answers prepared by the salesman prior to his presentation. This would certainly be a more realistic and

accurate way to answer the purchasing agent's unspoken query, "What's in it for us?" It would be more convincing and dynamic than the customary sales talk.

FINAL PREPARATION FOR MEETING THE PROSPECT

Having acquired and prepared all possible advance information, the professional salesman sells the prospect *in his own mind* long before he calls on him. "Selling him in his own mind" means that the salesman rehearses his presentation before he actually sees the prospect. He makes definite decisions as to the sales strategy he will use.

Physical Preparation for the Sales Call

In addition to his "book" containing his planned route for the day and data about the people to be interviewed, the salesman may have other materials. It is best to assemble these things the night before to assure a prompt and orderly departure with the self-confidence that can only come from knowing that the preparation is complete in every respect from attitude and planned route, planned presentation and personality data.

Samples, brochures, product and other visual aids should be packed so that their sequence in the actual sales talk is orderly. This prevents fumbling and stumbling which distracts from the power of the presentation and loses the attention and interest of the prospect.

Among the many decisions the salesman makes is whether to leave his sales portfolio in his car or to keep it out of sight during the first few minutes of the interview. The salesman reasons that the new prospect may be annoyed if he appears with a pile of selling accessories. The prospect may mentally defend himself by offering excuses and alibis to avoid being sold.

Seeing is believing and the sample

case or briefcase should be bulging with visual aids which have the *convincers* needed to close sales. It may be possible to sell without visual aids, but if they are available the salesman has them for those situations where they may tip the scales in favor of him, his product or his service.

If *testimonials* are to be used, they should be arranged in the most effective sequence, with the significant sentence and paragraphs underscored. It is the rare prospect who will read even one testimonial letter in full, much less a series of them.

A written testimonial may never be needed, but occasionally a prospective buyer is convinced by written testimony if it is presented to him on the spot. Information sent later from the home office is never as effective as proof presented immediately.

If *catalogue* or other publications are used as part of the presentation, the place at which they are to be used should be marked to avoid fumbling and backtracking.

As preparation for this kind of presentation, it is advisable to study local conditions through newspapers, calls at banks and other sources of local information. These sources of information will provide facts so that the salesman can localize his sales talk and fit it to his customer's particular base and needs.

A good first impression should be of concern to the salesman.

Planning for Interview Time

Before a salesman interviews a prospect, he should make an appointment by telephone or mail. If he has an appointment, he should be on time. It is a good idea to make appointments flexible within a half hour, offering both the salesman and the client some leeway. However, even a good excuse for being late cannot entirely erase the salesman's apparent disregard for the prospect's time.

Sometimes a prospect will "come out to the gate" instead of inviting a salesman into his office. He does this to find out if the salesman really has anything to offer that is of interest to him. The salesman must therefore quickly present the benefits of his product or service.

"Too Busy" Problem

If the prospect says he is too busy to talk, the salesman must ask for a firm appointment. Some salesmen give up as soon as a buyer says he is busy or shows impatience. The salesman who quits so quickly is not a salesman, he is a peddler.

At the other extreme is the salesman who barges ahead every time, continuing with his sales talk in spite of danger signals from the prospect. This person's determination must be admired, but he cannot be called a salesman, either. Through lack of experience and perception, he antagonizes many buyers.

What is the answer to the "too busy" problem? Probably it is the telephone appointment. Some salesmen are reluctant to state their business by telephone, but if they believe in what they have to offer it should be natural for them to ask for an interview.

When a personal call is made, only the salesman can decide if the prospect really is too busy to see him or if he is only trying to avoid him. If the salesman is in doubt, he can offer to return at a more convenient time, leaving literature for the prospect to peruse. If the prospect really is not busy, this is the salesman's opportunity to interest him.

"Gate" Selling

The rule is that a salesman should never sell "over the gate." Many sales managers warn their salesmen against talking to any prospect over the gate or office railing, in hallways or in any place other than the buyer's office.

When such a situation is unavoidable,

the salesman should try to win the prospect's interest so that he will be invited to sit down to talk with him. The salesman will never gain the prospect's full attention and neither will be at ease discussing business in a hallway or reception room.

Meeting the Receptionist

When calling on a new prospect the salesman will probably be met by a secretary, switchboard operator, office boy or receptionist. This person will ask him whom he wants to see and the reason for the call. Sometimes the receptionist will tell the salesman that another person does the purchasing or that several people are involved in it. If the salesman is alert, he will acquire information that might have taken him some time to discover.

The receptionist's job may include protecting the prospect from peddlers and order-takers who needlessly take up his time. The salesman should prepare to sell this person one idea: that he has such constructive benefits to offer that Mr. Prospect cannot afford *not* to hear him.

POWER POINTS

Scouting for prospects requires as much method and system as selling. It is as important as any other part of the selling job. For example, most salesmen receive a sales quota which they are expected to meet. It is equally sound practice to establish a *prospect quota* which should not be less than 10 percent of the number of customers, preferably more. Too many prospects are better than too few.

As already stressed, the really *live* prospects will be those the salesperson discovers by himself. They are kept live by being placed in a prospect file, one card for each, noting results and comments on every call.

The prospect-minded salesman will rarely have to ask himself, "Where can I find a prospect?" His plan for the day, week or month will always include prepared calls on one or more prospects.

Locating prospects and qualifying them are almost the same process. Both activities require leg work, footwork and good thinking. To qualify a prospect the salesman must determine whether or not he is a potential buyer, if he has a need for the product or service.

Need for the product or service is the first qualification. A need may be known or it may be unknown. Sometimes need varies among prospects, but any *real, live* prospect has a need.

Ability to pay is the second qualification. It may be necessary to overlook those with insufficient income or purchasing power, but deferred payments and various finance terms give ability to buy to many who would otherwise not qualify.

Authority to buy is the third qualification. Salespeople can afford to deal only with those prospects who are responsible for buying such as business partners and proper company officials, husband and wife, minors with parents.

Accessibility is the fourth qualification. Prospects must be available for interview.

Sympathetic attitude or *empathy* is important.

The *business history* of the prospect, whether he is a price or quality buyer, as well as whether he deals only with one supplier, also helps to qualify a prospect.

When the salesman takes time each day to plan where he is going and whom he will see, he realizes that there is a relationship between proper use of time and effort and attainment of success in selling.

Unused plans are useless, a waste of time. Successful selling is nearly always the result of systematic planning. Plans should be made, and, then they should be followed. In short, plan your work, then work your plan.

DISCUSSION QUESTIONS AND PROBLEMS

1. Select any business in which you are interested enough to believe that you could be a success.
   a. List at least ten *standard* sources for new prospects and state why you selected them.
   b. List ten miscellaneous sources for new prospects and state why you selected them.
2. Design a prospect card capable of recording the information mentioned on page 63.
3. What is meant by qualifying a prospect? What are the values of qualifying a prospect from the salesman's viewpoint?
4. How would you qualify prospects in your community for the following products?
   a. A complete unabridged Webster's dictionary.
   b. Accident insurance.
   c. A course in conversational Spanish.
   d. A new hand soap for cleaning especially gritty-greasy hands.
   e. An industrial cleaning compound which is applied by a spraying apparatus. Approximate cost of apparatus, $150.
   f. Small plastic desk calendars which can be personalized.
   g. An electric mousetrap costing $15.
5. Select ten products and determine where and how you would locate prospects for them.
6. Assume you are selling one of the following products:
   a. A set of high quality picture encyclopedias for elementary and junior high school age children.
   b. A central heating and air conditioning system for business firms (usual installation costs approximately $22,000.)
   c. A health, exercising and reducing system for business men.
   Write at least two dialogue-style situations for each product example illustrating how you would use the endless chain method to obtain additional prospects.
7. Describe and explain the meaning of creeping vine selling. What should be included in a creeping vine approach?
8. What questions would you ask in the pre-selling activities of the creeping vine approach?
9. What are the advantages to the salesman of a survey approach?
10. State in detail the preparation which might be required to sell a professional buyer through the medium of the ideal sales call described in the chapter.
11. What would you do to prepare to meet the prospect? What decisions should you make before seeing the prospect?
12. When a prospect says he is too busy to arrange an interview what procedure should the salesman follow?
13. Why should a salesman try to avoid selling over the gate? When he must sell over the gate, what should he do?
14. How can the receptionist be helpful in prospecting for customers? Explain *why*.

15. Salesmen who make ten or fifteen calls each day are not always able to perform detailed planning as set forth in this chapter. What method would you suggest they use? What would you do under such conditions?
16. A few buying offices insist that salesmen talk to the buyer over the phone from the reception room. Others insist that the salesman make his introductory presentation by filling in a printed form. If you were requested to do either of these things, how would you react? Explain what you would do and tell *why*.
17. How could a salesman get the information referred to under the four points in Personal Data?

PHENOMENOLOGICAL PROJECTS

Finding New Faces H. F. Silver (Case)

The prospect has a right to expect that we know. our business and that we are capable of developing an accurate picture of his business situation, that we plan for his needs with care and look at the purchase from his standpoint, not ours.

As a salesman, I must be willing to invest a great deal of time in my work. I must study changing conditions and economic developments; I must know competition; I must prepare plans which permit the prospect to buy the best he can afford; I must review these plans before each interview. And, after spending all this time on his behalf, I must *not* pressure him to buy.

I look for people who are compatible. The prospects I want are open-minded, generous, and want to do as much as they can for their families as well as for themselves.

I do not let prospecting drop just because I'm busy on other work, because sooner or later it would tell. I need a constant stream of new faces.

My job in contacting prospective clients is to weed out those who don't want my services. If a man shows any hesitation at reviewing his problems with me, I simply leave my name and ask him to call me when he wants to see me.

If he doesn't give me all the information I need to provide him with good service, I stop the discussion and no longer consider him a prospective client.

After I analyze his problem, if he shows any unwillingness to have me carry out my recommendations or indicates a lack of confidence, I end the interview. I feel a prospective client has a right to choose the person with whom he is going to do business, and I reserve the same privilege to myself. I find that a client-salesman relationship develops only when there is mutual confidence and liking.

After he has my recommendations and he knows what he can buy with the amount he is willing to spend, it's up to him. If he wants the product, I'll arrange the details and close the deal.

Questions:
1. What are the basic factors in this case?
2. What do you think of this salesman's ideas about qualifying and locating prospects?
3. How would you do this differently?

Bronson Brothers Department Store (Case)

Many retail department stores limit their buying hours and thereby inconvenience and often discourage salesmen who wish to present their products. The reason behind this store regulation is that buyers must have sufficient time to perform a multitude of other duties. Often a buyer is forced to see so many salesmen during the day that he does not have time to plan advertising, check invoices, work on markdowns, tabulate sales reports and attend to many other merchandising duties.

Rules to guide salesmen have been listed by some department stores. Here they are:

"Salesmen should strive to time their visits to stores so that they interfere as little as possible with the other duties a buyer must perform. The best time for a salesman to call upon a buyer is between 9 and 11 A.M. Do not arrive before 9 A.M.

Question:

1. Do you believe that there may be exceptions to the 9 to 11 regulation? *Why?*

Busy Periods

In one large department store the busiest selling hour is at noon, since the store is located near a large factory and those who work there like to shop during their lunch hour. At that time the buyers like to be on the selling floor getting consumer reactions. Each department store has its own special "busy periods," especially Saturdays, when all buyers are too busy to see salesmen.

Questions:

2. Why should a salesman study individual stores so that he can determine their busy periods?
3. Would it ever be advisable to attempt to sell a department store buyer on Saturday?

Staff Meetings

Most department stores also advise against salesmen calling late in the afternoon. At that time the buyer must work with his sales staff, checking daily sales reports. It is a great inconvenience to all concerned, including the buyer, if he must sandwich in reports between salesmen's interviews or if he must discuss the day's sales with his staff in a salesman's presence.

Where out-of-town salesmen are concerned, it is to everyone's advantage if the salesman telephones the buyer when he arrives in town. The buyer can then make a definite appointment with the out-of-towner, and avoid missing him during his trip.

Questions:

4. How many hours during a day are available for selling department store buyers?
5. Are evening, holiday and Sunday contacts advisable?
6. What can you suggest for improving the situation?

Chapter Five

Words that Sell

One of the secrets of successful selling lies in the effective use of words. Words express ideas, paint vivid mental pictures in the customer's mind, stimulate imagination and set the emotional mood. Words answer questions, present facts, overcome objections, convince customers so that they will buy merchandise or services. Nothing is more effective in selling than the authoritative use of persuasive language in a judicious way.

In the actual sales presentation, whether it is in an office, at a front or back door, in literature, in a letter, over a telephone or over a counter, the use of words must be skillful enough to induce buying action.

Whether written or spoken, language is the vehicle used by the salesperson to reach and penetrate the customer's mind. All language, particularly the spoken word, must have clarity, power and good taste. The salesman's sales talk must be clear, convincing and vivid in order to attract attention and arouse interest. His words must be colorful but accurate and descriptive to convince the customer that

he should buy. In closing the sale, the salesman must select his words carefully so that his presentation has fluency and continuity.

In all selling, the importance of good speech cannot be overestimated. Good speech means not only correct grammar, effective vocabulary and good taste, but also pleasing tone of voice, clear enunciation and proper pronunciation.

The salesperson should realize that what he says and how he says it speak for his whole company, and that words and speech are the tools with which he is able to:

1. Win respect and attention.
2. Communicate ideas.
3. Gain an acceptance of ideas.
4. Close successful sales.

There is power in words, and the right words at the right time can exert a vital influence on the thoughts and actions of others.

IMPORTANCE OF WORDS

In every psychological test used to determine an individual's potential as a company representative or salesman, emphasis is placed on the vocabulary test. Research in this field has established that, other things being equal, the man with the better vocabulary becomes the more successful person. An adequate vocabulary is important in practically all of the professions: for teachers, lawyers or physicians, as well as for salespeople. In each group the effective use of words is a necessity, and the means of acquiring that proficiency are identical. The only difference is that each profession has its own group of specialized words, with the physician as a conspicuous example.

The vocabulary of the average person falls into two classifications:

Kinetic, or active speaking vocabulary, consisting of words used freely in speaking or writing, words which are instantly available for use when need arises.

Latent, or inactive vocabulary, consisting of words which the person recognizes in his reading or hearing, but which he does not ordinarily use in his own speech or writing.

The well educated man uses about 15,000 words in his daily speech, and recognizes at least 70,000 more that he does not employ. The kinetic, or speaking, vocabulary of the typical adult American, exclusive of proper names, is estimated at about 3,000 words — an almost unbelievably small figure when we consider that there are more than 400,000 words in an unabridged dictionary. One's stock of kinetic and latent words is easily ascertainable if he is willing to spend a half hour with a dictionary.

How to Build a Larger Vocabulary

There are three good sources for acquiring new words:

1. By listening to good speakers — on radio or television, at your church or on the lecture platform.
2. By reading.
3. By a concentrated course in vocabulary study.

In both the listening process and the reading program it will not suffice simply to hear or see the new word. Newly-learned words should be listed. They should be looked up in a good dictionary, for both meaning and pronunciation, then repeated until they become a natural and familiar part of the individual's vocabulary. The final part of this acquisition program is to make use of new words in one's conversation or writing. An inactive word is like a ten-dollar bill in a forgotten inside pocket: it is of little value until it is discovered and put to use.

Pronunciation

Learning to pronounce words correctly is as important as acquiring new words. By using a new word improperly or mispronouncing it, one risks being stamped as illiterate. The only way to begin to correct errors, in both pronunciation and grammar, is to be conscious of them. This involves an attentive ear in listening to the speech of educated men and leads again to the dictionary.

Unless one is entirely familiar with the diacritical marks used in all good dictionaries to indicate correct pronunciation, it is well to read the introductory pages in the dictionary where these marks are explained.

Because of the many common errors in grammatical usage, a refresher course in grammar, repeated at intervals, would prove helpful to any salesperson.

Practice

There is no magic way to build an adequate vocabulary. It requires an acceptance of one's particular needs, a sincere desire to improve and a will to succeed. Best of all the recommended exercises is (1) recording in a pocket notebook every day one or two words that one wants to transfer from his latent to his kinetic vocabulary; (2) looking them up each evening to make sure of their exact meaning and derivation; and (3) consciously using these newcomers to one's vocabulary whenever possible until they become part of one's stock-in-trade. The important thing is not the words one knows but the words one easily and habitually employs.

Words For A Selling Vocabulary

Each industry has a certain terminology of its own which the alert person will acquire during his job experience. However, the salesman must give particular attention to his "selling" vocabulary.

Use only words the prospect or customer understands. The seller must evaluate the buyer's vocabulary scope. If the terminology used is over his head, a selling presentation is made in vain.

Speech must be forceful to sell anything. Forceful words for the most part are concrete rather than abstract. An example of an abstract statement is "This automobile is in perfect condition and is a wonderful purchase." A concrete version is, "This car has been driven 8,000 miles. The rubber on the pedals is unworn. There's not a scratch on the body. Feel the tires; the tread is like new."

This example is sufficient to indicate the principal that abstract or generalized words are usually undesirable in selling, because at most they convey only a vague impression of a judgment in the salesperson's mind. They fail to create in the buyer's mind a picture of the thing or service under discussion. Concrete words, on the other hand, tend to create a series of visual images that enable the buyer to make his own judgments.

Forceful words are generally concrete words. They are also exact, conveying to the listener the precise meaning intended by the speaker. For example, when you say "large," do you mean big, huge, immense, colossal, gigantic, stupendous, extensive, vast, massive, bulky, wide, fat, tall, high, towering, deep, thick or steep? When you use the word "said," do you mean commanded, insisted, begged, whis-

pered, murmured, implored, cried or demanded?

The forceful word is the word that conveys exactly what you have in mind. This is particularly true of verbs, the backbone of every sentence. Use dramatic, even romantic words, that fit your product and help impress it on your customer's thinking. Elmer Wheeler, a noted authority on "magic words" for use in selling, expressed it by saying, "Don't sell the steak, sell the sizzle." Hunt for vivid, sparkling words — words that sing, words that are alive, words that appeal to the ear — and put them in your sales story.

Modernize your vocabulary: keep your story up-to-date while remembering that many new words are short-lived.

Choose words that will tell your story in the shortest possible order. Many salesmen talk so volubly that they tire the listener and lose the sale.

Write out the presentation you intend to make. In this way you are able to weigh the words you will use, to determine whether they can be improved upon in order to paint the quickest, clearest, most appealing picture. The successful salesperson must have his presentation ready before he is face-to-face with the buyer. When the person who sells needs a word, he needs it immediately.

Words to Avoid

Misuse of words is usually evidence of fuzzy thinking. Why say "splendid," which means shining or brilliant, when you mean to say "enjoyable"? Probably the most commonplace example of two words that have almost identical dictionary meanings but differ widely in connotation are "house" and "home." The first work carries the idea merely of a physical building without any emotional atmosphere; the second word implies the intense personal relationship of the people who occupy the building and consequently, as every real estate man knows, is a word with far greater emotional impact.

Words of exaggeration are damaging. Habitual use of superlatives suggests immaturity. The person who boasts does so because he has little to offer.

Remove useless words, such as "see," "you know," "get this," and similar expressions. They represent vocabulary weaknesses. Slang and trite expressions may serve an occasional purpose, but they soon become ineffective. Profanity may lend color in man-to-man talk, but it likewise betrays vocabulary weakness and may prove offensive to the prospect or customer.

It is more difficult to correct bad speech habits than to acquire new words, but it can be done. As a means of eliminating exaggerations, trite expressions, slang and profanity, it is a good idea to list those which one is conscious of using habitually or frequently and make written and mental notes to replace them with more effective words.

Technical Terminology

There are some situations and prospects which demand technical terminology for best results. Doctors and lawyers are obvious examples of men who must use technical terms in their everyday work.

Salesmen of technical products should learn twenty or thirty technical words to use in their planned sales talks whenever needed. Many professional buyers insist that the salesman employ technical terminology in order to express exact meanings.

If you are selling to agencies that book lectures, musicians or other artists, you know that a "sliding scale" doesn't mean a slide-rule or a piano exercise, but a graduated price range to fit the pocketbooks of clubs with memberships and budgets of different sizes. Gradually you can familiarize yourself with the trade terminology of the specific field in which you are employed.

Educated speech does not mean the use of long words like apportionment for quota or share. It means using simple words understood by those to whom you speak and expressing exactly what you mean.

Idiomatic terms or jargon used in one trade or business might be out of place in another. All salesmen must exercise good taste in determining when such jargon is acceptable and when it might be offensive or inappropriate.

Accents and Tone of Voice

A salesman should always speak naturally. If you have a Southern accent, a "down-East" twang, or a Western drawl, or if you have a British, Scandinavian or other foreign accent, remember that it is not the accent that matters so much as the voice itself. The tonal impact of your voice on the prospect is what counts—its clarity, its sales message.

An accent or regional manner of speech, which might prove distracting to some customers, can be eliminated or softened by conscious effort.

A low, distinct tone of voice is easy to understand and pleasing to the ear. It is not necessary to raise your voice in order to project it. We cannot all have melodious or powerful voices, but we can all speak in natural tones, pitched so as to be easily heard.

Enunciation

When you talk, speak clearly and carefully so that you will be understood the first time, saving both yours and the customer's time. Speak slowly enough so that your phrases do not run into one another because you are too hasty, too eager or have a "lazy larynx." One way to slow down is to remember to put all the endings on such words as going, wearing and buying. Pronounce all the syllables in a word: say recognize, not reconnize. Do not use extra syllables: say athletic, not ath-a-letic. When you enumerate, pronounce your words clearly, not pernounce. Do not say faks and figgers for facts and figures.

Factual Words

Salesmen should avoid the pompous word, the high-sounding phrase. For example, someone selling a preparation for repairing walls should refer to cracked plaster, not "household blemishes." If someone means dandruff, he should not say "intolerable scalp condition."

The simple factual word is basic to good communication. The urge in some beginners to use fancy language is often hard to curb. It is not a problem of over-education, for good salesmen cannot know too much about their subject.

A revised style sheet for newscasters on WAVE-TV, Louisville, makes some points which are valuable for salesmen. The WAVE admonitions are as follows: Avoid cliches. Rather than *you see,* use *understand.* Rather than *kids,* use *children.* Rather than *folks,* use a word describing the target of the message, such as *homeowners, mothers, fathers,* etc. Rather than *contact,* use *see* (contact means to collide with). Rather than *you know,* use *remember.* Rather than *like so,* use *for example.* Rather than *hi there,* use *hello.* Avoid teen-age expressions or other expressions from an insular source. Avoid delaying words and phrases such as *yes, well, but first, and now, of course.* Avoid ponderous words. Instead of *precipitation,* say *rain, snow* or *sleet.* Instead of *gubernatorial,* use *governor's.*

It may require time to rid oneself of poor speech practices and learn to make a sales presentation that is correct and objective, as well as interesting and beneficial to the prospect. However, the result will be worth the effort.

Cliches

Overworked words and trite phrases leave the buying public unmoved. Such words have lost their impact through overuse. Their meaning has been diluted. We bore ourselves and our prospects when we use them.

Some beginning salesmen think that they should employ similes, metaphors, puns or jokes, company slang and extravagant analogies. They should be avoided.

When you find yourself falling into the pattern of a cliche, try to turn the phrase into another which is more expressive or more personalized. For example, a prospect may remark to you that his father, who lives in Sioux City, Iowa, has a car exactly like the one you have in the showroom. Restrain yourself from sighing and murmuring, "It's a small world, isn't it?" Turn the situation to your advantage with a comment such as, "What a coincidence! Your father has excellent judgment. That car is one of the Italian sports car originals."

Here are some words and phrases which salespeople tend to use, often ill-advisedly:

party (for person), dearie, honey
guaranteed to give satisfaction
let me call your attention to
at your earliest convenience
as per recent date
smart, heavenly, nice
cute, terrific, slick
stunning, marvelous, wonderful
gorgeous, beautiful, elegant
stout or skinny

Words That Spell Trouble

It is frequently difficult to distinguish one twin from another. It is also a challenge to identify "word twins" which are not only look-alikes but also sound-alikes.

Word twins are a little like salt and sugar. An aged cook's failing eyesight frequently caused confusion. One day she picked up the salt, thinking it was sugar. Being uncertain, she exclaimed: "Looks like it, smells like it, feels like it," and, on tasting it, "but it ain't." Check for yourself which is which so that you will never again need to hesitate, even momentarily, when confronted with what "looks like it, sounds like it, but isn't."

Do not mix up these word twins. They spell double trouble! Learn the differences in their meanings:

stationary — stationery
dyeing — dying
counsel — council
desert — dessert
principal — principle
affect — effect
compliment — complement
pedal — peddle
alter — altar
adapt — adopt

These doubles come from mutual word origins but differ in form, usage, and meaning:

canker — cancer
reprove — reprieve
pungent — poignant
indite — indict
inapt — inept
maximum — maxim
movable — mobile
plaintive — plaintiff
complacent — complaisant
amicable — amiable

Slang Usage

Though slang is frowned on by many educators, the fact remains that slang is frequently used by Americans. Some slang has found its way into our dictionaries after general usage has made it a part of our language. Some expressions are so colorful, so eloquent in expressing their meaning, that they are more effective in use than formal terminology. Here are a few expressions classified as slang but generally accepted—or, at least, generally used and understood:

charley horse: muscular ache
double-cross: to deceive or betray
cheesecake: news photos emphasizing feminine charms
doubleheader: two ball games the same day; two of anything
hard-boiled: tough
small fry: little children
stuffed shirt: a pompous man
pushover: easily defeated victim or opponent
bullpen: pitcher's practice and warm-up place

TALKING *TO THE* CUSTOMER

In selling to people from top executives to shop laborer use the trade language of their industry to show that you understand their problems and are one of them. Do not let ignorance of their shop talk betray you. It is easier to get your point across if you can talk with prospects in their own vocabulary. For instance, know the hours for factory "changing of the guard" and what it is locally called, whether it be the "four to eleven," the "swing" or "graveyard" shift.

If your contact is with drivers for laundry, milk, towel, uniform, grocery or cleaner-and-dyer services, you may find that such men call their territories a route. In many parts of our country, such workers pronounce the word so that it rhymes with scout, though dictionaries show that the preferred form rhymes with root. If you are selling to a route foreman, do not risk offending him by pronouncing "route" differently from the way he does. That does not mean that you should use bad grammar, but it is good psychology to speak in a way that will put you on friendly terms with a customer rather than antagonize him.

Though it is not always possible to use the terminology of doctors or lawyers when selling to them, you will engage their interest more quickly if you present your proposition in their respective vocational languages. This has been referred to as the "you" attitude—talking in terms of the prospect's interests. If you plan your interview in advance, you can start the conversation by referring to a fact or event bearing on the prospect's vocational interest. Tie this in with your service or product and then proceed with your sales talk.

Here is an actual experience which illustrates the effectiveness of speaking the customer's language and getting his viewpoint:

An insurance salesman was interviewing a farmer. The salesman said, "That is a fine flock of chickens you have there; I guess you must get a lot of eggs."

"Oh, about 150 a day."

"What price do you get for your eggs?"

"I sell 'em for fifty cents a dozen."

"For about three eggs a day, I'll give you a $1,000 life insurance policy; for fifteen eggs a day, I will give you a $5,000 policy."

Without hesitation, the farmer said, "I think I will take a $5,000 policy."

When the salesman returned to deliver the policy, the farmer said, "Me and my wife have been thinking over this matter, and I think I will take one of them thirty-egg policies."

Your Selling Voice

Your voice makes your prospective customer feel welcome through its friendliness, pleasant tone, and enthusiasm. It is your voice which directs attention, arouses interest, and ultimately convinces him. Not only is what you say important, but also how you say it.

What You Say Is Vital

When you sell in a retail store, be brief. Sift things down to their essentials. Try to use a kind of oral shorthand when selling. You can get your sales message across more effectively if you use a sensibly brief technique which gets in all the facts in a brisk, interesting opening statement.

Keep it conversational. Keep your speech fluent, but not glib. Fluency allows the easy progression from one idea to another, so important in the continuity of a sale.

Keep it interesting. At every point in the sale, from the start through the close, the salesman must be interesting. This is not difficult when you are well informed. The information you have about your merchandise can be made interesting to the customer if you can tell your story in an interesting manner.

More Effective

A salesman who is fluent can give a smooth, accurate, sensible presentation of ideas and information. He progresses from one point to another without hesitation, never groping for something to say. He talks confidently and in an alert manner because he is sure of himself and his knowledge.

Practice is the solution for a salesman who needs fluency in speech. He can begin by reading aloud some well-written passage in prose or verse every day for a period of five minutes or more. He can also practice extemporaneous speaking every day. For example, he might select a subject and talk on it for two minutes. He could describe it, comment on its size, shape, color, weight, uses, or why he likes or dislikes it. He should keep going for two minutes without a break. If he continues with these spur-of-the-moment exercises, fluency will come. He might get practice by reading newspapers aloud, too, as well as books, magazines and reports—always being careful to avoid reading in a hesitant and halting manner.

When a prospect is greeted and throughout the sales presentation, the salesman's voice should reflect warmth and friendliness. The greeting should show that the salesman sincerely means to wish the prospect a "good morning."

Monotony is the common fault of an uninteresting voice and the voice that follows a mechanical pattern is monotonous. Conversational variety can be injected into the voice. Try to avoid monotony in both pace and volume. Speak rapidly when the subject matter permits, then emphasize an important point by speaking more slowly. Make good use of pauses to let the ideas presented take root and to give the listener plenty of time to follow the lead. Variations in pace and tone, conscious at first, later become subconscious and add life and action to one's diction.

Since a person's voice carries his message, it is important that it be pleasing. If the person's voice is loud and raucous, it annoys; if it is weak, it fails to get the message across; if it is rasping, it exasperates. If the voice is clear and pleasantly pitched, it is easy to listen to: it persuades, convinces, and gets results.

One way to determine just what kind of voice one has is to arrange for voice recordings. Another method is to develop "voice consciousness" — to pay attention to other voices in order to formulate a pattern of one's own. A third suggestion is to practice oral reading, expressing exactly the qualities one feels the material requires.

Of major importance in clear, pleasing expression is correct breathing. When talking, one should make every bit of breath count. It will give one's tones a quality of vitality, a contagious feeling of aliveness. Many salespeople have found that a moment's pause at the prospect's door, just time to fill the lungs to capacity several times, removes the "flutter" experienced during those opening moments. It removes the strain and tension that make effective speech impossible.

Combining this deep breathing with a squaring of the shoulders and a lift of the chin and chest helps to improve voice quality. Good posture is necessary for effective speaking.

And, finally, it is equally important to learn when to stop using words—when to stop talking. The fact that many people "talk themselves out of a sale" is reason for stressing this point. According to research conducted by Warner Brothers Studio the average person says 20 million words a year. In most instances that's 19 million too many.

Good Telephone Usage

Since much of the average salesperson's preliminary talking may involve the use of the telephone, it is important to practice the principles of good telephone usage and manners. The following points are based upon the Bell Telephone System Handbook.

Speak directly into the transmitter. Your lips should be half an inch from the mouthpiece. Words should be distinctly enunciated.

It is unnecessary to shout. Shouting distorts your voice over the telephone. The instrument is tuned to a normal tone of voice and loud tones cause it to blur. A loud voice sounds gruff and unpleasant over the telephone. It is equally unpleasant to listen to someone who whispers or mumbles.

Try to visualize the person. Speak to the person at the other end of the line, not at the telephone.

Say "Thank you" and "You are welcome." The use of such phrases is the way to "smile" over the telephone.

Be attentive! The person to whom you are talking will appreciate your listening politely and attentively. You would not interrupt in a face-to-face conversation, and the same rules of etiquette apply to telephone conversations.

Address the customer by name.

Explain delays. The customer cannot see you or what you are doing; he has to depend on what he hears. If you must leave the telephone, do not drop it on the desk.

It is well to identify yourself, your firm, and your department. For example:

"Roberts Company, Mr. Jones speaking."
"Shipping Department, Mr. O'Brien speaking."

Who should end the call? It is courteous always to allow the person who places the call to end it.

POWER POINTS

When a salesman feels that his words have failed to transfer conviction or a mental picture from his mind to the buyer's, it is perhaps because his stock of words is insufficient or his speech not as fluent as it should be.

Conscientious effort to improve vocabulary, speech and voice will bring gratifying results. A program of vocabulary building and practice in correct use and pronunciation of words is both interesting and profitable. Skillful use of words encourages exact thinking and increases sales.

Skill in the use of words that sell, like other skills, is the result of effort and practice.

DISCUSSION QUESTIONS AND PROBLEMS

1. Why are words important to the salesman?
2. Explain the difference between a kinetic and a latent vocabulary.
3. What are three ways to build a larger vocabulary?
4. Evaluate the phrase, "Speech must be forceful to sell anything." Discuss its meaning.
5. Using a tape recorder, practice enunciating the following lines:
   A big black bug bit a big black bear; it made the big black bear bleed blood.
   Fanny Finch fried five floundering fish for Francis Fowler's father.
   The sun shines on shop signs.
   She sells sea shells by the sea shore.
   Three gray geese in the green grass grazing; gray were the geese, and green was the grazing.
   The seething sea ceaseth, and thus the seething sea sufficeth us.
6. Using a tape recorder, practice saying the following paragraph taken from a sales brochure. Pronounce each word distinctly and try to achieve emphasis and force wherever you feel it is needed. Be prepared to play your tape before the instructor for constructive advice and criticism.
   "Mrs. Cogswell, whether the game of your choice is poker or parchesi, this contemporary tub chair is the perfect mate for your game table. Notice how the cut-out arm enables you to pull up comfortably close to the table when the blue chips are down. And when the game is over you can use it as an occasional chair, or even in a boudoir. Notice how beautiful it looks here on our floor. The fabric is a wide-wale corduroy velvet on a natural wood base with antique brass casters. As you can see, the casters are hooded. The construction is top-quality by Fine Arts and designed to last a lifetime."
7. Page 77 provides you with a list of words. Consider each word in the list and substitute a word which you feel would be more effective.
8. Look up the meaning of the word twins on page 77 and prepare a list of definitions, naming the dictionary from which you obtained your definitions. Remember, there will be forty words in all.

PHENOMENOLOGICAL PROJECTS

Easy Speech Exercises

A. *Find a quiet room with a full-length mirror if possible.*
Listen to your own voice: observe your mouth and facial expression in action.

How good is your voice now? Keeping in mind that prospects and customers will notice your voice and speech, try this exercise. Cup your hands behind your ears and say the following lines:

"I want a voice with full, round, melodious tones."
"I want a clear, mellow voice."
"I will practice every day."
"Hear it, see it, say it ten times and it's yours."

B. *Warming Up the Voice*
Much of the tension felt by novice salesmen can be avoided if they will practice speaking the following sentences, with gestures. Experienced salesmen can also use the exercise to advantage.

Do these exercises, with gestures, in front of the group:

I kicked the cat.	I waved good-bye.
I said no emphatically.	I saw a big gorilla.
I said yes reluctantly.	I rolled a seven.
I picked up the phone.	I pointed to the moon.
I opened the door.	I put up the umbrella.
I yelled, then listened for the echo.	I include you all.
I smiled my assent.	Good night, dear.

"Hear it, see it, say it ten times and it's yours."

C. *A E I O U*
This project will help you to eliminate a dull, flat, lifeless voice. Use this exercise as a means of developing resonance and quality of tone. First say the vowels, then go through the "maining, meaning, mining" routine that follows. Try to push the sound up through the nasal chamber.

Then go to "min, mean, mine" and so on. When you finish, say the vowels again and you will notice a perceptible improvement. Practice this two minutes a day for improved quality of tone.

A	E	I	O	U
maining	meaning	mining	moaning	mooning
main	mean	mine	moan	moon
may	mee	mi	mow	moo
A	E	I	O	U

D. *Read the following Y-O-U equals you aloud and practice frequently to avoid running your words together.*

1.	Don't you	7.	Told you
2.	Did you	8.	Heard you
3.	Won't you	9.	Missed you
4.	Could you	10.	Understood you
5.	Would you	11.	Beat you
6.	Can't you	12.	Wrote you

Your enunciation will improve only if you learn how to control your breathing and proper use of your jaw, tongue and lips. When you have gained enunciation control, your sales power will increase.

E. *Lip and Tongue Exercises*

Here are some exercises for your lips and tongue. They provide enunciation practice. Watch vowel and consonant sounds:

"For distinct enunciation, every word, every syllable, every sound must be given its proper form and value."

"Think of the mouth chamber as a mold in which the correct form must be given to every sound."

"Will you please move your lips more noticeably."

"The teeth should never be kept closed in speech."

"As your voice is the most direct expression of your inmost self, you should be careful, through it, to do yourself full justice."

"You may know what you are saying, but others will not unless you make it clear to them."

"Through practice we can learn to speak more rapidly, but still with perfect distinctness."

"Good speech is within the reach of everyone through conscientious practice."

F. *Try This For Painless Practice*

Test your ability to speak distinctly by uttering the following sentence through teeth tightly clenched: "Three or four minutes of speaking twice a day for a month in this manner will improve the average person's distinctness of speech."

Part Two

Practical Sales Techniques

Chapter Six

Starting the Successful Sale

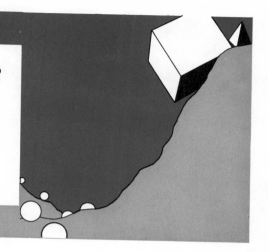

THE FIRST FIVE MINUTES

What is done and how it is done in the critical first five minutes of the presentation will probably determine the final result of the interview. Sales trainers point out that, at this time, the salesman is on trial to win the prospect's approval for the continuance of the interview. Because it is natural for every buyer not to want to be sold, gaining the opportunity to continue the interview is the first hurdle to be surmounted. It is also maintained that the salesman will not receive a brush-off if he is successful during the first five minutes.

The first few minutes of the sales interview is referred to as the "approach." During this time, the salesman starts conditioning the buyer and establishes the fact that he has something to say that the buyer wants to hear. Surely the first five minutes is not the time to exhibit weakness or stumbling in speech or manner, nor is it the time to launch into an unorganized sales talk.

Because of the vital importance of these opening minutes, the professional salesperson makes definite plans for his approach. He knows what he intends to say and do to arouse the buyer's interest; he

makes the start of his presentation clear, concise and intriguing enough to gain favorable attention and to establish empathy.

How to Establish Empathy

Empathy is the capacity to feel for others. The salesman with empathy has the ability to put himself in the position of others and to see things the way they do. Empathy is not charm or exuberance, nor is it sympathy or pity. Empathy can be acquired by anyone. The salesman who appreciates and understands the prospect's concern about a buying problem can deal more effectively with this prospect and can quickly establish communication with him.

To create empathy between himself and his prospective buyers, the modern salesperson deliberately tries to create an atmosphere of friendliness. He does not wait for friendliness to be shown by the buyer. Also, the salesman is earnest about his job and the other person's problems. He reveals enthusiasm for his proposition. He stimulates sufficient curiosity so that the prospect is willing to buy, rather than to be sold. Above all else, he has developed the capacity named empathy.

To be empathic in relation to his prospects, the successful salesman is always aware that he should never center attention on himself or his company. He knows that the buyer is interested in only one thing: How he can be helped? In other words, the buyer wants to know "what's in it for him." It is the salesperson's function, especially during the first five minutes, to establish empathy with the buyer by telling him, showing him and proving to him that the salesman understands the prospect's problems. The salesperson unmistakably reveals that, to him, selling means solving problems and benefiting the buyer.

The salesperson's first job is to convince the prospective buyer that what he has to say is worth the prospect's time and attention. His opening statements should make the buyer feel that his search for a wanted product or service is at an end, or that he is going to benefit in some way.

Sales resistance is said to go up in direct proportion to the apparent sales effort employed. Therefore, to make the customer believe that he is selling himself, the salesman must see his proposition as the buyer sees it. The seller cannot think as an outsider and force his views on the buyer. Such an attitude places the buyer on guard against being sold. The seller will then have a difficult time convincing his buyer of the benefits to be gained from his goods or services, no matter how closely they may relate to his needs. A salesperson is truly empathic when he is able to put himself in the buyer's place by identifying himself and his product with his buyer's needs, wants and motives.

Making People Feel Important
The start of a successful sale often begins with the simple act of making the prospect feel important. This ability has great advantages to the salesperson and it makes transactions much more pleasant for both parties. Psychologists know the desire for

recognition is a basic human need. Building up a prospect's good opinion of himself is one of the most useful tools a salesperson has.

Compliments make people feel bigger, better and more important. However, unless a compliment is sincere, there is danger in its use. Obvious flattery warns the prospect that he is being "buttered-up" or "kidded" and his mental guard goes up.

A compliment must be subtle. It should create a feeling of commendation without causing the prospect to wonder, "What's this character after?" If it is recognized, it is clumsy. Subtle compliments, for example, are expressed in these statements by an unknown author:

BIG LITTLE WORDS

Five most important words:
  "I am proud of you."
Four most important words:
  "What is your opinion?"
Three most important words:
  "If you please."
Two most important words:
  "Thank you."
Least important word:
  "I."

BEGINNING THE PRESENTATION

It is practically impossible to outline forms of address that will serve all purposes. It is always advisable, however, to avoid uninspired, commonplace openers and stereotyped phrases in getting the sales interview started.

Every successful salesperson avoids trite openers, because he knows that he cannot open a successful sale until he has:

    Captured favorable attention
    Won favorable interest
    Created confidence

A professional opening to a successful sale may require only sixty seconds, if the salesman has properly prepared himself. For example, the following opening statements have been highly successful when used to sell a product to a new prospect:

Salesman (smiling): Good morning, Mr. Prospect. I'm Joe Brown of the Pocano Process Company. I know you're a very busy man, Mr. Prospect, and I appreciate the time you have given me. So to save your time, I'll get right down to business. Here is an interesting sample of a product that we have just brought out and, from what other customers have told me, I'm sure it will save you time and money. Here's the way it works.

Note the technique Joe Brown employed to make a fast, favorable impression and actually start toward a successful sale:

Pronounced the prospect's name correctly.
Gave his name clearly.
Gave the name of his company.
Complimented the prospect.
Had a business-like appearance and attitude.
Demonstrated — showed something.
Showed friendliness but not familiarity.
Asked questions.
Listened.
Got down to business quickly.

This salesman's opening presentation centered around three factors: he sought to gain empathy with his prospect; he emphasized that the prospect would receive benefits; and he recognized the buyer's importance. When a prospect's attention and interest are obtained in this way, he will listen to the salesman. This kind of opening statement can be adapted to almost any product or service to obtain favorable attention at the start of a sale.

Recognition

Running through the salesman's words in the foregoing example, is the principle of making the prospect feel important. There is a sales advantage in making people feel important, because one of the basic human needs is the need for recognition, or receiving approval and attention from others.

Praise is a form of recognition, and the start of a sale is an excellent place to use that selling device. The good salesman offers praise to his prospect whenever he can honestly do so. Praise builds up the prospect's ego; it makes him feel important; it recognizes his position as an individual who deserves attention.

When a salesman gives a buyer a better opinion of himself, he earns his goodwill because he has satisfied one of his prospect's basic wants: the desire to be recognized as a person of importance.

Prospect's Needs

Early in the presentation, the alert salesman will tell his prospect how he will benefit from his products or services. He emphasizes benefits throughout the sales presentation, because he realizes that a propect is interested only in what a salesman can do for him. Some professional salesmen start an interview by saying, "Everyone knows how busy you are, Mr. Brown, and it is nice of you to give me the time I asked for. You will be interested in this product, because . . ." Obviously, this is a far better approach than "I just happened to be in this neighborhood and thought I'd drop in." It offers the prospect recognition while starting the presentation from the "need" and "problem-solving" aspects.

Businesslike Approach

Relatively few prospects like discussions about the weather, baseball or politics. The salesman knows and the prospect knows that the call is about selling and buying, and any other topics are mere time-wasters. Comments about topics not related to the prospect's interests do not

command favorable buying attention nor
arouse interest.

Too often the salesman starts talking
about the size of his company, how fast
it has grown or how much he wants to sell
his product, without pointing out specific
advantages for the prospect.

Prospects are never interested in such
vague generalizations as, "This is a nice
piece of goods," "This is a good seller,"
or "Mine is one of the largest and strongest companies." The salesman should describe a specific benefit to the prospect
or suggest the solution to a specific problem. All prospects are primarily interested
in "what's in it for them," and the approach which answers this query will
command attention. For example:

SALESMAN: Mr. Jones, my name is Don
Stevens with the XYZ Company. I
imagine that like all businessmen you
are trying to find some way of increasing your sales. Am I right?

PROSPECT: You bet you are.

This is a good approach because the
salesman endeavored to do three things:

1. He planted an idea.
2. He translated the idea into a benefit.
3. He got a response from the prospect.

In an industrial sales situation, the
presentation might begin in this way:

SALESMAN: Mr. Williams, how would you
like to cut your milling costs by approximately 25 percent?

PROSPECT: Fine, but how?

SALESMAN: Our new chemical milling
process can achieve that savings for
you.

In specialty selling to a consumer, the
salesman might use this approach:

SALESMAN: Mrs. Bosworth, I imagine that
like most women you are interested in
keeping your hands soft and young-
looking, aren't you?

PROSPECT: Naturally, but what has that
to do with water softeners?

SALESMAN: Just this, Mrs. Bosworth: your
present hard water system requires the
use of substantial amounts of deterg-
ents which are harsh to the skin. Isn't
that right?

PROSPECT: I hadn't thought about it that
way.

SALESMAN: By softening the water in your
home, you reduce the need for deter-
gents and protect your hands. Of course
this is only one of many benefits. May
I step in and show you how you can
live better with all of the other advantages soft water brings you? It will take
only a few moments.

Pedestal Questions

"Pedestal questions" are closely related to
the compliment. By asking the prospect
questions on subjects of interest to him,
the salesman "puts him on a pedestal."
The prospect is flattered to discover that
the salesman is interested in listening to
his ideas and opinions. This kind of conversation also frequently discloses to the
salesman information useful to him in the
interview.

That often leads to a successful sale.
Questions might be phrased like these:

"How long have you been in this business?"
"How did you come to choose this fine
location?"
"How do you attract so much business?"
"Where did you get your idea for inventory control?"
"How do you maintain such high morale
in your sales force?"

"How do you keep your trucks so clean?"

"What do you think about this product?"

"What do you think is the most important part of selling?"

"What do you think business will be like next year?"

Showing deference to a prospect is another way to place him on a pedestal. For example, many people like to pretend that they are very busy. The salesman might start an interview by saying something like: "Everyone knows how busy you are, Mr. Black, and it's mighty nice of you to give me the time I asked for."

Refusing to argue wins people to the salesman's side. By not arguing we show that others have a right to their opinion. People do not argue with facts, such as testimonials or success stories, but they will fight hard to support their own opinions. Arguing puts prospects on the defensive and arouses resentment.

Pronouncing a *prospect's name* correctly and distinctly is important in selling. The one thing a person really owns is his name, and he feels complimented when people remember it.

"Something New" Techinque

When possible, good salesmen use the *something new* technique because it has a strong sales appeal. The something new might be a product or service to be introduced, or it might be an exclusive feature. This selling device gains attention and breaks the ice. It permits the salesman to maneuver and explain while adding interest to the presentation.

The something new technique might be used in this way:

SALESMAN: Last year, Mr. Purchasing Agent, your firm spent $200 with our firm. I thought you would like to see an itemized statement of these repairs so I brought one along. You can save $160

or more of that amount this year and every year from now on if you use my product. Are you interested?

Attention Getters

Where does a salesman find a good attention getter? This question is easily answered: the best of all attention getters is the product itself. A close examination of any product or service will reveal features and benefits that attract attention. If a salesman studies a list of the benefits, values, advantages or exclusives of his proposal, he will be able to develop a presentation linking a buyer's interest to the product.

Consider a steel product as an example. Its features such as size, shape, color and finish can be presented visually to gain attention. If the article is portable, it can be shown to the prospect.

Almost any marketable item has characteristics that can be presented as attention getters. A professional salesman constantly seeks attention getters related to his products to aid in demonstrating benefit points.

For example, there was the salesman who attracted attention quickly by bouncing electric light bulbs on the desks of purchasers to prove that they were strong and durable. Another salesman carried a gasoline blowtorch to demonstrate the virtues of his flameproof fabrics.

Demonstrating

Showing the product at the start of a sales interview transfers attention from the salesman to the product itself and to the prospect's needs, wants and desires.

If a necktie salesman, calling at offices, told his prospects that he would like to show them the merchandise in his case, they would all probably say they were not interested. However, if the same salesman entered offices with several neckties hanging over his arm, attention would switch immediately from the salesman to the neckties; and if he held them out to buyers, they would probably take them in their hands for closer inspection. In this way, "no attention" would have been transformed into "active attention."

Showing something concrete to the prospect such as the product, a sample, a model or the material of which the product is made will usually attract the prospect's favorable attention when the salesman's oral presentation will not.

Prospect Participation

It is good practice to get something solid into the prospect's hands as soon as possible after the presentation is started. The product may be placed in front of the prospect, or the salesman may hand him a sample, a book, or model or a piece of advertising matter. When an interview is opened in this manner, the salesman attracts the prospect's attention and participation, and can lead smoothly into the sales presentation. When a prospect participates in a presentation, his attention and interest is secured. Interruptions by other matters will then be less likely to terminate the interview prematurely.

QUESTIONING AND LISTENING

Asking questions and listening attentively to the answers is a useful technique in stimulating a cordial relationship between salesperson and prospect. For instance:

SALESMAN: Mr. Prospect, I have told you how others are stepping up sales, making more money and building satisfied customers by selling our products. Frankly, I do not know all I should about your particular kind of business. Would you be good enough to tell me about it so I can decide whether or not our product can give you the increase in sales that others are getting?

The salesman must listen to the prospect's response, guiding the conversation in the direction he wishes by asking further questions. Salesmen often talk too much; it is better to ask questions and listen.

Intelligent use of questions can promote friendliness, increase the prospect's understanding of and interest in a product and obtain his participation in the selling process.

Listening attentively is one of a salesman's most important functions. Salesmen are often told that in selling it is important to talk well; however, it is just as important to know how to listen well. A salesman can often listen his way to a sale when he cannot talk his way to one. As one expert salesman put it, "If I let the customer do the talking at first, he tells me how he wants to be sold."

Successful salespeople talk to prospects in terms of benefits for them and ask questions to gain agreement. Then, they:

Listen, to show courteous attention.
Listen to learn the prospect's needs.
Listen in order to learn what to say.

A university professor once asked a student, "Why don't you join in the discussions?" And the student replied, "I learn more by listening. Anything I would say I already know."

Discovering Needs and Problems

The value and effectiveness of planned questions in starting an interview is shown by a recent study of the sales force of a large company. The survey revealed that a majority of its salesmen started their presentations by telling their prospective buyers what their product is designed to do. A smaller group in the same company launched their presentations with questions concerning the prospect's needs and problems. The second group consistently averaged more than 50 percent higher in ratio of successful sales to calls than the first group.

The following are some examples of planned questions which might be used to start sales interviews:

"Would you be interested in cutting down your losses by 25 percent?"

"This is our new product. An improvement over our previous one, isn't it?"

"How would you like to give yourself a raise in pay?"

"Would you be interested in cutting down your losses?"

"Do you have customers who would appreciate a product like this?"

"You are interested in saving money, aren't you?"

"Would you be interested in stepping up the number of satisfied customers, Mr. Prospect?"

"Have you ever heard of a glass bottle which won't break when dropped on a cement floor?"

"We're calling on dealers to offer a free checkup. May I see your installation, Mr. Prospect?"

"Would you be interested in making $100 extra this month?"

"Do you have time to learn how to cut down on your operating expenses?"

"Will you try this out, Mr. Jones?"

These are attention-getting questions. Have you noticed how each one promises a benefit to the prospect?

The Listening Technique

In Washington, D.C. there is a men's store known as Raleigh Haberdashery. There is a salesman in the store who uses the "question-listening technique" with customers who want to buy a suit. He greets the customer, then asks about his needs and tastes: the size, color, style and fabric he would prefer in a suit. The salesman brings out a coat and places it on a hanger, turning it to show both front and back. He says nothing, but he watches the customer. If he thinks the man is interested, he removes the coat from the hanger and holds it for the man to slip

into. As the customer views himself in the mirror, the salesman calls the customer's attention to the fit, weave, color or pattern.

The advantage of this method is that the customer is not bombarded with words and he has no feeling of being pressured; confidence is built. The prospect is able to "think" himself into buying. The demonstration also does some powerful selling.

In any sales presentation it is worthless to generalize. In less than two minutes the Raleigh salesman asks enough "need" questions so that he knows what the customer wants. He keys a few words to specific benefit points, demonstrates, receives the customer's attention and goes on to conclude the transaction.

Another example of need-satisfaction questions is revealed by a prospect who went into an automobile showroom intending to buy if his needs were met. He did not realize that he had any specific needs or desires in a car beyond the need for transportation.

The salesman greeted the prospect with a smile and launched into a canned story about the virtues of the car's appearance. He talked at length about several body features in which the prospect was not interested and emphasized things that were definitely not wanted. The prospect listened with growing resentment while the salesman talked and talked. Even though the prospect really wanted a car he left without buying one. Why? Specific needs were not established through questions and listening.

A few days later the prospect walked into another auto showroom. A salesman approached him and asked what he would like to see. Learning that the prospect was actually interested in purchasing a car, he asked what kind of performance was expected; if it was to be used to transport a large family; if it was to be used to call on customers; if economy was a factor; what color was preferred; which accessories were wanted. The salesman asked many more questions regarding the needs and wants of his prospect and listened carefully to the answers. He then showed and demonstrated a car best suited to the needs of this prospect.

The man bought the car because it satisfied his needs, as well as his vague wants and desires. This salesman sold by satisfying needs. He uncovered the needs by asking questions and listening.

Clarity of Expression

Clarity of expression is important in presenting benefit points to a prospect. Benefits must be outlined clearly; hazy ideas and vague generalities are to be avoided.

Your prospect must understand everything you tell him. If you know what you want to say, there is power in your words. If you have not carefully planned your presentation, it is apt to contain generalities and lame trade expressions.

Express the benefits and proof points in a conversational way. Simple language is the most forceful of all.

The product-minded salesman often makes the mistake of using technical language to describe the product to a nontechnical prospect. The salesman must avoid using technical terms that have no meaning for the prospect and tend to confuse him.

Understatements are more effective than overstatements because they are more believable. Exaggerations breed misgivings, understatements build confidence. Blunt statements of superiority often irritate the customer. A good rule is to speak cautiously.

Aids to Clarity

1. Keep your prospect's interests constantly in the foreground.
2. Introduce selling points one at a time, allowing time for the prospect to consider them.
3. Associate every new point with ideas already familiar to the prospect. It is

difficult to grasp anything entirely new. The demonstration affords an opportunity to associate the new with what is already known.

4. Use simple words. Clear language carries the most conviction.
5. Reach the prospect's understanding through his eyes: use demonstrations, printed articles, copies of letters, photos of jobs and other visual aids.
6. Make your presentation as brief as possible—but don't hurry. Cover every essential detail. Leave out information that doesn't help sell.
7. Guard against trade expressions that mean little or nothing to the average prospect and which mislead salespeople into believing they are delivering a strong sales statement. For example, a salesman might say, "This is a nice product," and consider that he has presented benefits to the prospect. Another salesman might say, "Our floor enamel wears a long time on any surface, is easy to apply, fast drying, with great covering ability and high gloss." Which approach conveys a better picture of the product to the prospect?

HOW TO REASSURE PROSPECTS

It would be fine if prospects would believe everything salesmen told them, but prospects have had too many experiences with exaggeration, resulting in disappointment or loss of money and time. Since most prospects fear being misled, the salesman must reassure them.

A salesman might say, for example: "Mr. Prospect, I realize that this may sound unbelievable, but Dick Jones of the ABC Company said to me yesterday, 'We've increased our sales more than 27 percent since we put in your product. We haven't had a single complaint!'"

In effect, the salesman is telling the prospect, "I realize that you do not know me and are afraid that I might mislead you; so I'll tell you what others, who would have no interest in misleading anyone, have had to say about my product." In using the assuring statement, "I realize that this may sound unbelievable," the salesman is trying to quiet the buyer's fears and open his mind for further selling.

When you make an unusual claim, no matter how true it is, it is wise to preface it with an assurance. Admit that "it sounds too good to be true." For example:

"This may sound unbelievable, but..."
"If you question this I won't be surprised..."
"From what others have told me..."

The Importance of the Receptionist

At the start of a sale, the prospect's receptionist may be of utmost importance to the salesman, because she can help him get in to see his client, or she can keep him out. The manner in which the receptionist announces the salesman can either block his way or smooth his path.

If she says: "There is a man out here selling something. You don't want to see him today, do you?" the answer is pretty sure to be, "Too busy now, try later." On the other hand if she says: "There is a gentleman out here who says he can save you time and money. Shall I send him in?" she is assisting the salesman to secure an interview. Therefore, it pays to be very courteous to this person, for she can ruin a sale before it actually starts. Often the prospect asks the receptionist what kind of person the salesman appears to be. If the buyer is not available, she can advise the salesman to see another person, or suggest a better time to see him. Since she can be of help, it is important to treat her with courtesy and respect.

The salesman can help the receptionist by properly introducing himself: "Please tell Mr. Prospect that Mr. Jones, of the Blank Company is here to see him." If a letter has been sent or if the salesman has a firm appointment, she should be informed of it.

The reasons behind an introductory approach worded in this manner are fourfold: (1) The salesman infers that he is expected; (2) he reveals no fear of stating his business; (3) he makes sure that he is not mistaken for another salesman; (4) the name of his company may be well known and, therefore, lends prestige to the call. This kind of introduction increases the salesman's chance of obtaining an interview.

It is advisable to discuss the purpose of the call with the receptionist so that she will be able to outline the salesman's errand if the prospect asks her, "Why does he want to see me?" Sending in a business card to a prospect usually does not have much value, but a card clipped to a pamphlet or brochure can be helpful.

If the prospect is not in or is busy, the salesman should ask the receptionist to suggest a time when he might return. He should also leave a business card with a message written on it or clipped to advertising material.

The salesman should always thank the receptionist when he is admitted for an interview and when he leaves. A courteous salesman is favorably remembered.

CONTROLLED TELLING TECHNIQUE

Did you ever watch a sports event on television and become irritated at the announcer because he talked too much?

Sports announcers and salesmen have at least one thing in common: both must be careful not to talk too much. An excellent sales presentation is worthless if the prospect is not allowed time to consider the information and ask questions about it.

"Controlled telling" means a two-way discussion between the salesman and the prospect. It is never a monologue by the salesman. This kind of selling is planned so that both salesman and prospect may ask questions and listen. When the prospect is encouraged to express his ideas and opinions, the salesman has a more relaxed and receptive buyer.

Ben Franklin, who was considered to be something special as a salesman, frequently stressed the importance of questioning and listening as a method of steering conversation in the direction he wished. This old skill is as valued today as it ever was.

The Champagne of Selling

Controlled telling is the champagne of selling. Like that lively beverage, it should sparkle.

"The man who converseth well," said Cato the elder, "may change his world." Likewise, controlled telling can change a salesman's world, for it can help him make friends, win customers, increase sales volume and advance on the job. In order to accomplish these things, the salesman must know how to control a conversation.

"The pitch" used to be considered the most important part of a sales presentation. Today, it has been replaced in importance by the ability to listen constructively.

Why do some salesman think they are not selling if they are not constantly talking? Watch these spielers and you will find that when they talk too much, it is for one of two reasons: (1) they lack sensitivity for the prospect's feelings; (2) they don't understand the nature of the selling process. They are afraid that if they stop talking, the prospect's interest may be lost and the deal will fall through.

Listening is the keynote of controlled telling. Listening helps the salesman find out what is actually on the minds of his prospects and customers. An industrial salesman does not talk about performance

if the prospect is interested in imitating a competitor. He listens for possible buying motives. Does the prospect reveal motives of fear, curiosity, envy, rivalry, pride or monetary gain? To discover buying motives, the professional salesman listens.

Conversational Art

Imagine a powerful automobile capable of traveling at 150 miles an hour, but with a solid steel windshield. With a car like that you could get places in a hurry, but you never could tell where you were going.

All of us have met salesmen like that high powered car — plenty of ability and courage but handicapped by a "solid steel windshield."

Salesmen like that forget an important fact: one of the greatest compliments that can be paid another person is to ask him questions and then listen attentively to his replies.

When salesmen question and listen, they are learning whether their presentation was understood, how it affected the prospect, and what else must be done to get the order.

Verbal Clues

Studying a person's use of words is helpful in learning about his attitudes and behavior.

For example, a word or a group of words used repeatedly by a prospect can give clues about his attitude or point of view. What a person is thinking about can often be determined by listening for and counting the number of times an idea is mentioned. These are described as "fingerprint words" by John K. Lagermann in

Today's Living.

Metaphors, similes and analogies used by a prospect can reflect his background as well as his attitudes. Repetition of thoughts such as "a penny saved is a penny earned," "security is a thing called money," "money in the bank" or "the good word is save your money," might mean that the prospect has had financial reverses or that he is a careful buyer and spender.

Adjectives used by the individual to express approval or disapproval can be revealing. Some prospects use words such as practical, functional, profitable, useful or feasible to indicate approval. Things they do not like are described as unworkable, stupid, useless or tiresome.

Prospects who judge everything on the basis of size and power, use words such as overwhelming, strong, powerful, gigantic. Things they dislike are often said to be weak, tiny or insignificant. Those prospects who have artistic interests, usually employ terms such as beautiful, gay, colorful, charming.

A discomfort relief quotient or emotional barometer, has been devised by Doctors Mowrer and Dollard. This device is employed to compare the number of words a person uses to express discomfort-annoyance, boredom, ill-health; with the number of words he uses to express comfort, relief, fun or satisfaction. If within a few minutes a prospect has used no optimistic comfortable words, but has called the weather "terrible," the new headlines "deplorable"; the traffic tie up "dreadful"; his associates as "crumbs," he does not need to add that he is "sore" at the world.

Self-References

When we count the number of favorable self-references in a prospect's statements he usually has an attitude of high self-esteem toward others.

Verb tenses, may provide clues as to a person's attitude toward the past as compared with his attitude toward the present and the future.

A preference for passive expressions such as "I found myself lost in speculation" instead of "I was thinking about it"

may reflect a feeling of hopelessness, while active statements reveals a sense of strength.

A passive, discouraged attitude is unmistakably revealed by the following:

But we've always done it this way.
We tried it once and it didn't work.
They didn't do it that way where I came from.
What's the use of working too hard.
It's OK but they would never let me do it.
It's not in the budget.

An old-timer once said that he could size up a prospective customer from his hesitations even more than from his direct answers. For example, ask a prospect "How's business?" If it's good, he will not hesitate to say so; a throat clearing may indicate that all is not well. Pauses may indicate tension or anxiety. The old-timer claimed that such pauses helped to determine a prospect's attitude.

Clues such as these can aid salespeople to gain a better understanding of the people with whom they transact business.

The prospect's questions may reveal his problems. When the prospect asks questions regarding the performance of a product, whether it is economical to operate or how much service is provided, he is voicing positive buying clues. Such questions prove that the prospect is thinking about the proposition in terms of his needs and problems and indicate that he may be ready to buy.

The questions asked by the prospect furnish clues that will alert the listening salesman to *closing possibilities.* The following are examples of such questions:

"Is this the latest you have?"
"May I see it again?"
"Is this the best price you can offer?"
"I wonder if this is a good buy?"
"How safe is it?"

"Is this more effective than what I'm now using?"

"How much research has been done on it?"

"Are there any precautions I should know about?"

"How about chemical reaction?"

"How else can it be used?"

Anxiety, tension or pressure can spoil a sale. A modern salesman rarely hurries through his presentation. He gives his prospect time to express his feelings and opinions about the points being presented.

This is accomplished most successfully when *approval questions* are asked after each benefit point and by careful timing.

Modern salesmen plan and organize so that they can: ascertain a prospect's feelings and attitudes; ask control questions to discover needs; guide a two-way discussion toward a successful conclusion.

POWER POINTS

Benefits are one of the power points that make things click in the buyer's mind. If you analyze your successes and failures, you will discover the importance of benefit points. Professional salesmen always analyze their successful sales and spot the power points that made those sales click.

Other important points include: use of techniques that attract attention; assurances that develop interest; uncovering needs and problems; asking questions and listening to stimulate buying action and increase understanding. Use and revise the ideas, words and plans that get results. When you discover the power of these methods for yourself in your daily selling, you will continue to use them.

To increase sales success, here are ideas that need emphasis:

Be sure to have benefit facts and be sure they are accurate. Statements which cannot be proved should never be made.

Sprinkle the presentation with a lot of the "you" attitude.

Sell personal and business benefits: people do not buy products or services. They buy gain, profits, comfort, satisfaction, values and advantages.

A good presentation aims directly at the buyer's interests, desires, yearnings and wants. The prospect does not want to be bored with technical terminology unless it can be directly related to his own interests.

Benefit facts should be pictured as well as described and explained. Every point should be visualized. Models, exhibits, photos, charts and the like should be freely used. An appeal should be made to the eyes as well as the ears.

Oral presentations should be simple. Fifty-cent words should never be used when penny words will do it better. The presentation should be made slowly, allowing time for the buyer to ask questions and clarify his understanding.

Presentations should be tied in with success stories or testimonials. The prospect should be told about the prestige accounts that have purchased the products, the satisfied users who have expressed favorable opinions. The salesman should be prepared to back up his oral success stories with written testimonials.

Naturally, there can be no sale without a desire for the product or services. Interest is the basis for desire, so it is necessary for the salesperson to arouse the interest of the prospective buyer.

The salesperson, too, must be interesting throughout the entire interview. Unless the salesperson can arouse and stimulate interest in himself as well as in his proposal, a successful sale is not likely to result.

DISCUSSION QUESTIONS AND PROBLEMS

1. How would you know when a prospective buyer is really interested in your proposal?
2. What are three things which help to gain favorable attention?
3. What was the keynote of the attitude of Joe Brown toward his prospect? Did he establish empathy and recognition?
4. Why is it important for a salesperson to ask questions and be a good listener?
5. What are six important factors in starting successful sales? Why are they important?
6. What are several successful attention getters and how may they be used to increase sales?
7. Why should salespeople obtain the prospect's participation when demonstrating?
8. Suppose you are selling fire extinguishers. What are some of the questions you might ask prospects to be sure they thoroughly understand your benefit points?
9. "The first few minutes in a buyer's presence may be vital to some salespeople, but my selling is different because I call on only a few people whom I know well or have met before." Comment.
10. What effective openings or methods can you suggest to make your first five minutes original and to create in the buyer's mind a desire to hear you through?
11. Explain how call-backs and repeat calls on old customers affect the beginning of a salesman's presentation. Should he employ different methods in such presentations?
12. What sales aid can be used effectively to arouse a prospect's interest to the point where he will give you all the time you want to tell your story?
13. Some buyers do not want to pay attention because they are moody, negative, pre-occupied, too busy or simply bad mannered. Briefly explain how you would deal with each of these attitudes.
14. What are the "big little words"?
15. Explain how you would recognize the importance of a prospective customer.

PHENOMENOLOGICAL PROJECTS

Pocono Process Company Case

Sam Smiles sells specialty equipment and is now making his first call of the day. This is the way he starts his sale presentation:

SAM (smiling): Good morning, Mr. Prospect. I'm Sam Smiles of the Pocono Process Company. I know you're a busy man, Mr. Prospect, and I appreciate the time you have given me. So to save your time, I'll get right down to business. Here is a sample of a product we've just brought out and from what other customers have told me, I'm sure it will save you time and money. Here's the way it works. Isn't that interesting?

Questions:

1. Exactly what did Sam do in his presentation?
   Why did he "enter smiling"?
   Why did he refer to his prospect as a busy man?
   Why did he say "get right down to business"?

Why did he show a sample?

Why did he mention "save you time and money"?

Why did he ask the question, "Isn't that interesting"?

2. What would you do to improve this method of starting a sale?

Dick Jansen Tractor Sale Case

Meet our salesman P. C. Spades, known as Paul to his customers. Note the features the customer wants in a tractor and how Spades describes his product to meet his customer's wants. This case does not represent a complete sale; it merely shows portions of a sales talk designed to illustrate meeting customer wants. Spades has just driven into Dick Jansen's farmyard. Spades recently has sold a tractor to Jim Briscoe, one of Jansen's neighbors.

SPADES: Hi, Dick.

DICK: Hi, Paul, how are you?

SPADES: First rate. Just delivered a new tractor to Jim Briscoe and thought I'd stop by to see how you're getting along. How are things going?

DICK: Oh, so-so.

SPADES: How's the corn crop look?

DICK: It'll be all right if we get some more rain.

SPADES: Well, how many acres do you have in corn this year?

DICK: I figure about thirty.

SPADES: Say, that's about the same as Jim. How many acres do you have altogether?

DICK: About the same as Jim — 120 acres.

SPADES: That's what I thought. Jim decided that he needed more power to handle the farming. And that new tractor I delivered him this morning is going to fill the bill.

DICK: That's fine. He's been wanting one for quite awhile.

SPADES: When did you buy your tractor, Dick?

DICK: Oh, gosh, it must have been about fifteen years ago.

SPADES: How is it working?

DICK: I can't complain.

SPADES: Dick, what would you like to have in your tractor to make your work faster and easier?

DICK: Oh, I don't know. I suppose I could use some more power, and it is kind of slow. But I'll be able to get along with it for awhile yet.

Questions:

1. What is Spades trying to do in starting this sale?

2. How does Spades find out how to start?

3. How can Spades use his knowledge that Dick is interested in performance? Let's watch how Spades uses this knowledge.

SPADES: You said you could use more power. What jobs do you need extra power on, Dick?

DICK: Well, the plowing on some of my land is rough. I have some heavy clay on the back end of the farm that's really hard to plow. And I certainly could use more power on that No. 6 hammermill with all the feed I have to grind.

Questions:

4. Why does Spades ask Dick where he needs more power?

What have we found so far? We've seen that Spades discovered his customer's buying interest. We've also seen that Spades has found exactly where his customer's interest lies. Let's watch Spades move in.

SPADES: Dick, your plowing problem is pretty general around here. Many of our customers have decided that they need more power for plowing, and that old hammermill problem — you can always use more power on it! A number of farmers in this area have found that our tractor really licks those problems, and I'm convinced it will lick yours, too. Here's why . . .

Questions:

5. Is Spades moving in the right direction? Why or why not?
6. Why does Spades associate Dick's problem with that of other farmers?

SPADES: . . . and I'm convinced it will lick your problem, too. Here's why! Shortly after you bought your old tractor, Dick, you found it did a much better job than your horses. By the same token, this new tractor, with more than 19 drawbar horsepower, and 22 belt horsepower, can do a much better job of plowing and operating your hammermill than your old job. As you know, your tractor will give you the additional power you need for both those jobs.

DICK: Paul, it probably has more power, but wouldn't it use a lot more gas?

Questions:

7. How does Spades convince the prospect about performance?
8. Does Dick show any other buying interest?

SPADES: Dick, offhand it seems that you would have to use more gas to get more power. However, since your present tractor was built, a great many improvements have been made in carburetion, materials and compression. These improvements actually will give you more power on about the same amount of gas your tractor uses. You will use very little more gas, if any, and still have the extra power you need.

DICK: If it won't use more gas, how will I get more speed out of it?

SPADES: That's a good question, Dick. As you know, your tractor has a gear range of $2\frac{1}{4}$, 3 and $3\frac{3}{4}$ miles per hour. Through an improved method of gearing, the new tractor has working speeds of $2\frac{1}{4}$, $3\frac{1}{2}$, and $4\frac{1}{4}$ miles per hour in addition to a ten-mile-per-hour road speed.

Questions:

9. Would you have handled this point differently?

Let's see where Spades goes from there.

SPADES: Dick, in this new tractor you have the added power you need and the speed you want with no more operating expense. I know you are busy now, so you think about that extra horsepower and the added speed our new tractor will give you and I'll bring one out tomorrow. Have your son, Johnny, here. We'll go over the new tractor with a fine tooth comb. Then you can see for yourself the other advantages the new one has over the old one. Will nine o'clock be all right, Dick?

DICK: O.K. See you tomorrow.

Questions:

10. What were the various points brought out as the sale progressed?
11. What major buying interests does Dick have?
12. What features and benefits of the new model does Spades use to sell performance?
13. What is your reaction to the "benefit by benefit" selling method?

Chapter Seven

Arousing and Stimulating Interest

Why one salesman is not as interesting as another is not easy to summarize. However, the interesting, effective salesman begins his presentation skillfully and plans each successive point. He displays both enthusiasm and knowledge of his subject, and makes use of interest-drawing techniques featuring benefits and advantages. He believes in what he is selling, and plans his presentation carefully.

THE IMPORTANCE OF EMPATHY

As was discussed in the previous chapter, the salesman with empathy appreciates the feelings of his prospects or customers. Since empathy means the capacity for participating in another person's feelings and ideas, the salesman with empathy finds it effortless to match his presentation to the personalities of the people on whom he calls. He does not use force or pressure. He understands the other person's problems, conflicts and attitudes, and therefore easily arouses their interest.

A salesman with too much empathy, however, can find himself in trouble. It may be difficult for him to control the interview sufficiently to close the sale if he identifies too completely with the prospective buyer.

If the buyer is not empathic, he might regard the salesman as an intruder. If he is able to see the sales situation from the salesman's point of view, he is exhibiting empathy, and a productive relationship will result.

PRINCIPLE OF HOMEOSTASIS[1]

The principle of homeostasis explains that it is natural for people to resist ideas presented by salesmen, for thought and action patterns are not readily changed. Usually, the prospective buyer is satisfied with what he has or has not, and a sale will not take place until his complacency is disturbed.

The salesman must realize that the prospect may resent efforts to disturb his habitual manner of thinking or acting. It is the salesman's responsibility to stimulate a prospect's interest so that he will realize his need for the suggested idea, product or service. When the prospect's

---

1. Homeostasis is a word coined by Walter B. Cannon, a psychologist at Harvard University. Of Greek derivation, the word comes from *homeo* meaning same and *stasis* meaning stand still.

103

need is latent, or unrecognized, the sales-man's job is to make the prospect dis-satisfied with his current status and en-courage him to improve it.

CONCENTRATING ON NEEDS

While it is true that people do not want to have their complacency disturbed, the majority will be interested when told "what's in it for them." If homeostasis did not exist, there would be no need for sales-men, only for order-takers.

Whether a need is latent or active, rec-ognized or unrecognized, the chief activ-ity of a salesman is to stimulate interest and arouse a desire to buy. To accomplish this feat, the salesman must be able to find the need, and demonstrate how the pro-posal will satisfy it.

The need-satisfaction principle assumes that prospects buy to satisfy needs. It follows, then, that to make a sale the sales-man must uncover the prospects' needs and reveal how his products or services will satisfy them. In other words, this is a prospect-customer oriented approach, rather than a company-salesman oriented one.

Uncovering Problems and Needs

After obtaining the prospect's favorable attention and naming general benefits prefaced by assurances, the salesperson's next move is to find a way in which these benefits can be applied to the prospect's problems or needs. He is ready to pass from the general to the specific, but to do this he must know as much as possible about his prospect's problems or needs, both realized and unrealized.

Surveys of a prospect's problems before the interview will help to uncover many needs. Another way to discover unrealized needs is through conversation, which is usually initiated by asking questions and listening. The salesman may say, "Mr. Prospect, I have told you how others are stepping up sales, making more money

easier and building satisfied customers by selling our product, but frankly, I don't know a great deal about your particular trade here in Centertown. Would you be good enough to tell me about it, so that I can decide whether or not our product can give you the increase in sales that others are getting?"

STARTING TO AROUSE INTEREST

Ordinarily, a prospect is interested only when convinced that he will gain a bene-fit. Prospects rarely offer reasons why they should buy a product; this is the salesperson's job. While he talks, the sales-man must realize that the prospect is say-ing to himself, "What's in it for me?"

Here is how a professional salesman who sells to manufacturers might intro-duce the benefits to be gained from his proposition:

SALESMAN (smiling): Good morning, Mr. Cartwright, I'm Jack Smith of the American Box Co. I appreciate your seeing me and to save your time, I'll get right down to business. I have an interesting little booklet on a new prod-uct that we have just brought out. Be-cause of what others in your line of business have told me, I'm sure it will save you time and thereby save you money. Many of my clients tell me that it has brought them many new custom-ers; yes, and made those same cus-tomers enthusiastic boosters. Doesn't that sound interesting?

PROSPECT: Yes.

SALESMAN (opening booklet): This is how it works.

Note how this salesman started his sale. He greeted his prospect by name, told who he was and the name of his company. He followed with an assurance phrase that carried the benefit, "to save your time, I'll get right down to business." Then he introduced the new product and told the prospect what he could do for him in terms of these benefits: "save you time" — "save you money" — a "lot of new customers" — "customers enthusiastic boosters." He did not give the benefits in his own statements but attributed them to others. Finally, he checked his prospect for his real business interest by asking, "Doesn't that sound interesting?"

The plan is to tell the prospect what can be done for him and then to explain how it can be done. Salespeople should ask themselves before they call on a prospect, "Why should I ask this prospect to buy this product now?"

An example of how to employ the same approach to create dealer interest is revealed by a manufacturer's salesman calling on a dealer who is already a satisfied buyer. The salesman follows the same form as in the previous example: greets the prospect by name, introduces himself and his company, assures the prospect that he will quickly state his business. But because he is calling on a dealer instead of a manufacturer, he emphasizes different benefit points.

SALESMAN (continuing): I'm sure this new product will increase your turnover, bring in new business and raise your profit. Many of my customers tell me that it has not only brought them many new customers; it has also made those same customers enthusiastic boosters. This is how it works.

Note especially how this salesman mentioned three benefits that will interest practically all dealers:

More consumer business
More repeat business
Faster turnover

When prospective customers are asked what they like best about salesmen they invariably mention the exact things in the above approach. For example:

He pronounced the prospect's name correctly.
He gave his name clearly.
He gave the name of his company.
He complimented the prospect.
He had a businesslike appearance and attitude.
He demonstrated his product.
He showed friendliness but not familiarity.
He asked questions.
He listened.
He got down to business quickly.

Assurances to Arouse Interest

The use of assurances help to introduce benefits and reasure the buyer. They make a concession to the buyer's possible doubts by admitting that the salesman's claims may be difficult to believe.

The following are examples of assurances which salesmen use to preface benefits when they attempt to stimulate interest:

If I hadn't seen it myself, I doubt if I would have believed it . . .

This may sound like just another sales talk, but . . .

Here's something that you may question, but . . .

You may not agree with this, but try it and see how it works . . .

You may be surprised at this, but . . .
I won't be surprised if this seems hard to believe, but . . .

I was amazed myself when I first heard this, but . . .

This may seem impossible, but . . .

Many of our customers were skeptical when I first told them about this, but . . .

This is a practical example of how assurances are used to stimulate interest:

SALESMAN (after he has introduced himself) : Mr. Prospect, I am sure that you want to increase sales, get more repeat business and make a good profit. Now I don't want to make any wild claims, and if you question my next statement it won't surprise me, but we have a product that is helping hundreds of our customers get more new business, more repeat business and make additional profits every month. If I can prove this to you, you would be interested, wouldn't you?

Silence May Be Golden

Experts usually agree that the successful salesperson says the right thing in the right way at the right time, but they warn that he must listen part of the time. He must sense when to remain silent and what not to say. Silence is often golden.

The salesperson can determine what is the most effective sales appeal to use in each case by listening to the prospect's remarks. The salesperson must listen and learn, hoping that the prospect will reciprocate by listening to his sales presentation and becoming a buyer.

Problem-Solving and Ideas

There are probably no prospects or customers who would not be interested in new ideas about their businesses, or who would not welcome help in solving some of their vexing problems. In many situations, no one is better equipped to do these things than the salesman.

Frequently the customer will ask for help. For example, a wholesale salesman once asked, "How can I eliminate monotony from my business? I call on the same customers each week, fifty-two weeks a year. It becomes very much the same story on each call. Once in a while we have new products or new deals on old products; but, for the most part, it

is a case of taking orders, copying down items from the grocer's 'want book.'"

Most of the monotony will be eliminated if this salesman suggests items that the prospect may have overlooked, and if he tries to have one new idea to present on each call. Successful salesmen know that merchants are eager for profit-producing ideas if they are tactfully suggested. Every merchant has problems needing solutions. A professional salesman identifies these problems and tactfully offers his suggestions and ideas for solving them.

When a salesman reads this he will possibly ask, "But where am I going to get the ideas and the suggestions?" The answer is, "From trade magazines and merchandising books." "But what magazines or books can I read that the prospect can't read?" he might persist. The answer is, "None," but the prospect is usually too busy operating his store or his plant or his service to read all the periodicals available to him.

Customers

Interest can be aroused sometimes by placing prospects or customers under obligation to the salesman, perhaps by the salesman disclosing information of value to the prospect.

In selling to lumbermen, for example, a salesman might offer information regarding permits that have been issued for the erection of new buildings. After the salesman shows tangible interest in the prospect's business, he feels under obligation to show interest in the salesman's presentation.

Tactful Minimizing

In convincing a prospect, the salesperson may tend to minimize any weakness in his product or service and to build up the outstanding qualities. However, a sincere and honest approach builds confidence in the salesman and his proposition. It is always advisable to tell the

truth. It is ethical to minimize, but not
to deny, poor quality. For example:

A jewelry salesman is confronted by
a young couple who plan to buy a modest engagement ring and wish to select a
stone. The salesman displays a nicely cut
fifty-nine-point diamond, sparkling and
clear. The young man hesitantly inquires
about the price. The young lady asks
pointedly, "Is the stone perfect?"

The salesman, dealing first with the
question of price, answers promptly that
the value of cut diamonds increases with
every point. The price he asks is fair on
the current diamond market — a fact
which he explains satisfactorily. Knowing that many people are more concerned
with show rather than true quality, pre-
ferring a larger stone with a slightly yellow cast and some flaws for the same
price, he explains the difference in the
appearance of this small but beautifully
cut blue-white stone.

The young lady appreciates these facts
but is persistent in asking whether *her*
diamond, even though fairly small, is
perfect. The salesman has an answer for
this. He says truthfully that this stone is
"commercially" perfect. He explains that
to most laymen, "perfect" means just
that. The young people are satisfied. They
feel that they are getting quality and
beauty at a fair market price, and they
are happy with their purchase.

To the discerning buyer, however, the
salesman's device for belittling the bad
points and magnifying the good points
of the stone would be insufficient. Some
people would prefer to own a smaller,
perfect stone rather than a larger one
with any flaw, even an unnoticeable one.
It is the salesperson's job to judge the
individual buyer and proceed accordingly. The honest salesperson tells his customer the facts.

Success Stories

"Success stories" is a more meaningful

term for testimonials. People like to hear
success stories. In them, the motives of
gain and imitation are especially prominent. For example, the salesman can tell
a prospect a success story about another
customer who is making more profits selling the salesman's merchandise. The businessman will probably apply the idea to
himself by thinking, "I can do what he
is doing and make more money, too."
Many prospective buyers are imitators
of other businessmen.

If a salesman is selling fire insurance,
he may appeal to the fear motive by telling a story about a man who suffered a
heavy loss because he postponed buying
protection; however, it might be more
effective to relate a success story about a
client who had money in his pocket because he had purchased adequate fire
insurance. If the salesman is selling a
trust-company service, he may tell a success story of an estate left in excellent
condition because of his firm's compe-
tence. If he is selling real estate as a
speculation, he may tell a success story
of someone who made big profits by buying property similar to the kind the salesman is selling.

In each of these cases, the customer
becomes the central figure in an imaginary
playlet of his own creation. His interest
is in himself as the chief actor in the
scene. If the customer is the star, the
salesman is the producer, having supplied
the script, properties and audience. Also,
by using the success story to bring in a
disinterested third party to offer testimony, the salesman can avoid making
blunt factual statements, which are often
discounted by the prospect.

Another advantage of the success-
story method of giving sales information
is that stories are more easily remembered than mere statements of facts. Success stories, or testimonials, are to the
listener what pictures are to the reader.
Just as illustrated books and newspapers

are more interesting than solid printed matter, so a sales presentation filled with anecdotes holds the prospect's attention, arouses his interest and impresses itself on his memory.

The novice salesman might be unaware of the importance of telling an interesting success story and might too often bore the customer with lengthy statements of fact. The professional salesman never misses an opportunity to tell a success story, because he knows that it is an excellent method for stimulating interest.

THE VALUE OF QUESTIONS
It has been said that there is only one reliable way to determine what a customer wants, and that is to have the prospect tell the salesman. This may be done by asking the prospect questions; for example, "What do you have in mind?" or, "How would you like to stop your worries?" When the prospect answers, the salesman can decide on the appeals which will most effectively influence him to buy.

Asking questions and listening is also a good method of stimulating interest in unrealized and latent needs. Uncovering hidden motives and unrealized needs calls for expert selling.

The salesman can say, "Mr. Prospect, I have told you how others are stepping up sales, making more money and building satisfied customers by selling our products. Frankly, I do not know a great deal about your particular kind of business. Would you be good enough to tell me about it, so that I can decide whether or not our product can give you the increase in sales that others are getting?"

Then the salesman listens, guiding the conversation by asking intelligent questions and showing interest in the prospect's comments.

Many of the better salesmen ask questions to induce the prospect to agree with them. They do this to check the prospect's

understanding, his interest, to obtain the prospect's active participation in the selling process and to obtain "yes" answers as the sale progresses. These salesmen may say, for example:

"Does that check with your experience?"
"Have I made that clear?"
"How does that look to you?"

A skillful salesman does not ask questions as if he were the prosecuting attorney with the prospect on the witness stand. He invites dialogue by posing a question when conversation lags or when a point needs clarification. Until two-way communication is established, the salesman has not really begun to influence the prospect to buy.

There are other advantages to this approach. For example, the salesman flatters his prospect when he asks him questions, because he indicates that the prospect is an authority. In other words, when a prospect is questioned, he is encouraged to talk, and to him this means that the salesman is interested in him and his problems.

Timing and Questions
Timing the pace of a presentation and asking questions about the key points in it are important.

For example, a salesman may talk to a prospect and not be heard because the latter has his mind on another topic or because he has not had time to consider a previous statement. The salesman should delay each point in his preparation until he is sure the prospect understands what has already been said. If the prospect fails to grasp each point as it is made, he may not have a desire to buy because he will not know how the proposal will benefit him. The best way for a salesman to determine if he is communicating with the prospect is to ask questions and listen to the answers, or answer questions from the prospect.

Questions and their answers can also serve as a timing guide to indicate to the salesman whether his presentation is too fast or too slow. He can then adjust his timing of key points to a pace that will be perceived and understood by the prospect.

Listening is a part of the question technique. Successful salesmen not only ask questions and listen, they also listen when they do not ask questions. They listen for complaints, objections, references to competition, gossip, stories and the like, so they may receive clues to the prospect's wants, needs and desires.

Questions to Check Belief

Questions help the salesman discover if benefit claims are believed, since some claims sound exaggerated even when they are not. There are buyers who silently answer every point made by the salesman with the comment, "Yes, if it is true."

Most prospects will not say that they do not believe a salesman. They will not be that frank. Therefore, it is advisable for the salesman to check on the acceptance of his claims with such questions as, "That sounds reasonable, doesn't it?"

Statements as Questions

Many statements can be changed into questions. For instance instead of saying that blue and chrome go well together, the salesman might ask, "Don't you think that the blue and chrome go well together?" By being asked such questions, the prospect is brought into active participation in the presentation. Often he will add other comments and suggestions, and sometimes proceed to "sell" the salesman.

Control over a prospect's decisions is always desirable, and one way to achieve this is to use statements as questions. Statements are often more effective when they are phrased as questions, particularly when the questions call for a "yes" answer.

Questions for a Wandering Mind

For any one of many reasons a prospect's mind may wander. The alert salesman will know when the thought thread is broken because he will sense, or see, that the prospect is not mentally following him.

When the salesman loses the prospect's attention and interest, he must act promptly to regain them. He might call the prospect's attention to a new feature or benefit, and then ask a question about it.

For example, "Did I make it entirely clear to you, Mr. Jones, that this product will save you 27 percent each month on your operation?" or, "Incidentally, have you noticed this unique feature on our new model?"

Such questions are useful for drawing a wandering mind back to the subject. However, it is better to prevent the occurrence of wandering minds than to have to bring them back to the topic. The prospect's attention can be held by the same means used to recapture it: by asking questions to obtain agreement as each benefit point or feature is explained.

Questions to Obtain Agreement

Many salesmen ask questions to induce the prospect to agree with them on every point they make. They do this to encourage empathy, to check the prospect's understanding and interest, to promote his active participation in the selling process and to obtain affirmative answers as the sale progresses. These salesmen may ask for example: "Does that check with your experience?" "Have I made that clear?" "Doesn't that sound interesting?" or, "How does that look to you?" Questions such as these assist the salesman in closing successful sales.

Poison Questions

Although the salesman wants his prospects to talk while he listens, he must do everything possible to avoid questions which may create a negative atmosphere.

Prospects may reflect a negative attitude when they think they are going to be asked to part with money. They'll say

"Business is lousy," "I have no need for your product," or "We have stopped buying for awhile." These negative statements are natural responses when the prospect's real need is not discovered through proper questioning.

When the salesman realizes that the wrong questions will bring negative replies, he will avoid like poison such questions as:

Things picking up much?
Anything doing?
How about giving me a break?
Need any of my stuff?
How's business?
Why can't you see my side, Mr. Prospect?
How are things moving?
That's simple enough, isn't it?
Do you see what I mean?
Could you afford this?

Poison questions will start the prospect talking, but the salesman will probably listen to the prospect talk himself out of buying. Poison questions ask for "No" answers.

Suggested Response Questions

When salesmen ask suggested-response questions, they are employing a technique that requires practice before use. These are questions intended to gratify the prospect's ego and cause him to react favorably to the salesman. For example, "Doesn't that check with your experience, Mr. Brown?"

The following will serve to offer additional examples of how to suggest the response the salesman wants:

1. To suggest friendly attitude and common interests to a prospect:
2. To refer to a person who is a satisfied user of the salesman's product or service:
3. To suggest the prospect's response after the salesman replies to an objection:
4. To use a trial close, suggesting that the prospect buy:

5. To suggest that quality is more important than price:
6. To build buyer confidence:

"You were in business with your brother for a few years, weren't you?"

"You know Bill Brown, the owner of Bill's Pharmacy, don't you? He's a good manager, isn't he?"

"When you evaluate the savings this product offers, as well as the service, the price is relatively unimportant, isn't it?"

"Mr. Jones, you seem to approve everything about this item. When would you like to have it delivered, this week, or would next week be soon enough?"

"But you realize, don't you Mr. Black, that this is a quality product?"

"Mr. Jones, I'm glad you had enough confidence in our product to examine it. I just want to ask you one question. What success have you had with it?"

Retriever Questions

Retriever questions are those which are formed by rephrasing statements made by the prospect. They bring him back into the conversation and may be used at any time during the interview.

Retriever questions are used when a prospect's eyes go blank, when he has a faraway look and a confused expression showing that the salesman has lost his attention and interest. If the prospect does not listen, it is the salesman's fault, because the salesman should control the interview. Here is an example of a retriever question:

SALESMAN: Would you like to see a chart that shows successive reductions in cost? Note that the reductions were observed in a situation similar to yours after my product was added to the manufacturing process. Isn't that important to you?

In this example, the salesman has regained the prospect's attention by asking a question, tying it in with the prospect's own interest while offering proof of statements.

Easy Manner

In addition to listening, the salesman will want to have a relaxed manner, a friendly smile, a thoughtful expression and a pleasant tone of voice. The use of these simple devices can smooth out questions and not only make them acceptable, but induce the prospect to disclose his needs.

POWER POINTS

Why people buy certain products is relatively easy to understand when it is understood that they are seeking the answer to the question, "What's in it for me?" When prospects ask that question, they want to know *how* and *why* they will benefit if they buy. The most successful salespeople never forget that a prospect is not interested in them, their company, or their product or service. They know that prospective customers are interested only in what the salesman can do for *him*. Unless the proposition appeals to the prospect's interests, unless it satisfies *his* desires, unless it shows *him* a gain, *he* will not buy.

Usually a prospect will be interested only in a money gain, which means added profits or savings, or both. Some prospects are also interested in safety, pride, competition, increased efficiency, comfort, dependability or employee satisfaction. There are other reasons for buying, but the chances are that these are the most important. The success of all selling activity will depend on the direct, selfish appeal the proposition has for the prospect. When the proposition appeals to *his*

interests, satisfies *his* desires, shows him a gain, *he* will surely buy.

It is also valuable to know that people do not buy things. They buy status, prestige, safety, security, satisfaction, enjoyment, recognition, solutions to their problems, profits, values, savings and advantages. To repeat: people do not buy products, features and services; they buy what products, features and services will *do* for them. One of the basic jobs of the salesperson is to translate product features into prospect benefits.

It is well to note that not all the benefits of a particular proposition are of equal interest to various prospects. One prospect may be interested only in economy of performance; another may be interested in safety; another, in increasing his status in the community. Therefore, a salesperson needs to discern a prospect's individual needs and decide which of these his proposition can satisfy.

During the presentation, searching questions about benefits should be asked. Questions that appeal to the other person's self-interest evoke the best answers but the salesperson must also be interested. He should take care in asking questions; too many may not obtain the desired response. There are times when silence is more rewarding than another question. In every situation, the value of the answer depends upon the quality of the salesman's attention.

A salesperson's questions must spring from honest inquiry, not from attempts at flattery or obvious efforts to manipulate the prospect's thinking. Questions that deal with a prospect's feelings are more revealing than those dealing with facts.

DISCUSSION QUESTIONS AND PROBLEMS

1. Explain the influence of empathy on personal marketing.
2. What is your understanding of the meaning of the need-satisfaction principle?

3. Explain the principle of homeostasis.
4. Why is it important for a salesman to emphasize buyer benefits in his presentation?
5. What is said to be the unspoken question of all prospective buyers?
6. Explain how features are translated into benefits.
7. What is meant by predicting needs and how could a salesman perform this activity?
8. How may buying motives be used to stimulate interest in the mind of a buyer?
9. What are the advantages of success stories? Give examples of this device in use.
10. Explain how and why placing a prospect under obligation often assists salesmen to stimulate interest in the sales proposal.
11. Explain why assurance words and phrases can be used to increase a prospect's interest and desire. Provide five examples of assurance phrases and tell why they were chosen.
12. Explain and give examples to show how listening and questioning on the part of a salesman can help to create buying interest.
13. Explain how a salesman can help solve problems and bring new ideas to customers. Why will such activities help both salesman and customer?
14. Name and explain the side effects which may accrue to salesmen who use the benefit approach.
15. Explain in detail why you believe one salesman sells more than another. Base your explanation on everything you have studied up to this point.
16. From the presentation viewpoint, what value do you see in outlining features and benefits a step at a time followed by questions, rather than subjecting the buyer to a nonstop presentation?
17. Assume that you are talking to a dealer prospect whose account you especially hope to win, when he suddenly says, "Your prices are too high." Write five benefit points which you could have used to ward off this objection, or at least to minimize its impact.
18. In relation to timing and questions, please answer the following questions:
    a. Do you believe that a salesman should ever leave a prospective customer without trying to close?
    b. What are some of the manifestations that would indicate that the salesman has "lost" his prospect's attention?
    c. You were told in this chapter to check on the prospect's understanding of each sales point. How does this advice relate to the "selling formula," or standard sales presentation?

PHENOMENOLOGICAL PROJECTS

The Bill Anderson Sale (Case)

While reading this case, note the features this customer wants in a truck and the way Short describes his product to meet his customer's wants. It is not intended to represent a complete sale, it merely shows portions of a sales talk to illustrate the points we have discussed previously.

Short is calling on Bill Anderson, a general contractor. Short knows that Bill has been awarded a state highway construction contract. Short has just entered Anderson's office.

SHORT: Congratulations, Bill. I just heard you were awarded that Rock Valley cutoff job.

BILL: Yeah, I was afraid Wilson's bid might be under ours.

SHORT: Well, it was pretty close. I noticed there was very little difference in your bids. It looks like a good job. If you don't have too much trouble with your equipment, you should make some money on it.

BILL: Yeah, it ought to be a profitable job, but you never know what'll happen.

SHORT: Well, as you know, Bill, anticipating breakdowns often means the difference in the amount of profit in any job. When do you plan on starting?

BILL: Well, we're going to move some of our equipment over right away.

SHORT: That's a big job, Bill, and you'll have to hustle to meet the September first deadline.

BILL: Yes, it looks like I'll have to move in eight road gangs and all my local equipment.

SHORT: In view of that deadline and the size of the job, isn't there a possibility that you might get into trouble with some of the old equipment you have here?

BILL: Oh, I don't know. We take pretty good care of our equipment. Most of it's still in pretty good running condition.

SHORT: No doubt it is, Bill. You do take good care of your equipment. But aren't a couple of those old bulldozers pretty well worn out?

BILL: Well, I have some that are getting pretty old.

SHORT: It could cost you plenty in time and money if those babies broke down! I'd like to fix you up with a couple of new models to help you make more money on this job.

Question:

1. What is the significance of the remarks Short makes in the opening conversation? We have seen how Short approached his customer. Now he continues with the sale:

SHORT: . . . I'd like to fix you up with a couple of our new models to help you make more money on this job.

BILL: That's darned nice of you, Paul, but I've always used Pixies, and they've been pretty satisfactory. If I do replace those two, I'll probably get Pixies again.

SHORT: Pixies are good scrapers, Bill, but this new model of ours has some improvements that I think you'll be interested in.

BILL: How did they improve that thing?

SHORT: They have improved many things, to give you better operation and at a lower cost than other bulldozers.

BILL: What did they improve to do this?

Questions:

2. What is this customer interested in?
3. How does Bill indicate this interest?
4. Do you think Short planned this sales approach? Why?

We have seen how Short found Anderson's interests and encouraged him to ask for information. As we interrupted, Bill was saying:

BILL: What did they improve to do this?

SHORT: Let's take the starting system. That's always been a headache to you, and you've got some cold weather coming up soon.

Short opens his briefcase and takes out a folder, which he shows to Anderson, using the cutaway drawings as he begins to talk about the starting system. Short fully describes the operation of the new gasoline-conversion starting system.

SHORT: . . . and another advantage, Bill, is that the pistons and cylinders are warmed with gasoline heat at an idling speed. Then, when you switch it to diesel, it's ready to go. With our system it's impossible to have half-burned fuel forming carbon around the rings. Do you agree that this is an improvement over other starting systems?

BILL: Yes, I can see where it might be.

SHORT: Bill, in addition to saving you money in repair costs, this starting system saves you plenty of time, too. It's as simple as starting your car. All you have to do is climb up and step on the starter. No other operations are needed. The time you can save, plus what you can save on repairs in both time and money, add up to a real improvement that will be valuable to you. Do you agree, Bill?

BILL: It sounds like it might eliminate some of our troubles, especially in cold weather.

Questions:

5. What is the value of the folder in Short's presentation?
6. How does Short follow up on Bill's two interests?

We have seen how Short found Bill's interests and how he explained the sales features of the starting system in terms of those two buying interests.

BILL: It sounds like it might eliminate some of our troubles, especially in cold weather.

SHORT: You bet it will, Bill. And it'll make your operators happier, too.

BILL: You mentioned several other improvements. What are they?

SHORT: Take the drawbar arrangement, for example . . .

Short opens a folder with a cutaway drawing and explains the advantages of the new model's drawbar arrangement over that of the Pixie. After giving Bill a full explanation, Short says:

SHORT: So you see, Bill, this gives you the proper balance between weight and power. This means you can move more dirt in a shorter time with less fuel cost. That's important to you, isn't it?

BILL: It certainly is.

SHORT: And you can see how this drawbar arrangement will make this possible can't you, Bill?

BILL: Yeah, that makes sense.

Questions:

7. How does Short appeal to buying interests when he tells about the new drawbar arrangement?
8. How does Short end his appeal to the benefits and advantages of the new model drawbar?

SHORT: You really have to operate this new model to appreciate these two advantages I've explained. I know you want to get started on this job, and time is short. I'd like to bring one out for a demonstration this afternoon or tomorrow. Which would be better for you, Bill?

BILL: Better make it in the morning. I'm busy this afternoon.

SHORT: OK. See you about nine o'clock tomorrow morning.

Questions:

9. Why was it helpful for Short to plan his call before seeing Bill?

10. Why was it important for Short to know his customer's buying interests?
11. What is your reaction to this selling method?

Dick Jansen Tractor Sale (Role)

While reading this case, notice how salesman Spades builds up his case and how he wins Dick Jansen's agreement. We shall interrupt from time to time to ask questions and discuss Spades' selling technique.

As we look in, it is 9 A.M. and Spades has just driven into Jansen's tractor yard and is unloading the new tractor from the trailer. Johnny, Dick's twelve-year old son, comes running up.

JOHNNY: Is this ours?

SPADES: It might be if we can sell your dad on it.

JOHNNY: Oh, boy!

SPADES: Jump up and see how it feels. . . . How do you like it up there?

(As Dick walks up, Johnny bounces around in the seat):

JOHNNY: Boy, this seat's a lot better than our old one!

SPADES: Well, Dick, I brought one of our new models out like I said I would yesterday, and we'll try it out in the field in a few minutes. But first I'd like to show you a few things about operating it that are different from your tractor. Why don't you get up in the seat while I show you?

Spades leans against a rear tire while Dick looks over the tractor, bounces on the seat a few times, looks around, stands up and then sits down. Then Spades says:

SPADES: How do you like that seat, Dick?

DICK: It's a lot more comfortable than mine.

SPADES: You know, Dick, it took a long time before we got around to making a tractor seat that's really comfortable. That hydraulic seat certainly would be a lot easier on you, wouldn't it?

DICK: It sure would.

SPADES: And notice, too, Dick, this seat is higher than yours. This way you're out of the dirt and dust.

Questions:

1. What selling technique is Spades using in this sale?
2. How does he discover the new buying interest?
3. How does he present this feature and benefit?
4. How does he get Dick to agree?
5. Why does Spades spend time talking about the seat?

DICK: I see you have foot instead of hand brakes on this tractor.

SPADES: Yes, that's another improvement you'll appreciate during this demonstration. You know how inconvenient the hand brakes are on your tractor, Dick. On this new model, you've got two foot-operated brakes for making sharp turns — one for each wheel. When traveling in the ten-mile-per-hour gear, they can be locked together for quicker stopping and safe operation. These brakes certainly will be more convenient than the hand levers on your tractor, won't they?

DICK: Yeah, they might be. But the hand brakes aren't too much trouble.

SPADES: Dick, that's one feature you won't really appreciate until you use it.

Questions:

6. Why does Spades talk about brakes?

7. What two buying interests does Spades appeal to while explaining the brakes?
8. What does Spades say to show that these benefits exist in this feature?
9. When will Spades get complete agreement on the brakes?

SPADES: And here's another operating difference from your tractor. It's also quite an improvement. Remember, I told you yesterday that this new model would do 10 m.p.h. on the road. Well, here's why. It has four speeds forward, and the fourth gear is the road gear. This marking here on the housing cover shows you the position of the different gears.

DICK: That looks pretty simple. It won't bother me.

JOHNNY: Let's crank it up, Pop!

DICK: Let's hear how it sounds.

SPADES: Johnny, you don't have to crank this new model. It has a self-starter. Climb up on the drawbar while I show your dad how to start it. All you do, Dick, is pull out the ignition switch button, advance the engine speed control lever one-third, push the clutch pedal in and pull on the starter rod.

DICK: Boy, it sure starts easy.

SPADES: And you can be sure it'll start just as easy winter or summer. This self-starter surely beats cranking the old model, doesn't it?

DICK: Sure does. Do you think you could start it, Johnny?

JOHNNY: Sure I can! Turn it off and let me show you.

DICK: Not now. I want to take it out and work with it.

SPADES: OK, Dick. Put it in third and drive it out to your back field. We'll hook up the trailer and see how it works. Johnny and I will follow behind. Come on, Johnny!

Questions:

10. What benefit is Spades selling now?
11. How does he present this benefit?
12. How does he get Dick to agree?

Chapter Eight

Analyzing and Guiding Buyer Behavior

PEOPLE PROBLEMS

Human beings are the most complex machines in existence. They cannot be labelled or classified; they cannot even be accurately analyzed. However, when we know enough about human behavior to understand the reasons for it, we can often predict the way people will act in the presence of salesmen. Salesmen deal personally and continuously with human beings, each of whom must be persuaded and motivated to act upon a sales proposal. This process requires skillful manipulation of the prospect's mind and emotions, in addition to the presentation of goods and services. Salesmanship is not solely a matter of selling *things*, it is also a matter of understanding people; it requires "people knowledge" as well as product knowledge.

Reasons for Problems

There are a number of common problems leading to difficulties and obstructions between salesman and prospect.

Bad attitudes
Prejudices
Honest reasons
Bad buying habits
Alibis, excuses, stalls
Defense mechanisms

Bad attitudes may exist because the prospect dislikes the salesman. This dislike may be caused by his manner of talking, his behavior, his mood, his attitude or his manners; or the salesman may remind him of someone he does not like.

Buying habits. A prospect may be in the habit of paying a certain price, using a certain brand or quality of product or wearing a particular style or color. Many prospects do not like to change their habits, but it is part of a salesman's job to jolt such prospects out of their complacency.

Prejudices. Prejudice may be based on bias, misinformation or misjudgment of the salesman, his proposition or his company. From the moment the salesman starts his presentation he may need to work toward overcoming the prospect's prejudices.

117

Alibis, excuses and *stalls* arise because the salesman has not obtained the prospect's real buying interest. The answer to the question: "What do you do when the prospect says, 'No'?" is " What did you do *before* the prospect said 'No'?"

Honest reasons. Prospects have the right to reject a salesman's claims. They may be fearful of poor quality and high price. They may be fearful of getting something less than they are paying for. These fears may not prevent a sale, but they often reveal that the prospect wants more and better solutions for his problems.

Defense mechanism. A defense mechanism is a device — a way of behaving — that a person uses unconsciously to protect himself against ego-involving frustrations. Actually, it is not so much the frustration he defends himself against as the anxiety that stems from frustration. The common view is that defense mechanisms may be regarded as defenses against anxiety. For example, a person may conveniently forget about things that make him feel uncomfortable or anxious. He can forget to make a decision to buy wall-to-wall carpeting because spending $4,000 for carpeting means foregoing $4,000 of profit for his firm. Or a person can find himself refusing to accept delivery of an article because, he says, he "forgot" he had ordered it. Behavior of this type is called "repression."

There are a number of other defense mechanisms besides repression. The following list gives you an idea how these mechanisms operate. We sometimes ascribe motives for our own frustration to someone else (projection); we identify ourselves with people who have the qualities we admire (identification); we bawl out someone, a salesman for example, because we have had an unpleasant experience with the salesman's superior (displaced aggression); we explain our behavior by concealing the real motive

and saying that some other motive has made us do what we did (rationalization); we shrug off frustration in one area of our lives by turning to a satisfying type of behavior in another area (compensation).

Advantages of Defense Mechanisms
Almost everybody uses defense mechanisms some of the time. Actually, moderate use of these mechanisms is a harmless and convenient way to dispose of conflicts. When defense mechanisms make us feel better and make others more comfortable, as they often do, their value in reducing tension and letting us get on with important problems more than offsets the trivial self-deceptions they entail. However, when we encounter people who use their defense mechanisms on *us*, we are not likely to appreciate their value nor enjoy the experience. We are more likely to become anxious and frustrated ourselves unless we understand the behavior of such people and know how to counsel them.

HANDLING DEFENSE MECHANISMS
There are many ways to handle problems of the type we have discussed. The folowing points might be considered as a general pattern:

1. *Take time to listen.* Whenever a prospect evidences behavior cues such as *repression, projection, displaced aggression, rationalization* or *compensatory behavior,* it pays us to give him our time whenever possible. This effort will rarely prove to be a waste of time. It will help him clarify his thinking and establish better communication.

2. *Be attentive.* If the prospect launches into a violent tirade, it is best to let it flow uninterrupted until it is exhausted. Let him siphon it off; employ emotional catharsis. We should make every effort to understand what he says

and to sympathize. In other words, be emphatic and attentive.

3. *Provide proper verbal reaction.* As the buyer talks, the salesman may employ what has been called a series of "eloquent and encouraging grunts" — "Humm," "Uh-huh," "Oh" or "I see." If the buyer pauses momentarily, the salesman should nod his head indicating understanding until speech starts again. In the field of psychology, this is known as the "non-directive" counseling technique.

If the buyer becomes unreasonable, the salesman should restate what has just been said, putting it in the form of a question. Examples of such questions are: "'Do you actually believe that our products are no good?" or "Do you believe our products are not produced under quality control?"

4. *Do not probe for additional facts.* There is a difference between willingness to listen and nosiness to get more information. In nondirected counseling, there can be no inquisitiveness. We don't want information for ourselves; we want to help the prospect siphon off his aggressions.

5. *Do not evaluate what has been said.* We must refrain from passing judgment upon statements heard from a buyer. In no case should we give a buyer advice about his emotional problems, even if he requests it.

6. *Do not lose faith in the ability of the buyer to solve his own problems.* As the buyer talks, we are witnessing a human phenomenon. He is really talking things over with himself. If we refrain from injecting ourselves into *his* conversation, the chances are fairly good that the buyer will work things out for himself, to our benefit.

7. *Relax.* When dealing with problem people, we cannot afford to grow tense. Tenseness brings anxiety, anxiety stimulates fear, and fear causes nervousness and often failure. Fear and anxiety are

easily communicated to the prospect, causing him to react with obstacles to prevent buying. Obstacles are the last thing a salesman needs. His real need all through a sale is agreement, assistance and consent.

Counselor's Technique

Talk less and listen more.
Make few or no suggestions.
Give little advice.
Never judge the buyer's ideas.
Give the buyer nothing to fight against.
Relax emotionally and physically.

PREDICTING THE BEHAVIOR OF CUSTOMERS AND PROSPECTS

How may a salesperson learn to observe, analyze and manage the various behavior traits revealed by his prospects and customers? A successful starting point is to accept and use six basic principles:

1. People cannot be typed; typing is the most common error made in judging people.
2. First impressions of prospects and customers are unreliable, and the salesman cannot depend on their accuracy.
3. The use of psychology in the marketplace can be learned only through *practice* and *application.*
4. People are much more alike than they are unalike; therefore, problem people are in the minority.
5. There are profound psychological antagonisms which divide people more absolutely than differences of creed, race or income.
6. When prospects are qualified and the proposition properly presented, few obstructions to a successful sale will arise.

All salesmen, either consciously or unconsciously, attempt to classify or type their prospects and to adapt their approaches to fit each individual. The salesman observes the prospect's outstanding behavior characteristic and focuses the greater part of his attention on it. He then generalizes his impression of the prospect from the single outstanding trait. For example, the salesman says, "This prospect is a jovial fellow," or, "He's the biggest grouch I ever met," implying in each case that this is the prospect's predominant characteristic. Typing is a poor way to evaluate people.

COMMON BEHAVIOR TRAITS
The behavior of people is indicated by common traits which are seen or heard. The following discussion of these traits should help us in our study of behavior in the marketplace.

Anger	Timidity
Skepticism	Over-Sociability
Indifference	Vacillation
Reticence	Irritability
Hesitation	Impulsiveness
Procrastination	Affability
Disorganization	Thoughtfulness
Self-Importance	Insincerity
Insincerity	Fearfulness

The Angry Customer
The person whose overt behavior is revealed by this trait is touchy, cranky, cross, mean and easily angered. He is easily provoked, has an inflammable temper or a disposition to be incensed on slight provocation; is excitable, unreasonable, impatient, irritable. He is usually difficult to please or satisfy; has fixed notions and standards.

This person is not really a good thinker, although he believes he is. His responses are largely impulsive and emotional. Quite often he likes to bluster and argue for the pleasure he gets from it. He may like to annoy and dismay a salesman whom he believes is vulnerable to abuse.

Ill-health, either emotional or physical, may be the cause of irascibility. Bad attitudes, habits, prejudices, set, aggres-

sions, projection and certain defense mechanisms may contribute to this person's behavior.

It is advisable to study each prospect as an individual and then formulate a process for dealing with him. We cannot succeed if we argue with a person whose irascibility dominates his behavior. We can usually succeed if we remain calm, ask questions and listen. In this way the prospect's inner drives and feelings may be made apparent, and the salesman can then learn how and where to focus his presentation.

Although there may be a natural inclination on the salesman's part to get tough in return, he cannot reciprocate in kind and still close a sale. This is the time for the salesman to remain friendly and poised. A good presentation, tailored to suit this individual's basic needs and desires, plus quiet self-control will tend to calm the prospect down until he acts rationally.

The Skeptical Customer
The person whose chief behavior characteristic is that of skepticism is one who doubts that anything is certain. He is distrustful, suspicious and dubious. He has a lack of faith in the truth, reality and fairness of our statements and of ourselves.

The skeptic's critical or incredulous attitude leads him to doubt, disbelieve and inquire into everything said or shown by a salesman.

This individual is probably a skeptic because of past disillusionment. No matter what he is told, he criticizes and discounts it. It is difficult to pin him down to what he thinks he wants. He ordinarily does not reveal his reactions to the presentation and perhaps avoids the issues of the sale.

Once his confidence is gained, however, this person usually becomes a regular buyer.

The technique for handling the skeptic may start with sympathy in the salesman's own mind. The prospect's doubts may be removed through a conservative, sincere and simple presentation. Understating and overproving will count here because this man will realize that testimonials and proof of benefits mean more than unproved oral claims.

Another technique for handling skepticism is to build up areas of agreement on minor points in the presentation, while at the same time building confidence in the proposition. The more he can find to agree with, the more confidence the skeptic will have in what the salesman says. Any questions or criticisms should be met with assurance, because the salesman knows that the product or service offered is right. The prospect's skepticism can be neutralized when the salesman remains sincere, honest and helpful.

The Indifferent Customer

This behavior trait means that the prospect is unconcerned, incurious, aloof, detached, not feeling or showing interest in the salesman's presentation.

The indifferent prospect handles his job or business well enough, but apparently has no interest or initiative for anything. The salesman's ideas may be sound, but this detached prospect hardly seems to think it is worth the effort to act on anything suggested to him. He is probably emotionally and mentally inert.

Often this indifference is assumed, because there is no one who can really be indifferent to suggestions that can benefit him. The salesman's job it to give this man his best presentation and watch for clues related to his motivations. Just as there are hidden values in products, so there are hidden motives and interests in seemingly indifferent buyers. When they are discovered, they can be appealed to with the proper benefit facts.

Sometimes these individuals have to be jolted. They must be shown the losses and dangers they are facing through their indifference and inertia. While this procedure is dangerous for use with most prospects, the salesman must consider that he may not close the sale anyway, and therefore he has nothing to lose even if he makes this prospect angry.

The Reticent Customer

Reticence is a trait which indicates that the prospect is inclined to remain silent or uncommunicative.

The reticent prospect refuses to commit himself. He often reveals a poker face and tries to leave the salesman in the dark as to his reactions. Actually, this trait may be possessed by an individual who is either shy, timid and retiring, or a capable executive who is really paying strict attention and sharply analyzing everything the salesman says.

When a stone wall of silence is encountered, it may be breached by asking questions and listening for the answers. Every time a benefit fact is mentioned, the prospect should be asked a question to obtain his agreement; for example, "Isn't that interesting?" "How does that sound to you?" "You agree with that, don't you?" Reticent individuals like questions, becouse it permits them to air their views to an interested, receptive listener. To give them a start, they may be asked why they refuse to talk. Ordinarily, when they do begin to talk, they convince themselves that they need to make the purchase.

The Hesitant Customer

This behavior trait indicates that the prospect vacillates, wavers, falters, shows irresolution or uncertainty.

The hesitative buyer is somewhat different from the procrastinator, because he has a reason for his hesitation. He may hesitate because he wants to talk to a partner or his boss, or because he is afraid of making a mistake. Many hesitant buyers think of themselves as careful shoppers and want to see several items and talk to several salesmen before they buy. They may have been previously sold on a single product benefit by a competitor who gave a good demonstration; or they may have received better demonstrations on everything except one point, which still concerns them.

These prospects may hesitate because they have not been convinced; they want to compare and judge relative merits. They really want the salesman to banish their doubts and prove that his proposition is the best, planning to obtain approval of the order later if their questions are adequately answered. The salesman could say, for example, "Let us approve this order while I am here, Mr. Jones. Then if we find that everything is all right, we can arrange for delivery."

This method is effective if the salesman is fairly sure that the prospect really wants the product or service, but is not sure of the opinion of others. The salesman should try to get the order signed before he leaves and while the prospect's interest is warm, or loss of a sale may result.

Another method which can be used when the prospect hesitates is to show him that it is costing more to be without the product than to buy and use it. Whenever the prospect hesitates to make the investment even though he knows he needs the product, the salesman can use this technique:

SALESMAN: Of course, Mr. Jones, you want to be sure it is a good investment for you. But you and I agree that you need this product. Isn't that right?

JONES: Yes, I could use it.

SALESMAN: And we have agreed that this product could increase your business by 25 percent. You cannot afford to throw that amount of money away, can you? Well, it is actually going to cost you more to do without this product that it would to buy and use it. Getting

25 percent more business is certainly profitable for you. So let's go ahead and complete the deal. Right?

The Procrastinating Customer

The individual who is dominated by this trait is one who puts things off from day to day; who defers and postpones; who puts off decisions again and again.

Usually, the procrastinating prospect agrees with the salesman that something should be done, and he may· sometimes offer little or no objection during the presentation, but he rarely acts. He may say he is sold, or he may encouragingly tell the salesman to come back on his next trip.

Sometimes the person with this trait is termed "mentally soft." It is not that he has any difficulty with the process of arriving at decisions; the difficulty lies in his distaste for making any decision at all. He does not often question what is said by the salesman—he simply does not have the courage to say "Yes" or "No." Possibly all his life this man has had someone to make decisions for him, or he may have suffered loss as a result of previous unfortunate decisions which he made without adequate evidence.

To handle a procrastinator, the salesman will usually need to use dynamic selling. The salesman must provide answers as to why he should buy now.

This prospect could be offered a desirable proposition and told that the opportunity may be withdrawn within a short time. The salesman might tell him that many people are inclined to delay making a decision, and then add, "I know that you are a man with the courage of your convictions. You don't dilly-dally, you act." It usually requires extra pressure to push the man having this trait toward decisive action.

If the prospect admits that the proposition is a good buy, but that he still wants to wait, the salesman might bring out his pencil and sales book and ask if he can write up the order for later delivery.

When the prospect admits that the proposition is a good buy, he really wants to purchase but he hesitates to act, every effort should be made to help him make up his mind by supplying him with adequate reasons for buying at once. In any event, the alert salesman will not congratulate himself when the prospect tells him he will think it over, for the chances are that the prospect will not recall the promise after the salesman leaves.

Rationalization is also used by the procrastinating prospect. When he rationalizes, he may be evading the salesman's questions, so that when he says he will think it over he is really showing that he is too lazy to think. He may say that he is not interested, when he is really trying to conceal his procrastination. The salesman will usually need to do something startling to shock the rationalizer out of his attitude.

The Disorganized Customer

A prospect who has not systematized or planned his activities and who believes that he is too busy to settle down and regulate his buying affairs possesses the trait of disorganization.

There are prospects who sometimes actually are too busy to interview a salesman; there are others who delude themselves into believing that they are too busy. The latter may often be identified because his desk is piled high with accumulated correspondence and memos which should have been disposed of weeks before. He frequently has two or three telephones on his desk, a secretary who constantly interrupts and vitamins in a top desk drawer. He is always in a hurry and constantly interrupts salesmen while they are making their presentations. This person has difficulty concentrating on one thing at a time for more than one or two minutes.

Obviously, a sale cannot be consummated if the prospect does not listen attentively. A desire to buy cannot be aroused if the prospect's mind is far away. The salesman could start by commenting on how busy the prospect is, how burdened with responsibility, and how much he accomplishes. This prospect will often listen to a little praise and he likes condolences about how hard he works. The salesman could remark that he knows that the prospect's time is valuable and that time will be saved if he will give a few uninterrupted minutes so that the proposition may be explained quickly.

This prospect should be shown that his ability is respected. The salesman should place strong emphasis on the prospect's need for the product or service and stress the importance of making a decision now.

The disorganized individual often will pay attention if he is encouraged to discuss or comment on a topic. He may respond favorably to an adventure story, a joke or a question. If these devices do not accomplish the desired result, it might be advisable to arrange a future appointment. Usually the salesman is in a better position if he does not try to pressure the prospect who is disorganized.

Another method for handling the prospect whose attention wanders is for the salesman to stop talking when he observes that the prospect is not listening, for the silence may bring back the prospect's attention. The salesman might also try lowering his voice or speeding up his delivery, and from then on attempt to tell a more interesting story and make a better explanation.

Long interruptions may occur with this kind of prospect. At this point, the salesman might use the time to bring his sales strategy up-to-date and to formulate a possible closing technique. When the interview is resumed, the salesman should summarize what was said before the interruption and then proceed with his

presentation. If interruptions are too frequent, another interview should be arranged for a more propitious time.

The Self-Important Customer

Self-important describes a prospect who
has an exaggerated estimate of his own
merit. The self-important individual believes that he is superior and important
because of the implied consequences of
his buying decisions.

Such a prospect is often patronizing
in manner, making salesmen feel that he
is doing them a favor when he grants
an interview. Sometimes this prospect is
domineering and tries to show that he
knows all the answers and that the salesman cannot conceivably give him any
information.

This egotistical person might be seeking recognition of his desire to feel important. He is not really sure of himself,
but he makes a special point of letting
salesmen know how important he is.

A reasonable approach to use with this
kind of person is to cater to his ego. First,
the salesman should show respect for this
individual. The salesman should appear
to accept him as an important person,
while keeping in mind that what is really
important is a successful sale.

Second, the salesman should pretend
that this prospect's time is valuable by
acting alert and businesslike in his presence. The prospect might be complimented on his vast knowledge and understanding; he might be asked for advice
on a minor matter, or even to do a small
favor for the salesman. Finally, he should
be induced to prove his importance by
making a brisk decision to buy what is
being offered.

The *bluffer* is closely related to the
self-important prospect. The bluffer is
essentially an uninformed person who
feels that he must disguise his ignorance
by pretending to be more effective than
he actually is.

Dealing with this trait requires dignity on the salesman's part so that he
will not be completely dominated by the
prospect. He should feed the prospect a
diet of cold facts, which ordinarily penetrate the coating of bluster and lead to
an understanding. The bluffer's pretense
should never be challenged. The salesman can afford to let this person try
to impress him and let him think he is
a successful bluffer: what really counts
for the salesman in obtaining the order.

The Timid Customer

When a person's behavior is hampered
by timidity, he lacks courage and self-
confidence. He may be fearful, apprehensive, uncertain, timorous. He shrinks
from any action or activity which requires
independence or self-assertiveness.

Many salesmen consider an individual
who is unassertive, retiring, quiet, courteous and shy to be a "sitting duck" for
a high pressure sales talk. This prospect
conveys the impression that he is a weak
person, so that many salesmen mistakenly
offer a hard, fast sales presentation.

It is possible that this person's behavior has developed from past experiences
of having been misled, and consequently
he finds it difficult to place confidence in
what any salesman says. Another reason
may be his lack of self-assurance when
meeting people. Many capable and brilliant people in responsible positions are
sensitive, shy and embarrassed when they
meet strangers. Also, signing the order
requires a decision, and the timid individual may fear to take the step.

The chief aim in handling this prospect is to build his confidence in himself
and in the salesman. Loud, pushy sales
talks are especially disagreeable to this
buyer and a direct approach may cause
him to react negatively. This person cannot be regarded as an "easy mark" simply because he is slow to decide. He wants
to study every angle of the proposition,

for he feels that he cannot afford to make an error in judgment. Patience is needed to win this sensitive prospect over to the salesman's side. He should be shown testimonials and hear success stories from satisfied users. He will also respond favorably to other kinds of proof material, such as graphs, charts, tabulations and demonstrations of the product.

The Overly Sociable Customer

Over-sociability means that a person is friendly, affable and inclined to like companionship with others. He likes to converse and chat. He may chat about everything except the product or service being suggested, but the salesman should not delude himself into believing that talking with this kind of prospect cements a beautiful friendship. Usually, the prospect is simply amusing himself — and wasting the salesman's time — for he likes the sound of his own voice and the feeling of superiority which he acquires from voicing his opinions.

The method for dealing with this behavior trait is to use the prospect's remarks to lead his thinking into the desired channel. This may be done by interjecting something like, "A while ago you said that . . ." When the prospect stops for breath or reaches a place that indicates a pause, the salesperson might say, "You mentioned something a moment ago that seems to me to have an important bearing on your present problem."

Strict attention should be given to what this prospect says, and the salesman should ask frequent questions and listen to the answers. Somewhere in the prospect's chatter the alert salesman will find a place to interject suggestions, as explained previously. The salesman cannot often make a direct sales talk to this person nor can he force this prospect to listen to him.

If possible, the salesman should try to use a presentation based on his idea sequence, with many questions in it designed to obtain affirmative answers. In this way, the presentation may seem to spring spontaneously from the prospect's own thinking, so that he may talk himself into buying what is offered. If the salesman cannot obtain control of the interview within a brief time, and if he cannot pin the prospect down to a discussion of his proposition, it may be advisable to leave and try again at a later date.

The Vacillating Customer

This trait means that the person wavers in mind, will, feeling, conduct and purpose. He is changeable and irresolute.

The prospect who is fickle, changeable and unreliable decides to do something and then quickly undoes it. He agrees one minute and disagrees the next. One day he likes people, the next day he dislikes them.

The basis for vacillation may be that the prospect simply lacks the power or authority to make a decision. He may have a fear of making a decision and standing by it, or he may not have been fully convinced of the proposition's merit.

To handle this man, the salesman must first qualify him. Has he the authority to make the decision? Has he the power to sign the order? If he is the buyer, the salesman must use patience and try to sell him on the need for his proposition. He should be given a quantity of facts and information, while the salesman emphasizes every benefit point in the presentation. As each sales point is made, the prospect should be asked if it is clear, if he understands it and if he believes it. In this way, agreement is obtained for each benefit point and when the time comes to ask for the order, the agreements usually add up to a successful sale.

Finally, it should be explained that the prospect is not merely being sold something, he is really being helped to work out a problem. His contribution to the solution of his problem is making a decision and sticking to it.

The Irritable Customer

Irritability suggests a person who is easily provoked and displeased; momentarily impatient and outraged; easily exasperated and nettled; sometimes roiled and peevish. This prospect is inclined to anger, easily excited, rather impatient, unduly sensitive to small irritants.

Such behavior directed against the salesman may have been prompted because the prospect has a complaint against the salesman's company, or because of personal problems, or because he may enjoy heckling salesmen in order to make himself feel more important, or because of ill-health.

The salesman must answer sarcasm and heckling with courtesy and patience. He can often shame this individual into decency and perhaps win him with kindness, but he cannot arouse interest and desire by losing his temper or retaliating in kind.

The irritated prospect has also been described as a grouch, a crank. He should be listened to with respect, offered sympathy and helped in solving his problems. He can then be sold the salesman's idea by making it his idea. Offers of help in correcting whatever bothers him is effective, especially if the salesman's company is at fault. Another part of the formula for handling him is to leave his presence as soon as possible, keeping in mind that the grouch today may be friendly tomorrow.

The Impulsive Customer

This trait dominates those who act without deliberation, under stress of emotion or spirit of the moment, unconsciously or as if by instinct.

Those who possess this trait also move fast, talk fast, think fast and give the impression that they are always a step ahead of the salesman. Usually they are

difficult to manage because it requires considerable selling skill to get them to sit still and listen. These men are proud of their snap judgments, which they call quick decisions. The hazard is that it is just as easy for them to decide quickly against the salesman as for him.

Many times these men take chances, almost like gamblers. They tend to like good food, good clothes, and buy what they want without reflection because it has momentary appeal. They may have later regrets, but this does not worry them. These individuals will often insist on helping to sell themselves and they should be allowed to do it. Usually they are loyal customers, since they must defend their choice and judgment to others and to themselves and they do not want to prove themselves wrong.

The best way to deal with the impulsive prospect is to make the offering as attractive as possible. They want not only quick, concise presentations, but also testimonials and success stories. They appreciate good jokes. These men can be rushed more than some buyers, but timing is very important when presenting to them. After summarizing the benefits, and before the close is attempted, the salesman may pretend to retreat a bit and state that he wants the prospect to be sure he is doing the right thing, because he is making an important decision and the salesman does not want to rush him.

The Affable Customer

The person who possesses this behavior trait is one who is easy to speak to, courteous and amiable in response to the salesman's approach, mild and gracious in bearing and appearance. If this is a prospect's true basic behavior, all is well and a sale should be easy. Unfortunately, these people do not always respond as expected.

Affability may be possessed by a person who is completely agreeable and who has no apparent resistance, objections or problems. He may help the salesman set up his proposition, supplement the proposition with some choice benefit points, and say "Yes" to everything the salesman proposes up to the point of closing, when he says "No."

The basic skill of the affable prospect, more often than not, is to squeeze every possible bit of information out of the salesman without spending any money. This prospect is always friendly, always happy to see a salesman, and always tells him he is giving the proposition every consideration. Meanwhile, he tries to pick the salesman's brains in every way possible, ranging from technical data to merchandising ideas. He invites him to come back the next time, but rarely buys.

One way to overcome this behavior trait is to establish an issue, which could be an objection or a point of disagreement, then close on settlement of the issue through answering it or reaching an agreement.

Another procedure for dealing with affability is to use the method proposed for handling procrastinators. The salesman might tell the prospect that his friendly spirit is appreciated, and that he realizes that the prospect understands the value of the information and help he has received. The sales proposal should be presented constructively, with the hint that there are many people who show a friendly spirit but do not conclude by placing an order. He might be placed in a position in which he either has to buy or admit, by inference, that he has been putting on an act. However, his agreeable attitude should not induce the salesman to leave with the expectation of a future order.

The Thoughtful Customer

The prospect who is attentive and who also cogitates, reflects, reasons, deliberates, considers and thinks before he purchases is showing thoughtfulness.

This prospect has trained himself to think logically and to employ reasoning before he buys. He is deliberate, slow to reach a decision, and cheerful in considering all the facts before he decides. He is shrewd, moves slowly and cannot be rushed into buying.

Usually he is a quality buyer and is not inclined to worry about price. He is sincere in manner and action, and deliberation is not a pose to impress salesmen. Often he is shy; more often he is merely a careful person who is willing to make a decision, but dislikes making a mistake.

When dealing with this prospect, the salesman must be thorough in his presentation and let the prospect know that it is a pleasure to deal with a man who takes his time to reach the right decision. He should be told that because of his analytical ability, he will appreciate what the salesman is trying to do. He should be offered evidence, figures, facts and visual proof. He cannot be pressured into buying, but his thinking can be guided and helped toward arriving at answers and solutions for his problems. The salesman's attitude should be one of patience.

If the salesman is not sure that "the thinker" is ready to buy, he should ask a test question: "Have I made that perfectly clear?" "Does it not seem logical that this should solve your problems?" This method helps the salesman to discover any obstacles which may be in the prospect's mind and gives him a chance to overcome them. When the salesman has obtained agreement on every point, there is no reason why the prospect should not buy. The only requirement at this stage of the sale is for the salesman to ask for the order.

The Insincere Customer

All prospects do not possess unblemished moral characters. All do not conform to recognized standards of morality or business conduct. Some prospects exaggerate about the subject at hand in the hope of gaining an advantage of some kind.

Some prospects are sharpshooters who want to shop around, but do not want to admit it. They want to make a comparison between the features and benefits of the salesman's product and competing products, and for that reason use excuses, stalls and alibis in the hope of obtaining lower prices.

This kind of buyer is a questioner and can skillfully attack a salesman's claims. He is able to present his ideas in an adroit manner, with the intent of obtaining a concession of one kind or another from the salesman.

This individual should be treated courteously and his attacks met with facts and proof. Eventually he should tire of his tactics and listen to the presentation. If the prospect's behavior has not rattled the salesman so far, he can conclude quickly and ask for the order. Such "sharpness" and unethical tactics usually wear thin in the face of a salesman's enthusiasm and sound product knowledge.

The Fearful Customer

This prospect's behavior is fearful, apprehensive, afraid, timorous and worried. Often the cause of fearful behavior is a vivid imagination. *Apprehensive* implies good reasons for fear and is, therefore, a state of mind. *Afraid* may or may not imply good reasons for fear, but it usually suggests weakness or cowardice. There are fearful prospects who stall and try to avoid making a decision. They offer excuses that are not the real reason for their fear. However, stalls and excuses tend to follow certain patterns and it does not take long to become familiar with most of them. For example, a fearful prospect will sometimes say that he has to consult his partner, his boss or his wife. Actually, he may really want to buy and can easily obtain immediate permission if he wants to. Often he is fearful because the salesman has not made him want the item strongly.

The fearful buyer may also make ex-cuses and employ rationalization. For example, he may say, "Bill Brown bought from you and he received terrible service." The salesman may discover, however, that the prospect has a vivid imagination and little regard for the truth: He does not know a Bill Brown — he only heard about him; Bill Brown had not bought the product anyway, but another product which had not been on the market for fifteen years.

The salesman needs to find out the prospect's real reasons for stalling, rationalizing and excuse-making, so he *qualifies* him. If he *qualifies* on the following points, he is probably a good prospective customer:

He has a need for my product (or service).
My product will fill that need.
My company is reliable.
My price is right.
He can pay for the item.
He should buy now.

If the salesman knows that these are the facts and becomes convinced that the prospect is fearful, he will need to introduce an exclusive feature to increase his interest. Therefore, the salesman will give him another convincing benefit fact and then ask for the order again. He may say, "Mr. Jones, I have shown you many benefits, advantages and features about this product that I believe you want. It is true that you obtain some of these benefits from other products, but here is something you can find only with mine, and it is so exclusive that no other product has it."

Professional salesmen know the impact of an exclusive and they save it until last because they realize that it gives their proposition a boost and often clinches the sale when they are dealing with a fearful prospect.

POWER POINTS

All of the "people problems" that have

just been mentioned can be handled so that they work for the salesman instead of against him. For example, prior to the interview the experienced salesman makes a thorough study of his prospective customer; he analyzes his needs, and studies his personality, his interests, his plans, his problems and his behavior. In this way he is able to present interesting benefit points and avoid confusion and pointless arguments which so often enter into the presentation of an untrained salesman.

Salesmen who have analyzed the obstacles which they have encountered in the past find that a new one seldom occurs. Sometimes obstacles may be expressed in a different way, but basically they are recurrences of ones they have heard before. Further analysis reveals that whenever a prospect objects to something, he is inclined to defend his objection. Having committed himself to a negative attitude, the prospect's pride prevents him from changing his opinions and he will continue to defend his behavior to the end.

Reasoning from that premise, one of the major efforts of a salesman must be to anticipate objections, alibis, stalls, excuses and defense mechanisms. The right idea planted in a buyer's mind is the most effective antidote to the objections and other obstructions which all salesmen dread.

When interesting benefit facts are worked into a strong, convincing presentation, a prospect usually will be too interested to raise barriers to further progress. He will be too concerned about the benefits he can obtain to raise impediments. This skillful selling will give the salesman a new eagerness for his job, and he will no longer be fearful of defense mechanisms and other obstructive behavior patterns.

The salesman must proceed slowly with his presentation until he garners enough clues to judge his prospect's behavior pattern. If a certain buyer were not too self-assured, for instance, he might welcome success stories, testimonials or survey materials; an overconfident person, on the other hand, might resent this approach.

Should the salesman use his standard presentation on the buyer or should he hit only a few high points? The best answer seems to be that the same planned presentation cannot be used with every prospect, since each prospect has his own traits, behavior patterns, and needs. It is better to start the sale with a brief statement of the proposition and to mention only outstanding benefits as they seem to apply to the individual buyer's needs.

DISCUSSION QUESTIONS AND PROBLEMS

1. What are the six chief reasons for "People" problems?
2. What do we mean by "defense mechanisms"?
3. How can the salesman recognize a defense mechanism in a prospect? Provide examples.
4. What are the techniques recommended for handling defense mechanisms?
5. "All salesmen, either consciously or unconsciously attempt to type their prospects." Explain this statement.
6. What are the dangers or pitfalls in attempting to type a prospect?
7. What are the six basic principles that a salesman should accept in learning how to manage people?
8. What are the common buyer traits as seen by salesmen? How are each best handled by the salesman?

PHENOMENOLOGICAL PROJECTS

Review of Trait Descriptions

This chapter analyzed and described eleven behavior traits which are often encountered by salesmen. Review these trait descriptions, selecting those which you believe are difficult to understand and those which are easy. Did you select the "difficult" traits because they described the kind of prospect you know best? Would your answers have been the same if you had selected the "easy" traits?

Diagnosis and Treatment of Prospect Behavior

A method for learning how to observe, analyze and deal with prospect behavior traits has been used with success for many years. It employs a convenient form like the one which follows. The form headings are similar to those which may be used by physicians to observe, analyze and prescribe for ills.

Directions:

Rule a sheet of 8½ x 11 paper following the form shown below and write in the main headings. Next to the heading "Procrastination" in the first column, write the symptoms of the trait. In the third column, describe the treatment called for by the trait (how you would handle the prospect).

Repeat this procedure for other behavior traits which you encounter during your daily calls.

PROSPECT BEHAVIOR FORM

I. Behavior Trait Name	II. Diagnosis of Trait (Analysis of Characteristics)	III. Treatment Indicated
1. Procrastination		
2.		

The Topeka Wholesale Hardware Company (Case)

The buyer for a wholesale house regarded the salesman thoughtfully for a moment and said, "Joe, you are welcome to come into this office as often as you care to, but I will never buy anything from that company you represent!" Joe smiled and said, "Well, Mr. Smith, I'm glad that you let me come in and see you. Naturally, I'm sorry you don't regard my company favorably because I make my living selling their products. If you don't want to talk business or learn about our products when I call on you, that's okay with me. But you should know that if I call on you, I'm going to try to get your business."

For many months Joe called on this company as faithfully as he did any of his regular customers. The manager would occasionally listen to his story, nod his head and say, "It's too bad you don't work for a good outfit." Or, he would listen to part of it and say, "There's no use of your trying to sell me that stuff," and switch the conversation to the weather, fox hunting or local gossip.

After about six months of apparently getting no place. Joe walked in one day and the manager said, "Well, Joe, we need a carload of material and I'm going to give you the order. We'll show those people in your office that you're doing a good job in this territory."

Questions:

1. What psychological principles are involved in this case?
2. How would you have handled this buyer?
3. Do you believe Joe could have succeeded in winning an earlier favorable reaction if he had pressed the prospect to buy?
4. What other sales strategies can you suggest for situations of this kind?
5. Does selling to wholesalers involve any behavior traits that do not apply to selling on other levels? Why?

Chapter Nine

Motivating & Persuading Prospective Customers

MEANING OF MOTIVATION

Motivation provides the impulses and inducements that incite people to action. To a salesman, motivation means creating interest and arousing a desire in the mind of the buyer for whatever is being sold.

How buying behavior is motivated is a difficult but interesting subject. It is important to the salesman because he cannot be a professional unless he understands what makes people behave as they do in the marketplace. According to Crissey and Cash, "It is safe to say that success in selling depends largely upon a knowledge of customers' and prospects' motivation . . . the reasons why they behave the way they do."[1]

It is important to know that people, generally speaking, have the same basic motives for buying, and that each person wants to satisfy a want or need. Some of these motivations are dormant or unrealized, and an important part of the sales-

man's job is to help float them to the surface of the prospect's consciousness so that they will become active and arouse him to buy.

With the exception of simple reflex activity, all human behavior is motivated; that is, directed toward the accomplishment of a *goal*, usually named a reward or incentive, that will satisfy a particular need. The motives, or stimulus conditions, that direct our behavior may be classified as *biological drives* and *psychological* and *social drives*. The word *drive* refers to any condition of the organism which creates internal tensions and thus impels it to activity.

We are most concerned with *psychological* and *social drives*. Among the most important of these are the need for security, the need for liking and esteem, the need for recognition, approval and prestige and the need for new experience.

Most of our drives are said to be acquired as the result of past experience. They may result from a learning process in which *symbolic rewards* or punish-

1. W. J. E. Crissey and H. C. Cash, "Motivation In Selling," *The Psychology of Selling* (New York: Personal Development, Inc., 1957), p. 9.

ments are important in producing behavior. We may be motivated by acquired fears and the desire to *avoid* certain experiences, as well as by the desire to achieve rewards and incentives. Often our behavior is directed by acquired, learned motives of which we are not even aware.

The importance of learning and social factors in motivation is clearly shown by the different manner in which people express their need for social approval. Social learning also determines the development of individual *interests* and *values,* important motives in everyday life.

RATIONAL AND EMOTIONAL BUYING MOTIVES

Rational	*Emotional*
1. Economy in purchase	1. Pride in appearance
2. Economy in use	2. Pride of ownership
3. Efficient performance	3. Desire to feel important
4. Increased profits	4. Desire for recognition
5. Durability	5. Desire to imitate
6. Accurate performance	6. Love of family
7. Labor-saving	7. Romance
8. Time-saving	8. Comfort
9. Simplicity in construction	9. Desire for adventure
10. Simplicity in operation	10. Desire for variety
11. Ease of repair	11. Health
12. Ease of installation	12. Safety
13. Space-saving	13. Fear
14. Increased production	14. Desire to build or create
15. Purity	15. Desire for security
16. Availability	16. Desire for companionship
17. Complete servicing	17. Convenience
18. Low maintenance cost	18. Amusement and pleasure
19. Good workmanship and materials	19. Desire to be different
20. Thoroughly researched and tested	20. Curiosity

Buying motives are both *rational* and *emotional* in nature. Rational buying motives are based upon reasoning things out objectively or thinking things through. Emotional buying motives are based upon the way we feel. The accompanying chart provides examples of these two types of motives. Notice that the rational motives include economy in purchase and use, efficient performance, durability, increased profits. The prospect generally rationalizes or plans these things. Emotional motives include pride in appearance, desire to feel important, love of family, desire for comfort. These describe feelings. We feel proud, important, loving, comfortable.

The industrial buyer generally attempts to purchase on a rational objective basis, while the household buyer tends to place emphasis on subjective emotional factors. Even a supposedly rational buyer, however, may be influenced more by emotion than by reason. People show inertia when forced to think, and even a small amount of deliberation and decision making is tiring for them, particularly when they can substitute emotion for the pain of logical reasoning.

While the professional salesperson appeals to the customer's reasoning mind to a certain extent, he does not expect decisions to come from it alone. He knows that appeals to the emotional or subconscious mind often motivate the customer toward deciding in his favor.

Needs and Problem Solving

Throughout the preceding chapters, it was stated that among the most important psychological and social drives are *needs* of various kinds. The salesman, therefore, should be capable of determining a prospect's buying needs and problems and be able to satisfy and solve them. A prospect's need may be known or unknown, latent or felt. It is the salesman's job to discover the need, and if it is not realized by the prospect, to call it to his attention. A felt need varies in intensity with different people, but any real prospect has a need of some kind; otherwise he cannot qualify as a prospective purchaser.

Wishes and Needs

While a sharp distinction cannot be made between an individual's wishes and needs, there is no doubt that they exist. The difficulty in recognizing them arises from the fact that they are not always specific in nature. Some of the wishes and needs are latent and some are active; some are not realized and some are vividly felt by prospective buyers.

Wishes and needs arise from many complex sources, such as habit, custom, conformity or individuality. The demand for a new automobile, for example, might be caused by a genuine *need* for transportation, but it may also be caused by the wish to keep up with one's neighbors or to be the first person in the neighborhood to own a new car. In most cases, there is an overlapping of many causes, so that it is difficult to isolate the predominant one.

Needs and Motives

The prospective buyer of anything is an individual who has: (1) a need for the product or service, and (2) the means to pay for it.

Since every sale presupposes a buyer with need, it is logical to begin the study of motivation by investigating what causes a person to become a buyer. If the prospect's need is active, he is aware of the need and will probably attempt to satisfy it. A dormant need, on the other hand, will not be felt by the prospect until it is brought to his attention, usually by advertising or by a salesman.

A salesman is concerned with both kinds of prospective buyers. When the need is active, the prospect usually, but not always, lets the salesman know of his requirement. When the need is dormant, the salesman must make the prospect aware of the need and let him know how his product can satisfy it.

The needs of people are expressed through different motivating factors. Sometimes one motive alone is sufficiently compelling to cause a purchase, but more often the decision to buy is caused by a combination of motives. Salespeople know that the prospect, of his own volition, will rarely state the basic motive that will cause him to buy. However, he may express his motives by his reactions to the presentation, by asking questions, by handling the product or by other similar clues. The salesman must determine from such hints what buying motives are most important to the prospect in order to find the most effective method of inducing buying action.

PSYCHOLOGICAL MECHANICS OF MOTIVATION

Three theories have been advanced to aid the salesman in his efforts to motivate people to buy: (1) the selling formula theory; (2) the stimulus-response theory; and (3) the need-satisfaction theory.

Each theory has its adherents, and the selling approach may be based on any one of them, depending on the particular circumstances. The motivation methods employed by most salesmen are usually guided by one or more of these theories.

The Selling Formula Theory

The most common expression of the selling formula theory is in the words *atten-*

tion, interest, desire, action (A I D A). Possibly a more complete way to express the formula is in the words *start, tell, explain, prove, summarize* and *close* (S T E P S).

This formula implies that all prospects

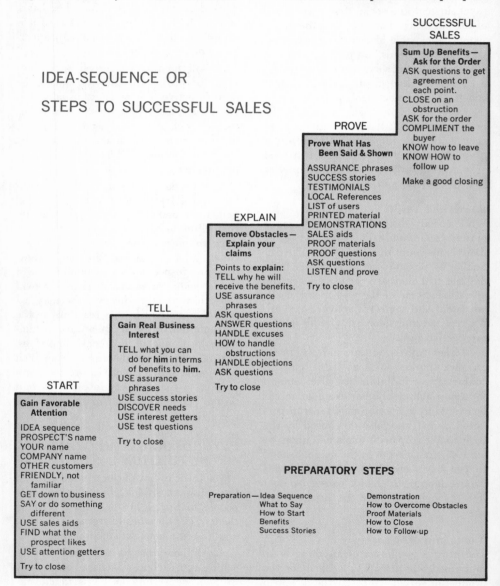

Figure 2. Idea-sequence for successful sales.

should be treated alike and that successful sales are made by taking prospects through the successive mental stages of attention, interest, desire, action, and perhaps, satisfaction.

Those who oppose this method believe that it approaches the motivation process from the salesman's point of view, rather than from the prospect's. They believe that the application of the formula tends to make the salesman feel that he is an engineer who, with a standard operating procedure, can motivate a prospect to make a purchase. Opponents of the selling formula also point out that a prospect does not necessarily experience the mental steps of a sale in logical sequence and that the steps are not of equal importance in motivating and selling.

Nevertheless, this method has value when salesmen are too inexperienced to develop a presentation based on a prospect's individual motives and needs. It is also believed to have value when prospects have motives and needs similar to those of the salesman. The basic reason for the wide acceptance of the selling formula, however, is that it may provide a logical framework within which ideas about selling techniques may be presented.

The Stimulus-Response Theory [2]

Based on the psychological principle that for every sensory stimulus there is an appropriate response, the stimulus-response theory is probably the simplest of the three approaches.

The application of the principle of stimulus-response to motivation and selling means that the salesman must have certain things to say and do (stimuli), so that the prospect will buy (response). Obviously, it is believed that if a salesman

uses the appropriate stimuli, the prospect will be motivated to buy.

Cybernetics, as it relates to sales communication, is one aspect of the stimulus-response theory. The meaning of cybernetics is "steersman" or "governor."[3] In addition to being a mechanism for personal development, cybernetics helps us to understand the stimulus-response theory more thoroughly.

The selling concept of cybernetics means that the sales communicator is enabled to (1) transfer his fund of knowledge to the prospect's storage place of knowledge; (2) ask questions and listen to the feedback revealing the effect of his presentation; (3) adjust his continuing presentation to fit the needs of the situation. This is the process by which a salesman presents his information, asks questions, listens in order to keep himself informed of the success of his communication, and then adjusts it to suit a particular prospect, customer or situation. Cyberneticists point out that man is not a machine, but that he has a machine and uses it. They see the subconscious mind as a mechanism consisting of the entire nervous system, including the brain, which is used and directed by the mind. Since man is capable of storing information or memorizing, the prospect's mind may be said to work with the data that salesmen feed into it in the form of perceptions, interpretations, beliefs, understandings, thoughts and attitudes.

Through his planned presentation, the salesman feeds this data into the prospect's storehouse of knowledge. If sound information is fed into the prospect's nervous system, it will be processed and used in solving related problems. Thus, according to some psychologists, whatever is fed into the prospect's nervous system will auto-

---

2. Adapted from Kenneth B. Haas' *Professional Salesmanship, Persuasion and Motivation in Marketing* (New York: Holt, Rinehart & Winston, 1962), pp. 180-181, 443-444.

3. Norbert Weiner, *The Human Use of Human Beings* (New York: Doubleday & Company, 1965).

matically bring an appropriate response when the proper sensory stimulus is set in motion by the salesman.

The stimulus-response and cybernetic theory is useful when the selling situation is simple, when the selling price is low and when little time can be spent with a customer. Its weakness is that a stimulus which motivates and influences one customer may not motivate and influence another. This means that not only does the salesman lose sales but also that he cannot analyze the reason for his success or failure. Since the salesman who uses this approach may be working in the dark, he is not likely to improve his selling skills as the result of his experience.

The Need-Satisfaction Theory

When it is assumed that prospects buy to satisfy needs, it follows that to make a sale we must uncover the prospect's psychological and social needs and motives. We then match our proposition's features and benefits with the prospect's needs and motives and reveal how we can satisfy his needs and solve his problems. Obviously, the need-satisfaction theory is a prospect-oriented approach, while the other two theories are usually salesman-oriented.

Since the need-satisfaction theory begins with the discovery of a prospect's motives and needs, the salesman cannot talk about his product or service until he knows what those motives and needs are. This situation is the reverse of the selling formula theory, by which the salesman tries to point out all the outstanding features of his proposition. The application of the need-satisfaction approach requires greater skill and maturity than do other methods, for he must be able to dominate the sales situation through motivating, questioning and listening, rather than merely through a sales talk.

When a sale is complex, the need-satisfaction approach is preferable. It may be more time-consuming, as some salesmen

claim, but it may actually save selling time. It may be advantageously employed in all selling above the canvassing level.

Actually, all three theories can be combined for effective use by the salesman.

PROSPECT MOTIVES

The prospect is not motivated by the salesman, by his company or by the product or service being offered, but only by what the salesman's proposition will do for him. Unless the proposition appeals to *his* interests, unless it satisfies *his* desires and shows *him* a gain, he will not buy!

The prospect may not be influenced by a pure monetary consideration in all instances, for there are other important buying motives — practically all selling involves more than one. The prospect must be motivated by a *gain* of some kind that will satisfy his own interests. Salesmen spend more time planning appeals to motives of gain than they do on any other phase of their sales presentation.

Very few prospects will announce what motives prompt them to buy. When a prospect does make a direct statement, such as, "My present trucks cost too much to operate," it is probable that the salesman should appeal to the *economy gain* motive. However, the real reason the buyer is considering new trucks may be because his competition is buying them. The salesman, therefore, should touch upon the benefits of his proposition in such a way as to appeal to the prospect's fear of loss of business as well as to the more obvious economy gain motive. The salesman can see if the prospect reacts more favorably to some appeals than to others. He then concentrates on those motives by showing how his proposition will fit the prospect's need.

A useful way to learn what motivates prospects is for the salesman to determine his own buying motives. For example, he may ask himself, "Why did I really buy that sport jacket or that auto?" Was it to imitate, for pride of possession or to gain something? Was it rational or was it emotional?

Plainly, motives for buying are mixed; they spill over; they are combined. But it is certain that a buyer never makes a purchase unless he believes he will *gain something* in some way.

Frequently Cited Motives

gain	pleasure-comfort
pride	curiosity
imitation	rivalry
fear	envy

The Gain Motive

A great many sales are decided within the first two minutes of the interview. Unless the salesman can successfully appeal to the gain motive within that time, the prospect will usually decide that neither the salesman nor his proposition are of any interest to him.

A salesman's success will largely depend on how well he answers the prospect's familiar unspoken question, "What's in it for me?" All good motivation carries a promise of *gain*. In general, all personal marketing can be reduced to this one phrase: "The planned and constant promise of *gain*."

There are four kinds of *gain*: money, economy, happiness and utility.

Money Gain

Naturally, many salesmen appeal to the prospect's desire for savings and profits, since this is the motive that causes the most favorable responses from buyers.

In appealing to the money gain motive, the salesman emphasizes not only price and financial gain, but also high quality, performance, economy, savings and profits. To make his attempts to motivate more effective, he offers proof for everything he claims. The salesman's discussion could be so illuminating and so authoritative

that the sale might be consummated solely on one point — how the customer would gain from using the salesman's proposition. Both the money gain and the following economy gain motives are important industrial and commercial buying motives.

Economy Gain

The economy motive, properly handled, is said to be a potent appeal in overcoming the prospect's objection to the price of the new product, as well as in giving him additional reasons for deciding to buy. For example: manufacturers, thinking in terms of profit and loss over a long period, often replace machinery and equipment in excellent condition with newer equipment that, because of improvement in design, will perform more efficiently and more economically. This is done because within a reasonable period the new equipment will pay for itself and will result in a net saving. For example:

SALESMAN: Mr. Prospect, I know you are interested in cutting costs wherever you can without having to lower the the fine quality work that you give your customers, isn't that right?

PROSPECT: Certainly is.

SALESMAN: And lower costs mean that you can lower bids on printing to your prospects and customers. Lower bids mean more jobs for your plant, and more jobs in your plant mean more contribution to overhead as well as more dollar profit. Doesn't that make sense?

PROSPECT: Yes, it does. But how will a new Harris-Jones offset press accomplish all this?

SALESMAN: By allowing you to turn out twice the amount of work on a new H-J press that is now being turned out on your present equipment. The key to it is your high wage costs. Let's do a little figuring and I'll prove this to you.

PROSPECT: I hope you can. This sounds like the proposition I've been hoping for.

Happiness Gain

Appeals to the prospect's desire for a money gain should be turned, whenever possible, into what may be called the happiness gain. A store manager who is worried about operating costs, for instance, and is therefore losing sleep and mental ease is interested not only in saving money, but also in obtaining peace of mind. The industrial buyer is interested in added profits, or savings, or both, but he may also be vitally interested in the dependability of the product. He may be motivated by safety reasons, such as wanting to prevent accidents or property damage. He may also be interested in satisfying his employees so they will take greater pride in their work.

Happiness, contentment and peace of mind are also motives in the consumer goods market. Listen to the following sales interview between a roofing salesman and his prospect:

SALESMAN: A new roof on that house would certainly put your mind at rest.

PROSPECT: Oh I don't know. How do you figure that?

SALESMAN: Have you noticed any ceiling leaks yet?

PROSPECT: No, I haven't.

SALESMAN: But if you let that roof go any longer you will begin to experience leaks. Notice the deterioration on your shingles all along the ridge line. Also look at the bare spots next to the hip

where your bedroom juts out. Those spell trouble spots that could cause anxiety and inconvenience when winter comes.

PROSPECT: Why couldn't I get by with just a patch-up job?

SALESMAN: You could get by, maybe. But wouldn't you rather have the feeling of comfort and security that a new, well-installed roof will provide? Why live in constant fear that you will have to cope with an obnoxious leak or two and perhaps even a complete repatching and painting job because you waited too long?

Notice how this salesman established the general problem and attempted to create dissatisfaction with the existing situation. As soon as the prospect was aware of his problem, the salesman attempted to motivate him by appealing to an increase in his happiness and related this happiness gain to the idea of putting on a new roof.

Utility Gain

Any new product is presumed to have utility not possessed by previous products of its kind. A prospect who owns an older product, therefore, stands to gain utility if he buys a newer one. This applies when a new product is offered in place of an older product of a different form and also when a new and improved product is offered in the same form.

By pointing out added utility in his product, the salesman not only appeals to an important buying motive but also justifies the price. Further, when he is selling for replacement of an old product, he must emphasize the gain in utility over the product now being used if the prospect is to justify in his own thinking the expenditure required to make the purchase.

The Pride Motive

There are six basic methods for appealing to the customer's pride: (1) offering praise; (2) referring to the prospect's opinions; (3) asking the prospect questions about himself; (4) calling the prospect by name; (5) liking the prospect and showing it; (6) appealing to his pride of possession. These motives are just as important as *gain* to many people.

Praise

Praise is something we all like. Anything distinctive about the prospect or his possessions should be praised. For example, outstanding features of the prospect's store, office or factory provides good motivation, and the salesman should single these items out. Offering praise enables the salesman to meet the prospect on common ground and to produce the first agreement in the interview, as well as to bolster the prospect's ego. An appeal to pride is not flattery and it is effective only when it is honest. Flattery is an imitation of genuine praise and its hollowness is often detected.

Seeking Opinions

The following statements illustrate one of the effective methods of complimenting the prospect: "That was a very interesting point you bought up. I am very much interested in getting your viewpoint. You certainly hit the nail on the head when you said that. Very few people understand the situation as you have just described it." The prospect usually reciprocates with a high regard for the salesman who employs this technique because he feels that the salesman understands him and, of course, everyone likes to be understood.

Questions

A different way of appealing to the prospect's pride is to ask him questions about things he has done or in which he is interested. The purpose of these questions is to condition him to accept the proposition and to prepare an environment of friendliness and agreement for a successful sale. Such questions are presented in Chapter VI.

The Prospect's Name

A person's name is important to him; it is his identification and one of his most valuable possessions. It pays the salesman to use it at every opportunity, and to be able to pronounce it and spell it correctly.

Liking the Prospect

If there is anything about a prospect that a salesman does not like, he should try to eliminate it from his mind quickly. If the dislike is allowed to remain, it will unconsciously affect the expression on the salesman's face, thereby announcing his true feelings. If the salesman dislikes him, the prospect will know it and his pride will be hurt.

Pride of Possession

Pride of possession takes two general forms. One is the *sense of achievement* that an individual may derive from a possession; the object may be the realization of an ambition that the prospect has had, or it may be so valuable to the owner that it is a source of great pride to him. Many people like to feel that they have the best that is made, the most expensive item, the brand that means top-quality all over the world. The salesman should recognize that many people seek status through the possession of such items, and should, consequently, appeal to their pride of possession using such assurance phrases as:

"You won't have to worry about having the best with this."
"This is recognized the world over as the leading brand in its field."
"This is the 'Cadillac' of kitchen ranges."

A second form of pride of possession is what is known as *keeping up with the*

Joneses. What friends and neighbors say is of great importance to many people. First, the salesman must realize that pride of possession comes from the qualities that can be seen and immediately appreciated by the prospect, as well as by his neighbors and friends. The salesman must enable the prospect to anticipate exactly how he will feel when he has possession of the product. He does this by the adroit use of descriptive phrases which set up an imaginative response in the mind of the prospect.

When the salesman says, "You can see how the distinctive beauty of this refrigerator will improve the modern appearance of your kitchen," the prospect visualizes her pride and satisfaction in having the impressive new refrigerator in her kitchen in place of the old refrigerator which reveals its age all too clearly.

When the salesman says, "You may buy this turret lathe with the confidence that its features offer you the last word in performance and economy, and you can be sure that there is nothing finer available," the prospect should feel confident that he will receive features that competitive products do not possess.

When the salesman says, "The precision-built mechanism of this superb television set will not go out of order at the slightest provocation and leave you embarrassed before your guests," the prospect thinks of her assurance in the presence of guests because the set has prestige and quality.

Miscellaneous Motivators

Imitation Motive

People imitate all the time. All of us do it. If a salesman tells a truck operator about the advantages of Blank trucks, he could include in his presentation a statement such as: "John Smith was telling me some time ago that he would use no other trucks because he had proved the superiority of Blank trucks by actual road tests similar to the ones I have described to you." The salesman then goes on with other portions of his presentation.

The advantage of this method is that the appeal to imitation is made in a subtle way and the prospect is not aware that he is not making an independent decision, his pride is not hurt, and he does not realize that he is an imitator.

Imitation is extremely important in the consumer goods market. In fact, the fashion industry bases its success upon this motive. A *fashion* is any style which is popularly accepted and purchased by several successive groups of people over a reasonably long period of time. A *style* may be adopted by an elite group of people who seek distinction. The distinction catches on among the taste-makers in various social strata, and finally is taken up among the masses of people, the emulators. The teen-age market is especially sensitive to the imitation motive: For example:

SALESLADY: May I help you?

TEEN-AGE PROSPECT: Gosh, I hope so. I'm looking for those sweater dresses that come in those weird colors.

SALESLADY: Surely. Here are some of our most popular designs in this rack. Here's a shapely wool chenille in lemon that would look well with your complexion.

PROSPECT: Gee, it's sure bright. I don't know. It's so different from what I've been wearing. I wonder if I could wear it.

SALESLADY: I'm sure you could. These cables and stripes are extremely popular right now. My daughter wore one like this to her sorority dance (shows a lime color), and the fellows flipped. Her boy friend wants her to get a frosty blue, also.

PROSPECT: Well, maybe it would be OK.

SALESLADY: Here's a design that's popular with the Grossmont College girls. It's a size eight. Like the many other girls who wear these, you have just the figure for it. I'll show you to the dressing room.

Fear Motive

At first glance, the motive of fear may appear to be a negative factor which might prevent a sale. However, *fear* can be a positive factor in selling. An astonishing number of articles are sold on the basis of the fear motive: dental and medical services; automobile, casualty and fire insurance; paint, cosmetics, insecticides; automobiles with seat belts; lubricants, dry cleaners and hundreds of other items.

Protection is another aspect of the fear motive and it is a powerful reason for buying, since it embraces protection of health, property, loved ones or anything that the prospect may value. Life insurance, burglar alarms, sales, seat belts and similar products and services are purchased solely for the reason that they protect and provide security. Consider the example below of how a salesman uses the fear motive in selling automobile tires.

SALESMAN: I imagine, like thousands of others, Mr. Smith, you spend a great deal on auto insurance, most of it designed to protect you against lawsuits from injury to others.

PROSPECT: Yes, I do. It seems like quite a bit.

SALESMAN: Driving these freeways like you do in rainy weather could mean a serious accident and injury to yourself and others if you don't get those smooth tires replaced. I'd like to spare you that anxiety by putting on a set of Guardian treads, now.

Pleasure-Physical Comfort Motive

Anything that saves time and gives a person more leisure makes a strong appeal to the pleasure motive. Household electrical appliances are good examples. To the industrial buyer, any equipment which can function in the absence of an operator makes an important contribution to the manager's pleasure, comfort and probably to other motives.

Everyone likes to be comfortable, to eat good food, to lie back in an easy chair, to have ease of mind and to have the conveniences of modern living. If a salesman can show a prospect how a product will make his routine easier and help him gain these pleasures, he can often motivate him to buy.

Curiosity Motive

A salesman can utilize the curiosity appeal in numerous ways. To obtain an interview, he may disclose some facts that make the prospect want to learn more; for example, "Mr. Buyer, I am sure you will be interested in our new gear assembly which will increase your profits."

Two motives are appealed to in this example: money gain and curiosity. The prospect wants to make more money, of course, but he is also curious to know more about the new gear assembly.

Intriguing phrases may also be used to motivate. The salesman might refer to "our new development," "our success plan," "our profit-making scheme," "our plan for reducing operating costs," or he might say, "Mr. Prospect, I have a message for you from twenty other satisfied users."

It is often possible to motivate curiosity by asking questions which induce a reply, such as: "Mr. Businessman, when you buy you are interested in just one thing, getting the most for your money. If I could show you proof that you could make a considerable saving by using our products, you would be interested, wouldn't you?"

Rivalry Motive

Nearly everyone has a desire to surpass others. This reason for buying may not be as strong as pride or gain, but some people are motivated by rivalry, especially when they are stimulated by the proper appeal.

Suppose two merchants were competitors, one of them more aggressive than the other. If a salesman offered the latter a product or service that he could show would increase profits or attract a high-income clientele, he could probably stimulate this merchant's spirit of rivalry.

Envy Motive

Envy is a trait which varies with different people and is not as universal as the motives of pride and gain. With a prospect in whom the trait is strongly developed, envy can be a powerful inducement to action.

The salesman usually thinks of envy as the reflection of the prospect's discontent because a neighbor or a competitor possesses what he would like for himself. Most salesmen know of neighbors and competitors who may be envied for their success. If they happen to be his customers, he has the foundation on which to build a sales talk which will give the prospect a reason for attempting to gratify his envious attitude.

Combined Motivating Appeals

Ordinarily, salesmen must try appeals to several motives before they find the *chief* motivating forces which impel, invite and urge a prospect to buy. It is a rare sale which is motivated by only one factor. Nearly always there is a complex of motives and appeals. The trick is to find the chief benefits which supply the motivating force.

How a combination of motivating appeals may be used is revealed in the following example. The salesman relates the experience himself:

"My sales manager first appealed to my motive of gain, but without success because I did not feel that I had the ability to sell something which people did not want. He then appealed to my pride without success, so he reversed his approach and risked injuring my pride by ridiculing my low earnings and my lazy work habits. This depressed me, but did not change my attitude.

"Then he appealed to the motives of imitation and envy by naming other salesmen who were earning enough money in six months to spend the remainder of the year vacationing in Florida. That did it! I envied men who were no smarter than I, but who were able to take a six-month vacation. I became discontented with myself. I found myself wishing that I could do what they were doing. A further appeal to pride in my own ability lifted my morale to a new high and I decided that I would really try to sell."

All motives aided in the decision, but it is possible that envy of the other salesmen's prosperity was the chief motivating force, supplemented by the motives of gain, pride, imitation and rivalry.

The following example illustrates how five different motivators were used to stimulate buying action in retailers. The first four motives were appealed to once, and the fifth received four different appeals:

"Joe, you are losing money every day with your present set-up *(money gain)*. Pete Jones on Beech Street, whose location is no better than yours, is outselling you two to one *(rivalry, imitation)*.

"Now, Pete is not a better businessman than you are—probably not as good *(pride)* — but he is using our sales promotion plan to move his products and he is making more money than he did with his old setup *(money gain)*.

"You could use some more money, Joe, couldn't you? *(money gain)*. And probably you are making plans for expanding your business. That's going to make you some money, isn't it *(happi-ness gain)*? Why not make your business produce it *(curiosity)*?

"Let me show you the modern merchandising plan that has made more profit for other dealers *(curiosity, money gain)*."

POWER POINTS

The process of motivating and persuading prospective customers is important for gaining favorable decisions. However, there is more to this process than has been presented in this chapter. A salesperson also needs to know something about analyzing and guiding the behavior of problem people; the principles of counseling people who are difficult to handle; how to predict buyer behavior; and understand common behavior traits as observed by salespeople. These appreciations, skills and understandings will be presented in Chapter XII.

DISCUSSION QUESTIONS AND PROBLEMS

1. What do you understand by the word "motivation" as it is used in this chapter?
2. From the salesman's viewpoint, what is the significance of understanding and using buying motives?
3. What is the relation between buying motives and buying appeals that are used in personal selling?
4. What buying motives would you appeal to in each case if you were selling the following items:

   life insurance   Cadillac cars
   reducing pills   filter tip cigarettes
   winter coats   rebuilt auto tires
   wheelbarrows   fur coats

5. Name five logical and five emotional reasons for buying.
6. In your opinion what social class and what intimate group influences might motivate an individual's buying behavior?
7. What do you consider to be some of the characteristics of good appeals? How might the effect of various appeals be tested?
8 Under what conditions may a negative form of presentation be effective?
9. Briefly explain how you would appeal to the following buying motives:

   gain   pleasure and physical comfort
   pride   curiosity
   imitation   rivalry
   fear   envy

10. It is possible that a prospect's or customer's motivation may be influenced by his occupation or his home and social life. Using your readings as a guide, list the clues which would help you to know when to emphasize occupational or "off-the-job" factors.
11. Suppose a salesman were able to identify immediately a buyer's motivations. Would it be advisable to let the buyer know he had such knowledge and understanding? What would you do in a situation like this?
12. If your file records and advice from older salesmen indicated three different buying motivations for one of your customers, how could you use such information?

13. "No two persons are likely to have identical motives for buying a particular product or service." Do you agree or disagree? Give examples or reasons to support your position.

14. "Very few people respond to logical, reasoning appeals. People buy on the influence of prejudice, emotions and habit more than on good sense." Explain this quotation.

PHENOMENOLOGICAL PROJECTS

The Bing Surfboard Case: Los Angeles City College

Study carefully the following sales dialogue. In the spaces indicated, write in the type of buying motive which you think the salesman is appealing to. Then rewrite the dialogue to improve the salesman's presentation by linking the sales features more closely to the buying motives you listed in the blank spaces. Pay close attention to lines 1, 5, 9, 11, 13, 15, 17, 19, 21 and 25. A suggested change in the salesman's dialogue on line 7 is offered as an example, below.

SALESMAN: You certainly can, Bob, and let me tell you a little about this product," (walking customer over to a surfboard on display) "the world-famous Bing Surfboard."

The annual sports show is now in progress, with representatives from many distributors of surfboards and other marine equipment. A salesperson from the Bing Surfboard Company is presenting his product to an inquisitive customer.

1. SALESMAN: Here is one of the finest hand-crafted custom surfboards made locally here in Los Angeles.

2. CUSTOMER: Los Angeles? I thought that the best surfboards were made in Hawaii.

3. SALESMAN: No sir, Mr._____?

4. CUSTOMER: Bob Smith is my name.

5. SALESMAN: Well, Mr. Smith, that is a false assumption, because fine surfboards are made throughout the world.

6. CUSTOMER: I certainly am glad to know that. Then I can buy a good quality board right here in the city?

7. SALESMAN: You certainly can, sir, and let me tell you a little about my product, the famous Bing Surfboard. ————————
buying motive

8. CUSTOMER: Please do.

9. SALESMAN: The Bing Surfboard is made of polyethylene foam, with a thin wood laminated strip in the center to give maximum buoyancy and strength. Covering the polyethylene foam are two layers of ten-ounce fiberglass and resin.
_____
buying motive

10. CUSTOMER: Why is all that necessary?

11. SALESMAN: These extra layers give the surfboard a hard and lasting finish which also insures impact resistance.
_____
buying motive

12. CUSTOMER: That sure is good to know, because I'm just beginning to learn how to surf-ride.

13. SALESMAN: Oh, then since you are a beginner, may I suggest our Standard Board

Model, with a style of fin that gives maximum stability and makes it easier for learning.

_____

buying motive

14. CUSTOMER: That's great! That is what I want; but if I should improve my surfing ability, what other types of boards are there?

15. SALESMAN: We have designed the nose-rider model which is best for riding small waves. This board gives better maneuverability than the pipe-liner, which is for larger waves and has either the shark-shaped fin for fast turning or the pop-out fin for riding in rocky waters.

_____

buying motive

16. CUSTOMER: That's good to know in case I do continue to surf. But now, what about the board I'm buying today?

17. SALESMAN: We have decided that the Standard Style Board is best for you, but we have to decide about size and color.

18. CUSTOMER: Size and color, you mean I have a choice?

19. SALESMAN: Of course you do! Our surfboards come in different lengths and weights according to your height and weight

20. CUSTOMER: Well, I'm 5'11" and weigh about 160 lbs. What do you suggest?

21. SALESMAN: Those are the perfect specifications for our 10-foot 30 lb. Bing Surfboard. You have a choice of several color combinations to add to the beauty of your new surfboard.

22. CUSTOMER: No, I think that for my first board I'll just keep it in the standard clear-resin color.

23. SALESMAN: Now Mr. Smith, why don't we step over to my desk to discuss price and delivery arrangements?

24. CUSTOMER: That will be fine with me, and thank you very much for helping me make my decision on buying a Bing Surfboard.

25. SALESMAN: Not at all. I hope you'll be back when you decide to buy your next board.

A Look at Buying Motives

1. Clip advertisements from magazines and newspapers illustrating each of the seven major motives for buying goods. Paste each ad in your notebook and write a brief discourse explaining how the advertisement appeals to that particular motive.

2. Write a testimonial for one of the following products:

    (a) a fountain pen
    (b) a shirt
    (c) a television set
    (d) a baseball glove
    (e) a refrigerator
    (f) an educational toy

3. Clip several testimonials from periodicals and evaluate each one. Paste your testimonials in your notebook.

4. What are the probable buying motives in each of the following cases:

    (a) Mr. Johnson, a traveling salesman, purchases a Cadillac.
    (b) Mary Jones enrolls in an evening class in college.
    (c) William Smith buys a piece of land.

(d) Dr. Clark purchases an expensive set of office furniture.
(e) Barbara White buys a ticket to a football game.
(f) Mrs. Green purchases expensive carpeting.
(g) Mr. Larkin purchases an annuity insurance policy.
(h) Mr. Brooks purchases a second-hand car.
(i) Jim buys a ticket for the sideshow.
(j) Mrs. Lane purchases an evening gown for her daughter.

The Mortgage Insurance Case

A salesman, seeing that he was getting nowhere in outlining the advantages of life insurance to a farmer, changed his tactics by appealing to the individual's immediate problem — a $3,000 mortgage — and presented a life insurance policy as a solution.

"How much interest are you paying on the mortgage?" asked the salesman.

"Six and a half percent," replied the farmer.

"Would you be willing to pay me 2½ percent additional if I agree to cancel the mortgage and give your wife clear title to the farm in the event of your death?"

The farmer immediately agreed.

Question:
What buying motive did this salesman use?

The David Company Case

When a certain company was first organized, it was necessary that it change its trade name from the David Company to the David Dry Goods Company because another firm in the state was operating under Mr. David's firm's name.

After two years of negotiation, arrangements were made for the purchase of the trade name, enabling the David Dry Goods Company to operate as the David Company. Three months after this change had occurred and the new name had already appeared in its advertising and on the store, an advertising salesman representing a large daily newspaper solicited Mr. David for some ads. Mr. David was favorably impressed with the man and was on the point of buying when the salesman in his closing remarks referred to Mr. David's store as the "David Dry Goods Company." The salesman lost the account.

Question:
Why did this salesman lose the account?

Chapter Ten

Proving, Demonstrating & Dramatizing Claims

THE NEED TO PROVE CLAIMS
The salesman must be ready to back up every claim and suggestion that he makes. The shift from the claim-suggestion phase to the proof phase usually entails an overlapping and blending of one into the other. It is an easy transition to make, provided the salesman uses the proper techniques, materials and devices. Proof usually combines both oral and visual presentations.

Sales are consumated every day without actual proof that the buyer will receive benefits, values or advantages. This may be due to the buyer's genuine need for the product or service; because of his earlier acceptance of the proposition or because of his confidence in the salesman and the company he represents. However, even when the salesman assures his prospect that the benefits claimed will be forthcoming, it is only the salesman's word that is presented as proof. Something more is usually necessary to verify a salesman's statements and thereby bring about conviction, belief and buying action.

Selling to industrial users is not only more competitive than other kinds of sell-

ing, it also requires more presentation skill and much more "proof facts," usually in the form of sales aids. The industrial salesman calls on mining companies and oil producers; manufacturing and processing industries; the transportation industry; power and public service companies; construction firms and many specialized industries.

How does a salesman approach those who purchase for these concerns? What must he do to close sales? David Seltz states, "Unlike the consumer sale, the industrial sale is always made on the basis of cold, hard facts, concretely proved by test, research, experiment and experience rather than through appeals to emotions. Another difference exists in the amount of time necessary to complete the industrial sale as compared with that needed to sell the average consumer product."[1]

The industrial sale is not often made in minutes; therefore, the industrial salesman must make thorough advance prepa-

1. David Seltz, *Successful Industrial Selling* (Englewood Cliffs, N.J.: Prentice-Hall, 1958), p. 5.

149

ration. This preparation will include sales aids, materials and devices to help him present his proposition swiftly and dramatically. Many companies spend millions of dollars on these sales aids.

It may be assumed that any prospect is normally skeptical and cautious and his mind is often closed to the salesman's presentation. A good salesman, nevertheless, can quiet many of his fears through the use of the *suggestion selling technique* described in Chapter XV, as well as through the use of *proof materials*. A salesman's proof materials may be divided into two broad categories: oral proof and visual proof.

ORAL PROOF

Evidence is an oral presentation of facts which aims at producing conviction and bringing about favorable action.

Facts are more impressive than hearsay, and when many facts are presented in a positive fashion, they bring conviction to a prospect. A salesman's method of presenting his facts is important, because an alleged fact stated positively is often more convincing than a known fact stated weakly.

One kind of oral evidence is known as *user proof*. When a salesman is representing a well known and reputable company, he can offer evidence of the reliability of his proposition by referring to the reliability of his company. If the salesman is representing the distributor of a dependable and recognized manufacturer, he can also bring in its trustworthy name to help establish confidence and conviction.

Another kind of evidence is *authoritative proof*. It is furnished to the salesman by a person or organization recognized as an authority. Evidence drawn from the expression of the sales representative is known as *personal proof*. This evidence is drawn from the experience of the sales-

man and is usually satisfactory for use with customers whom he has been serving for several years and who have faith in his personal assurances.

Simple Words

The oral presentation of benefits and proof of claims must be carefully planned and skillfully made to arouse conviction and the desire to buy. One of the rules for making a clear presentation is to avoid technical words and phrases. It is difficult for a prospect to pay attention to someone whom he cannot understand. On the other hand, if every word uttered produces a clear-cut picture of the idea in the customer's mind, he will listen because he is interested.

Technical terms scattered throughout sales talks may produce confusion and cause a lack of interest. For example, some salesmen who sell to small garage owners may say: "Precise unfluctuating gas flow eliminates oxidized and carbonized welds; has large gas channels and eliminates restriction of second stage diaphragm, having relief valve and compound springs." Do such technical terms arouse the interest of small garage owners, or should the salesman employ simple English? The answer is obvious: Technical terminology should be used sparingly and then only when the prospect has sufficient experience or education to understand what is being said.

Avoid Generalities

A generality is a vague and hazy general statement. To say that a car is a "good" car is to state a generality and proves nothing. The descriptive word "good" might apply to the entire car, or the engine, or its appearance. To be convincing, the presentation must make clear statements about specific features and benefits.

For example, "This engine is dependable, powerful, economical." This specific statement enables the prospect to visualize the engine very clearly. One salesman says: "That is nice upholstery in this car." Another says: "Just sit in the rear seat and feel the luxurious comfort that has been built into this car."

One salesman says: "This table has a pretty design." Another salesman says impressively: "You will be proud to have this table in your home because its unusual design is fashionable." One salesman says: "You cannot go wrong on this suit." Another salesman says: "You will always feel distinctively well-dressed in this suit."

It is not strange that buyers are skeptical about generalizations. They may even believe that salesmen mean well, but the buyer is interested only in a clear-cut picture of benefits such as economy and profits. Buyers want facts and the proof that they will receive the specific benefits if they buy. Generalities do not offer convincing proof.

Using Questions to Prove

Successful salespeople know that it is easier to prove, convince and gain understanding if the prospect or customer will participate in the sales talk. Therefore, salesmen often ask questions during their presentations. Questions, properly used, are powerful proof. Salespeople cannot look into their prospect's mind, but they can discover his misgivings when they induce him to talk, and can then offer proper proof. Inducing a prospect to answer questions, however, requires both tact and good judgment.

The tone of a salesman's voice can smooth out the question and not only make it acceptable, but actually make the prospect want to disclose the information that the salesman desires.

Salesmen can use test questions not only to offer proof, but also to find out where they stand in an interview, especially when they encounter a reticent prospect. For example, test questions can be used to discover:

If the prospect is listening.
If the prospect is interested.
If the prospect's reaction is favorable or unfavorable.
If the salesman's presentation is clear.
If enough proof has been offered to support claims.

Examples of Test Questions

The following are examples of test questions used by successful salespeople to determine where they stand in an interview:

Have I made that perfectly clear?
Does this check with your experience, Mr. Brown?
That is what you want, is it not?
How does that look to you?
We are agreed on that, are we not?
How does that strike you?
Isn't that just good common sense?
You have had that experience, haven't you?

Oral Success Stories

During the presentation, the prospect can be given added proof and assurance by citing the successful experiences of satisfied customers. These experiences are known as oral success stories, or testimony. They are powerful proof materials, because they tell of someone similar to the prospect who has used the product or service, likes it and has benefited from its use. Success stories can be even more effective when the prospect goes with the salesman to visit a satisfied customer and hears about the benefits at first hand.

There are right and wrong ways to use success stories, and to obtain the best results, the following points should be included:

Tell where it happened. The salesman may start by saying, "All over my territory," but he should be very sure that he can also give definite names, the street address and the town or city.

Tell when it happened. He must be definite: was it last month, last week or yesterday?

Tell who knows it happened, and will back him up. For an unbiased witness, the salesman should choose somebody in similar circumstances to the prospect or someone known to be favorable to him. If the user is not known to the prospect, the salesman must be sure to explain who he is. For example:

SALESMAN: It is happening all over my territory.

PROSPECT: Well, just where?

SALESMAN: Well, take Elgin. You know John Ore at 228 Main?

PROSPECT: Yes, I know him.

SALESMAN: Do you think he is a smart businessman?

PROSPECT: Sure, John does a swell job.

SALESMAN: Well, only last Tuesday, John said to me, "Bill, I never had anything work better for me than this device!" So I asked him to put it down in writing. Look what he says.

The salesman started with a general claim and supported it with a definite example. He made sure how his prospect felt about John Ore. If the prospect's reaction had been unfavorable, the salesman should have shifted to another testifier. He was definite about his location and date. He also had a testimonial letter to add proof to his statements and he could have suggested a telephone call to John Ore.

Telephone Calls
Closely related to the oral success story is the telephone call which can link the prospect at his place of business with a satisfied user. Quite often the value of a telephone call is more than the cost, if the testifier represents a prestige account that is substantial.

VISUAL PROOF
It has been stated that *oral proof* will assist the salesman to open the prospect's mind and quiet his fears. Many prospects, however, insist that the salesman offer more substantial proof, such as visual proof. The prospect may insist on being *shown* valid, reliable proof before he will commit himself to a purchase. He may want a demonstration; he may want to test the product; he may want written testimony; he may want visual sales aids. When these proof materials are skillfully used in their proper place, they can be the most substantial way of revealing to the prospect what benefits he will receive when he buys.

"Constant use of visual aids is the key to volume sales and profits." This quotation states briefly what salesmen learn through costly experience. Since the prospect possesses five sensory receptors, each of which helps him select and comprehend messages, it is wise to appeal to as many of those receptors as possible when communicating with him.

Advantages of Visual Proof
Demonstrations and visual aids enable salesmen to understate their claims while proving them, an advantage in selling. If salesmen had a true appreciation of the value of visual sales aids, they would use them more often. Visual sales aids help salesmen in these ways:

By simplifying the features and benefits related to a product or service. The proper visual aid will enable a prospect to understand more quickly by eliminating nonessentials and spotlighting benefits of real importance.

By obtaining and holding the prospect's attention. Only the most gifted salesmen can hold the attention of prospects for more than a few minutes because of fatigue and monotony. Visual aids keep prospects alert and interested.

By using additional sensory organs to assist the prospect in the assimilation of facts. Without sales aids, the salesman can only tell his story, depending entirely on the prospect's sense of hearing to carry his message to the prospect's brain. When sales aids are added, the prospect is stimulated not only by what he hears, but also by what he sees and feels and sometimes smells and tastes.

By creating more vivid impressions. Sales aids properly used can dramatize a presentation, drive home the important points vividly and leave the prospect with permanent impressions.

Attention of the prospect is attracted more easily and quickly when visual aids are employed. Also, what prospects see is more believable to them than what they hear. A salesman cannot gain a prospect's understanding until he first obtains his attention, and a sale can start only after attention has been gained.

The relative attention-attracting power of each of the five senses is shown in the following tabulation. The salesman should note that sight has about seven times the attention-attracting power of all other senses combined.

Sense	Percent
Sight	87.0
Hearing	7.0
Smell	3.5
Touch	1.5
Taste	1.0
Total	100.0

Retention. What prospects see attracts their attention, but how much do they retain after they have seen a visualization and listened to the oral part of a sales presentation? Here are research findings on this topic published recently by Sales-Marketing Executives, International:

People retain
    10 percent of what they hear.
    35 percent of what they see.
    65 percent of what they see and hear.

Therefore, for the best results, oral appeals should be combined with visual; a skillful combination of the two will produce more successful sales than either method used alone.

HOW TO SHOW AND DEMONSTRATE

The easiest, quickest and most effective method for a salesman to communicate claims and prove assertions is to show and demonstrate the product itself. This is true for five reasons:

1. Seeing a demonstration is more convincing than hearing words.
2. A demonstration is easy to remember.
3. Demonstrations translate abstract ideas into concrete form.
4. Demonstrations paint pictures quickly, and save time.
5. Demonstrations produce strong impressions: because many people are "eye-minded," they tend to learn more quickly through sight than through hearing.

Product Demonstration

People need help in visualizing the salesman's product or service; therefore, it is usually best to show the product itself, or a sample. Because it is often necessary to demonstrate the product or service, the salesman must train himself to demonstrate the item effectively.

Before he demonstrates a product, it is important that the salesperson check carefully to be sure that the product will be shown most favorably. If it is a food, it must be served at proper temperature; if a machine, it must be cleaned, well serviced, smooth-running; if a safety razor, it must be sure to click-click when it is supposed to do so. Both the salesman and the item must perform smoothly in the demonstration, or a sale will be lost instead of gained.

Before the salesman demonstrates, he must decide what he wants to prove. The professional salesman does not emphasize economy if his customer wants speed. He first demonstrates speed, and then goes on to the other plus values: economy, safety, performance, construction features or beauty in terms of the product or service he is selling.

As he demonstrates, the salesman makes sure his prospect is grasping what he is saying and doing by asking questions. Sometimes a failure results because the prospect does not understand. The presentation may be too fast and the salesman gets far ahead of the prospect's understanding. The salesman should emulate the teacher who explained his success in teaching this way:

"I tell them what I am going to say;
Then I say it;
Then I tell them what I've said.
Then I ask questions and listen."

The top-tier salesperson uses the same principle. He tells his prospect what he is going to demonstrate. Then he demonstrates. Then he tells the prospect what he has demonstrated. Finally, so the prospect will never forget it, the salesman hands him the product and lets him repeat what he has just seen. Then he asks questions and listens.

The salesman should not ask the prospect to perform tasks beyond his capability; it is important not to confuse or embarrass him. A failure during a sales-man's demonstration will ruin a sale, but it is also important that mistakes do not take place when the prospect is attempting the demonstration.

Dramatic Demonstration

In a dramatic demonstration, the salesperson shows exactly how his product works. He runs floor polish on a board, or auto cleaner and polish on an automobile. He takes out spots with a clothes cleaner. He kills flies with insect spray. He heats lubricating grease to prove its tenacity and body; he stretches a fabric; puts rugs and furniture into a demonstration room; shows a washing machine washing clothes; holds a necktie against his shirt; shows how an automobile operates; has a floor lamp connected for actual use; cleans a rug with his vacuum sweeper.

Nearly all products lend themselves to proof by demonstration, regardless of their size, nature or value. The following examples will serve to illustrate this point; proof and assurances can also be shown for many other products.

Tire   A cross section is shown to prove superiority of construction.

Vacuum cleaner   Demonstrate how it will easily pick up sand, lint, cotton and other debris.

Necktie   Place it against a shirt, or hold it against the customer's suit to prove its attractiveness when worn.

Aluminum utensils   Boil water or cook something to show its practical uses.

Electric Dishwasher   Show it in actual operation.

Aluminum siding   Build a model to prove the merit of the materials which may otherwise be too abstract and difficult to visualize easily.

Shoes Cut a shoe in half lengthwise to prove superiority of construction.

Life insurance Show a sample or facsimile policy.

Hosiery Stretch to prove its tensile strength.

Furniture Make a room setting to suit the customer's idea of comfort and taste. Show a cross-section of construction.

Fabrics Make acid and burning tests to prove all wool content and wearability.

Electric Stove Strike the enamel with a coin to prove its non-chip quality. Operate the switches and burners.

Washing machine Fill with laundry and operate it to prove its quietness, speed, economy and cleaning power.

Prospect Participation

Another way of proving the superior advantages of a proposition is to induce the prospect to participate in the demonstration. Have him test the product. When he handles, sees, smells, hears and perhaps tastes it, he will find it difficult to remain unconvinced about its benefits: "when they try it, they will often buy it!"

When the prospect or customer participates in a demonstration, he is receiving the strongest kind of proof material. A self-demonstration brings him into the picture. The salesman is talking about him, his business, his worries and showing him solutions to his problems. The prospect actually experiences the benefits when he participates in the demonstration.

Prospects can be induced to participate in many demonstrations; in fact, the possibilities are almost unlimited. The following are only a few examples of the many ways in which prospects can be induced to participate:

Clothing Have the customer try it on to prove its fit, style, comfort and wearability.

Automobile Have the customer drive it to prove its acceleration, flexibility, comfort, control and speed.

Aluminum kitchen utensils Have the customer cook in a utensil to prove its benefits to her.

Shoes Have the customer try them on to experience their style and comfort.

Food products, beverages Have the customer taste them to prove delicious flavor.

Furniture Have the customer sit in a chair, push the drawers in and out of a dresser, push down on the springs of a bed, to prove their comfort or convenience.

Book Open to certain pages and have the customer see the pictures or read to prove that it is worthwhile.

Perfume Have the customer smell and try it to prove its distinctive quality.

Typewriter Encourage the prospect to operate it to prove its light touch and efficient operation.

Ball-point Pen Have the customer write with it to prove that the point and shape are suitable.

Tools Let the customer handle and operate them to prove their merit.

Musical Instruments Have the customer play them to prove their tone and pitch.

When the prospect participates in the demonstration, when he tries it out himself, he experiences the advantage of using the product or service. His participation conveys to him a feeling that the salesman is there to help him, not just to sell him something. While he is participating, the prospect may make a comment or suggestion indicating that he feels that he is solving his own problem and that he appreciates and believes in the promised benefits. This is the appropriate time to try to close the sale.

Competitive Demonstrations
Demonstrations that compete against other products or companies should be avoided. If a customer insists on a competitive test, he should select the competing product and an impartial person to conduct the test.

A better way to show improvement and superiority and thereby interest a prospect in a product or service is to compare its operation or uses with his previous or present product or service.

Demonstrations are so important in selling that they cannot be overemphasized. It is not only profitable to demonstrate, it is also easier for a salesman to demonstrate than to explain to a salesmanager why he did not obtain the order.

VISUAL SALES AIDS

A visual sales aid is any visible device or material that assists salesmen to transmit and communicate facts, knowledge, understanding, appreciation and skills to a prospective customer. According to this definition, there are many visual aids with merit, including:

blackboard
catalogues
demonstration kits
display windows
direct view slides
exhibits
flash and flip cards
graphs
table viewer

manuals and booklets
maps
mock-ups
models
motion pictures
photographs
paper and pencil
portfolios
transviewers
presentation books
samples
sand tables
scrapbooks
sound slide and
    strip films
specimens and models
success stories
turnover charts

Advantages of Visual Aids
After using visual sales aids over a reasonable period of time, salesmen have offered laudatory testimony about them. These salesmen stated that visual aids:

Enabled them to understate and overprove
Helped them to avoid blunt or contradictory statements
Never irritated prospects
Helped to close more successful sales
Furnished a track on which to run sales talks
Anticipated the prospect's objections
Made presentations more interesting and thereby encouraged the prospect to listen to the whole story
Often gave the prospect an opportunity to participate in a demonstration
Revealed product uses, values, benefits and features in a way that the prospect did not expect to see
Helped focus the prospect's attention on the sales points
Told a complete story about each benefit, feature, value, advantage or exclusive

In short, wide utilization of sales aids and demonstrations is one of the keys to volume sales and profits, according to the statements of the salesmen interviewed by Kenneth B. Haas.

In their advertising, Williams and Myers, Chicago photoprinters, say, "A well organized sales portfolio or presentation, with a few words and many pictures, may present in five minutes what the most swift-tongued salesman could not successfully prove in half an hour. A picture never mumbles, never forgets, never confuses. Present it visually and in a flash the prospect has received and perceived the idea."

Use of Visual Sales Aids

Visual sales aids, including the product itself, are used to prove oral claims, as well as to enhance, amplify and clarify the entire sales presentation. The value of visual aids has been so widely accepted, in theory at least, that no salesman or prospective salesman needs to be persuaded that "see power is sales power." However, many salesmen, although convinced that visual aids are useful, use them less frequently and less effectively than they might. Too many adopt a "Yes, but" attitude: "Yes, but I haven't the money to buy materials." "Yes, but the company doesn't furnish them and I'm no artist or mechanic." "Yes, but where do I find the things and what do I need?" "Yes, but I wouldn't know how to use them anyway."

Two key points should be kept in mind: good sales aids need not be costly, since some of the best are homemade; artistic and mechanical skill is much less important than common sense in choosing sales aids and being alert to opportunities for using them.

Examples of Visualized Proof

Visualizations of both tangible and intangible products or services is effective because the broadest highway to a prospect's mind is through his eyes. Think how much more powerful the suggestions in the following visualizations are when compared with oral claims or evidence:

A newspaper clipping about the death of a prominent, respected person

A sample stock certificate, a bond, an insurance policy

A graph or photo illustrating the increased efficiency that would be realized from the use of the product

A photo of a worn sprayer nozzle to show sturdy construction

A photostat of a check made in payment of an insurance claim

A college catalogue to help in selling an education insurance policy

A diagram showing how intricate equipment operates

A photograph of an automobile wreck in selling accident and liability insurance

METHODOLOGY FOR USING SALES AIDS

Relating Oral to Visual Proof

When offering proof of claims, the salesman should make his oral presentation first, then introduce the related visual material. To illustrate how this is done, the salesman could be saying: "Mr. Black, when I came in here, I said that hundreds of dealers who handle our products are increasing their sales, making higher profits and enjoying a faster turnover. I am now going to prove to you that what I have said is true, and that our products can do thé same for you." The salesman then proceeds to offer his proof in the form of a demonstration, written testimony, exhibits, charts, photos or other sales aids.

Presentation Outline

While a presentation is being made, visual aids arranged in sequence serve as an outline for the salesman to follow. An outline aids the prospect in remembering facts and figures. It also helps the salesman remember his strategy, and frees his mind to concentrate on his presentation while allowing him to watch for opportunities to close the sales successfully.

Quantity of Aids

The presentation of visual materials, or sales aids, should never become more important than the person who is conducting the interview. This may happen if several visual aids are in evidence at one time. To avoid losing control of the interview, the salesman should offer for the prospect's attention only one item at a time, and then only to prove a specific point made in the oral presentation. When the proof material has emphasized the benefit point, it should be removed from the prospect's sight. Otherwise, the prospect may object to the clutter on his desk, or be confused by the amount of material confronting him and be unable to make a decision.

Timing

There is no predetermined point at which visual aids should be introduced into an interview. Professional salesmen meld them into their presentations, especially during explanations and as a help in dealing with obstructions. Sales aids should be used with economy, and only when specifically required to influence a prospect's wavering judgment.

Good timing indicates that visible proof is necessary to confirm oral statements, but only after the salesman has explained briefly the importance of the facts, features or benefits that he intends to prove. He should not talk while the prospect is looking at the visuals, because he cannot look and listen at the same time.

For example, suppose the salesman observes that the prospect is not agreeing with his claim that the product will provide a solution to his problem. The salesman's procedure might be this: "Mr. Black, I understand perfectly why you believe that your problem is different from others. Actually, I am glad you brought that up because it offers me the chance to prove that we can help you. I have with me some user experience reports, from many different sources, but I want to show you just one that I selected when you told me over the phone that you could see me this morning."

At this point, the salesman extracts a specific letter from his carefully indexed file of success stories. He handles it with respect and as something of value, while he directs Mr. Black's attention to the exact paragraph containing the proof of practical benefits.

Handling Visual Aids

All demonstration and testimonial material is given higher value in the prospect's mind if it is handled impressively by the salesman and is carefully framed, mounted or otherwise arranged so that the prospect is impressed with its quality. People judge the value and worth of the things the salesman shows them by the value *he* places on them.

Portfolio Management

People often need help in visualizing and perceiving the benefits they would enjoy if they possessed a certain product. Obviously, the actual product, a miniature or an exhibit is best for showing and demonstrating, but the salesman may not be able to use these visuals. In place of those devices, he should provide himself with a portfolio, a binder or a folder in which to keep testimonial letters, photostats, photographs of the product or service in use, lists of satisfied customers, specification sheets, brochures, survey charts, graphs and many other items that help to prove his claims. In addition to these visual materials, there are others of equal value for specific presentations.

Competition. No success letter or other evidence of value should be placed in a salesman's kit which could be used equally well by a competitor. Such material is usually colorless, uninviting or unconvincing.

Cross-Indexing. When the salesman must carry with him a quantity of success stories and similar material, it requires careful indexing. The form of this indexing will depend on the character and diversity of the salesman's line, but in general the best system is a simple cross-index.

One general heading might be "Demonstration Materials." This heading might include photographs, company advertising, newspaper and magazine tear sheets and clippings. A second heading could be "Success Stories," which might include user letters, photostats of repeat orders and charts and graphs summarizing user-group experiences of satisfaction. Cross-indexing also includes an analysis of all these materials under subject headings like "Names of Customers" and "Applications of Product," as well as others, depending on the character of the line and the salesman's job requirements.

Preserving Materials. There are several ways to keep proof materials fresh, clean and attractive so that the buyer will receive a good impression. Proof materials are often kept in a common three-ring binder with separator tabs on division pages. To preserve typed or printed materials in spotless condition, many salesmen use ready-made clear acetate envelopes which can be purchased already punched for three ring binders, or in large sheets for large items.

Portfolio Size. Portfolios of visual materials should not be so bulky that they cause the prospect to fear a lengthy interview. In all situations, it is wise to keep sales aids on the floor besides the salesman's feet with only one item on the prospect's desk at any one time.

Filing. Following the interview, it is good practice to restore every item of proof material to its proper niche. This should not be done in the prospect's office, but in the reception rom, or in the salesman's car as he reviews his plans for his next call.

Dramatization. In order to dramatize proof materials, the salesman must display enthusiasm and conviction in his bearing, facial expression and tone of voice.

Picture Books

Closely related to *portfolios* are "picture books." As the name implies, photographs make up the bulk of the content and the method of presentation is substantially the same. It is not difficult or expensive to build up a picture book. One successful salesman carries a small camera on his travels, photographs installations made by his company, then places his pictures in a loose-leaf binder. He also acquires suitable photos from other sources, as well as tear sheets from periodicals, and includes both in the picture book with his photographs. These visuals present the merits of his proposition more vividly than a mere oral presentation. Many salesmen in many lines use photographic materials to advantage in proving claims and illustrating benefits.

Written Testimony

Written testimony is synonymous with written success stories and letters. The best testimony bears a recent date and describes as specifically as possible the experiences for which success is claimed. The testimonial letter which the salesman likes best and which the prospect respects most is one that meets the newspaper requirements of *who, what, why, when, where* and *how.* With few exceptions, a prospect is far more interested in the experiences of a competitor a mile or a few miles away than of an unheard firm a thousand miles distant. For this reason, a salesman might have his portfolio cross-indexed to include one heading for "Industries" and another for "Location."

When the customer does not have time to write a testimonial, the salesman might ask for his letterhead, type the testimony and have him sign it. It might also be profitable to make a scrapbook of testimonials, accompanying each one with a picture of the satisfied user and the company name to give it authenticity.

Route books, or order books, have been successfully used by salesmen as testimonial proof. It it convincing to many prospective customers to see actual orders and the names of those who have already purchased. In addition, the route book can show what and how the salesman sells, what service is provided, how deliveries are made and supply other details of interest to a wavering prospect.

Maps, charts, graphs and similar materials can illustrate increased production, savings or increased turnover for which the salesman's product or service is responsible. Visual materials of this kind should be small, simply constructed and readily understandable.

Scrapbooks

Closely related to portfolios, the scrapbook most often contains material related to the general prestige of the salesman's organization. It may be made up of tear sheets of his company's national advertising in trade papers, general magazines, newspapers and the company's annual report. Some salesmen have reproductions made of letters received from their customers. With these they attach photographs of the customer and his office, store, building or other items of interest.

Pencil Selling

The simplest and easiest form of visual proof for the salesman to prepare and use requires only a piece of paper and a pencil. Every benefit topic of a sales talk may be jotted down on a sheet of paper in outline form. When the salesman has completed his presentation, the prospect has before him a written outline of benefit points. This device is often helpful in proving claims.

Presentation Books

Closely related to picture books, scrapbooks and portfolios, the presentation book consists of professionally prepared graphic materials and illustrations.

Maps, Charts, Graphs

Maps, home-made or professionally made, are indispensable in selling many products.

Charts are used chiefly to analyze a problem or situation. They show proper sequence and relationship. Flow charts, for example, can be used to show each division of a business and its breakdown into individual or functional departments.

Table charts are indispensable in many selling situations. They are effective, for example, in presenting a breakdown of financial statements. They may also be used for comparisons and for listing advantages or disadvantages of a business organization.

Strip-tease charts are specially successful in focusing attention on one point at a time in developing a sales talk. Each important point on a chart is covered with a thin strip of paper that can be removed as the sales presentation unfolds.

Process charts are adaptable to many kinds of selling. They may illustrate the complete production process of a product or they may depict the channels of distribution for various kinds of merchandise.

Graphs are especially useful for making comparisons and contrasts or for presenting complicated facts to prospects and customers. A long column of figures or statistics appears impressive, but is usually skipped over by a prospect. A graph of the same figures may make the prospect stop, look and think.

Flash cards are small, compact cards flashed before a prospect or customer to bring home an idea. The message contained on the cards must be brief and to the point to be effective. Flash cards may be used to summarize, to review, to repeat the sales talk or to emphasize and highlight important points.

Posters

Posters have been defined as "visual combinations of bold design, color and message . . . intended to attract and hold the attention of the prospect or customer just long enough to implant a significant idea in his mind."[2] For effective use, posters must be simple, since they are used to transmit an idea or an image at one glance. Posters can utilize graphs, charts, pictures, cartoons or almost any item that will help to present facts or emphasize a selling point.

Sales Manuals

A sales manual is a book or binder containing complete information related to a certain product, service or line of merchandise. Some manuals may contain information on a number of products. A manual should contain all possible information pertaining to a specific product, service, object, device or type of merchandise. A manual will enable the salesman to talk intelligently about his products or services; answer customer's questions concerning the products or services offered; give suggestions on how to use

2. Walter Arno Wittich and Charles F. Schuller, *Audio-Visual Materials* (New York: Harper & Brothers, 1957), p. 127.

and care for the product; and help the salesman to display and prove more effectively.

Easel Portfolio

The easel portfolio is usually placed on the buyer's desk, although it may be used with a floor easel. In either case, it has papers which are flipped over as they are shown. The pages are arranged to appeal to the prospect's point of view.

The easel portfolio serves two purposes: first, it helps the salesman to keep on the track and bring out salient facts in the proper sequence; second, it helps to dramatize the presentation and arouse interest. This sales aid is useful to salesmen who sell to business executives, dealers, purchasing men and others who sit at a desk when buying. It is effective in building up interest in a specialty or technical product to engineers and purchasing agents who do not care for emotional appeals.

Company Advertising

According to David Seltz, advertising by industrial companies has a twofold purpose: first, to educate the company's most logical market in the use and benefits of its products; second, to stimulate inquiries from prospects interested in learning how the company's products might be of use to them. In addition, some large companies buy space in popular publications to assist their public relations departments. Salesmen can use these advertisements in several ways.

First, advertisments help salesmen obtain prospects: Second, advertisements often assist the salesmen to emphasize his company's status, reputation and policies. A prospect may feel that a company large enough to advertise would be a good one with whom to do business.

Third, advertising may be used to show product and service features, benefits, values and advantages. Fourth, advertising can help a salesman when it indicates to a prospect that the company is interested in his industry. For example, a steel company might run an advertisement showing the use of steel sheets in the manufacture of lockers, thereby boosting that particular industry. Also, the customer's plant might be photographed and used in an advertisement by the vendor's company.

Catalogues

Catalogues may consist of from one to several hundred pages presenting the various products of the company in an informative and eye-appealing manner. Catalogues are often sent to prospects in advance of the salesman's call and can, therefore, serve as an entry for the salesman. They can also serve as a conversation piece when the salesman says, "By the way, have you seen our latest catalogue?" or "What do you think of the new product shown in our electric appliance catalogue?" They may also be used as a presentation manual.

Business Cards

A salesman's business card can be an important sales aid, for it is the first contact the prospect has with the salesman and through him, his company. It may be the first impression the prospect receives of the salesman and it may also be the most lasting. Business cards contain the name and address and telephone number of the caller; they may also contain messages, illustrations or symbols related to the salesman, his company, his sales proposal and other imprints designed to attract and impress potential buyers. Business cards left with the buyer serve as constant *reminders* of whom he may call for certain products and services.

Guarantees and Warrantees

Printed guaranty and warranty forms may be used as sales aids. The simple fact that a product is guaranteed or warrantied to perform according to specifications may attract attention, arouse interest and stimulate conviction in the buyer.

Visual Devices

Blackboard

There are times when a salesman may want to use a portable blackboard to drive home important points about a product or sales problem. The blackboard is a good tool for emphasizing the key points of a sales talk. A portable blackboard can be used to advantage in presenting proof materials.

Films For Selling

There are certain products and services that can best be sold by showing films. A salesman may find it desirable to have a room arranged for projecting films or have a portable projector for field presentations. Films for selling include motion pictures, sound slides, strips, motion-slides and slides. Each of these film types is useful for offering proof in certain kinds of creative selling.

Motion pictures may be black-and-white or colored, silent or sound. For selling intangibles, the motion picture is a valuable selling aid. For selling appliances, devices, or other products that have motion, the moving picture has great value. For appealing to emotions, building appreciation and encouraging understanding, the motion picture is an effective device. The motion picture is not so effective for portraying facts, skills, knowledge and for proving a point. It also is more expensive and difficult to acquire, transport and use than other sales devices.

Sound-Slide Film. The portable sound-slide projector is light and easy to carry. Sound-slide film is valuable for selling certain products. First, it helps to picture products or services to a prospect. Sound-slide film never omits, never exaggerates, it is not overawed by a customer, never suffers from fear and never has a poor memory.

Also, sound-slide projectors and film are easy to transport, use and acquire. Pictures can be shown in sequence with a sound recording or as strip film without the recording.

Strip film is a continuous strip of film consisting of individual frames or pictures arranged in sequence, usually with explanatory titles. Each strip may contain from ten to one hundred pictures or more, with suitable copy. For most sales use, the silent strip film is best because it permits questions, answers and discussion. For many items, it offers excellent proof of values. It is easy to transport and use. It is the most economical of all film media.

Motion-Slide Film. The motion-slide film combines the values of the motion picture with the strip film. Where motion is needed, it gives motion; where motion is not needed, or where motion is not good, the picture is frozen until motion is again required. For certain kinds of products or services, this dual feature is a valuable aid in proving benefits.

Slides. Slides are easy to make, versatile, easy to select, low in cost and easy to transport and use. When used with a portable projector, they furnish many salesmen the answer to the proof problem and open the door to successful sales.

Overhead Projectors. For illustrating details that sell better when enlarged, such as work sheets, charts, graphs, pictures, maps, operational sheets and sales checks, an overhead projector is an advantage. However, all materials to be projected must first be transferred to transparencies. Transparencies are inexpensive and may be made by professionals or by the salesman. Intricate details requiring draftsmanship in art work should be done by trained experts. For spot work, the salesman can prepare the transparency by writing on it with a china marker or grease pencil.

Transviewer. This device is a variation of the overhead projector. It uses the same kind of transparencies and gives a brilliantly lighted background for dramatic effect. It can be plugged into any outlet and set up on a dealer's counter or a prospect's desk in a few seconds. This is an effective, easily used devise for getting attention and proving oral claims.

Direct-View Slides. Direct-view slides can add the potency of full color, three dimensional sight-selling to a sales talk. This is the modern selling version of the stereoscope. It is useful for showing products, services, installations, manufacturing processes and other selling factors. It is pocket-size and uses film to show objects and designs in relief or three dimensions.

Table Viewer. This sales presentation device uses ordinary two-by-two inch slides and operates by electricity. It is small: only nine by twelve inches. The slides are dropped into a chamber where they are automatically inserted for projection and restacked in their original order. This device is a creative selling tool for salesmen of all types of products and services.

Presentation Board

The presentation board — also known as the felt board, flannel board or slap-on board as well as by several trade names — is a simple but effective device for controlled disclosures. With this modern version of a blackboard, a salesman can build up his story visually at the same rate as his accompanying sales talk. This is done by emphasizing the chief sales points with a series of pictures, designs or symbols made of stiff cardboard. Flock or sandpaper in then glued to the back of each unit. The board itself is wood covered with a felt material to which flock or sandpaper adheres when pressed against it.

Transparency Portfolio
The transparency portfolio performs the same task as the model. Working parts of the product are illustrated on separate transparent sheets. As each sheet is placed in position, another part of the product is added. The item is completed while the prospect watches and listens to the explanation.

Used most often by salesmen of industrial products, the transparency portfolio is excellent for showing the construction of a product or demonstrating an engineering principle.

Plant Trips
Plant trips may be one of the best selling aids a salesman can use. He might talk about a product, service or production process at great length, and yet fail to get his story across even when he uses all other available visuals.

When other methods appear to be inadequate, a trip through the plant, mill or factory will give prospects a firsthand view of the things the salesman wants them to know about his product or process of manufacture.

When such a trip is considered, plans should be prepared regarding what prospects are to see and why. They will then know, before the start, what they should look for and where they will find it. Likewise, there should be a discussion with the prospect after the trip, to review what has been learned and to answer questions.

Trips by salesmen through the plants of customers are also valuable, because salesmen learn how the products are made. Such knowledge helps them to sell more.

Recordings
Wire, tape and disc recordings are not visual aids, but they are aids to sales presentations. They can be used to pre-sent speeches, skits or any staged situation where sound alone can transmit a message to a prospect. It should be noted, however, that recordings rank lowest of all the sales aids in effectiveness.

Recordings may be used to reveal the wrong and right way to start questions or to conduct a conversation. The start of an actual sales talk can be recorded up to a certain point, when it is stopped and the salesman continues the conversation with the prospect. Recordings may also be used to convey personalized messages from individuals in top management who are unable to meet prospects. They may also be used to entertain prospects and customers.

Sales Trailer
One of the most useful sales devices for manufacturers of furniture, durable goods, machinery and certain appliances is the *sales trailer*. It is not only a good visual device, it also reduces sales costs by allowing the salesman to make more calls more efficiently, since the salesman brings a showroom to the buyer who does not have the time to go to it.

These rolling sample rooms come in various sizes, but the most popular is the large or medium-sized trailer attached to the salesman's car. It is usually fifteen to twenty-five feet long and may carry up to a 2,500 pound load. The latest trend is to devote part of the trailer to sales demonstrations and the remainder for sleeping accommodations for the salesman.

Miniature Models
The miniature model ranks next to the actual product in effectiveness in a sales presentation. Models are constructed to scale and are often working models. Salesmen of engineered specialties use a cutaway model to show construction and a working model to demonstrate engineering principles and benefits. A model can

be transported and displayed where the actual product could not because of its size.

Demonstration Kits

A demonstration kit may be a briefcase, an attache case, a small suitcase or a specially constructed container. It may contain miniature models, exhibits, specimens, the actual product, graphs, charts, booklets and any other aids needed to help sell the product or service.

Demonstration kits are good devices for highlighting sales presentations. The variety of materials provided helps to retain the prospect's attention. Some kits include a humorous "gimmick" to amuse the prospect. Kits are among the oldest sales aid devices and also among the most effective.

Kits should be kept in good order with everything carefully arranged and dis-

played to the best advantage. Items should be easily removed for handling, sampling and testing.

POWER POINTS

A dramatic presentation of proof of benefits through visual aids saves time, helps avoid misunderstandings and disagreements and adds power to the sales talk. While the visual sense organs are many times more powerful than the auditory sense organs, visual materials and devices must be carefully chosen, with thought given to their timing as well as to the specific points to be stressed for each buyer. When a salesman explains his sales proposal clearly to a qualified buyer, supporting his presentation with oral and visual proof of benefits, he will be on his way to overcoming obstructions to the close of a successful sale.

DISCUSSION QUESTIONS AND PROBLEMS

1. a. Distinguish between the content of a "presentation book," a "scrapbook" and a "portfolio."
   b. Describe the technique you would employ when using each of them during a presentation.
2. Scrapbooks are often useful as sales aids. (a) Explain why and when they may be of greatest value; (b) describe how you would use them.
3. Some salesmen find uses for company posters, manuals, booklets, advertising tear sheets and brochures. *How* would you use these materials and *why* might they be of aid to a salesperson?
4. Films of various kinds, as well as overhead projectors and transviewers, are useful aids for some salesmen. What kind of salesman and what products or services would be aided by these visual devices?
5. When might it be desirable to take a prospect on a tour of the salesman's plant or home office? Do you believe that a plant tour is really a visual sales aid? Why?
6. Describe a situation in which a disc or tape recording would prove to be a valuable sales aid.
7. Exactly why are visualizations of both tangible and intangible products or services said to be effective?
8. What is the relationship between visual sales aids and suggestion selling, as described in Chapter IV?
9. Imagine yourself as the salesman for a company selling a cleaning compound used in hotels, restaurants, institutions and industry. Would you *demonstrate* this product

or would you use visual sales aids? Tell how you would use or employ the method you choose.

10. How would you arrange and organize your own file of proof materials or evidence for efficiency and accuracy during your presentation?

11. A salesman for a manufacturer of welding and cutting equipment sells his product to metal manufacturers, junk dealers, garages, trucking companies, earth-moving operators and many other concerns. His products are technical and intricate in construction.
   a. Should he use visual aids to help his presentation? Why?
   b. Should he demonstrate his products while he talks? Why?
   c. Should he use both? Why?

12. Several years ago a large insurance company had picture books prepared for use by its salesmen. The salesmen were to place the picture book directly in front of their prospects and point to the pictures while they supplied the oral presentation. Although the method was successful, many salesmen did not like to use the picture book and the company finally abandoned it.
   a. Why did some salesmen dislike it?
   b. What are the advantages of this kind of visual selling? The disadvantages?
   c. (1) Would you like this method? (2) Would you prefer other visual aids? (3) Would you like to make straight oral presentations? (4) Why?

13. You are a salesman for a company which manufactures and distributes projectors. To assist you in your sales presentations, you have been given a sound-slide projector and appropriate film about your products.
   a. Is this device likely to be an effective sales aid for your purpose? Why?
   b. What might be some of the disadvantages from using this kind of visual aid? Why?

14. One of the most effective visual aids of all is the physical appearance of the salesman himself. The salesman's facial expression, mannerisms, bearing and grooming are often the deciding factors in a sale.
   a. Why might these physical attributes be considered good visual aids?
   b. When might they be considered liabilities as compared to visual aids?

15. Think of ten visual aids which might help you if you were selling canned fruit and preserves for a large food cannery. (1) After deciding on the ten visuals, which would be best for this kind of selling? (2) On the other hand, would product demonstrations be more effective? (3) In either case, tell why you selected visuals or the demonstration and explain *how* you would use the aid, or aids, you selected.

16. What is your opinion of success stories or testimonials? Do you believe that such proof materials are more effective when they are from people located in the salesman's own territory, possibly someone the prospect knows? Or is testimony more valuable when it comes from a well-known person located a long distance away?

PHENOMENOLOGICAL PROJECTS

The Merryweather Plastic Company (Case)

John Merryweather is the owner, production manager and sales manager of a small plastic manufacturing concern that specializes in extrusion items such as toys, tableware, advertising novelties, containers, bottle caps and similar small products.

He has three salesmen who regard themselves as plastics engineers rather than salesmen. These men call on manufacturers, wholesalers, jobbers, agents and specialty houses. Since much of their work involves figures and planning, all have college degrees. They are intelligent, use good speech and make an excellent appearance. They regard themselves as members of a high echelon in the sales field. Because of their education and morale, they do not want to carry samples nor do they want to demonstrate. They feel that such activities would imply that they were peddlers or identify them as belonging to a lower level of salesmanship.

Their sales are only fair. Mr. Merryweather is not making much money but he is not losing any. He feels, however, that his operation is close to the breaking point and that he must increase sales volume to have a financially safe operation. The only method that he can think of that might increase sales is to have his salesmen show samples and demonstrate the actual products to supplement their oral presentations.

Since Mr. Merryweather cannot afford to spend much money on a visual presentation, he would like his salesmen to compile their own books of facts containing photographs and charted information concerning their large products. He would also like them to carry kits containing the full line of small items. He thinks his salesmen would give more effective sales presentations and increase their sales volume with the use of presentation books and sample items.

Questions:

1. What is the problem in this case?
2. What should Mr. Merryweather do about the problems?
3. Do you believe that, since the expense of visuals is important, presentation books and the actual products will be sufficient for demonstration purposes?
4. Do you believe that these devices would help his salesmen to increase sales?
5. What other visuals can you suggest which might help close more sales?

Chapter Eleven

Overcoming Common Obstacles

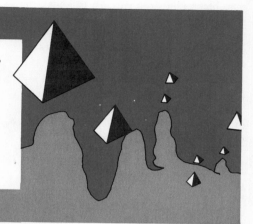

A GOOD PRESENTATION OVERCOMES OBSTACLES

Through practice and training a skillful salesperson establishes a pattern of behavior so ingrained that he is able to discuss and explain his product without conscious thought, hesitancy or concentration. Even though he cannot take time to consider all factors, the professional salesman reacts fast and in language understandable and pleasing to the buyer. He knows that his presentation will not be successful when he backtracks, fumbles or corrects himself. Therefore, before he even attempts to sell, he organizes his presentation in an idea sequence.

When a salesman uses the idea-sequence presentation he is organized so thoroughly that he not only knows what he will say and what benefits he will emphasize, but also in what order he will present them. The idea-sequence is similar to the planned sales talk discussed in an earlier chapter, and is neither the verbatim nor the off-the-cuff sales talk.

Whether canned or planned, the presentation should be so firmly ingrained in the salesman's mind that he will react without conscious thought. Because he has an idea-sequence he will be able to pick up his presentation at any point. Thus,

when a prospective buyer interrupts his presentation with an abrupt, "How much does it cost?" the salesman with a carefully planned idea-sequence will not be side-tracked. With his mind free of other details, he is able to detect questions before they are asked and is prepared with an automatic answer. This ready reply will also help to deter the buyer's questions about prices until their proper place at the end of the interview. The sales presentation is retained as a unit in the mind of the professional salesman. His primary purpose is to be prepared to make his presentation in its entirety and in the most effective way. Because he is habituated to present and react according to a definite pattern and because he employs the idea-sequence to present the benefits, he neglects nothing and is able to use his ingenuity and resourcefulness in manners most becoming to a professional salesman. In other words, he is able to overcome with relative ease any obstacle to a successful sale.

Obstacles may also be handled in such a way that they work for the salesman instead of against him. The experienced salesman makes a thorough study of his prospective customer. He analyzes his needs, studies his behavior traits, interests, plans and problems. In this way he is able to present interesting points and thereby avoid confusion and pointless arguments which so often reflect the presentation of an untrained salesman.

When salesmen analyze objections they find that new ones seldom occur. Sometimes objections may be expressed in a different way, but basically they are simply recurrences of the same old, tired objections. Also, further analysis of objections has revealed that whenever a prospect objects to anything, he is inclined to defend his objection. Then, having committed himself to a negative attitude, the prospect's pride prevents him from changing and he will continue to object to everything the salesman says.

Reasoning from that premise, one of the major jobs of a salesman is to anticipate obstacles such as alibis, stalls and excuses. Therefore, the alert salesman presents convincing proof of his claims before the buyer thinks of anything negative to say. The right idea planted in a buyer's mind is the most effective antidote to the objections and other obstructions.

It would be logical for the salesman to make a list of all the obstacles he might possibly meet and then ask himself what kind of behavior pattern the prospect showed, or what kind of mental dodging or negative remarks influenced their attitudes. He could then write out his best prescription for dealing with each behavior pattern, based on the behavior trait explanation in Chapter VIII.

Convincing buying reasons can be advanced to offset every possible negative reaction and possible loss of business. When a salesman is pushed, pulled and punched around the selling ring, it is more often his own fault, because he did not prepare himself.

When interesting benefit facts are worked into a strong, convincing presentation, most prospects will be too interested

to raise barriers to further progress. They will be too concerned about the benefits to raise impediments. Also, this kind of skillful selling will give the salesman a new eagerness for his job and he will no longer be afraid of negative, discourteous and hard-boiled prospects.

OBSTACLES: ATTITUDES, HABITS AND PREJUDICES

Many of the obstacles which impede successful salesmen have already been explained in Chapter VIII. However, there are other obstacles and they are commonly known as objections, resistance, obstructions, rejections and impediments. These obstacles are attitudes, habits, prejudices, requests for information and either sincere or insincere objections.

Prospect's Attitudes

Some prospects may resist a sales pitch because they have a dislike or aversion to a certain salesman. Their dislike may be caused by the salesman's speech, his behavior, his mood, his attitude or his manners. The salesman may remind them of someone in their past with whom they clashed, and for that reason they are wary of him. For any number of similar emotional reasons, there may not be a rapport between the prospect and the salesman. A brief analysis of the prospect's attitude will usually reveal the cause of the difficulty. If possible, the salesman should correct it. If the difficulty is caused by the prospect, the salesman should be prepared to deal with it.

Prospect's Buying Habits

Buying habits may also obstruct a sale. For example, the prospect may be in the habit of paying a certain price, using a certain brand or quality, or wearing a different style or color. It is part of a salesman's job to jolt them out of that attitude of complacency, satisfaction and laziness. This can be done through relaxed explaining, interesting presentations, and by using human relations techniques.

Prospect's Prejudices

Another cause of personality conflict is prejudice. The prospect may be biased or misinformed about the salesman, his proposition or his company. The salesman, from the moment he starts his presentation, may need to drive out prejudices the prospect may have. The salesman can do this if he employs the ideas revealed in this and other chapters.

OBSTACLES: REQUESTS FOR INFORMATION

One of the most common obstacles to the sale is the request for more information from prospects who want answers to their questions and explanations for their problems. Fortunately for the salesman, this is merely a small obstacle and need not worry him providing he applies the procedure suggested here.

He should aim to win the prospect's liking and respect.

Replies should be made in such a way that they indicate respect for the prospect's attitude and viewpoint.

The salesman should answer the prospect's questions with a short review of the major benefits.

Success stories from satisfied users are always impressive.

Questions should be asked by the salesman as each benefit is mentioned, to gain acceptance as he goes along.

The salesman should ask for the order.

The prospect usually raises sincere questions and problems when he does not understand or is fearful that what the salesman says sounds too good to be true. When a salesman encounters something that is difficult to explain, what should he do? There is a simple method of explaining which will eliminate these things: relax, listen, understand the prospect, use assurances.

First, the salesman should relax, emo-

tionally and physically, but not mentally. He should never be afraid to make explanations. He should recognize that questions are signals that the prospect has certain fears and wants the salesman to make him feel that they are groundless.

Second, he should listen to the question so that he understands what is on the prospect's mind. The prospect wants to be understood. He does not want an argument. The salesman should let him know that he believes his thought is worth careful listening. The prospect should be encouraged to express himself. The salesman should show by his attitude that he respects the stand the prospect has taken.

The salesman should never forget that by allowing the prospect to siphon off his aggressions or questions, he deflates the obstacle. The salesman can then quiet the prospect's fears. If the prospect represses his doubts, on the other hand, he will inflate the obstacle and force the salesman to probe in the dark. A salesman cannot change an opinion which he does not know exists. The salesman should, therefore, welcome questions and recognize in them an opportunity to clarify sales points, review advantages, meet competition and to fill unsatisfied needs for information.

Third, he should understand the prospect's viewpoint. He should respond to the prospect's questions by providing the information asked for clearly, completely and with an understanding of his viewpoint. Here is the core of the whole explanation bugaboo: answer to the prospect's complete satisfaction and with an understanding of his viewpoint. When the prospect has a receptive mind, the salesman can provide the information he wants. In providing that information, one thing should be remembered: no prospect resists being turned into a customer when he feels certain that he will benefit.

The only time a prospect resists is when he feels that something is being taken away from him. He resists when he feels that he is giving something without getting back an equal or a greater value from the seller. Anyone would feel this way under similar conditions. A prospect does not want a salesman's goods or services. He wants what they will do for him. If the prospect is made to concentrate on what he will receive rather than on what he is giving, the salesman is more likely to be successful. Likewise, when the salesman answers questions, he must remember to add benefit point to benefit point, each one more closely related to the prospect's primary motive of gain.

The fourth thing a salesman should do is use assurances like these: "Mr. Jones, I can understand why you feel that way. In fact, several of our most satisfied customers felt exactly as you feel. But now that they have seen the extra profits that they are making from their purchase, they are very happy about their decision to buy."

When these assurances are used with explanations, the salesman shows that he understands the prospect's problems. He shows that he sympathizes with the prospect's position, although he may not necessarily agree with him. He quiets the prospect's fears and reopens his mind for further selling while figuring out a solution for the prospect's questions.

Finally, the salesman must recall what Charles Schwab once said, "Winning an argument never put a dollar in my bank account."

Knowing Answers

Giving an explanation, and answering questions to the prospect's entire satisfaction, implies that the salesman knows the answers. Certainly, he should know the why, where, when, what, who and how of his product and his competitive products. Certainly, he should know about his company, its personnel, its policy and other

details if he hopes to overcome the question and problem obstruction.

When a salesman does not know the answers, he should say so. If the question is technical and he does not know the answer, he should never hedge or bluff. Nobody knows all the answers and a "fishy" answer destroys confidence in the proposition. On the other hand, the prospect's confidence is often increased if the salesman says, "Well, Mr. Jones, that's a new one on me. Frankly, I do not know. However, I will look it up and get the answer for you just as soon as I can."

If the salesman appears to be sympathetic with the prospect, he will quiet the prospect's fears and go a long way toward closing a sale.

OBSTACLES: OBJECTIONS

It is important for the salesman to recognize a prospect's excuse, alibi or "stall," and to discover the reasons for them. In many cases, he will discover that the prospect does not qualify and therefore is not even remotely interested in the salesman's proposition. It is important to know where the target is located before one starts to shoot. An unqualified buyer is not a target. He is, therefore, almost compelled to offer excuses.

The time to qualify a buyer is before the call is made. He qualifies as a prospect when he: has a *need* for the proposition; has the *authority* to buy; *can pay* the price; is *accessible* to the salesman; has *common interests* or a *close relationship* to the salesman.

When a salesman starts with a qualified prospect, he can offer things that are so important and beneficial to him that the prospective buyer would be foolish to offer insincere excuses. When the salesman shows a qualified prospect the facts and figures, the prospect's excuses, alibis and stalls are greatly decreased.

Advantages of Objections

Salesmen should not entirely believe the

old saying, "salesmen should welcome objections." Salesmen know, or at least suspect, that some objections can lead toward lost sales. And they also know that skillful handling of objections identifies a professional salesman.

Objections cause some salesmen to become confused and nervous. They lose confidence in their ability to answer objections and they may backtrack in confusion. They may even descend to offering a lower price, when their prospective customer is actually sold and simply wants more information about the product or service.

Successful salesmen know that objections offer them the chance to:

Clarify their sales presentation points.
Review benefits and advantages.
Offer more information.
Discover the real objection or real needs of the prospect.
Meet competition.
Gain a favorable buying decision.

When to Answer

The prospect sometimes interjects objections at any time and on any subject. Often these objections are unrelated to whatever the salesman is presenting. In this case, the salesman can stop at once and dispose of the objection, or he can ask the prospect's permission to hold it in abeyance until he can answer it completely.

Generally, it is better not to answer an objection until a complete presentation has been made. Meanwhile, the salesman may classify the objection as one of need, product, company, price or when to buy. He can fit his answer into the most suitable place in his presentation. A delayed answer gives him time to give a more realistic and more acceptable reply to the prospect.

When answering any objection the salesman must guard against being too

fast with his replies. When an answer is given too quickly, the prospect may receive the impression that he is being rushed into making a decision. The yes-but method, as explained later, is a good way to pace the reply.

How to Answer
Explaining Method

No one can give in a book the absolute, fool-proof answers to all objections for specific products or services. Only the salesman, his sales manager and other company officers can offer the product and background knowledge to do that. But the following basic outline, or method, can be profitably used to present explanations which will suit many prospects:

Learn the real objection and why it is an objection.
Restate the objection, then answer it completely and concisely.
Do not evade or minimize objections.
Avoid arguments.
Discuss objections positively.
Use the "yes-but" technique.
Use the objection as a reason for buying.
Do not let the objection deflect the main issues.

Certainly these are not all the ideas, but they capsule eight of the best and most important methods used by professional salespeople to counter objections.

Asking Questions and Listening

If the salesman has the ability and willingness to ask questions himself, he will find that dealing with objections is not difficult.

The salesman will need to know how to ask questions to test the objection; in this way seller and buyer reach agreement and speak the same language. Sometimes this process is not necessary; for example, when a prospect says, "But your product is not well built," the salesman knows that the prospect is making a product objection. On the other hand, a prospect may say, "I just do not know how I can use it right now." Does a salesman know what he means? The salesman can find out only by asking the prospect a question to clarify the statement.

A salesman's sharp listening ears are like selectors on a television set, which pick up phrases that tell the prospect's hidden interests or motivations. For example, a prospect might tell a salesman that the new company cafeteria is saving employees time, trouble and money. The salesman might think his prospect is motivated by convenience, unless his ears are tuned in to hear him say, "It cost us plenty to install it!" The salesman would then realize that the prospect is really bragging about the high construction cost.

Re-Stating Method

When a buyer voices an objection, the salesman can often restate it and feed it back to him in the form of a question. This technique not only places the prospect slightly on the defensive but it also gives the salesman extra time to phrase better answers. The technique is simple but effective. The objections and questions occur somewhat like this:

OBJECTION: Your price is too high. The product we use costs 10 percent less than yours.

QUESTION: Then you are wondering why you should pay 10 percent more for a similar product? Is that your question, Mr. Jones?"

BUYER: That's the question, all right.

SALESMAN: Well, I can answer that in a few words. Competitive products appear the same, but in this case there is a difference. Research tests show that our product lasts longer. Note this demonstration. See how it works. You

try it. Our customers say you'll save on labor costs with our product. Next, you can reduce your inventory because our warehouse is in this city. These add up to logical answers to your question, don't they, Mr. Jones?

Smooth-Over or Yes-But Method

Whenever most objections come up, the smooth-over method can almost always be used to good advantage. It is one of the strongest methods in salesmanship and the nearest thing to being scientific. The smooth-over method overcomes either real or insincere objections. If a salesman thinks of the smooth-over method every time his prospect raises an objection, he cannot go wrong and he will close more sales.

When the customer says, "Your product costs too much," all the salesman need do is say: "Yes, I know just how you must feel, Mr. Customer. No one likes to pay more money for anything than it's worth. You can buy a lower priced product, that is true. But . . . let me tell you about the built-in economy and comfort values of this . . ." Then the salesman should continue to tell the prospect why his product offers the best investment in service, safety, comfort and economy that he could make.

An analysis of this method of handling objections reveals that the salesman first agreed that price is important, then he gave the prospect all the reasons that his product is fairly priced and an excellent investment. This is how the smooth-over method can be applied in solving real and imagined objections.

Suppose the prospect says, "Most of my driving is around town. I think a less expensive tire would serve my purpose."

The salesman should try answering with something like this: "Yes, you're right. I can understand how it would appear that way. But have you ever stopped to think of it this way?" Then he retells the benefits — protection against skidding, safety from blow-outs in fast traffic — stressing the great importance of these features in driving in city traffic and along high-speed highways.

Other examples of the smooth-over technique are:

"Yes, I know how you feel, but if you should find that . . ."

"Yes, that is the way it may look but after you see . . ."

"Yes, I can understand why you should feel as you do, but when you consider . . ."

"Yes, that is perfectly natural to think so, but an investigation of the consumer group has shown . . ."

The fact that the smooth-over method is very useful does not mean that the words "yes" and "but" must appear in a sales talk. To use the method, the salesman: (1) acknowledges that he recognizes the position of the prospect in making the objection; and (2) goes on to show the prospect why he did not have enough adequate information. For instance, if the prospect said, "I prefer the XYZ brand," the salesman could reply, "I know that you want the safest and most economical product. That is why I feel so confident in urging you to depend on our product which your engineers have determined will give you greater performance than the next best." Here, as in most cases, the words "yes" and "but" are not actually used.

Although the smooth-over technique will apply in most instances, there are a few exceptions. Suppose the prospect says, "The only time I ever used one of your products, it gave me such poor service that I swore I would never buy another." His trouble could likely have been caused by poor use or care of the product. Therefore, the salesman can handle this situation by encouraging the prospect to tell all about this experience until he gets it off his chest.

While getting it off his chest, the prospect often convinces himself that what he thought so important was not worth mentioning after all. In any event, if the prospect is allowed to unload his emotions, he will more than likely accept the salesman's suggestions as a cure for his trouble. His mind will be clear to decide whether the salesman's product will fill his need.

There is another situation where smooth-over does not apply. For example, a prospect interrupts a presentation with the statement, "I don't need a product as good as that one. I never had trouble with the one I use." Very often the best solution to this problem is to say absolutely nothing. To give a serious answer would possibly provoke an argument. But a smile from the salesman will probably result in the prospect having a higher opinion of the salesman's common sense.

Sometimes an ordinary explanation will not work and a genuine objection will have to be answered. Naturally, no salesman can hope to overcome all objections, but if he can develop his skill in many areas, he can also increase his sales.

Analyzing Prospect's Objections

Before he goes out to call on prospects, the salesman might as well admit that he will encounter obstacles in the form of different objections. Since objections are inevitable he should be ready to deal with them. Analyses of constantly recurring objections indicate that the prospect is usually thinking something like this: "I'll not buy unless you convince me that —

It will pay me to give you an interview.
I need the benefits you offer.
Your proposition is better than competitors.
Your company has prestige and I like you.
Your price and terms are right.
Now is the time for me to buy."

Objections are voiced in an infinite

number of ways, but analyses have indicated that these six categories embody practically all objections. When these objection categories are used as memory hooks and centers of knowledge by the salesman, he may be well on his way toward high skill in dealing with them.

"I Don't Want an Interview"

"Convince me that I will benefit if I give you time for an interview." How may a prospect by convinced that his time will not be wasted? The answer is that everything at this point depends upon the prospect's first impression. If the salesman's appearance is poor, if his approach is awkward, if the idea is conveyed that the prospect's time will be wasted, his excuse "I'm too busy" is actually a legitimate objection. It is always important that the salesman convince the prospect that he has something of real value to offer.

The excuse, "I'm too busy now" when uttered by an insincere buyer should not be confused with the honest, polite objection of a person who is truly busy. One is a disinterested dismissal, the other can be an honest invitation to return. In the latter case, all that is needed is an agreement on when it will be mutually convenient for an interview. To explain more fully methods of dealing with interview objections, the following examples are presented.

OBJECTION: *I'm too busy to talk to you now.*

ANSWER: I certainly do not want to take up your time when you are busy. When is the most convenient time for you? Would next _____ be convenient? (Make appointment.)

OBJECTION: *I'll let you know when I'm ready to buy.*

ANSWER: Eventually, why not now? (Find out the reason in back of this objection.) If I can save you time and money

eventually, why not start now to get these advantages? Let us make an analysis. What are you using now?

OBJECTION: *I want to think this over before I place the order.*

ANSWER: Certainly, you want to be convinced that it is to your interest before you buy. Perhaps I have not made certain points clear to you. If you will let me know what your questions are on these points, I can answer them while I am here today. If you wait to think it over while I am not here, you might forget some points important to your advantage. (If it must be delayed, make an appointment for the answer.)

OBJECTION: *Not interested.*

ANSWER: At first glance, Mr. Jones, I don't blame you for not being interested, knowing the great number of these items that are on the market. Here, I'll demonstrate to you exactly how this compound will save you dollars each month you use it.

OBJECTION: *I'll phone you when I'm ready to buy.*

ANSWER: Thank you very much, Mr. Black, but you are a very busy man, with so many things to think of, besides my product, that I cannot reasonably expect you to keep me in mind. Suppose I call back and see you tomorrow.

OBJECTION: *Send me a sample.*

ANSWER: I have a sample here, and I'll be very glad to show it to you, or give it to you. Please remember, however, that a sample is not always sufficient to give you any idea of its value. I could come in with the worst product in the world and put on a good demonstration, because you might not use it right. In either event, you would have no way of knowing whether or not your employees could use the product, week in-week out.

"I Don't Need Your Product"

"Convince me I need your product or service." In other words, the prospect is saying "What's in it for me?" He wants to know about the benefits he will receive. If, at the start of the interview, when the prospect knows only the salesman's name, he says, "I don't need any today," he is making an excuse. The salesman should recognize this statement as an excuse and go ahead with his presentation.

However, if the salesman has presented his facts and then meets this objection, he knows that something is defective in his technique. The prospect may have a genuine reason for not buying. Either the salesman has failed to qualify the prospect, or he has talked about product features rather than benefits. Therefore, additional evidence may be needed to convince the prospect that he really needs the product.

Convincing proof of need and benefits may be done in many ways. For example:

A survey, personal inspection or inventory made by the salesman of the prospect's plant, business or situation.

Success stories and testimonials of people similar to the prospect who are already enjoying benefits from the product or service.

Frank discussion with the prospect regarding his needs. Usually, a purchase results when a prospects admits he has a need for the product.

"I'm Satisfied With the One I Have"

"Convince me that your product or service will benefit me more than any other." If the prospect says at the outset of the interview, "I'm satisfied with my present bryzlicker," he is often giving an excuse. He may be prejudiced, cantankerous, or just plain too lazy to want to improve his situation.

If the statement is made after hearing the salesman's story, either the proposition offered was no better than the one he had, or the salesman failed to convince him that he had superior benefits, values or advantages. The prospect buys only when "there's something in it for him." He never buys to satisfy the needs of others. He thinks only of himself and his problems.

The salesman can prepare himself in advance to meet this basic objection by listing the needs, hopes and problems that his product or service can satisfy. This list should then be checked against a list of similar needs and benefits for other prospects so that no important factors will be overlooked.

This listing may be made by (1) writing down all the things the product and the related service can do for the customer; (2) naming all the benefits that the customer can reasonably expect to derive from his purchase. Having fortified himself with such facts, the salesman can confidently answer the excuse, "I don't like the quality," with a reply such as, "What exactly don't you like about the quality?" This would place the prospect slightly on the defensive, smoke out the objection, and thereby allow both individuals to examine it and arrive at a satisfactory conclusion.

Claims should never be made to convince a prospect unless backed up with good proof in the form of a demonstration, a test report, photos of the product in action, paper and pencil figures and illustrations, testimonial letters, written guarantees and perhaps other sales aids mentioned in Chapter Ten.

Sample illustrations of the methodology employed to deal with this kind of objection follow:

OBJECTION: *Your product is wasteful and inefficient.*

ANSWER: So are paper towels, paper drinking cups, paper wrappers and other one-time products. The biggest cost of any operation is labor, and the chief reason for using my product is because it saves labor.

OBJECTION: *We have gotten along without it for years; I can't see any reason for changing now.*

ANSWER: That is quite true. Years ago all business got along without telephones, cash registers and other time-savers. You have to modernize, why shouldn't you use the best?

OBJECTION: *That's a good product for a big company, but we don't need it.*

ANSWER: Every business has the same fundamental key operations. The difference is only minor. The great majority of our orders come from relatively small concerns. (Show samples.) Perhaps we can take the good features and incorporate them into a product tailored to your needs.

OBJECTION: *We tried that years ago and it didn't work.*

ANSWER: That is interesting to know. Perhaps there was some good reason why it did not work. Perhaps it was not planned and installed properly? Maybe a different product or a few changes would make it work? (Here is an opportunity to analyze and suggest new ideas.)

OBJECTION: *Your stuff is a racket.*

ANSWER: (The salesman becomes a little angry; he lets the prospect know that he is not a mere peddler.) "Mr. Schackenpoofer, my company is no more a racket than yours. Here, let me show you what others have said about it. You see, they're making money and their worries have stopped. Does that read as if a racket is being operated? Now, as I was saying . . ."

"I Don't Like Your Company"

"Convince me your company is a satisfactory source of supply." This covers expressions of doubt related to company policy, service, the salesman's part in rendering the service and the reciprocity problem.

When the prospect says, at or near the start of the interview, "I'm satisfied with my present source of supply," he may believe that he is really satisfied, or he may not even think. He is usually interested only in being left alone and is offering an excuse. This excuse will become an objection if it is taken seriously.

If, after the prospect has seriously considered the facts presented, he says, "I prefer to continue with my present source," the salesman can again resort to his question technique and say, "Why do you believe that, Mr. Jones? How can your present supplier give more advantages than we are able to give?" The salesman then cites more benefits and repeats others. The salesman enhances his position when he asks honest, frank questions with the obvious intention of helping the prospect reach a wise decision. He can also ask questions to bring out attitudes, facts and viewpoints which reveal what is going on in the prospect's mind. Finally, questions free the salesman from the necessity of shadow boxing, a costly waste of time and effort.

Whatever a salesman says about his company is of vital importance: size of the company; age of the company; company personnel; company sales promotion; company methods and policies of conducting the business. Nevertheless, these are similar to product *features* and they mean nothing to a prospect unless they are expressed in terms of *benefits* such as better deliveries, fair treatment, prompt adjustments, promotional aids, profits and fast turnover. There is probably no stronger force for building prospect confidence than the enthusiasm of a salesman who is thoroughly "sold" on his own company.

"I Usually Buy from Another Company" (Reciprocity)

The reciprocity problem is increasing, and for many salesmen it presents a serious problem. However, the problem can be solved if the following simple, time-tested method is employed. The reciprocity obstacle may start something like this:

"A local firm buys from us and we like to reciprocate." "Sorry, I cannot buy from you because the Blank Company spends approximately $10,000 with us every year and we naturally feel we should buy from them exclusively." Although this is a difficult obstacle to overcome, the salesman may reply somewhat as follows:

ANSWER: I understand how you feel. However, if we can show you a product which the Blank Company does not manufacture and which will do a better job for you, will you buy it? As for local buying, was your automobile, your washing machine, your cash register made in this city? We have an office here, too, and we also spend money. I spend my money here, too...

Analysis: This salesman used an assurance statement to begin. Then he used the smooth-over technique. He also indicated that benefits were possible from the purchase of his product. He suggested that few items were made locally and that the wise buyer obtains his merchandise from the best sources.

The reciprocity "switch method" may also often bring success. For example, a salesman could say:

You are indeed fortunate to have such a good customer. We do not solicit business from a reciprocity standpoint, and I cannot therefore, offer you any of our business. However, is it not true that your business would suffer materially if you lost this one big account? And is it not true that you are banking rather heavily on their business? And is it not true that you have no assurance of its continuance? Under these circumstances, it might be well not to keep all of your eggs in one basket. Why don't you go on record with my company by purchasing at least a portion of your requirements from us, and then when your salesman calls on our purchasing department, he is more likely to receive favorable consideration.

Analysis: This reply may switch the customer's attention from the company's failure to give him an order to his failure to place himself in a position to get it. This twists the situation in favor of the salesman. While the salesman makes it clear that he cannot promise anything, he plants the seed of hope in the customer's mind and indicates that reciprocity is a two-way street.

Other obstacles related to company objections, together with answers, are the following:

OBJECTION: We've always bought from the blank company.

ANSWER: I admire your loyalty. However, we make the broadest line of products in our industry and, therefore, we are without prejudice on these products. Perhaps you should be using something that he does not have. Our business is founded on ideas. If I can suggest an idea that will save you time and money, would you buy from me?

OBJECTION: You require too much time for delivery.

ANSWER: If you mean we do not play favorites with our customers, you are right. Have you ever seen our line of stock products for immediate delivery? The fact that we have a backlog of orders indicates that many people like to do business with us. Our quality, service and price must be right.

OBJECTION: *I don't want to change companies; we're doing all right now.*

ANSWER: You do not necessarily need to change your system. Perhaps I have ideas on design and construction to save you time and money and make your present production even better.

"I Don't Need It Right Now"

"Convince me that now is the time to buy." This is the time when the prospect must make a decision; it means that the presentation has progressed to its climax. Presumably all obstacles have been overcome and the *time to decide* has arrived.

If the prospect states that he is not ready to buy, or that he wants to think it over or talk to an associate, the salesman may make one of two assumptions. Either the prospect wishes the salesman would abandon his talk and thereby give him an excuse for not buying, or he is revealing that he would like to buy if he could.

Making a decision to buy is very difficult for most people. Therefore, the professional salesman rarely pays any attention to delay or put-off decisions. He knows that the prospect has received enough reasons to make an intelligent decision, so he avoids being side-tracked. If he observes cues that the prospect has an urge to buy, he attempts a trial close. If the prospect repeats his objection "I want to talk it over with my boss," the salesman should say, "If the general manager gives his consent, you'll sign the order, is that our understanding?"

If the prospect says "yes," the salesman acts immediately on that agreement and arranges for a meeting. If the prospect hesitates about the meeting, the salesman knows the prospect is not completely convinced. But the salesman does have a clear pattern for checking on the uncompleted part of the sales talk. He knows that, when the prospect is satisfied on all six of the buying conditions previously outlined, he will say yes and mean it.

He may also ask the prospect, "Is there any question in your mind, Mr. Prospect, or any problem that I may clarify?" If the prospect reveals that he is doubtful about his reply to this question, the salesman knows that he must do more selling on that point. The prospect's needs must be analyzed, explained and proved until he fully appreciates his need and agrees to it. This may satisfy the prospect and, if so, the way is open for another attempt to close. If the prospect still hesitates, the salesman moves on to the product. He says something like, "You are fully satisfied, aren't you, that our product will do an effective job for you and give you the results you need?"

If the prospect wants to delay further, the salesman can summarize the advantages in favor of buying now and the disadvantages of further delay. When he can show the results in actual dollars and cents gained or lost, he has a particularly strong leverage for obtaining an immediate order, or at least in arranging a three-way conference for a final decision.

Additional factors and methods for dealing with the not-now objection are suggested in the explanation of the "procrastination trait" in Chapter VIII. However, there are so many variations of this obstacle that descriptions of several of them should clarify the topic and render the salesman better able to cope with it.

OBJECTION: *I can't afford to change all at one time and I have never bought anything on the installment plan.*

ANSWER: Mr. Customer, if you prefer, replace your machines one at a time, but actually buying on installment is about the same as signing a lease for a building. You sign for the full amount of the year's rent, but pay in monthly installments, letting each month's business carry its share of the rent. Further, the savings you make with the new equipment help pay the installments. Some of our largest accounts, who normally discount their bills, take advantage of our easy-payment plan because they like the idea of letting the equipment help pay for itself.

OBJECTION: *I'll have to talk that over with my manager.*

ANSWER: An excellent idea. However, he might have some questions that I have not covered. Might I suggest that we both see him together? Could we see him now? He will probably have some more questions and I'll be there to answer them.

OBJECTION: *I will buy this outfit later on, but not now.*

ANSWER: There is only one reason you will ever buy this outfit and that is: Will it be an expense or a profit? If an expense, you do not want it now, next week or next month, not ever. If you want a profit, you want it now because it starts making money for you the day you put it in. When do you want it installed?

OBJECTION: *Business is not good enough to warrant spending the money.*

ANSWER: Is it bad enough to warrant studying possible economy of operation? When things are slow is the time to make a thorough check-up.

OBJECTION: *We are making some changes right now; see me later.*

ANSWER: Perhaps I can be of assistance in helping you plan the new changes.

I make my living suggesting products to do the job my customers want done. All this experience is at your disposal. Shall we start now?"

OBJECTION: *See me next month.*

ANSWER: Make a definite appointment. Might be a good idea to suggest he check his inventory on any repeat product to save time.

OBJECTION: *We have a large supply on hand. We'll talk it over when we are ready to order.*

ANSWER: So much the better if you have a large supply on hand. That gives us plenty of time to look over your stock for possible improvement in design or construction. We can submit ideas and sketches. It is much better to do it thoroughly than wait until the last minute when there will be no time to consider changes. (Mention time needed for delivery.)

OBJECTION: *We have a contract.*

ANSWER: I can show you that you would save money through the use of my product, even though you may only use small quantities. You could easily do this, and at the same time, continue to use up your other product on this contract. When would you like to start?

OBJECTION: *The boss has a friend in the same business.*

ANSWER: Should it cost your boss money to keep that friendship? If that is the case, I might as well leave and not waste time. However, I'd like to compare my product with the other product and I can positively show you how much more it is actually costing you to buy that other product. If the other product is as good as mine, I would not blame you for buying from a friend. Is that fair?

OBJECTION: *All buying is done at the main office.*

ANSWER: Mr. Jones, your statement is true, for I know your company buys that way. But, I have looked your place over and you know that if you want anything very badly you could buy it. If you buy this product your manager will credit you with sharp buying, because you will save your company a lot of money. Isn't that interesting?

Doubt-Creating Method

The doubt-creating method is useful when dealing with *stallers* or *lookers*. The staller or looker is probably subject to ungrounded fears, prejudices, bad habits and bad attitudes. The following illustrates how they act and what the salesman can do to turn them into good customers.

Suppose, for example, an automobile dealer has shown his prospect a number of cars and one particular style seemed to please him. However, the prospect says, "I believe I'll look around and if I don't find something better, I'll be back."

A professional salesman will recognize the uselessness of trying to get an outright reversal from this prospect, so he will employ a time-tested technique and reply somewhat as follows: "That is a wise decision. When you buy a car, you want one that will give you pleasure when you drive it.

"Now when you look at other cars, note carefully if they have these features . . ." (The salesman then touches each item and points out each feature as he talks.) "Is it economical to operate? Is it a comfortable car? Is it a quality product? Is it the right size for your family, as this one is? How is the construction for long life? Does it have the conveniences this one has? Is it a well-known car? Note whether it has an adjustable seat, convenient arm rests, ample leg room, fine upholstery, sure-catch door handles.

Be sure to ask about the services offered. Finally, ask about guarantees and warrantees."

This salesman did not push the customer into buying, nor did he use "scaremanship." He did, however, fix in the prospect's mind the outstanding features of his car. If this prospect does go into a competitor's showroom to look at other cars — and he probably will not — he will wonder, "Is this as good as the one that nice person at Blank's showed me? Is it economical to operate? Is it easy to drive? Will it suit my family? Is it worth the price?"

The prospect will, in most cases, come back and buy from the first salesman. The *looker* and the *staller* are interested in benefits, and when the salesman has the proper facts and figures he will be able to convince the staller that he will gain if he buys.

Reverse Position Method

Let's suppose that the customer looking at an appliance says, "I know this won't last long." The salesperson says, "You evidently know a great deal about appliances and I am interested in your opinion." This reverse position on the salesman's part is usually very effective. This is because people like to feel that their opinion is important. The more positive and opinionated they are, the more easily they can be won over by a creative salesman.

Questions for Favorable Reactions
Rolling Action Questions

Good questions can be used to stimulate favorable prospect reactions. The best salesman can "roll with the punches" whenever obstacles arise. They never lose control of a situation. For conditions that seem to be impossible they use a three point formula:

They relax completely.

They concede points here and there with soothing remarks such as "Yes, I can appreciate your reasoning, but have you considered . . .?" They follow their soothing remarks with questions like: "On the other hand, isn't it possible that . . .?

"I agree with you completely, but if that were the only objection would you . . .?"

The salesman who takes pains to become expert in asking questions which tactfully, skillfully develop this technique make it difficult for prospects to become annoyed or angry. These salesmen rarely lose sales because of a stubborn stand by the prospective customer.

Questions for the Skeptic

Sometimes a prospect will put off a decision to buy because the salesman has used too much *expertise!*

A flawless presentation may render the prospect skeptical. He may think, "What's the catch?" He may wonder, "Is this too good to be true?" The salesman can convince the prospect by feeding him an objection in the form of a question. He could say something like this: "You seem to be bothered about something, Mr. Jones, could it be this [product benefit]?"

This kind of question often brings a denial, followed by a genuine objection from the prospect. This kind of question brings out the hidden objection that may be holding up the sales decision. When it's out in the open, it can be further examined and answered to the prospect's satisfaction.

"Why" Questions

One of the most wonderful little words to use in dealing with objections is that little word, "why?" Just tack on a question mark and the salesman can bore right in and get prospects to talk, to unburden themselves and to siphon off what doubts they are keeping from the salesman.

PROSPECT: Well, I just don't know. I think the Acme refrigerator would be better for us.

SALESMAN: Why, Mr. Roundtree?

PROSPECT: Well, it just seems to be a better buy.

SALESMAN: I hope you'll pardon me for asking again, but why do you feel it will be a better buy?

PROSPECT: Well, it boils down to roominess. It seems to me that you can store more large bottles in the Acme.

SALESMAN: I see, well, I guess I owe you an apology Mr. Roundtree. I didn't explain that fully enough. I believe that I can show you how our refrigerator can afford you even more space than the Acme for tall bottles.

Asking "why" is usually a good method for handling the opinionated, positive person. For example, a customer is looking at a living-room chair and says, "I know this fabric won't wear well." The salesperson could counter with, "You evidently know a great deal about furniture, Mrs. Gray, and I'm interested in learning your opinion. Would you mind telling me why the fabric won't wear well?"

At this point the customer usually begins to express positive opinions, and before she knows it, she has talked herself out of the objection and the salesperson gets another chance to prove that the item is of very good quality.

This method is effective because it flatters the customer; it makes her feel that her opinion is important.

Side-Track Questions

The principle use of the side-track question is to guide the prospect's mind away from objections and toward an analysis of his statements. The side-track question also may be used to control resistance because of its value as a retort or retaliation.

Side-track questions make good buffers with which to soften up prospects. When the objection, "I'm not interested" comes over to the salesman, he can often guide and control the interview if he replies with, "Wouldn't you be interested if I could show you how to make $1,000 next week?"

The obstacle, "No demand for your goods" would certainly fall flat if the salesman asked, "Is every item on your shelves in demand now?" In this way, sidetrack questions can be devised to guide and counteract any objections the prospect may make, as well as to discover his real needs.

Very often the side-track question will bring a self-conscious grin as the prospect realizes the stupidity of his statement. The salesman should not reveal that he notices this self-detection, since it may embarrass the prospect and make him angry.

Turnaround Questions

Turnaround questions probe for a prospect's needs and make his objections a reason for buying. For example:

OBJECTION: I'm too busy to talk to you, now.

SALESMAN: Are you too busy to learn about something which will take away most of your worries?

OBJECTION: I wouldn't pay that much for a dress shoe.

SALESMAN: But you want to look your best, don't you?

OBJECTION: I can't afford a car that costs that much.

SALESMAN: Honestly now, can you afford to be seen in a lower-priced car?

OBJECTION: I am satisfied with my present source of supply.

SALESMAN: May I explain to you why satisfied customers are joining our ranks every day?

OBJECTION: I'm not interested.

SALESMAN: Are you interested in getting lower operating costs?

OBJECTION: I don't want anything to do with your company.

SALESMAN: That's why I'm here. Are you interested in a new business building merchandise plan?

OBJECTION: I'm satisfied with the product I am already using.

SALESMAN: We, too, have many satisfied customers; would you be interested in learning how my product can earn you a lot of money?

Retort Questions

Many salesmen fear the opinionated ill-mannered person who is sure he knows all about everything and likes to say so in a nasty manner. This person can often be handled through a retort question.

For example, a customer in a men's apparel store was looking at shirts and said to the salesman, "You've got a lot of nerve asking $5.00 apiece for this garbage." The salesman retorted by saying, "I can see that you are an authority on garbage, but you know nothing about shirts. What kind of a shirt do you have in mind?" This retort usually renders the customer speechless, sometimes ashamed of himself, often ready for further selling. The question keeps the sale open. The retort and question is often the only way to gain the respectful attention of an ill-mannered person.

POWER POINTS

Sometimes an interview starts with the salesman telling the prospect all about his proposition. Because the prospect was interested, he listened attentively. He watched the salesman's demonstrations and visual aids, because they were important to him. Then, like a flash, he thought of an objection. If he was like many prospects, he said something like this: "Your product is more expensive than others."

From the moment he voiced that objection, he wanted an answer. If the salesman tried to pass over his objection and go on to another part of the presentation, he would probably leave his prospect behind. The prospect will continue to think of that objection and he will eventually want an answer to it.

Quality is the keynote usually used to combat price objections. The quality answer really means that the salesman must give proof of value; proof that his price is right in terms of the benefits he will receive. Since he must convince the prospect that he will benefit, he must be well prepared to offer proof of value before he can guide his prospect to a positive decision.

The salesman may say to himself, "That old price objection again! How shall I answer him?" First, he must recall that he does not want to argue with the prospect. However, the salesman does want him to feel that he has raised an honest objection that deserves an honest answer.

There are many ways to answer the price objection. What the prospect has said is possibly the result of a misunderstanding. When he says, "Your product costs too much," a good salesman would not say, "Ah, you don't know what you are talking about." Nor would the salesman ask, "Are you crazy?" A salesman may be able to tell a prospect what he thinks of him, but the customer can refuse to buy. The salesman may win the argument, but lose the sale.

The man who spends money wants to feel he is important. When he says, "Your product or service is more expensive than others," he is really asking to be convinced that the salesman's product or service will benefit him more than others. His statement is not meant to be insulting. It actually means he is challenging the salesman to convince him about its worth, value or benefit to him. The prepared salesman can easily meet his challenge!

No matter how the seller thinks his prospect feels, the salesman should always assume that the customer does not understand the point he has tried to make. The salesman may also assume that the prospect does not agree with the way the salesman has tried to make it. Maybe he still is not completely convinced that what the salesman said was right. The salesman must constantly visualize his target. He is not trying to fight the prospect, he is trying to make a sale.

DISCUSSION QUESTIONS AND PROBLEMS

1. Explain why the idea-sequence presentation helps salesmen to overcome obstacles to favorable buying decisions.
2. State and explain the procedures for how to answer objections described in this chapter and explain how you would use them in actual practice.
3. What is the general procedure for answering valid objections, as explained in this chapter?
4. Explain the values of asking questions and listening to the answers as a useful method for handling objections.
5. You have read that the yes-but method for handling objections is one of the strongest in salesmanship. Do you agree? Why?

6. What are some of the variations in the use of the yes-but method?

7. When should the yes-but method not be used?

8. What categories embody practically all objections?

9. Describe and state how you would deal with objections to interviews.

10. Describe and state how you would deal with prospects who say they do not need your product.

11. "You don't pay the freight and your competitor does; he also gives me a discount on quantity orders. I'll stick to him." Make a pro-con chart to show this prospect proof of the benefits your proposition offers, compared to those of a competitor. Your chart form should look like this:

Objection

pro	con
1.	1.
2.	2.
3.	3.

12. Don Mason, one of the better sales trainers, says that there are three chief causes for honest objections. "First, is an inadequate knowledge of what the salesman proposes. Second, prospects object because they misinterpret the salesman's statements. Third, they doubt the salesman's proposals." Do you agree with Don Mason? Why?

13. Following are a number of resistance phrases. According to your readings and experience, which are excuses, stalls, alibis or honest resistance? Give your reasons.

Too busy to talk	Same supplier for years
You sell everybody	No call for your product
Not interested	We're overstocked
I'll think it over	Too many suppliers now
See me later	Not buying today
Let me sleep on it	

14. State which of the following objections may be honest, which may be excuses and which may be stalls? Give reasons for each answer.
Doesn't meet budget requirements.
Competition is too tough to buy now.
Lack of finances.
Consult with associate about price.
Poor service for top prices.

15. When a procrastinating buyer is stumped for an honest answer he often wiggles out of a situation by saying, "Your price is a little out of line, I'll have to think it over." Exactly how would you eliminate this impediment?

16. When answering a prospect's objections, the salesman's attitude, facial expressions and general deportment should indicate immediately that he respects the prospect's viewpoint. At this time, phrases like the following are:
I can understand why you feel that way. On the other hand . . .
Under normal conditions you would be correct in that opinion, but . . .
Your suggestion has much to recommend it. On the other hand . . .
Your plan certainly has its merits, but when you consider . . .

There is a lot of truth in what you have to say, but have you ever considered this angle?

    a. What is your opinion of this method of answering objections?
    b. What makes this method of answering questions easier?
    c. Would you employ this method to answer all kinds of objections?
    d. What is the name of this objection answering method?

17. Quite often it is good practice to overcome an objection by turning it into a question. Study the following objections and then turn each one into a question. After converting each objection into a question, write an effective convincing answer to the question.

RETAILER: Our customers say the price is too high.

WHOLESALER: Your discount is too low.

MANUFACTURER: We can buy better quality for a lower price.

FARMER: I haven't sold my crops yet, so see me next spring.

    a. State the objection.
    b. Convert the objection into a question.
    c. Answer the question.

18. What is a retort question? Evaluate its usefulness in selling.

PHENOMENOLOGICAL PROJECTS

Dick Jansen Tractor Sale (Role)

P. C. Spades is selling a new model tractor to Dick Jansen. Spades has already presented certain benefits in terms of Dick's main interests — performance and economy. He has also shown the benefits of the seat, the brakes and the starting system. In each case he determined the buying interests, presented the benefits and got Dick to agree. ·

Now, we look for Dick's objections and see how Spades tries to overcome them. Our characters are on their way to Dick's back field to try out the tractor. By the time Spades reaches the back field on foot, Dick has just finished plowing around the field once. As he pulls up to a stop, Spades says:

SPADES: How did it do, Dick?

DICK: I'm kind of disappointed. It sort of hung up in that clay bank there.

SPADES: What gear did you have it in?

DICK: Third.

SPADES: Well, put it in second and try again. That's pretty tough stuff you have out there.

DICK: O.K. I'll try it again.
Dick makes another round.

SPADES: How did she go this time?

DICK: Well, she went through fine in second, but it didn't go as fast as I expected.

SPADES: You say it doesn't seem to go as fast as you thought it would. Is that it, Dick?

DICK: Yes.

SPADES: What gear do you use on your old tractor?

DICK: I've been using first.

SPADES: Well, let's look at the facts, Dick. In the first gear on the old model you can get $2\frac{1}{4}$ miles per hour. With the new model you can use a second gear which will give more than $3\frac{1}{2}$. Actually, you can go $1\frac{1}{4}$ miles per hour faster. Do you see the difference?

DICK: Well, that's the way it adds up.

SPADES: Probably the reason you didn't think it was going that fast, Dick, is because this baby handles so easily. Remember, too, you only have to use second through this heavy stuff. For the rest of your plowing you can use $4\frac{3}{4}$-mile per hour third speed. So, having the additional power, you've also got extra speed. This will save you time, won't it, Dick?

DICK: Yeah, I guess you're right. That old model is kind of slow.

Questions:
1. What is Dick's first objection? *got hung up in clay*
2. How does Spades meet that objection? *tells him to try it again*
3. What is Dick's second objection? *Speed of tractor*
4. How does Spades meet this objection? *Compares old with the new model*
5. How else could Spades have answered this objection?
   At this point, Dick shuts off the tractor, climbs down, walks around it, and then says:

DICK: Sure is a lot better than my old model. How much are you asking for it, Paul?

SPADES: Dick, that depends on what attachments and implements you need. You can use the pull-type plow you have now if you like, but you'll need a cultivator. This tractor is going to give you that added power and speed you need on your farm with little, if any, extra fuel cost. The way this tractor is equipped, and the cultivator, will cost you only $1,695.00.

DICK: Paul, that's a lot of dough, and why the cultivator?

SPADES: Sure, that cultivator is all right for your old model. But it won't fit this new model. You see, Dick, this new cultivator is operated by Touch Control. That means you won't have to stop every time you want to lower or raise your cultivator. You can keep right on going, operating your new cultivator merely by moving the Touch Control levers.

Questions:
6. What is Dick's objection now? *Cost & why the cultivator*
7. What method does Spades use to answer this objection?
8. What does Spades talk about to meet this objection?

9. How else could Spades have handled this objection?
   Now let's go back and see what happens after that.

SPADES: I'll admit, Dick, that on the surface it does look like an extra purchase. But you are primarily interested in the added power and speed of this new model. This Touch Control cultivator will make your job just that much faster by eliminating the starting and stopping at the end of each row. Without this cultivator, you're not really getting the full advantages of your new model. And it's so simple to use that even a child can operate it.

DICK: Yeah, it looks like it might be easier.

Questions:

10. What is Dick's objection this time?
11. What does Paul say that makes you think he is meeting this objection?
    Now, let's go back and see what Dick was going to say when we interrupted him.

DICK: Yeah, it looks like it might be easier. But it still seems like a lot of money. I can buy a Charley Horse outfit for $1,500.00.

SPADES: Sure you can, Dick. But, remember that you've had your old model for 15 years now, and it always has given you dependable, low-cost service. And you can expect the same kind of service and dependability from your new tractor. Furthermore, with the new model, you get the added benefit of Touch Control, which you agreed would save you a lot of time. It gives you instant control at the end of the rows, both up and down, and you can use it with other implements, too. The slight difference in price is more than offset by the time you will save with Touch Control. And time is money to you, isn't it, Dick?

DICK: Darn right! But it's still a lot of money.

Questions:

12. What is Dick's objection here? *Too much money*
13. What method does Paul use to meet this objection? *Smooth over*
    Well, let's move on. Remember, Dick was saying:
    DICK: Darn right! But it's still a lot of money.

SPADES: You're right, Dick. It is a lot of money. But you saw the new model pull through that clay in second gear 1¼ miles per hour faster than your old model, and that Touch Control on the cultivator will save you a lot of time. The difference in price between our equipment and the Charley Horse outfit will be returned to you in time saved alone. In addition, we can offer our top-notch parts and service facilities. You remember how important it was to you last year when we were able to replace that broken spring in a few hours. You realize how important efficient services are, don't you, Dick?

DICK: Yeah, I guess they are.

Questions:

14. What is Dick's objection now? *Still cost to much*

15. How does Spades meet this objection?
16. Would you try to close the sale now?

Rambler Manufacturing Company (Role)

This project begins at the place where John (the salesman) is telling Phil (the customer) about the engine in the truck he sells. After listening to a few details, Phil says:

PHIL: Looks all right. But of course I couldn't use it for out-of-town deliveries. It's too small.

JOHN: That's right, Phil! This particular truck may be too small for your out-of-town deliveries but we have several sizes to solve every delivery problem you have.

Questions:
1. How does John answer Phil's objection that the Rambler is too small?
2. How would you handle this differently?

PHIL: You mean you have more than one size body?

JOHN: Oh, yes. We have eight basic sizes — four with a curved back and four with a flat back. We will match the truck to your delivery problem to save you money and make it more convenient and more comfortable for your salesmen. And then there's all that extra space we talked about. Just look at these figures to see how much more payload space you will have in a Rambler.

PHIL: Yeah. But do these cubic foot figures mean actual loading space, John? Look at all that wasted space in front of the side doors.

JOHN: Those cubic feet figures don't cover the total loading space — only the minimum. When we talk about the length of the body and cubic foot dimensions, we measure from the back of the driver's seat to the rear doors. That's the minimum space, but you have additional space up front here. For instance, the space over this insulated engine cover can be used for storing the first deliveries, and this compartment over the windshield holds the salesman's reports and invoices.

PHIL: Then it really will give me twice the payload space of a panel?

JOHN: Very nearly, Phil — and a shorter wheelbase and with a shorter turning radius. This truck has several other features you can use in your business: plenty of vision through this massive windshield, ease in getting in and out, plenty of height, and it is easy to service.

PHIL: That all sounds good, but I don't think I can use that body. It's too flimsy for my work.

JOHN: What do you mean, Phil, too flimsy?

PHIL: Come here, I'll show you. Look at the inside. I have to have something I can fasten racks to, otherwise I'll waste all the space from the floor up just like a panel.

JOHN: Those sides seem thin, Phil, but that's a camouflage. They hide many of the features of this body. This truck is built somewhat like a house. In a house, you have floor joists, ceiling joists and wall uprights. We have the same construction in our Rambler body. This panel is just a finished inside wall. You can remove it with these cadmium plated screws which, by the way, are rust resistant. We use lightweight but strong high tension steel for the floor, side and roof joists. The outside panel is sheet steel. The roof is insulated with glass wool, and the air space between the inner and outer body panels insulates the rest of the body. Won't that insulation help keep your peanuts and potato chips fresher, Phil?

PHIL: Seems like it would.

JOHN: These body features will give you strength and durability and allow you to have almost any shelf arrangement you want, The Rambler is adaptable to your requirements.

Questions:

3. After John mentions the four sizes, he shifts immediately to space advantages of the truck. Do you agree that this was a wise move?
4. What do you think of the way John mentions several other features?
5. Would you answer Phil's "too flimsy" objection differently?
6. How does John tie body features into the prospect's business?
   (Let's return to our salesman. As we interrupted, he was saying:)

JOHN: The Rambler is adaptable to your requirements.

PHIL: John, if this truck is built the way you say it is, I imagine the price is way out of line.

JOHN: Not considering all factors, Phil. The first cost is a little higher than for a panel truck, but the greater payload space will enable your salesmen to cover longer routes, call on more customers, and sell more merchandise. This increased profit-per-truck will make the Rambler far cheaper in the long run.

PHIL: Well, let's go in the office and figure out how much it would cost me.

JOHN: Swell, Phil. And we also want to figure out your routes.

PHIL: Why the routes?

JOHN: So that we can fit a truck to each route. You will want different chassis, body sizes, tires and gear ratios for different routes. This will help keep your maintenance costs down.

PHIL: You mean different trucks on the various routes will lower maintenance costs?

JOHN: It usually does, Phil.

PHIL: Well, you can work with Harry Morley. He can give you all the information you want about routes, payloads and number of stops. Figure out something for our northwest route. I'll be with you in a little while — I have to make a few phone calls.

John and Harry figure out the details. As we look in again, Phil is returning.

JOHN: Here's what Harry and I have worked out, Phil. We figure that you need an LM-150 with a 134-inch wheelbase and a 12-foot flat back body on that route. This body has a spare tire rack in the rear stepwell. Take a look at this shelf-arrangement.

PHIL: Looks all right. How much?

JOHN: Just $2,500.00, including painting and lettering, this shelf arrangement and tires. We can deliver it in two weeks.

PHIL: All right. Where do I sign?

Questions:

7. How did John close the sale?
8. What do you think of John's overall sales talk? What parts of it would you handle differently?

Chapter Twelve

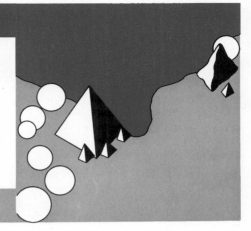

Coping with Price Resistance

PRICE FACTORS

More than one hundred years ago John Ruskin wrote, "It's unwise to pay too much, but it's worse to pay too little. When you pay too much you usually lose only a little money. When you pay too little you sometimes lose everything because the thing you bought fails to serve its function. It is impossible to pay a little and get a lot. The law of business prevents it."

All salesmen believe "you can't get something for nothing," because it is common sense. However, very few salesmen agree with the equally common-sense statement "price-selling is the penalty a buyer demands for a salesman's mistakes and inefficient selling methods." Failure to accept this statement occurs even when salesmen realize it is a factual statement. But they refuse to admit it.

The price problem presents a hurdle which many would-be salesmen are unable to surmount. These types of salespeople are unfortunate; they are mere order-takers. They are the kind who call on customers with the sterile inquiry, "How many feet or pounds can I book you for?" Or, "How many can you use if I give you a good price?" Or, "I can give you a low price if you buy today." These men sell price, not benefits, values, advantages and exclusives.

Professional salesmen agree that price is not the most important deterrent in selling. Those who say it is are rationalizers, excuse makers, and lazy thinkers who use price as a device to move goods, rather than engaging in the strenuous practice of genuine salesmanship. They also use price appeals instead of benefit appeals and imagination. They hint at giving something away, but it does not require salesmanship to give something away at less than its real value. The problem of price revolves around attitudes, planning and selling ability and not around intrinsic values, cost or competitive factors. Obviously, price is important to every buyer, but it is not all important. A great many salesmen overemphasize price. Usually they have accumulated price fear and, therefore, complain about price troubles. A price-conscious salesman should ask himself these questions and give himself honest answers:

Do I have an ingrained price consciousness?
Do I like to haggle over price?
Do I like to horse-trade?
Do I take orders rather than sell?

Do I believe a product is bought, not sold?

Do I use selling handles other than price: benefits, values, advantages, modern selling techniques?

If a salesman has these viewpoints and attitudes toward price, then he himself is the direct cause of his difficulties with the price problem.

Price Is Secondary

Price is not the most important element in selling, but people who use price appeals are always ready to use an analogy or argument to prove this statement is wrong. Their analogy is stated something like this: "O.K., but why do you think women always mob a department store when bargains are offered if price is not important?"

They are talking about price appeal, not selling. Salesmanship is not necessary if merchandise is given away at something less than its real value. Profitable sales cannot be closed by selling on a price basis.

It is a certainty that a professional salesman will have price pride in his product or service. He will skillfully spotlight benefits, values, advantages, services, house policies and the like. He will prepare himself to meet the old price problem. He will take it for granted that prospects and customers are going to bring up price and he will plan all of his interviews to meet and solve this problem.

A salesman should actually believe his prospects when they say, "Your price is too high." They may be correct, because they are comparing the salesman's price with their estimate of the value. If the prospect's estimated value is lower than the price asked, the salesman usually has not made a good presentation.

Price Determination

A hundred, or even fifty years ago, prices were settled by the law of supply and demand. Today, instead of the exclusive use of the law of supply and demand to determine price, the industrial executive approaches his pricing problem in at least two different ways. First, to determine price, he adds up the costs of materials, labor, machinery and distribution, plus a "proper" loading for profit. If goods do not sell at the set price, then management intensifies promotional activity or curtails production. Business that does not pay its own way is refused. However, this kind of refusal is primarily intended to protect capital, not to price and sell.

Second, there is another type of price making, a more dynamic one. Instead of adding costs together to arrive at a price, executives start with the needs of the buyer and his ability to buy, and then set about finding a way to satisfy those needs at a price the buyer can afford to pay. In other words, the modern way to figure price is to start with the marketing-management concept, rather than with a supply, demand or cost accounting concept.

One part of the marketing-management philosophy which carries major significance for salesmen, as well as for management, is the *growth of profit-conscious volume*. This concept is giving way to an increasing awareness of the importance of *profitable* volume. More and more, management is teaching the salesmen that volume is meaningless unless it is accompanied by a corresponding increase in profit.

Of course the actual price policy followed by a particular firm may be a combination of many pricing considerations. Some items in the line, for example, may be priced on the basis of underselling competition, while others may be promoted by heavy advertising and priced high in proportion to their production costs. An item can be given a relatively low price and be heavily advertised in order to move a larger volume at a comparatively low-unit profit margin. Notice that marketing-management philosophy does not state that it is necessary to reduce the earnings of a company to get an order.

Non-Price Competition

Business firms often attempt to stress some factor other than price in their marketing program. In price competition the seller attempts to influence demand by changing the price, in non-price competition a seller attempts to influence the demand by product differentiation, promotional activities and other devices. For example, if the seller decides to differentiate his product, he may improve its quality, change its design or alter the ingredients in the product. In promotional activities, the seller may embark upon an aggressive personal selling campaign or an intensive advertising program designed to acquaint prospective buyers with the merits of the product. Other devices could include the use of trading stamps or the introduction of a lucky number contest. Both are designed to stir up action on the sale of the product without changing the price.

Among the major factors contributing to greater use of non-price competition are:

1. General tendencies toward price uniformity within industries.
2. Proven ways of holding satisfied customers.
3. Successful non-price firms imitated by less successful firms.
4. Adoption of the marketing concept and better trained salesmen.

Among the minor factors affecting non-price competition are these:

1. More advertising to promote sales and price acceptance.
2. Increased knowledge of customer motivation.
3. Growing doubt in many industries that price cutting will increase sales.

4. Growth of service and related sales promotion devices.
5. The benefits of quality and service as compared to price alone.

Benefits of Non-Price Competition

1. Eliminates meeting head-on competitive prices.
2. Promotes better understanding and goodwill with prospects, customers and even competition.
3. Leads to greater stability in production.
4. Earns a better net profit for each competitor.
5. Gives less grief and headaches to everyone.

There is an increasing use of non-price competition in marketing. Companies want to be masters of their own destiny. When a seller employs the strategy of non-price competition, he does not lose his advantageous position when a competitor undercuts him in price. This happens because customer loyalty has been built up for the product. That is, customers believe that the product possesses other virtues that more than offset a higher price. They will not want to change their affections to another product.

Regardless of the specific factors which influence the establishment of a price, and regardless of the care and study which goes into its determination, price is always on trial in the marketplace. No matter how logical the price may seem, if it attracts an insufficient number of customers, or if it loses money for the company, it is the wrong price. Unrestrained "price selling" is always considered to be the wrong price policy.

Competition and Price

During periods of merchandise shortages, price obstacles rarely occur. During such abnormal periods the buyer's chief interest is in obtaining merchandise. Its cost is a secondary consideration, thus price becomes much less important.

In a competitive market, however, competition grows more keen, and price becomes more of a factor which salesmen must consider. Salesmen hear such statements as:

"I want a better discount."
"Your price is too high."
"You're out of line on price."
"It costs too much."
"My customers won't pay that much."

The preceding obstacles are certain to occur and the alert salesman anticipates these by preparing to meet and beat them.

The salesman has little or no control over the prices of the things he sells. Nevertheless, he should know how and why the prices are set at certain figures and why these prices are justified. When he has this information, there is probably no need for hesitation or errors. There is always a reason for a price. A prepared salesman can use the reason effectively to turn price obstacles into a reason for buying.

Listing and Analyzing Price Impediments

The prospect may phrase his objection in many different ways. The salesman will need to know how to recognize each one. By making a list of all the price obstacles he encounters, and then proceeding to analyze them, the salesman will find that they are basically the same and each one can be successfully handled with its own appropriate method. If he is well aware of the benefits, values, advantages, how to deal with price, competitive prices and products his convincing presentation will overcome a price obstacle.

Planning Interviews

A good way to banish the price problem is for the salesman to take it for granted that customers and prospects will say, "Your price is too high." Then he should plan all his interviews to meet this objec-

tion. When a buyer says the price is too high, he may be right. He is mentally comparing the price with the value the salesman caused him to place on the product. If the value is lower in the prospect's mind than the price, it is usually the salesman's fault. He has not made a good presentation. The benefits and values, therefore, should be built up so that the price seems lower by comparison.

"An ounce of prevention is worth a ton of cure." If a salesman wants to succeed and close successful sales, he will spend a great many hours planning answers about price. That is the best way to prevent trouble. To overcome obstacles, a successful salesman will look at his product or service through the eyes of every prospect he expects to contact. He will know the benefits of that product or service from the prospect's viewpoint and his business needs. He will know the benefit claims and prices of every one of his major competitors. He will put his price appeals at the bottom of his bag of appeals.

Price Pride

The opposite of price fear, price pride is one of the essentials the salesperson wants to master. He should be so sold on his product, service and company that he will be unimpressed by anyone who tells him his prices are out of line.

It cannot be overemphasized that a salesman must work on the answers to price and quality questions before his interviews. Another good method is to write out the answers and then check them with a friend, a relative or another salesman, in order to discover how convincing they are. He should also check with himself to see if they would satisfy him if he were a prospect.

Price Proof

The successful salesman must offer acceptable proof of every claim and statement he makes. When a selling transaction is complete, including proof, a favorable decision from the prospect is not far off. In fact, if the sale is handled properly up to and including the proof step, a successful sale is practically guaranteed.

Timing

There is a definite time to introduce the subject of price. The time is near the end of the sales talk, after the prospect has been sold on benefits, values, advantages and exclusives. When price arises too early in the presentation, too much emphasis is placed on it. The entire purpose of a sales presentation is to build desire in the mind of the prospect to the point where he wants the product being sold regardless of the price. Then, price resistance will be less likely to occur.

When price becomes an obstacle, it is usually because the prospect has not been fully convinced that he needs what a salesman has to offer, and as a result, he feels he cannot afford it. Or price may become an obstacle when the prospect feels he can go to another source and buy what he believes to be an equally good product or service at a lower cost.

Price should never be treated as an objection until the salesman discovers that it is a genuine objection. How does he find that out? Usually, the prospect says something like, "I can't afford it." The salesman must decide how qualified his prospect is as to his need and his ability to pay for the product or service. If he qualifies, cost cannot be a genuine objection and the salesman should continue to prove to the prospect that he cannot do without his product or service.

The technique of answering the "I can't afford it" obstacle is one on which salesmen should do considerable practice. Such practice would involve practicing how to present thoughts so that the prospect will be convinced of the salesman's sincerity and interest in their problems. Quality, durability, service and satisfac-

tion when properly presented will usually defeat price arguments.

When the price obstruction arises it will generally be on these occasions:

At the very beginning of a salesman's contact with the prospect — usually as one of the prospect's opening remarks.

During the presentation when the prospect begins to have the feeling that the proposition has more values than he can afford.

At the end of the presentation — at which time the prospect feels he cannot afford the price at this time or he can buy a comparable product for less money.

When price arises during a demonstration, there are usually three reasons why: (1) the salesman does not know the prospect's needs and desires; and (2) the salesman has not pointed out the benefits and use values of his product; (3) the prospect may be ready to buy and it is now time for the salesman to ask for the order.

Sometimes a salesman may become so wrapped up in his demonstration that he may cause the customer to become bored enough to ask the price in order that the seller will transfer his talk to another topic.

In any event, when the prospect asks the price, the salesman should use the question as a signal. He should answer the prospect and attempt to close the sale by asking for the order.

When price is mentioned at the beginning of an interview, the salesman can sometimes postpone his answer. For example, if the prospect immediately asks the price, the salesman might postpone the issue by asking quickly questions such as,

"Do you think this will be big enough?"
"Do you have any particular one in mind?"

Such questions will not only deflect the

prospect's price obstacle, it will also give the salesman a better idea of what to say and do. The salesman should then be in a better position to appeal to the prospect's curiosity and interest.

If the prospect ever becomes suspicious that the salesman is trying to dodge naming the price, he will become even more price conscious and will likely hear nothing more until he is told the price. Postponing and side-tracking the price issue requires real tact and diplomacy on the salesman's part. Therefore, this device must be handled expertly.

REMOVING THE PRICE OBSTACLE
Selling Benefits Method

When a salesman sells benefits, the whole question of price becomes secondary and often unimportant. "But," as some salesmen say, "we can't sell our products if they are priced out of line or if the prospect can't pay what we ask." Consider the example of a woman shopping for shoes. She is easy to sell to because she was prepared to buy when she entered the store. The real question is, "What quality of shoes to sell her?" What quality of product or service to sell any prospect or customer? What is the relation of price to quality?

A professional salesman knows that if his prospects were willing to buy only on a price basis, they could buy direct from the manufacturer, or from a mail order house. They do not always buy direct because they want salesmen to help them decide the problems of what, how, when, where and why a product or a service can benefit them. Advertising cannot supply this information and, obviously, merely quoting a low price does not help.

Salesmen should realize that the responsibilities and opportunities of their jobs are *to sell people what they should have*. This result can be accomplished by

selling benefits, not by making price concessions.

Some salesmen like to haggle and bargain on price; they like to thimble-rig a competitor. They like to talk about price because it requires little thinking. The important point is that any competitor can act just as stupid and sell for an even lower price and soon both will be selling for less and less until both lose money or merely break even. Real selling is not a contest between the salesman and his prospect, or the salesman and his competition. The salesman should assume that the prospect is not an enemy, but a friend for whom the salesman wants to perform a mutually profitable service. In the selling process, the competitor may often be disregarded altogether.

Selling is a deal in which two minds meet on a common ground. Salesmen do not make sales because their prices are lower or because they are smarter than a prospect. They do not obtain orders by outwitting or overpowering a prospect. Instead, they tell, show and prove to a prospect that what they are selling will fulfill his needs and benefit him.

Strike First Method

There are some buyers who think only of price. Since a number of prospects feel this way, it will often pay the salesman to work out a short sales presentation like the following:

> Bring up — price
> Figure up — price
> Play up — price

These nine words can make sales work more enjoyable, raise the size of the order, and get orders which the salesman would otherwise miss. The "strike first" method is employed somewhat as follows:

Bring Up Price

"I suppose your product is all right, but it is entirely too high," is a remark which is very familiar to everyone who sells.

Usually it comes toward the end of the conversation and it prompts the salesman to begin justifying his price. Too often he settles for a trial order or goes away defeated. Fortunately, a salesman can anticipate the price obstacle and bring up the price himself very early in the presentation. For example, "Chances are, Mr. Smith, you buy the product that will do the job and cost you the least money, isn't that right?"

It should be noted that the suggestion question was asked as soon as possible after the hello's were over! The important thing to remember is that if the salesman brings up price before the prospect does, he steals the prospect's thunder and saves his time as well as the prospect's.

When the salesman who uses this approach can quickly bring up price, he is off to a good start toward a favorable decision from his prospect.

Figure Up Price

When the salesman brings up price, he needs a fast and accurate method of figuring. The method must be fast, because several minutes of fumbling with figures will mean a conspicuous delay at a crucial time. The method must be accurate, because it is embarrassing and unfair to present a larger amount than the estimate without a good reason for it.

On the other hand, any price figures must be considered estimates rather than guarantees. Too many other things can affect the out-of-pocket price. Differences in freight, market changes and different prices, cause the estimated prices to be revised.

The important factor is that when the salesman brings up the price and presents it with accurate proof, he can influence the prospect to see the price in relation to benefits.

Play Up Price

When the salesman uses this approach he leads with the total price as a sales point and reuses it later also. For example, when the prospect states, "Bill Moore says he likes your product, but he tells me it costs $310. Seems like a lot to me," the reply can be: "But as I said, Mr. Brown, you can save money on it and enjoy care-free performance for many years." The salesman can use this answer, since it was he who brought it up and figured the price. Otherwise, he would be on the defensive.

The salesmen who use the strike-first method claim that they influence many more favorable buying decisions when they bring up price, figure up price and play up price. According to those who have used this method, these advantages are realized:

> No bickering or arguing.
> No defeat over price.
> Less trial orders.
> More firm sales.
> More satisfied customers.

Kidney Card Method

Another way to take the prospect's mind off price is to use the "kidney card" method. It consists of two pieces of heavy paper specially cut in the shape of a kidney. One is labelled PRICE and the other VALUE. When one is placed on top of the other, they are exactly the same size. When they are placed side by side, however, the card at the right will appear larger.

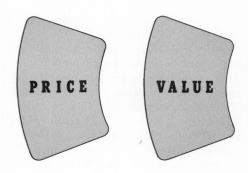

The kidney cards are especially valuable to the salesman when the prospect asks the price before the salesman has a chance to present or demonstrate his proposition. Under ordinary conditions, when price is asked first, the salesman will feel that it is necessary to quote the price and qualify it as best he can, even when he knows that he is at a disadvantage when he is forced to discuss price before mentioning benefits. The prospect will naturally feel that the price is too high if he has not heard the benefits of the product first. He will often decide not to buy in the beginning.

When the kidney cards are in the salesman's pocket, however, he has a device which can remove the prospect's mind from price and put it on value; the very thing he wants to prove in his demonstration. When using the cards, the salesman may say something similar to this:

"I am not surprised that the price may seem high to you, for you don't make a purchase like this every day. Naturally, you may not realize all the benefits and advantages this product will give you through the years.

"After all, even though everyone agrees that price is important, what you are most interested in is getting the biggest value for every dollar you invest, isn't that right?

"Now, when you ask me the price of a product without knowing the value it contains — the price and the value look to you like this (put Price card at the right of Value) — the price looks bigger than the value!

"However, after you have seen all the benefits and conveniences that it will provide and all the quality that is built into this product to assure your satisfaction throughout the years, then I am sure they will appear like this. (Put Value card to the right of Price.) The price will seem small compared to the value you receive!

"And so, for a minute, let us just forget the price while I show you . . ." (and lead into your demonstration and presentation).

The kidney cards may also be used to good advantage after a demonstration and presentation and an attempt has been made to obtain the order, but the prospect hesitates because of the high price. In this situation, the salesman uses the kidney cards to assist him. He says something like this:

"Naturally you want to be sure that the product you buy gives you good value for the dollars you spend. But I have two little cards here that I think will emphasize a point you want to consider.

"This card represents Value and this one represents Price. And if this product (or service) just gave you 100 cents of value for every dollar you invest, you would consider it a good buy. (Put Value card on top of Price to show they are the same size.)

"But in addition to the values I have already shown you, this product has many hidden values, values that result from the research, the manufacturing facilities, the service and all the great resources of my company. To maintain and enhance our enviable reputation, we build into our products so many extra values that mean dependability and low cost through the years that when you realize all the extra benefits this product will bring you, the Price and Value actually look like this (move Value card to the right), the Price is small in comparison to Value. And to prove that point, I would like to show you . . ." (proceed to demonstrate and present quality features).

Pays-for-Itself Method

One good method for convincing a price-minded prospect is to use the savings method. Salesmen usually have ample proof about their propositions. Salesmen should also be alert to pick up new, applicable success stories and examples from their own customers, when they want to prove that the product really does pay for itself. For example, let's listen to a salesman who is selling heavy woodworking machinery.

PROSPECT: I'd like to do business with you, Mr. Salesman, but $12,000 just seems too big an outlay of funds for us to consider at this time. I feel that the firm should continue buying our chair and desk legs out.

SALESMAN: I can understand your reluctance to take on an additional debt at this time, Mr. Jackson. This was the same way Mr. Patton felt. You know Mr. Patton, General Manager for the Uptown Desk Co.?

PROSPECT: Oh yes, I've heard of him. They have a very successful operation. Did Mr. Patton actually feel that way?

SALESMAN: He certainly did, and he was faced with the same kind of a problem that you are faced with today.

PROSPECT: What's that?

SALESMAN: Namely what to do about more intense competition and price sharpening at a time when production costs and especially factory wage levels are increasing.

PROSPECT: How did you handle it?

SALESMAN: Well, we worked out a cost analysis of Uptown's old method and then compared a projected five-year cost breakdown using two new AD101 machines. Do you know what we came up with?

PROSPECT: No, what?

SALESMAN: A savings of 16 percent a month in the cost of milling and finishing legs and rails alone, even after you take into consideration the amortized cost of the new equipment. This put Uptown back on a competitive basis

again. That savings meant that the equipment paid for itself in six years.

PROSPECT: Do you think you could achieve the same results for us?

SALESMAN: Sure, why not? Let's make a deal. Let's figure it out the same way I did for Uptown. If my figuring shows you save money even after you deduct the cost of the new equipment, I get the order; if I can't prove that I save you money, I don't.

PROSPECT: Let's get to work.

Breaking Up Price Method

Another good method for dealing with the "price prospect" is to give him the cost of the item per day over its normal period of life. Over a ten-year period, under this method, the price of a $500 item, for example, would be a mere 14 cents a day — less than half the price of a pack of cigarettes — certainly a very small and reasonable amount from the buyer's viewpoint. In this way the cost is made to appear inconsequential.

BUYER'S TECHNIQUE

Studying skills about the handling of the price obstacle is not enough. It is as important to understand some of the processes which may go on in the buyer's mind. It is also important to know that purchasing agents study the psychology of buying at least as much as salesmen study the psychology of selling.

The Squeeze Play

Shrewd purchasing agents prefer to use the squeeze play to obtain a lower price. One tactic, for example, is to tell the salesman that everything is fine, that his product is just what they want. They might tell him that placing the order is only a matter of routine, that in a week or two they will go ahead.

New salesmen might feel that they

were being stalled if this happened to
them. They might become a little anxious,
and this anxiety might put them in exactly
the frame of mind the buyer wants.

A week later the salesman may be asked
to call. Then he finds two or more men
in the office of the buyer and they insist
on going over the specifications again.
Then at the last moment, one of them
suddenly says that they would like very
much to do business but the price makes
it impossible. "Could you revise it down-
ward to suit?"

Now the salesman is on the spot. His
desire for the order has been deliberately
stimulated. He was certain that the order
was in the bag. From here on it is a case
of wits between the salesman and the entire buying committee.

When a salesman recognizes this strategy and refuses to budge, he will more
often than not have a good chance of getting the order.

If he weakly or foolishly cuts the price
or refers it to his company, he admits that
his quotation was elastic and can be reduced still lower. Professional salesmen
never permit themselves to succumb to
this buying device.

The Big Welcome Technique

Another clever buying method is to make
the salesman very welcome and give him
the flattering idea of how the buyer likes
him. The salesman might be told how
much the buyer wants to do business with
him, if it were not for one teeny-weeny
little obstacle. He is almost ashamed to
mention it, but it is too bad that the salesman's price is five cents more than his
competitor's.

If the salesman succumbs to this proposal, he may get one order, or perhaps
two, but in the long run he will lose out,
as will his company. No buyer respects a
salesman or a company which has flexible
prices and allows the price to be beaten
down.

The Quantity Order Technique

A third common buying technique is for
the buyer to start an argument about proportionate prices on different quantities
of the same product. "Yes," says the
buyer, "your price is fine, but not on the
quantity I want to order."

Then, to back up his demand for a
lower price, he may fire a few technical
facts and figures about the product and
speak with such assurance about the ratio
of price to quantity, that he may be believed. This is likely to happen if the
salesman is weak on product knowledge
and buyer stratagems.

The salesman may begin to feel that
he had better recheck his estimates, that
his company has made a mistake. But the
very minute he begins to recheck, he reveals his lack of confidence in his company. He shows that his prices may be
flexible and elastic and that he is easily
suggestible to price concessions. From
that point on, he will be fair game for
every sharp-shooting buyer who discovers
his weakness.

The Appropriation Dodge

A fourth buying technique might be called
the "appropriation dodge." The buyer
tells the salesman, "The product or service is fine and the price is reasonable, but
if we accept it, we will be forced to exceed
our appropriation for the item in question. We would like to buy it, but if we
did we would throw our appropriation out
of balance. How about trimming the
price?"

If the salesman does not have the courage and confidence to be loyal to his house
and his price, he may land the odd order.
But in the long run, he will command
greater buyer respect and make more
sales if he does not yield to pressure statements from buyers.

The Chiseler

The four buying methods which have just

been explained are used by chiselers. What is a chiseler? Is he the buyer who considers it legitimate to try to obtain the best price on his purchases? If this buyer makes purchases in great quantities, is he entitled to a lower price or a bigger discount?

When the salesman analyzes the prospect's behavior traits and tries to place himself in the prospect's shoes, he will be able to tell whether the buyer is working for his own benefit or his company's best interests. He will also be able to detect the individual who attempts to trick salesmen. The four types of buyers previously described in this section are chiselers.

A professional salesman realizes he will be rewarded according to the profitable orders he obtains. He knows that his company must earn a fair profit so that he in turn can earn more. He knows that when orders are not profitable, the business is not profitable. Orders cannot be sold on price alone and earn a fair profit for his management and commissions for himself.

There are salesmen who like to hold a price concession, a special price, a special discount or margin "up their sleeves" as a final "closer." These salesmen are very popular with chiselers. The chiseler knows that once a salesman gives him a special price or a larger discount, he is *committed* to repeat his actions in all future dealings with the buyer. The price-cutting salesman simply lets the chiseler know that his prices are flexible and from that point on he encounters trouble for future sales. It is usually very difficult to revert to the proper price later.

The chiseler usually says something like this, "I can buy it for less." If the salesman knows that he is dealing with a chiseler he can reply, "Very true. You can buy it for less and, if you wish, I can tell you where you can get it for half-price, but I don't think you'll get the same product, the same quality or the same service."

It is much better for a salesman to be inflexible about his price. The salesman should be aware that price selling encourages chiselers, and therefore he should adhere to his price.

POWER POINTS

Most customers buy only when they think they are getting the most value for their money. No matter what you are selling, you can never take it for granted that the customer will recognize the full value of your product. Be sure to describe what the product will do for him. Let him translate the facts in your sales talk into terms of his own intended use of the product. In this way, just by emphasizing significant sales factors, the salesman actually creates value for his product in the eyes of his customer. When the value is lower than the price, the customer ignores the merchandise. When the value is equal to the price, the customer recognizes that he is getting a fair deal. However, when the salesman has pointed out sales facts that build up the value of the product until it is higher than the actual price in the customer's opinion, then the customer feels he is getting a bargain.

Generalities don't sell quality, only specific sales facts can do that. If you put yourself in the customer's place and take his viewpoint, you know he wants to save money. He thinks he is saving money by buying a less expensive product than yours. You can show him that he isn't. It is the essence of true salesmanship to be able to persuade the customer that he should buy a better product — even at a higher price — if it will serve him better and longer and give him full value for his money.

Keep the quality points about your products or services readily available for instant use. To make selling easier and more pleasant, know why your product or service is of better quality. You then have a basis for more sales to dealers and consumers.

Much of the true value of products and services is hidden. To induce the customer to buy quality products, the salesperson must point out these hidden values and show the prospect what these values mean to him.

Many persons buy low-priced merchandise because they have no comprehension of a product's true value to them. Others do not have the money to buy anything else. However, there are always customers who will react to the quality appeal if it is properly presented in terms of serviceability and durability.

Customers are justifiably confused when two items of merchandise look alike yet have a wide variation in price. An alert salesperson can find the hidden values which account for these differences in price. Sales value is value only if the customer is able to see it.

After he has delivered his sales talk thoroughly, listened, questioned, motivated and coped with all impediments, the successful salesman is ready to start his decision-making activities. If he has performed well up to this point, he will have none of the nervous reaction so often experienced by novices. He is ready to try for a favorable decision from his prospective buyer.

There is no magic formula for closing sales. Obtaining a favorable buying decision from a prospect is the natural reaction to the proper approach and presentation. The time to ask for a buying decision is often so obvious that it is sometimes overlooked. The methods of asking for the order are equally obvious and simple. Learn and practice them.

It should be advantageous to recall that beautiful girls do not marry men who never reach the stage of proposing marriage. They usually marry the men with enough skill and courage to ask for a favorable decision. Likewise, asking for the order is probably the most important part of the decision-making activity.

DISCUSSION QUESTIONS AND PROBLEMS

1. Explain the statement, "Price selling is the penalty buyers demand for a salesman's mistakes and inefficiency."
2. How would you distinguish between genuine *selling* and *price appeals?*
3. Discuss one method of price determination.
4. What is the basis for price consciousness?
5. What is the best way to detect and prevent price troubles?
6. When may the price obstacle arise?
7. Explain the various methods employed to establish market price. Which is preferable? Why?
8. What are the major factors affecting non-price competition? What are the advantages of non-price competition?
9. What are the advantages to the salesman from listing and analyzing price obstacles that occur in his daily selling activities?
10. In relation to the price problem, what is the importance of *timing* in presenting a proposition to a buyer? Explain each point in your answer.
11. Explain and demonstrate the *strike first* method for handling price.
12. Select a representative specialty item such as a deep freeze, a vacuum sweeper, an automobile or a similar product. Common objections to these products are listed below. For each of these objections write the best answers you can devise.

    a. I won't pay the high dollar for anything.
    b. When your article is priced right I may buy, but not until then.
    c. I can't afford to buy now.
    d. If you could just shave the price to meet my budget, I may be interested.
13. "Your competition beats you on both quality and price" is a comment frequently heard by salesmen. How would you reply to this *obstacle?* How would you handle this comment if it were an *excuse?*
14. What is price pride and why should salespeople have it?
15. How would you anticipate price resistance all the way through your presentation, so that you might minimize its importance in the event it is raised at the conclusion of your presentation?
16. Explain and demonstrate the strike first method for dealing with price problems.
17. Describe and explain the following strategies employed by many professional buyers:

> Squeeze play
> Big welcome technique
> Quantity order method
> Appropriation dodge

18. Explain in detail how you would handle the chiseler and the looker. How are they related to those who use the strategies mentioned in question 17?
19. "We have no quarrel with those who sell for less. They should know what their product is worth." Explain this statement.

PHENOMENOLOGICAL PROJECTS

Kidney Cards (Case)

Make a set of the kidney cards illustrated in the text. Explain in detail how you would use these cards in an actual sale and prepare to demonstrate how you would use these cards in a selling situation.

Strike First Method (Role)

Refer to this topic and role play "Bring up Price, Figure up Price and Play up Price."

Laughinghouse (Role)

Prior to this time Paul Spades has presented certain benefits, values, advantages and exclusives to his prospect, Dick Laughinghouse. All seemed to be going well when Dick objects to the *price.*

    DICK: This thing costs a lot of money. I can buy a Charley Horse outfit for $1,500.00.

    SPADES: Sure you can, Dick. It is a lot of money. But the difference in price between our equipment and the Charley Horse outfit will be returned to you in time saved alone. In addition, we can offer our parts and service facilities. You realize how important efficient service facilities are in case of a breakdown, don't you, Dick?

    DICK: Yeah, I guess so.

Questions:

1. Would you start closing the sale at this point?

2. Do you think Paul is trying to close the sale now?
3. What method is he using?
   Let's continue. Dick's last line was:

DICK: Yeah, I guess so.

SPADES: They certainly are. Don't you think the added power, the added speed and the advantages of Touch Control are the answers to your problem?

DICK: Yeah, I guess you're right. I hate to part with my old tractor, though. It's been a loyal baby.

SPADES: Well, you'll forget the old one as soon as you get this new model. There's no reason why you shouldn't start using it today, is there?

Question:

4. What closing method does Paul use here?
   As we interrupted, Spades was saying:

SPADES: There's no reason why you shouldn't start using it today, is there?

DICK: I can think of 1,695 reasons — dollars, that is.

SPADES: Don't let that worry you. I'll write the order now and take the old tractor and cultivator in on down payment. We'll arrange your payments to match your income. Does that sound fair enough, Dick?

DICK: That's O.K., but what will you give me for the old tractor?

SPADES: Remember, Dick, we've already agreed that $400 was a fair allowance for the cultivator and tractor.

DICK: Yeah, I guess we did.

SPADES: Now, let's see, that's one new tractor at $1,486 and one cultivator at $209 minus $400 for your old tractor and cultivator, leaving a balance of $1,295. Let's sit down here, Dick, to figure out the balance of the down payment and work out the payments to match your income.

Questions:

5. Does Dick have any further objection?
6. What closing method does Spades use here?
7. What suggestions do you have for improving Spades handling of the price impediment?

Jim Jasper Sale (Role)

Sam Smiles had overcome Jim Jasper's objections about the durability and economy of the truck he sold. Just when Sam was ready to attempt a trial close, Jim delayed the sale by bringing up the *price* obstacle. This is the conversation between Jim and Sam.

JIM: Yeah, Sam, it looks like a good buy. But what will one of these rigs cost me?

SAM: Well, Jim, that will depend on the equipment you want on it. Let's figure one out and list the equipment on this blank.

Jim and Sam go over the list of equipment and attachments needed to do his job. After more emphasis on the benefits and advantages of his truck, Sam says:

SAM: Jim, you can have all of the advantages we discussed in a new truck for only $10,500.

JIM: Wow! That's a lot of money. Let's see . . . that's about $200 more than your competitor's Bulldozer rig . . . and more than I ought to pay. Why does your rig cost so much more?

SAM: Mostly because you're getting so much more tractor, Jim. It costs a little bit more to build in the exclusives like the track suspension system. Just look — one busted main shaft alone would cost you the difference. Beside that you have the advantages of a positive oiling system and the convenient starting device. Then, too, the track shoe construction and the draw bar set up will give you the maximum performance in your new model. Don't you think these combined advantages and savings outweigh the slightly higher price?

JIM: Yeah, I guess it would be cheaper in the long run.

Questions:
1. What is Jim's objection?
2. How does Sam meet this objection?
3. What offsetting benefits did Sam mention?
4. What other ways could Sam have used to overcome this obstacle?
5. What is your reaction to this method of handling price?
6. Would you try to close the sale *now?*
7. Why did Sam ask Jim a question at the end of his explanation?

Chapter Thirteen

Successful Closing Techniques

MAKING HOME RUNS

A successful sale is the ultimate goal of the salesman's presentation. It is the difference between crossing home plate and being stranded on third base. In selling, the principal aim is to make home runs. These home runs usually start with buying signals from the prospective purchaser.

The champion salesman knows that he is attempting to close the sale from the moment he starts it. He is watching for buying signals throughout the sales process.

Buying Signals Are the Tip-Off

It is easy to recognize buying signals because people cannot help but react to things they like or dislike. Some buyers develop a professional caginess where salesmen are concerned; expressionless, pokerfaced purchasing agents are fairly common. However, most prospects cannot maintain completely blank expressions throughout a presentation.

Very few people make any effort to restrain their feelings. Most people openly reveal their feelings of interest, desire and conviction by their actions, words, and facial expressions. There are dozens of buying signals which reveal the prospect's state of mind and his emotional bias. The most important of these tip-offs are:

Agreement

Does the prospect heartily agree with what the salesman says and does? In his answers to the questions from the salesman, does he agree that the proposition is appealing and that it offers him definite benefits, values, advantages? Does he ask for details?

Attention

Does he pay attention while the salesman presents and demonstrates? Does he convey the feeling that he is on the salesman's side? Is he complimentary, well mannered, patient, kindly? Does a sudden change of facial expression take place? Does his face suddenly show serious consideration after reflecting only pleasant passivity throughout the presentation?

Operation

When a prospect asks questions about the operation of a product, he probably wants to be told that he is not too ignorant or unmechanical to handle it. When these questions are asked, the prospect should be given full assurances and instructions. Then the salesman should attempt to obtain a decision. If the prospect picks up the item again and re-demonstrates it to himself, the salesman is justified in assuming that the customer is in the process of making a decision. Clothing salespeople agree that a customer who tries on a coat or a dress for the second time is signaling his (or her) interest in buying.

Storing

When the prospect asks questions about how an item should be stored, he has mentally searched for a place to install it. The salesman can safely assume that the prospect wants more information. He can feel sure that the prospect is ready to buy.

Service

The service inquiry is closely related to guarantee and warranty questions. It is a closing signal because it indicates possession in the buyer's mind. It indicates that proof of trouble-free operation will overcome the prospect's last resistance to buying.

Terms

Questions and remarks about terms reveal that a prospect is relating the benefits, the price and his budget. It usually indicates that the prospect is sold on the benefits, values and advantages of a product or service. After answering the queries, the salesman should ask for the order.

Particular Item

When a prospect more than once handles, points to, comments upon or indicates in some way his particular choice, he is hoisting a decision signal.

Guarantee

Questions about guarantees or warrantees indicate that the prospect has already mentally bought and used the product and only needs assurance that it has a long life, or that it will be replaced, if necessary. When a salesman hears the word guarantee or warranty he is receiving

strong signals that the prospect wants to buy. It is time to start moving toward the close of the sale.

Making It Goof Proof

In most selling situations, as soon as he has identified buying signals, the salesman should start to sum up the important benefits, values, advantages, exclusives. This will tend to make his presentation goofproof.

The summary is a way of making as sure as possible that, when the salesman actually asks for the order, the prospect will say "yes." It is his way of being sure that the prospect remembers and understands all the reasons for replying, "yes."

So the prospect should be given a quick, clear review of the benefits that seemed to interest him most. The sales talk should be made in terms of "you and yours," and the prospect is carefully watched to see how he reacts as each benefit is mentioned. Does he show approval? Does he seem to understand thoroughly? If the salesman is not sure he should ask a test question — "Have I made that perfectly clear?" "So doesn't it seem logical that this should get you new customers?" This method helps to smoke out any fears which may be in the back of the prospect's mind and gives the salesman a chance to explain them away.

When salesmen have obtained agreements on every point, why shouldn't the prospect buy? It is only natural when a goof-proof presentation has been made.

Pushing for Action

Asking for the Order

It has been said that more sales are lost because salesmen fail to ask for the order than for any other single reason. Probably sounds ridiculous, but it is true.

Ask for the order. This should be done without prompting. Why else do salespeople make their presentations? Professional buyers are shocked at the small number of salesmen who ask for the order.

There is an old example which illustrates this point rather well. It's about the salesman who worked hard at telling the story of his product. For over an hour he had told the prospect the entire story about his proposition. For more than an hour he had gone over it point by point. Finally, in desperation, because he could sense he was not going to get the order, he yelled, "Why in the heck don't you buy my product?"

"Why in the heck don't you ask me," replied the prospect. "I was ready to buy forty minutes ago."

Volumes have been written about closing the sale, but there is no mystery about it, nor is the process too difficult. Really, it narrows down to:

ASK FOR THE ORDER[1]

Ask for the order often,
That's what you're there to do;
Salesman have learned no dough is earned
From a "pleasant interview."
Determine to get that order,
Just wishing will draw a blank;
Guts count a lot, for wishes are not
Negotiable at the bank.
Prepare your prospect for orders;
You didn't drop in as a treat,
He must learn the look of your order book
If you plan to continue to eat.
Assume you will get the order;
Keep selling with tact and skill,
Some men will sign on the dotted line
When you take for granted they will.
You may know the Buying Motives,
And you may Approach like a dream,·
You may be good when the buyer's mood
Keeps putting you off the beam;
But unless you have conquered Closing
Your future is all behind;
Your fortune lies in the man who buys —
In orders filled out and signed.

---

1. *Sales Review*, October 1948, Vol. II, No. 10, p. 7.

Probing Questions

Pushes for action may also come in the form of probing questions. These are usually direct questions which check, explore or probe into the prospect's mind to determine if he is willing to buy. Probing questions are often called "test," "feeler" and "trial balloon" queries. At any point in his presentation, but particularly after making each benefit statement, the salesman·can probe for buyer willingness.

Answers to probing questions inform the salesman: (1) if he is on the right track; (2) if the prospect understands; (3) if the prospect agrees with the salesman. Sample probing questions are:

Will you O.K. this order now so that I can make delivery as soon as possible?
Is there any good reason why you should not have this just as soon as possible?
Would you mind okaying this order so we can take care of the installation?
Don't you think this will do the job?
Would you like to end your worries?
Have I made that perfectly clear?
Can I ship you this order?
Will you take this deal?
Doesn't that sound interesting?
Does that check with your experience?
That's what you want, isn't it?
How does that sound to you?
Isn't that just good common sense?
You've had that experience, haven't you?
How does that appeal to you?

It is not always necessary to smother a prospect with facts, figures and demonstrations before asking for his business. The prospect knows why the salesman is there. He knows that he is supposed to be asked for an order. He may even be waiting to be asked for the order. Valuable time can be saved when the order is asked for as soon as possible. In other words, the salesman should watch for buying cues, tip offs and signals. Then he should send out frequent feelers, or probing questions.

Slow Curve Questions

A successful sale can often be closed by throwing a slow curve to the prospect. This means that a direct question is asked and then a switch is made to a double question. Like this:

"Do you think this bryzlik will do the job for you?" If the prospect's answer is "yes," the salesman would naturally ask, "Would you like to pay cash or open an account?" "Which do you like best, the medium size or the large unit?"

If the prospect's answer is "no," the salesman could say, "Well, perhaps I don't understand exactly what you need. In your opinion, why don't you think it would work?" Then the salesman slides easily back into his sales points or benefits. For example:

SALESMAN: Do you like the idea of this built-in music center with all of your hi-fi components in one place, Mr. Smith?

PROSPECT: Not necessarily.

SALESMAN: Just what is there about this system that bothers you, Mr. Smith?

PROSPECT: Well, it's that tape recorder. Its just that I like the idea of record-playing better.

SALESMAN: I see. I'm sorry Mr. Smith I guess I just didn't make that point clear to you. Let's go back over that point and I believe that I can show you how the installation of a stereo tape recorder will give you more all-around music enjoyment than would a record-player. For instance, take the idea of recording some of the beautiful music you hear on your FM stations . . .

Slow curves give a prospect a choice between something and something, never between something and nothing. Successful salespeople do not ask *if* — they ask *"which."* Slow curve examples are:

Which do you like, the large or the small?
Which would you like, immediate shipment, or would next week be soon enough?
Which would you prefer, an open book account, or deferred payments?
Which would suit your needs best, freight or express?

The following examples show other uses for slow curve questions. The first set of statements are blunt facts which do not probe and would probably not identify a need. The slow curve questions on the other hand, gently probe for need-satisfaction information.

Blunt Statements
You need new shoes.
You're losing money.

Slow Curve
What color shoes would you like with your new suit?
How would you like to start saving money right now?

Alert salesmen use slow curve questions, because they keep the prospect thinking, but not critically. If the salesman had asked, "Do you want brown shoes?" he would have asked a closed end question, and a "no" answer would have ended the deal. Slow curve questions, like those above, would have revealed his needs and kept him talking. Also, the salesman would have avoided the possibility of critical questions and requests for explanations.

Slow curve questions indicate indirectly that the prospect should have the product or service. For example:

Mr. Prospect, when this service is installed, it will no longer be necessary to guess as to whether or not you are saving money. Won't that be a big advantage to you?

Mr. Merchant, I have no doubt that there are times when you have worried about your present————. When this new————is installed, you will be relieved of that worry and feel free to plan other things. Don't you feel that this will be a great advantage to you?

Questions Make It Easy for the Customer To Buy

To avoid a jarring "Do you want to buy this?" try something like:

"Mrs. Jones, we are delivering one of these beautiful items next Monday to Mrs. White who lives in your neighborhood, would you like to have yours at the same time?"

"How soon would you like to start preventing the losses you have just mentioned, Mr. White?"

"Our trucks make two deliveries each week, would you like delivery on the second truck, Mr. Black?"

"Do you prefer color or black and white television, Mr. Brown?"

The important thing is to avoid questions which are too direct and too blunt, regardless of the phrasing used.

THE PROSPECT'S QUESTIONS

Listening to the prospect's questions will also help the salesman to learn about his prospect's problems. When the prospect asks questions regarding the performance of a product, economical operation, service and guarantees, the prospect is voicing positive buying clues. Such questions prove the prospect is thinking about the proposition in terms of his needs and problems. He may be ready to buy.

The nature of the questions asked by the prospect furnishes buying clues that will alert the listening salesman to closing possibilities. The following are examples of such questions:

Is this the latest you have?
May I see it again?
Is this the best price you can offer?

I wonder if this is a good buy?
How safe is it?
Is this more effective than what I'm now using?
How much research has been done on it?
Are there any precautions I should know about?
How about chemical reaction?
How else can it be used?

METHODS OF CLOSING

Pro and Con Method

Many salesmen summarize their presentation and start their decision-making activities by writing out a list of the pros and cons of the proposition. For example, in one column they might include all of the prospect's reasons for wanting a later delivery. In another column they might itemize all of the reasons why the prospect will benefit from an immediate delivery. The salesman then asks the prospect to compare the two, in order to help him make the right decision. Then he asks for the order. Some students of salesmanship call this method the "close by contrast" since the salesman is helping the prospect decide by contrasting the advantages against the disadvantages of making the decision.[2]

For the prospect who wants to postpone or stall his decision, this method is usually effective. First, it is businesslike. Second, it is convincing to the prospect. Any salesman can think of more reasons for buying now than the prospect can think of reasons for buying later.

When competition must be met, this same technique can be used. In one column, the salesman lists all of the benefits, values and advantages of his own product. In the other column, he lists all of the features which the prospect likes about

2. John W. Ernest and George M. DaVall, *Salesmanship Fundamentals,* 3rd edition, pp. 295-296 (New York: Gregg Publishing Co. 1965).

a competitor's product. Again, the salesman asks the prospect to compare them,
item by item, and decide for himself
which has more advantages.

When the prospect cannot make up his
mind this technique is effective, especially when the salesman's column is longer.
When the prospect sees the lists next to
each other and the salesman reviews each
item, the advantages of the other product
become less significant. Here's how a
salesman selling a kitchen modernization
plan might do it:

SALESMAN: That about completes the
story, Mrs. Miller. In view of the many
benefits you will get from our new
Happy House Kitchen, may I have
your O.K. to go ahead now?

PROSPECT: Mmmm — I don't know. I
think I'd like to hold off for a while.

SALESMAN: Just why do you feel you
would like to hold off, Mrs. Miller?

PROSPECT: Well, I think it might work
better if we remodeled a small portion
at a time. Then it won't cost so much.

SALESMAN: This is a big decision for you,
Mrs. Miller, and I know you want to
get the most for your money. I'd like
to help you make the right decision.
So, why don't we think it over together.
Let's list the pros and cons of doing a
complete remodeling job against doing
it piecemeal on this piece of paper.
Let's start with the piecemeal method
first, O.K.? Just what big advantage
can you think of in doing it this way?

PROSPECT: Well, I wouldn't have to pay
as much.

SALESMAN: Are you sure about that, Mrs.
Miller? Isn't it possible that you might
be paying more over a period of time?

PROSPECT: Yes, that might be true. What
I mean is that I wouldn't be letting go
of a large amount of money at one
time.

SALESMAN: But under our convenient
budget financing plan you also
wouldn't have to pay a large amount
at one time. However, I'll write it down
as an advantage of doing your remodeling over a period of time. (Salesman
writes "no large debt contracted all at
once.") Are there any other advantages, Mrs. Miller?

PROSPECT: Well, as I mentioned before,
when I remodel a little at a time I can
take advantage of new developments
as they come.

SALESMAN: Yes, you are right, but I don't
think that there will be any significant
new developments in kitchen appliances in the next few years, Mrs. Miller.
However, let's write that down as a
point also.

Now, can you think of any other advantages of remodeling a little bit at a
time?

PROSPECT: No, that's about it.

SALESMAN: Fine. Now let's consider some
of the advantages of doing a complete
remodeling installation all at one time.
First, you get a completely new and
attractive kitchen with all the new and
modern appliances you want right
now, not years later. Isn't that important to you, Mrs. Miller? (As prospect
agrees, salesman writes it down on the
advantage side for complete all-at-once
remodeling).

Secondly, you have the services of
a kitchen planning expert and a skilled
interior decorator to insure that you
will get the right kind of a kitchen.
Don't you think this is a big advantage
over doing it piecemeal, Mrs. Miller?

PROSPECT: Indeed I do. (Salesman then writes it down as an advantage.)

The salesman then proceeds to bring out other important advantages such as an accurate, all-inclusive estimate of cost, written guarantee, convenient financing, the immediate increase in resale value of the house, the ease of selecting the kitchen built-ins all at once, the comfort and convenience of being able to get the entire job done in only a week. When he has finished, he has a list of advantages for his proposition over five times as long as that against his proposition. He asks the prospect to review the list saying "Now as you look at these lists, Mrs. Miller, which proposition offers you the biggest net total of advantages?"

Minor Point Method
To discover whether or not a prospect is ready to decide in favor of a proposal, many salesmen ask the prospect for a decision on a minor point. He takes for granted that the prospect is going to buy. At a favorable moment, the salesman seeks a commitment on a minor point instead of immediately asking the prospect to make a major decision.

This method is frequently used in retail selling. The salesman asks the prospect, for instance, whether he prefers a certain jacket in blue or brown. If the question is asked in a quiet, normal manner, and with a seeming desire to be helpful, the prospect will make his color choice and move one step closer to his buying decision.

Minor decisions may be of little consequence, but when a prospect has made several of them, the salesman has conclusive evidence of his readiness to buy. If the salesman does not obtain a favorable response on a minor point, he has not lost the way to a sale. He simply continues his presentation by offering additional reasons for the prospect to buy and continues

to ask for the order at frequent intervals. Other examples of minor point questions are:

Do you wish to pay cash, or is this a charge?
Do you prefer delivery on Monday or would Wednesday be better?
Would you wish this installed in the kitchen or service porch?
Do you wish this in mahogany or walnut?

Order Form Method
A standard technique, the order form method, is also known as the physical action technique. It is based on the principle known to every stage manager that there is something almost hypnotic in the well-timed motion of actors on the stage, even when no lines are being spoken. The salesman who, during the closing phase of his presentation, calmly and unhurridly fills out his order form, is using this principle. The prospect knows that he is buying the deal if he does not stop the salesman's physical action, but the suggestion to continue is so powerful that he usually finds it very difficult to resist.

When using this method, some salesmen offer the pen to the prospect and place the partially filled-in order form in front of him, to suggest a signature at the bottom. Other salesmen have found it effective to ask the buyer to fill in those portions of the order form which are directly above the signature line, thus making it easy for the prospect to add his name.

Some authorities also recommend using an order book in which many orders have been recorded. This may suggest to the prospect that many others have purchased and that he too will benefit if he decides to buy.

Some salesmen take back the order blank after having placed it before the prospect. They make the excuse that they want to verify terms or other details. The salesman then assumes that the prospect will want the form filled in, because its withdrawal makes him feel that something has been taken away from him. The prospect does not react pleasantly to subtraction when he has a mental image of the addition of something beneficial to his ownership. The withdrawal of the form, therefore, makes the prospect decide much more quickly that he wants the product.

Certain salesmen hesitate to use the order form method, because they suspect it is high-pressure salesmanship. Actually, it is not. No matter what decision-making method is used, no sale is closed until the prospect's name is on the order blank.

This method of closing a sale must be tactfully employed. Many prospects who are ready to buy will be upset if the order blank is suddenly brought into view. The professional salesman keeps his order form in sight during the whole presentation, so the prospect will become accustomed to it. When the time comes, the seller fills out the order form and presents it to the prospect for his decision.

Most prospects do not like to be asked to sign the order or contract. Instead, the salesman should request the prospect to approve or okay it.

Naturally, to use the order blank method effectively, the salesman must be aware of his prices, specifications and other details. He can then write up the order very quickly. He also will avoid looking up or figuring the price in the presence of the prospect. Either may confuse him and cause him to delay his decision.

Name-Spelling Method

The name-spelling method is a variation of the order-form method. When a salesman feels that his prospect is about ready to say "yes," he should start to write the order. After the customer has become conditioned to the order blank, the salesman says: "Let's see, Mr. Smith, are your initials "E.W?"

If the prospect answers, "No, they are W.E.," the salesman replies, "Oh, that's right." Then, he quickly follows this up with, "Your·address here is, ah . . ." Then, if the prospect gives him the address, the salesman hands the order blank to him and says, "Mr. Smith, would you just OK the order on this line?"

Mr. Smith is completely aware that the salesman is writing an order. If he has not decided to buy, he has to stop the salesman. But the act of writing the order helps the prospect come to a decision. Relatively few people will actually stop this kind of closing procedure.

Reversed Position Method

Sophisticated buyers who think that they know how to combat the appeals of salesmen can often be won over by the reversed position technique. When using this method, the salesman pretends to give up the sale as lost. The prospect then feels that he can relax. Then, the salesman quickly begins a new sales appeal before the prospect has a chance to develop new resistance.

In this way the prospect is forced to reflect. If the salesman follows up his lead energetically, the prospect's mind may be diverted from resistance to a consideration of the benefits that he will derive from the proposition.

In some selling situations, this method may be quite effective. For example, when a prospect wants the salesman to leave, the salesman may act as if he wants to leave and make preparations for leaving such as picking up his hat, gathering papers together, and reaching for his briefcase. Having thus conditioned the prospect to expect a certain action, the salesman suddenly reverses himself and surprises him with the exact opposite action. He does this by abruptly stopping his preparations for leaving and introducing an apparently sudden thought, such as, "Mr. Prospect, it just occurred to me that one important factor has been overlooked . . ."

The prospect is not prepared for this change of method and is off guard. This is exactly what the salesman wants. A moment before, the prospect was confident that he had dismissed the salesman. He knew exactly what he was doing and he was sure that the interview would be terminated at once.

Now the prospect is not so sure of himself because a new situation has developed which cannot be handled effectively in his usual manner. The reversed position method is often successful because it reverses the situation and places the prospect on the defensive. Successful sales are often made by keeping the prospect unsure.

Transfer Method

Life insurance salesmen, after building up the sale to a climax, often use the following technique: "In case anything happened to you," they tell a prospect, "can you transfer to your wife the responsibility for providing for your family? Do you really want to place that tremendous responsibility on her?"

A refusal to buy compels a "yes" to these questions —— an almost impossible answer for the prospect to give. He must say "yes" to mean "no" to the order, and a "no" would mean "yes" to the order. This method also places the prospect on the defensive. It also makes his objection appear to be somewhat ridiculous.

The same technique may also be used to change the meaning of words. When a prospect tells a salesman that he is already buying the product from a friend, the salesman could reply, "That is fine. Everyone would rather do business with friends, and nowadays we're all looking for business friends. The purpose of my visit with you is to establish your company and my company on that basis."

Since the prospect wants to do business with a friend, the salesman immediately puts himself in that classification and tries to qualify as a very good friend. In this way, the obstacle may often be rolled aside and the assumption method introduced to assist the prospect toward making a favorable decision.

Last Chance Method

Another useful method for closing a sale is based on the principle that people often want what they cannot get. Their inability to gain what they want may be due to their inability to pay or to the limited supply of the product or service.

When appropriately used, the last chance method is often advisable. It should certainly never be used, however, in a dishonest manner. Scaremanship is not related to salesmanship.

An example of this method is furnished by the earth-moving equipment salesman who tells his prospect about another buyer who wanted the equipment very much but was unable to make the purchase due to short supply. Thus the prospect realizes the inability of some people to purchase the item and this intensifies his desire to be among the successful applicants.

Another example is furnished by the salesman who says to a merchant, "It may be impossible to fill orders after today, since the demand for this item has been sensational and the stock is very low." Limited editions of books, limited bond issues, limited styles, limited time, limited sizes —— all of these claims illustrate the use of the last chance method.

Such limitations boost the value of the product or service, intensify the desire of many prospects, and help to crystallize desire into decisive action. It must be emphasized, however, that all statements regarding limited supply should be truthful. Professional salesmen know that it does not pay in the long run to use dishonest methods to make sales.

Focusing Attention Method

Many products and services have been sold on the value of one benefit or one feature. Often the resourceful salesman will sense, during the demonstration, that the prospect is very interested in one particular feature. When the time comes to close the sale, the salesman stresses the importance of that feature and emphasizes the benefits and values to be gained through its use. Then the salesman simply proceeds to use the direct or double question to complete the sale.

Sometimes it is difficult to determine the prospect's key interest. If the salesman has completed his presentation, yet has received no buying signals from the prospect, he could probe for the key point in the buyer's mind and then, having located it, drive the sale home by a last ditch sales effort. For example:

SALESMAN: Mr. Allen, during the last hour we've gone over a number of excellent features which our roofing installation will provide you. But, for the life of me, I can't figure out what you consider the most important. Is it the neat attractive appearance of our asphalt shingles?

PROSPECT: No, they're the same as your competitors.' They're all attractive.

SALESMAN: I see. Well, is it the careful and thorough installation?

PROSPECT: Well that's important, but I'm not particularly worried about it. I know you would do a good job.

SALESMAN: Uh huh. Well then how about the low maintenance feature we talked about? No need for oiling, tarring and no replacement for years to come. In fact, you just forget about roof care after we install.

PROSPECT: Yes, that's what interests me. If I could just be sure that I don't have to put up with any fuss or bother maintaining this roof, I think we could work out a deal.

SALESMAN: O.K. Let's concentrate on this point, Mr. Allen. Right here in my briefcase, I have a number of case histories of customers who specifically mention how satisfied they are over the easy maintenance on our roofs. Here's a letter, for instance, from Ronald Jones, right in the next block. Do you know him?

PROSPECT: Oh sure. I know him well. Great guy.

In this example, the salesman probed for the key issue in the prospect's mind and finally found that it was the low maintenance feature. The buyer's interest was immediately re-engaged. Now, the salesman has only to prove that the benefit does indeed exist; he intends to offer proof by using testimonial letters from satisfied users. If he handles this stage well, the decision to buy should be easy to obtain.

Implied Ownership Method

A very common selling device used by many successful salesmen assumes that the prospect has already made up his mind to buy. During the explanation the salesman makes such statements as these:

Mr. Prospect, when this service is installed, you will find it will be a great time saver.

You will be proud to tell your management that you can effect such a savings for them, won't you?

Your family will be delighted with this, won't they?

This would be a good location for the new————, don't you think, Mr. Prospect?

The salesman then goes on with a direct or double question close to bring about the prospect's decision.

A similar technique can be used by saying, "Do you usually approve your orders as Smith and Company, or just W.E. Smith?" Then the salesman begins to fill in the order blank and usually asks a double question.

Referral to Authority Method

Salesman may find that with all their powers of persuasion, they cannot persuade the prospect to arrive at a favorable decision. There are some prospects who will deal only with the sales managers or some other authority. These prospects feel that by so doing they are getting the best possible terms. It may be that they want a word of assurance from someone in authority. At such times, it is well to enlist the services of the sales manager, or perhaps a company officer, to help in closing the order. Frequently this note of assurance is all that is needed to obtain the prospect's signature.

Another form of this technique is to have the senior salesman or sales manager act as a consultant to determine whether, in his opinion, the proper item has been recommended. While some prospects may dislike this method, many others desire it.

"Assuming a Close" Method[3]

For many salesmen, the "assuming a close" technique is the best of all. The salesman assumes, even before he faces his prospect, that a sale is certain. He feels this confidence because he thinks of his proposition in terms of service and benefits. He knows that he would not be making the call if the prospect did not qualify and if he did not have something of value to offer. He maintains this positive, buoyant attitude through every phase of his presentation. Then, after summarizing the

3. *Ibid.*, p. 297.

benefits, he asks a double question. A dialogue similar to the following ensues:

SALESMAN: Do you want this shipped by rail or by express?

PROSPECT: Wait a minute, I have not bought it yet.

SALESMAN: I realize that, Mr. Brown. I was just wondering if you would be in a hurry and if we could give you good service. Now there are a few points that I am sure I have not made clear . . .

Actually assuming the order and asking for it is not high-pressure salesmanship. If the prospect is not completely convinced of his need for the product, he will tell the salesman so, and he will also commit himself by telling the salesman why he is not ready to buy. It may be because a point was omitted from the sales talk or because something was not made clear in the buyer's mind. If necessary, the salesman should go back and emphasize again the particular points on which the prospect has not been sold.

When the salesman has done this, he once more asks for a decision, assuming that he has agreement. In most cases, the salesman will conclude a successful sale.

Doubt Elimination Method

If the salesman is not sure that the prospect is ready to buy, he should ask a test question: "Have I made that perfectly clear?" or "So does it not seem logical that this should solve your problems?" This method helps the salesman to discover any obstacles or fears which may be in the back of the prospect's mind. When he has obtained agreement on every point, there is no reason why the prospect should not buy. The only requirement at this stage of the sale is for the salesman to ask for the order.

Free-Trial Method

Sometimes the salesman arranges for the prospect to sample or use the product and to demonstrate it to himself. "Take it home and try it," says the appliance salesman. "Take it out on the highway and get the feel of it," says the auto salesman. In many areas of selling the free trial method is being employed more often. Automobiles, motor boats, typewriters, newspaper subscriptions, electric appliances and many other items are being sold by the free-trial decision-making technique. This method is based on two principles: (1) the prospect will be too thrilled with the product to return it. (2) the prospect engages in a high degree of participation and actually sells himself.

Objection Method

Nine times out of ten an objection from a prospect is really a request for more information. When a salesman gives the information and explains the benefits to the prospect, it is time to try for a close. Note in the following example how an objection is turned into a sale.

JONES: I don't know; I am not sure whether I like that one particular feature.

SALESMAN: Well, Mr. Jones, that is a very important point. But, before my company builds any product, it researches for months, even years, to be sure that it knows just what is most desirable to most people.

According to an extensive survey on the feature you mentioned, most customers have actually preferred the item because . . . (Here the salesman retells his benefits, values and advantages.) I am sure you will be very happy with this product because of these benefits. That is really important, isn't it, Mr. Jones?

JONES: I never thought of it in just that way.

SALESMAN: That is understandable, Mr. Jones, and I am glad I have been able to clear that up for you. Would you want us to deliver this week or will next week be soon enough?

If at this point Jones says, "The price is too high," the salesman could answer, "I don't blame you for thinking so because a lot of my other customers felt this way until they used it and found out that . . ." Then the salesman tells more benefits and success stories. Then again he asks for the order, probably using a subtle question.

If the prospect tells the salesman he wants to think it over, he probably expects the salesman to give him a lot of reasons for buying now. This is a good time for the salesman to use the yes-but technique and say, "Naturally, you should be sure that you are right. Now, bear in mind, while you are considering it, that this product . . ." Then the salesman is back in his sales story again with more benefits and more success stories. Another opportunity has been created to ask for a favorable decision.

Similarly, if the prospect says, "I think I will stick to the Rainbow brand because that is what my customers want," the salesman should use his yes-but technique again: "I am glad you brought that up, Mr. Brown, because lots of people feel that way and it is important. We experimented with a similar product but we feel that our product has these advantages. We find that people like a balanced product . . ." This method offers the salesman still another chance to ask for the order.

This method of helping the prospect toward a favorable decision is considered good salesmanship and it illustrates how objections can be turned into real decision-making opportunities.

Show-Down Method

The show-down closing method has its values when used with the proscrastinating, the lazy and the fearful. It is effective with those who repeatedly tell the salesman "see me next trip," and those who say one thing but mean another.

The show-down close is a salesman's last resort. Everything else has been tried, and still he gets no order. He forces the show-down by confronting the prospect with: "Mr. Prospect, my proposition either fits your company or it doesn't. If it doesn't, please tell me and I won't take up any more of your time. If it fits, here is the order form which I would appreciate your okaying." Better than 50 percent of prospects will probably buy. The other people are probably mere *suspects* who weren't qualified prospects in the first place. The salesman was only wasting his time. The show-down close takes courage, but often it helps to close successful sales.

Other Methods

There are other, and somewhat special decision-making devices that can be used. However, enough has been written to indicate the range of possible decision-making methods. The salesman may vary his methods and even experiment a little to make sure that he is using the methods best suited to his personality, his prospects and his product or service.

Because there are such wide ranges of personalities and behavior patterns among both salesmen and prospects, it is impossible to state that there is one method suited for everyone. The techniques which professional salesmen find most profitable for their use vary according to the particular prospect, the product or service being sold, and many other factors. *Even the best salesmen do not win favorable decisions from every prospect, but they never allow themselves to be discouraged.* They profit from their errors and gradually develop the techniques which work best for them.

WHAT TO DO AFTER...

Salesmen have been told for years, "When you get the order, leave. Don't stick around and talk yourself out of the order." Granted, there is some truth in the statement. Still wide misinterpretation has caused many, many returns and cancellations.

Suppose, for example, you have approached a prospect and said, "This product will last as long as two of the ordinary kind. Let me show you," then you demonstrate. The demonstration appeals to the prospect, he is in somewhat of a hurry, he gives you an order and you leave.

Now let's see what is liable to happen. ... He may say to himself later, "I wonder if I didn't fall too fast for that product. It certainly looked too good to be true — I wonder if there isn't a catch in it some place? Maybe it needs a lot of servicing. Perhaps I can buy it elsewhere for less."

Perhaps a competitive salesman calls on him and is told the prospect has already ordered your product. So the competitor says, "Well, they are a good company, but that's a new product and I'm wondering whether it will do everything they say. It looks O.K. but will it do the job you want?" His boss or his partner may say to him, "Why did you buy that stuff just on the strength of a short demonstration? Why didn't you ask him to send one to test before you ordered? It may not wear, it may break down easily."

In any of these cases, the customer is liable to cancel his order. Why? Because he has been disenchanted by the very selling points which you could have used but didn't! Wouldn't it have been wiser, after the order was written up, to have said,

"Mr. Jones, I just want to say that you have bought a good product. Your employees will like it. It will do the job better than anything I know."

Praise His Judgment

"Mr. Buyer you have just made a wise purchase."

No prospect will ever object to his judgment being complimented. The salesman is talking about the prospect's product, not his product. The prospect is being told what a wise buyer he is and when he accepts that kind of statement he will be very unlikely to complain later.

Telling the whole story cuts down cancellations, but even more important, this kind of follow-up makes sure that the prospect is receiving the benefits he was promised. And the salesman will earn more money because he will, in effect, have customers working for him.

After the sale the salesman may touch upon some of the important selling features that were left unsaid because the sale was completed before the salesman had a chance to bring them out. One important aspect to go over with the buyer after the sale is care of the product. For example:

SALESMAN: Mr. Buyer, you have made a good decision. You will get a great deal of enjoyment and satisfaction from this new Moncata Impala motorcycle.

BUYER: I sure hope so.

SALESMAN: It will provide you with a lot of fun. Here's a few pointers on how to take care of this fine bike that I didn't get a chance to mention. First, always make sure you put the kick bar down when you are parked, this will . . .

POWER POINTS

Fear, the sensation of extreme nervousness that almost mows down many salespeople, is natural. It is similar to stage fright and, if mastered, is no deterrent to good salesmanship.

There is another type of fear that is not so easily subdued. It is the fear of asking for the order — fear of the close. A surprising number of sales managers state that many men who score high on almost every other phase of selling fall down on this part.

The enthusiastic beginner may wonder why it is necessary to lay so much emphasis on this point. Asking for the order seems the easiest and most natural act in the world. But after a few barrages of objections, excuses, and many uncompromising "no's," the question of how and when to close assumes a very different coloration.

As with most selling problems, the studious salesperson discovers the answer through trial and error. But he can at least compile a few pointers which will ease his way. Important among the pointers which have been offered in this chapter are these: *when* to close and *how* to close.

It may be proper to apply pressure when seeking an order, but never high pressure.

The order should be asked for when buying signals are flying, before the prospect shows signs of becoming cold.

If one opportunity to close is lost, or fails, another can be made. Opportunity knocks more than once in every selling situation. Opinions vary as to the number of times a close should be attempted. Some say three, some four, some more.

The greater the number of objections answered in the course of the presentation, the more likely there will be a favorable close.

If persistence antagonizes a prospect, try to make an appointment to discuss the matter again. Have a different approach for each call if possible.

Every "no!" leaves the way wide open for your competitor to reap where you have sowed.

Take pride in completing a finished job. The coping stone of a sales presentation is the order, the close.

Make sure that everything has been said and done to justify asking for the order.

When the close has been successful, the order signed and checked, a "thank you" offered, it is time to stop and leave.

DISCUSSION QUESTIONS AND PROBLEMS

1. When should a salesman begin to close his sale?
2. What are the three forms of buying signals that a prospect gives to the salesman? Provide examples of each.
3. The salesman should attempt to make his sales presentation "Goof-proof." What does this mean?
4. How do successful salesmen push for action?
5. Explain the pro and con method for closing sales.
6. Is it possible to achieve satisfactory results in a sale by an early close?
7. The customer is always right. Debate this policy.
8. Describe the minor point method of closing. Furnish examples for closing a sale on a color television, Honda motorcycle and an electric toothbrush.
9. How should a salesman treat the order blank in a sales situation?
10. In what way is the name-spelling method similar to the order form method? Explain how, why and when you would use the name-spelling method.
11. Explain how the reversed-position method of closing is used on sophisticated buyers.
12. The transfer method is used to answer objections from the prospect and then guide his decision-making. Explain how this is done. In your own words, tell how you would use the transfer method to sell a product or service with which you are familiar.
13. When properly used, the last chance method is often advisable. Give an example of how you would use this method. What might motivate certain prospects to react favorably to this method?
14. Briefly explain how the salesman would use the focusing attention method of closing the sale. Write a role-playing situation using this method.
15. Explain and describe how you would use the implied ownership method. What are its advantages and disadvantages?
16. Briefly describe and explain how each of the following closing methods work.

    a. The assuming a close method.
    b. The doubt elimination method.
    c. The free trial method.
    d. The objection method.
    e. The show-down method.

17. What should a salesman do after the sale?

18. How can a salesman handle procrastination in a sales presentation?
19. For each of the following, write appropriate closing statements:

   (a) sale of a camera to a high-school girl
   (b) sale of a set of dishes for a newlywed couple
   (c) sale of an automobile to a salesman
   (d) sale of an air conditioner to a housewife
   (e) sale of office furniture to an executive
   (f) sale of a textbook to a principal
   (g) service — beauty treatment to a matron
   (h) service — cleaning rugs for a housewife
   (i) service — interior decorating job
   (j) service — haircut to teenager

20. Study the following closing statements. Which statements would you consider acceptable? Which unacceptable? Why?

   (a) Will you please purchase this set of books? I am working my way through college.
   (b) I am sure that, if you do not purchase this lot, I can easily sell it to your competitor.
   (c) How soon would you want delivery?
   (d) And remember, we will be glad to service your machine absolutely without charge for the next three months.
   (e) I am glad you decided to take this shirt. But do you know that the style of tie you are wearing doesn't suit you?
   (f) Even if the color does not suit you, you are saving quite a lot by purchasing it.

PHENOMENOLOGICAL PROJECTS

The Gem Food Company (Role or Case)

This case illustrates the step-by-step procedure used by one of the nation's large door-to-door distributors. The salesmanship revealed in this case is that which is used by the *advance salesman*, not a routeman. The *advance salesman* is a true door-to-door salesman, since his job is literally a one-shot proposition.

Step #1 — The Knock — Walk right up to the door. Knock so it can be heard but not too loudly. Stand where you can be seen. Step back as door opens. If wearing a hat, remove it. Give a big smile and say . . .

Step #2 — The Introduction — "Good morning, I'm the Gem food man. I have some very new things that I want to show you." (Wait for reply.)

Questions:
  1. Why is the knock step procedure important?
  2. Why does the salesman introduce himself in this manner?

  Your reason for being there is to show the many new things that you have (emphasize words "new things"). This may bring an objection like "I don't think I'd be interested," from the customer. This objection can be met by the reply, "I can understand that you wouldn't be interested in something you haven't seen, but I'm sure you will be interested when you have seen these surprises." If you get another "disinterest" reply, you can meet it with the next step which is effective and important.

Step #3 — Getting Inside — "These are surprises and I can't show you here, but if I could step inside, I'll show you a lot of things that will interest you."

Questions:
3. Why is the word "surprise" used?
4. Do you believe that this approach will get a salesman *inside* the home?
5. Why is it important to get inside a home? Why not sell on the porch or front steps?

If it doesn't break the resistance, or get the next logical objection, "No, I haven't time," reply with, "Everyone is interested and I'm sure that I can make you happy just by letting you see my surprises."

The next objection may be, "I do not have time to talk to you." This is met logically and gracefully by, "I know you're busy, but if you'll give me just ten minutes, I'll guarantee to leave at the end of that time, if you're not interested." (Look at your watch here to indicate that you are ready to start timing yourself.) "Why don't you take a rest? You know, the boss at our office always insists that the girls in our office take a ten-minute recess in the morning and in the afternoon. Why not take your ten minutes now? I'll do the work, you just rest for ten minutes and then I'll be on my way." (Makes motion to enter the door.)

Questions:
6. How are objections handled? Do you agree with the technique?
7. What is the compliment expressed in this approach?
8. Why does the salesman ask for "just ten minutes?"

Step #4 — Presenting the Sale — "Thank you. If you'll sit here, I'll show you the bag of surprises. Here is our new premium catalog." (Show quickly —— don't let her look too long at each page, merely long enough to arouse her curiosity. Mention the items on each page as you turn it, don't try to sell anything —— yet.)

Questions:
9. Why hurry through the premium catalog?
10. Why is the use of the premium catalog important at this point?

Turn the page rapidly enough to prevent long, drawn out discussions. Answer any questions as you go along and take enough time to develop interest, but not enough to create desire. Then look at your watch or a clock and say, "Gee, I'll have to hurry. Several minutes are gone and I haven't shown you the most important things."

Question:
11. Why look at a watch or clock and suggest, "I'll have to hurry?"

Mention and show pet items and point to the prices: "bowl cleaner, almost three lbs. for only 59c, biscuit flour, Korex stove cleaner makes your stove like new, cleanser, hot roll mix . . ."

Step #5 — Explain the Proposition — "In addition to our everyday low prices, here is the biggest surprise of all . . . on all of our own brand products that you buy, you receive a bonus which ranges from $.05 to $.50 on an item. These bonus credits can be used to pay for the household article you select, and you need not pay any additional cash unless the premium you select is over $6.50.

"This bonus does not increase the price you pay for your groceries. We can give it, first, because we spend no money for expensive advertising and, second, because we manufacture a large number of the items we sell. We deliver all merchandise direct from Gem to you, eliminating the necessity of anyone else making a profit on the merchandise. Probably our best value and the one most of our customers use regularly is . . ."

Question:
12. What do you think of this explanation?

Step #6 — Close the Sale — "Would you use a two or three-pound package?" As soon as she mentions which package, write it in the order book and then suggest, "Won't you select the groceries on which you can save money and which you will need this week?"

Question:
13. Why does the salesman suggest "Would you use a two or a three-pound package?" Do you believe this is a good closing technique?

After receiving an order say, "Now if you will approve the order by signing your name here, your order will be delivered Thursday morning along with your neighbors' who buy from us. Thank you, Mrs. Blank for the order." Exit quickly, but courteously. You have other calls to make. Be sure you have picked up all your equipment.

Question:
14. Do you believe that the procedure in this case produces successful sales? Would the same general procedure apply to any kind of selling?

Joe G. Childs (Case)

Day in and day out I meet only a few different objections that delay my closing of sales. The first barrier is caused by the hesitant buyer. The second is caused by the procrastinating buyer. Here are the ways in which I close sales when I encounter these prospects:

1. The *hesitant* prospect. He is sold but is naturally cautious, hesitant. Such prospects need a little extra push, an additional urge. To him I say: "There is only one way you will be able to enjoy the extra dollar volume that my product will give you and that is to start it working for you immediately."

2. The *procrastinating* prospect. He wants to put it off, think it over. The job here is to get over the value, the reward of immediate action, the loss in putting it off. Here's the usual pitch: "Mr. Prospect, you've seen for yourself how our product can speed up your service and help you to serve more people than you do now. An increase of just 10 percent means 100 more people a day. As a businessman, can you afford to lose the profits this extra volume will give you between now and the time you suggest I call back? Can you afford to continue paying a premium on your operations? Don't you agree that it would be a good idea to plug these profit leaks right now?"

Then I try to isolate the one point that usually stands in the way of the order. Next, I review the chief benefits of my product. I, then, assume that he is sold and give him a choice. For example, a choice of delivery dates, of terms, of quantities, of colors. If the prospect remains hesitant I give him a strong personal close. Here, I build up the prestige and reputation of my company and the personal reliability of myself as reasons for the prospect accepting my recommendations. I say, "Mr. Buyer, I have been calling on you for years and our company has been doing business in this area for years, and we expect to keep on doing business not only with you but also your neighbors. We wouldn't think of recommending a single proposal to you that wasn't sound, because we value your goodwill and our past business relations too highly."

Questions:
1. Do most salesmen meet only two different objections? State your reasons.
2. What do you think of the devices for closing used by this salesman?
3. Do you think his closing statement results in sales?
4. Is it good practice to isolate the one point that may cause the procrastination? Why?
5. Are these closing devices used in a logical manner?
6. Will these closing devices be successful in every sales situation?
7. Prepare a sales dialogue in written form for the procrastinating prospect as you would handle him.

Part Three

Special Sales Situations

Closing on Call-Backs

LLOW-UP CALLS

principle there are two types of call-
ks: on prospects who have failed to
on previous calls, and on customers
salesman wishes to retain and de-
p into better customers.

Although a sale may not be closed on
first call, a failure should not be as-
ed. Many sales cannot be made in one
and this simply necessitates another
rview. Quite often the inability to dis-
of the proposition occurs because
prospect must consult with other per-
(husband, partner, top management)
re a decision may be reached. If a
sperson is satisfied that he has not
untered an alibi, stall, excuse or
sh-off, he should follow up by trying
rrange a definite time and place for
ther interview.

ing the Call

timing of the follow-up call should
lanned. If a follow-up is tried before
prospect has finished his considera-
of the proposition, it could have the
ct of delaying the decision. When such
tuation develops, the nature of the call
ld be changed to a summary of the
entation, or a review of the benefit

point. The salesman should not make an
attempt to close the deal at that time.

The idea of summarizing indicates
that additional calls should result in a
favorable response from the prospect.
When the prospect gives a buying signal
revealing that he has completed his weigh-
ing and judging of the proposition, an
attempt to close is advisable. If he does
not buy, still more calls may be necessary.
The salesman should remember that the
cumulative effect of many calls is greater
than the minor effect of a single call, providing that the calls are at short intervals
so that the prospect is able to remember
previous presentations.

When calls are too far apart, the penetration of the first call is lost, therefore,
the second call must be handled like the
first. Timing calls will depend on the
product being sold, the strength of the
impression made in the previous call, and
the prospect's recall power. While it is not
possible to state the length of time which
should elapse between calls, it is safe to
state that too frequent calls may not cause
deep penetration of the proposition into
the buyer's mind. Conversely, if a five-
year interval were to occur, it would be
necessary to conduct the interview as

though no previous call had been made. The right time to call is determined by examining the results of calls at different periods of time, until the pattern reveals itself.

Advantages of Follow-Up Calls

In the interval between calls, the presentation can be reviewed in the light of experience with the prospect. In this way the salesperson can determine where his sales talk was weak, where strong, at what point he had gained the prospect's interest and how his product benefits might solve the prospect's problems. This advance preparation should enable him to capitalize on the facts gained during his initial call, and use them as aids in future calls.

Methods for Follow-Up Calls

Nothing should be taken for granted on follow-up calls. Between calls the prospect has usually forgotten the salesman, his company and everything that he has said. The prospect has seen many other people since the last interview and he has had many problems to solve. Therefore, the salesman should supply him with as much sales information as he would offer a new prospect. Successful closers take nothing for granted.

The methods to be used on follow-up calls are practically the same as those to be used for the first call on a prospect. The salesman approaches and greets the prospect first, and then proceeds to build up real business interest, desire and conviction in the prospect's mind as a preliminary to the decision to buy.

Often, too much is taken for granted when making repeat calls, a natural reaction but a pitfall. On every call, new or repeat, a creative sales job must be done. At least one big benefit must be offered the prospect and the salesperson must be prepared to go through each step of the sale. The benefit must consist of a

new product, or idea, that will help b prospect and salesman earn more mon The job is not only to sell a product service, but also to help the prospect ma a success of his business.

Questions

On follow-up calls, if the salesman u a question to which the prospect c easily answer "no," he is unnecessar handicapping himself. It is better to st a follow-up presentation by saying "L time I talked with you, your problem v one of price. Is that still so, Mr. Brown

The prospect must say "yes." By p senting the customer's difficulty in form of a question, the salesman has moved the reason for the objection. a practical salesman would phrase it, "T steam was taken out of the prospec boiler."

Meeting an Obstacle

When the salesman knows that he is goi to meet an obstacle on a follow-up c: he should bring it up himself before prospect has a chance to get it out in open and create a difficult situation. T approach steals the prospect's thund while it offers the salesman an easy so tion. This approach is often useful dealing with the price-minded buyer.

For example, the salesman can say have been thinking about the price a I wonder if we should not look at it fr this angle . . ." Then the salesman ma a different and more interesting presen tion revolving around the topic of pri He also may mention new benefits to t prospect and thereby recreate his intere Most important of all, the salesman d not have a "no" to surmount before launches into his presentation.

Nearly all prospects like to say "n It is easier to say "no" than "yes" cause the word "yes" makes prospects f that they must make a decision. Decisi making, for most people, is a very di

It task. The chief job of the salesman to persuade and motivate the prospect say "yes" through helping him to make favorable decisions.

Typed Order Method

Salesmen often use the typed order form a follow-up when they have been unsuccessful in closing the order on a previous call. It may be that the prospect has put off the salesman by saying something like: "See me tomorrow"; or "See me next week"; or "I'm too busy now."

A neatly typed order has a compelling effect on many prospects since it indicates confident attitude on the salesman's part. Even more important, it saves the prospect from making a decision; the typed order form has done it for him. However, the typed order method, when used by young and inexperienced salesmen is a dangerous one. Many purchasing agents are extremely independent and resent this type of approach. Consequently this approach should be used only after the salesman has acquired the finesse and judgment that is accompanied by experience.

When using the typed order on a follow-up call, the salesman might say something like this: "Mr. Prospect, since I talked with you yesterday, I have worked out the details and I have them typed here for your consideration." Then the salesman shows the prospect the order form and requests the order by asking a new curve or minor point question, as explained in Chapter XIII.

New Angle Method

The new angle close can frequently be used on a follow-up call when the salesman has been unsuccessful previously. If he has failed to obtain the order, he should review again the needs of the prospect and tell him how the product or service can fill those needs. Many orders may be obtained from an apparently hopeless situation by presenting a new angle: "Mr. Prospect, in presenting our product to you the other day, there is one point which I entirely overlooked and I feel that this feature should be explained to you more thoroughly."

He then proceeds to show the prospect additional values, benefits and advantages which he thinks may bring about a favorable decision. It is usually well to concentrate on one feature when using the new angle close. If the salesman finds that this is not successful, it is easy to extend his explanation to other benefits of the product or service. And he always remembers to ask for the order before leaving!

REPEAT CALLS ON REGULAR CUSTOMERS

Repeat Call Approach

In calling back on regular customers, the salesman should be eager to continue his development of friendship, but on a business basis only. He knows that personal friendships lead to familiarity and familiarity may lead to trouble.

Only a few minutes at the start of the interview are necessary for reestablishment of the respectful relationship built up during previous calls. The procedure may vary, but after the friendly greeting, the salesman may offer suggestions about a new development in the prospect's industry, or a new merchandising or display idea which he has observed during his travels. Attention to such little things may distinguish the professional from the mediocre salesman.

In this area of thought, the importance of trifles should not be overlooked. Perhaps the salesman has certain *mannerisms,* such as nervously beating a finger on the prospect's desk or slouching in his chair. These mannerisms, in the course of repeated call-backs, may irritate the buyer. The salesman should guard against them and other unconscious mannerisms; business relationships are quite fragile, easily damaged or destroyed.

Persistency of Purpose

There may be times when the repeat call has served its full purpose, because the salesman has reestablished his friendship with the customer. He makes what is known as a courtesy call and in some instances, unwilling to trespass on the time of a busy man, the salesman departs without an order. Generally, this situation is not typical, because the salesman usually wants an affirmative decision regarding a new promotion, the ordering of new merchandise or additional items.

Persistency of purpose means that the salesman never loses sight of the fact that he is there to sell. In calling back on regular customers, the temptation is strong for the salesman to say to himself, "Oh, I've told this man my story before; I've told it ten times today and I'm tired of it." The best cure for this attitude is for the salesman to remind himself that a number of competitive salesmen have been working on the customer since he last saw him. Also he should be aware that man's memory is short and that very few customers remember more than a speck of what they are told on any one call. It is essential in every repeat call to establish again the prime reason for the call. A good salesman realizes that what may be old to him may be new and interesting to the prospect.

Refractory Phase

According to the refractory phase principle, there will be times when less sales effort will be needed than usual. At other times the prospect will buy if sufficient reasons are given him, but more sales effort will be required. The *relative refractive phase* is involved here.

For example, if a person has just purchased a new Cadillac and he is thoroughly satisfied with it, the salesman may

assume that he is in an absolute refrac phase. It is probable that no amoun persuasive appeals to buy will event in a purchase by him. However, as months and years of usage accumul the car owner's attitude changes and though he really does not need to bu new car, the time will arrive when he buy if a good salesman persuades h A good trade-in, a new model and o special benefits, or exclusives, may ca him to buy when otherwise he would even listen to a sales talk.

The auto owner is in an *absolute* fractory phase when his car is brand n he refuses to think of purchasing a car until he has used it for not less t one year. Even if great persuasive p sure is applied during this time, the sa man will ordinarily not close a sale. W new models appear, his attitude change a bit. During this time the bu would be in a *relative refractory ph* However, immediately after he has to have the car repaired or repainted would probably resolve to make the last for another year or more. When is feeling like this, he may again be ir *absolute* refractory phase and, theref need greater persuasive pressure to duce him to buy.

How much persuasion, how much p sure to apply will depend on a consid tion of the *refractory principle*. It sho be realized that at some intervals amount of persuasive sales effort will successful, while at other points differ degrees of persuasion will be nee When the salesman has properly quali the prospect, he will know about the gree of persuasion to apply. The amo of persuasiveness to use will be depend on the fact that the salesman is the mid man between his employer and the p pect. He cannot employ so much forc persuasion that he becomes obnoxiou the prospect and thereby prejudices fut

s. He cannot sell at a loss to his em-
yer; and he cannot waste his time on
spects who are not ready to purchase.

thods of Repeat Calls

stery of Idea-Sequence

relation to the body of the repeat call
sentation, the salesman should remem-
what was said in an earlier chapter
ut thorough mastery of the ideas he
ats to present. He must arrange them
n effective idea-sequence (see Chapter
), and have them so deeply buried in
memory that he is free during an inter-
w to watch customer reactions. He tells
sales story slowly, a step at a time, and
s adroit questions as he goes along, to
sure that the buyer understands what
eing said.

estions

s questioning technique may pay un-
ected dividends in revealing what is
med the "china egg" — the man on
om a salesman is not justified in wast-
his time. This man's firm may have
real need for the product or service.
perhaps he lacks the authority to make
desired decision. Again, the sales-
n's questioning may reveal that his
ying potential is so small that the pros-
t should be reclassified, and perhaps
en less costly handling.

ide In Persistence

lated to pride in persistency of purpose,
the salesman's determination to make
complete presentation as impressive
possible on every repeat call. It is im-
rtant to recall some of the facts related
Chapters IX, X, and XI. The heart of
sales presentation, as distinct from
approach and close, can be described
four statements.

That the salesman have the attitude
the problem solver.

That the salesman hold himself to a
slow pace with frequent questioning of
the prospect.

That the salesman achieve a complete
mastery of the idea-sequence.

That the salesman develop all possible skill in getting the presentation
back on the track following occasional
derailments.

CONCEPT OF THE CLOSE

In effect, this means that a repeat call is
made with the purpose of effecting a sale,
regardless of the friendship which may
have been developed with a customer. It
is recognized that there are frequent call-
backs when the purpose is merely to hold
the customer's business in the face of
competitive selling. But even here an affirmative decision is required, and the
familiar devices of proven closing methods
should be introduced. The concept of the
close is a professional method for bringing
the interview to a successful termination,
even when it is merely the customer's re-
affirmation that the salesman's line is
satisfactory.

In a previous chapter, the point was
made that many men make weak closers
because they fail to overcome their dislike
for facing up to decisions. This dislike
should be overcome, particularly during
repeat calls where friendship with the
customer may make it awkward to look at
an issue squarely.

Case Studies

No matter how excellent a presentation is,
the customer is likely to sit back and in
his mind say, "O.K., Mr. Salesman, I'll
admit you made your point. I agree that
your proposition will save my firm money.
So what do I do about it? And do I do it
now? Why not next week?" Consider the
example offered below. Salesman Sam is
trying to sell $5,000 worth of dictating
equipment to a supermarket chain. Notice

how Sam confidently meets the "so what" issue in each of his four calls.

Interview No. 1

Salesman Sam calls on the office manager of a large supermarket chain. He makes a convincing presentation, using facts and figures to show that the substitution of dictating equipment can produce material savings in the office of this firm. At the end of the interview, the office manager is mentally asking "so what?"

SALESMAN: Mr. Wilson, I don't expect you to reach a decision on this matter now. The issue is too important. I would appreciate your giving me permission to present this same material in the form of a cost analysis to you and your executive buying group next week. Let's say next Wednesday at 3 P.M. right here in your office?

Interview No. 2

At 3 P.M. next Wednesday afternoon, Sam appears before a group of executives and again gives his facts and figures using charts, graphs and other visual aids. Again, he senses that the men are thinking "so what?"

SALESMAN: Gentlemen, as I have shown you here today, over 1,600 business firms have saved thousands of dollars by introducing our type of dictating equipment for stenographers and secretaries. Just how much money my firm can save you can be easily determined. So, let's take the next step and find out by making a survey of your present correspondence costs. This survey won't cost you one red cent, and it will be made by experts in the secretarial field. Here is an invitation form authorizing me to begin that survey next week. It will take one week and I'll have the results of that survey for you on June 10th.

Interview No. 3

On June 10th, Sam again appears before the executive buying committee, presenting survey results which show th the equipment he proposes to install w effect important savings in the compan correspondence costs. Again, he gets t feeling the committee members are aski "so what?"

SALESMAN: Gentlemen, we now know th our dictating equipment should pr vide substantial savings in correspondence costs. But you want proof. At o own expense we are ready to put a trial demonstration of our equipme in any department you so choose. Wh I ask now is that you select that depa ment. On July 25th you will have t necessary proof for your decision.

Interview No. 4

On July 25th, Sam presents his pro showing unmistakably that costs ha been reduced 20 percent in the test depa ment. There is now an easy answer to t committee's "so what?"

SALESMAN: Gentlemen, you have seen t proof and you now realize the savin available to your firm by using mo 602 dictating equipment. Our surv shows that you need 200 such m chines. Here is an order already ma out.

METHOD BETWEEN CALLS

Keeping prospects "hot" between calls every bit as important as keeping pr pects alert during a sales talk. Experien has taught salesman that they must s their method of getting in touch wi prospects between calls to the individu Sometimes a letter is most appropria sometimes a telephone call and, occasio ally, a telegram suits the purpose be Salesmen learn to pace the attention th

ive to customers; some customers de-
erve more between-call attention than
thers. Remember that customers, like all
eople, enjoy knowing that someone is
inking about them. Man's memory is
ort; it is dangerously easy for an ag-
ressive competitor to wean away custom-
rs in the period between the salesman's
alls.

Letters are possibly the first and most
bvious method of recalling a salesman
the customer's mind. A note may merely
cknowledge a courtesy or express thanks
r an order. A letter that includes some-
ing other than routine matters is most
ppreciated — for example, outline the
ay your product can be adapted to the
ustomer's problem, or enclose a clipping
out an industry trend, or describe an
tstanding sales promotion or a window
splay that could be applied to the cus-
mer's own business.

Company sales aids, such as direct mail
d point-of-sale handouts, are also ap-
opriate at this time. This material can
ten be enclosed with an effective per-
nal letter, not with the idea that litera-
re can close a sale, but to remind the
stomer that the salesman is thinking
out him. Usually it is advisable to rub-
r stamp, or red pencil the literature to
rect the reader's attention to items of
ecial interest.

Greeting cards are sales aids for the
lidays, for a personal or business birth-
y or anniversary. It is well to keep a
rbon copy file of such mailings so they
y be reviewed in connection with other
ords in advance of the next call-back.

The occasional friendly telephone call
uld include a worthwhile message, to
tify using the prospect's time. The cus-
ner should be asked if he is free to talk.
herwise, the salesman may unwittingly
rude when the prospect is too busy to
k and thereby defeat his purpose.

Promises

Probably the most important factor about
these warm-up contacts is to be constantly
alert to fulfill the most trivial promises.
A promise made to a customer should be
kept. If, during the interview, a promise
was made to send the customer a quotation
on price, for example, a written note of the
commitment should be made and the
promise kept as soon as possible. Nothing
contributes more to the deterioration of
business confidence than a history of un-
kept promises.

It should not be understood that anything in the foregoing paragraph implies
that a salesman should be a sycophant, for
that is not the way to build high regard.
However, a good salesman never forgets
his role as problem-solver and counselor.
The customer-salesman relationship must
rest on a sturdy foundation.

RECORDS

The heart of a salesman's work is *system-
atization*. Throughout this text the need
for systematic review of personal attributes, of territory organization and of
selling time has been stressed. In the same
way, the successful salesman recognizes
that he cannot keep in mind an encyclo-
pedic index of information about a host
of customers, so he gives constant attention to the records on which repeat calls
are based.

Many records come to him at regular
intervals from his company. They are indispensable, because they show such items
as past purchases and credit ratings.
Equally important are his own records,
which relate to many details of no direct
concern to management. The salesman's
aim should be to make every customer
record card a complete history of all his
contacts with the customer, both in person
and by mail. Immediately following each
personal contact with a customer, the
salesman should record the nature of the

interview and include not only the transaction completed, but also the customer's personality, habits, motivations, hobbies, new business possibilities, new objections, when to follow up and many other factual details.

SELF-ANALYSIS

Customer record cards may contain evidence of self-analysis on the part of the salesman. They might show answers to such questions as:

Where was I strong during the interview?
Where was I weak?
Did I contribute anything toward helping the customer with his problems?
Was my presentation complete? If not, what was overlooked?
Did I work toward a favorable decision or am I softening up with this customer because of personal friendship?

COMMON COMPLAINTS

Credit refusal by the home office is a common complaint. For example, "Last year your company refused to grant me credit; my honesty was questioned; my financial standing was damaged. Why should I give you an order and be insulted again?" It is possible that this complaint was justified. The credit reference may have been handled as a routine affair and the refusal may have been due to carelessness or oversight on the part of a credit department clerk. The keynote for handling a complaint like this is to assure the complainant that a company credit policy and procedure is not a personal affair and that it is never used to insult a prospect or customer. The customer should also be assured that the situation will receive his personal attention and be corrected if possible.

Poor service is another common complaint. "Your service is terrible" has been heard by practically every salesman. "Service" embraces every phase of a business

operation, therefore, the salesman mu discover what was "terrible." Was it d livery, or refunds, or allowances, e changes or overcharge? What is the re cause of the complaint?

If the buyer has mistaken ideas abo the company's policies and services, t salesman should explain *why* they we adopted. He should promise to forwa the facts to the home office, to follow and try to have the situation correcte Service complaints should be taken se ously and the prospect given the und standing that the salesman is taking genuine interest in his problem.

Refund and allowance complaints a not only serious, they also represe wasted effort and they are costly. Nea always these complaints arise as the res of poor sales techniques and it is usua safe to imply that they occur because the salesman's lack of skill.

These are only three of the comm complaints, but they should serve as amples heard every day by salesm Furthermore, the technique for handl complaints can be reduced to somethi resembling a formula.

HUMAN RELATIONS FORMUL

Practically all complaints and gripes be handled through the human relati formula. Professional salesmen say t they have to give attention to the important factors of *human relatio* particularly when dealing with *compla* situations. These salesmen know that c plaint handling is an important part their work. If there were no complai (and gripes), much of their work wo be unnecessary and it would be diffi to justify their employment.

Professional salesmen know that t will never succeed in handling all c plaints, but they know that they will h a 90 percent better chance of succeed if they base their procedure on the foll ing human relations formula:

Relax, emotionally and physically —
but not mentally.
Listen to the complaint.
Protect the buyer's pride.
Show sympathy.
Use assurance words and phrases.

Relaxation
Prospects and customers usually complain
because they resent inconveniences and
loss of money and fear that the salesman
will not make a just settlement. When the
salesman relaxes emotionally and physically, it is contagious. When prospects
observe his relaxed manner, they too will
relax and lose much of their skepticism
and fear. The salesman should then
have little difficulty in making a good
presentation.

Listening
A professional salesman listens when a
customer or a prospect wants to air a
grievance. The salesman lets the prospect
do the talking because he can usually
siphon off most of his steam. Salesmen
can almost see customers deflate like a
balloon, while they listen. Actually, some
salesmen even encourage a customer to
get everything off his chest by asking
questions and then listening sympatheti-
cally to his answers.

Usually, a prospect's grievance or complaint is exaggerated. The salesman often
finds that it is imaginary. He may receive
many complaints, only to find out that it
was another salesman's product or service
that had given the trouble. Quite often it
is the way the customer used the salesman's product or service that created the
complaint. Relaxed listening allows the
customer to air his grievances and clari-
fies the atmosphere so that the salesman
can again start to close a successful sale.

Protecting Buyer's Pride
Most people dislike to admit that they are
wrong. Once they have taken a position,

it is hard for them to retreat; their pride
is at stake. A professional salesman will
never try to prove anyone wrong, particularly a customer, or a prospect for his
product or service.

If the salesman tries to prove that a
customer's attitude is unusual or silly, he
does the one thing that will certainly encourage the complainer to maintain it.
But if the salesman shows that he respects
the complainer's position and understands
why and how he happened to get that way,
he makes it easy for the complainer to
come down to earth and agree with him.

All salesmen must be careful to protect
the other person's pride. Even after the
complaint is satisfactorily solved, they
must guard against any impression that
might reflect against the prospect's good
opinion of himself. When a complaint is
handled in this way, the customer feels
that he was the smart boy who had all the
answers and the salesman nearly always
turns such a complainer into an enthusiastic booster for himself, his product and
his company.

Sympathy
People crave sympathy. When a salesman
has a sympathetic, understanding attitude,
he can take the complainer off the offensive. A professional salesman shows by
his attitude that the customer is worth
listening to. He always listens attentively
and when the complainer has unloaded
his mind, he gives the salesman a chance
to come in with his explanation and close
a successful sale.

The following solutions for complaints
are always used by professional salespeople and they seldom fail. First, when
things go wrong — when the customer is
in trouble — come through with super-
service; right then is the time to smother
trouble. A professional salesman will
jump into his car and rush over to see
the customer because he knows that the
trouble shooter can build real friends.

When the salesman himself is in a jam — in real trouble — he likes the person who will "be right over." Any salesperson likes to be treated this way and so do his customers.

The professional salesman gets to the trouble and stays with it while it is hot. He knows that someone will be burned and it may be him! A complaint, properly handled, can tip the scales in favor of the salesman and turn the resenter into a booster.

Experience has shown that in ninety-nine complaints out of each hundred, the product or service is not to blame. Most complaints are caused by misunderstandings rather than any failures of the product or service. Therefore, a professional salesman would offer a solution for a complaint, and then sell his solution in the same way as he did the first sale to the customer. Finally, the professional would never have an "I told you so" attitude when dealing with a prospective customer.

Using Assurances

In explaining away complaints, questions, excuses, alibis and stalls, the good salesman tries to use assurances. He uses assurances that suit his personality. He is never afraid of repeating his assurances. And he is sure that they are said naturally and expressed with quiet confidence. To smother complaints, to banish suspicion and fear, many successful salesmen use assurances like these before they give a direct answer . . .

> That is a perfectly natural thought . . .
> I can understand your viewpoint . . .
> Yes, I see your position . . .
> That is an important point to consider . . .
> I am glad you brought that up . . .
> That is certainly a logical conclusion . . .
> I can see how you feel. Others have felt the same way until . . .

HOLDING CUSTOMERS

Salesmen can often make their customers stay sold merely by using a little common sense and good human relations. One of America's top salesmanagers used to say, "Make the presentation stay presented." What he meant was that many an order that is written up is never delivered because the customer changes his mind. This would not happen if the customer had been thoroughly sold.

For years salesmanagers have told their salesmen, "When you get the order, leave — do not stick around and talk yourself out of the order." Granting that there is some truth in the statement, still it has been widely misinterpreted and has been the cause of many, many returns and cancellations. Successful salesmen know that a sale is not really closed until the customer knows how to use the product, or how to sell it to his trade. When a salesman tells his whole story his commissions increase because he will then have his customers working for him and his follow-ups and cancellations will drop almost to zero.

POWER POINTS

It usually pays to call back on both customers and prospects. Call Back is also spelled "repetition" and repetition is generally thought of as dull and unimaginative. However, repetition is imperative if you want your message to stick. There are some thought-provoking facts about repeat calls and call-backs. These facts were part of a study made of a group of people by Walter Dill Scott of Northwestern University and several psychologists. They discovered that:

25 percent of all people forget an impression in one day.
50 percent of all people forget an impression in two days.
85 percent of all people forget an impression in three days.

97 percent of all people forget an impression in four days.

Let's toss those facts around a bit and see what their implications are for salespeople. Salespeople, for example, will have to make a great many more call-backs to counteract this human tendency to forget. Teddy Roosevelt is reputed to have boasted about his simple but effective technique for making a good political speech. First, he would tell people what he was going to talk about. Then, he'd go ahead and talk about it. After that, he would sum up and tell them what he'd said.

The old Rough Rider was a true salesman. He had the right idea. Speak your piece at least three times, but with a different approach each time. That will make the message stick.

Plan it so that you will be expected and welcome when you call back. It is better for you to be able to say to a receptionist, "Mr. Chillicothee told me to come by to see him on my next trip to Pittsburgh. I phoned yesterday to arrange for a brief interview at about this time. Is he free yet?" Otherwise you might have to sell yourself all over again, even to get past the receptionist. Orders established through strong call-backs can develop into a salesperson's strongest accounts for the close of one sale can be the start of another.

If something has gone wrong, don't alibi, even if it is not your fault. To the customer you *are* your company; so go to bat for your customer. Listen to his complaints as carefully and attentively as if they were sales objections. Hear him out, don't interrupt. Then, decide on the proper adjustment procedure for his case.

Most people are honest and most complaints are genuine. However, when you do get a *deadbeat*, go to bat for your company. That kind of customer is not likely to buy from you again anyway. Actually, while a sale is a sale, one like this can be too costly in time, energy and damaged reputation. Settle the claim fairly, then write him off the books. You don't need him!

DISCUSSION QUESTIONS AND PROBLEMS

1. What are the essential differences between *follow-up* and *repeat calls* on prospective customers? Consider presentations; advantages and disadvantages; summation principle.
2. Describe each of the following decision making techniques and tell how they are used with call-back and complaint activities:
   a. Typed order
   b. Referral to authority
   c. New angle
3. What is the relation of the "refractory phase principle" to call-backs on customers?
4. Explain how the "idea sequence" is related to call-backs.
5. What is meant by "pride of persistency" and how is the concept used in call-back activities?
6. Explain and tell how you would use each of the five items in the human relations formula.
7. Why should the salesman introduce potential obstacles early in the follow-up or repeat call? Should a repeat call be handled like a completely new presentation? Why?

8. How are assurances used to relax prospects and win them over to the salesman's side?

9. During the first few minutes of repeat calls on established accounts, how would you keep the interview on the track, and eliminate any possibility of the buyer thinking, "I have heard your story before. Why tell it to me again"?

10. "A new stone must be laid during every follow-up or repeat call for the building of customer good will." From a salesman's viewpoint, what is your interpretation of this statement?

11. What methods might be effective for "keeping customers hot" or warmed-up between calls?

12. Most companies provide their salesmen with various reports *over and above* the reports received from the company: What can you suggest which would help salesmen to evaluate (1) the progressive month-to-month development and growth of their accounts; (2) their personal growth and development as salesmen?

PHENOMENOLOGICAL PROJECTS

The Perturbed Salesman (Case)

It was easy to see that this mild-looking gentleman was perturbed. He was raving mad, as a matter of fact — a thing no salesman, whose life is involved in being pleasing to others, should ever be.

I calmed him down, and asked him to tell me what was bothering him. It was routine — an old customer had become a "quit."

When the salesman had called earlier in the afternoon, for what he expected would be an easy order — what is called in selling a "wrap-up" — he received, instead, the information that the customer had just placed the order with a competing firm.

"I've had that fellow for ten years," the salesman told me. "He was my best customer. I did my best to keep him. No one ever gave a man better service. And now that's all the thanks I get out of it."

He was bitter toward the duplicity of his best customer. "The idea that a guy I've treated like a brother would cross me up like that!"

I pointed out that losing customers is no sin. All salesmen lose customers.

"But there's one sin in connection with losing a customer that I hope you never commit," I told him.

"What's that?"

"The sin of not going back and inviting the customer to be your customer once more."

"Do you mean I should go back and ask that heel to buy from me again?" he demanded. "What do you think I am? I wouldn't go back to call on him again if he were the only customer on earth."

"And if you persist in having that attitude," I told him, "pretty soon there won't be any customer on earth — for you, anyway."

Then I told him the philosophy of the really topflight men in selling. It boils down to this:

There isn't any thing more important that a salesman can do than to hold a customer once he gets him. If a customer, for any reason at all, or for no reason at all, decides to quit, it's the salesman's duty to go to him — at once — and ask him to come back, no matter how humble he must be, how much saying the words stings his throat.

After all, a salesman is a professional manufacturer of customers. Every time he loses one it is a black mark on his shield.

Questions:
1. What is the basic thought in this case?
2. How would you deal with this kind of customer? Why?

Dundee Mills (Role)

This case begins in the thriving little farm community of Red Dog, U.S.A., population 2,201, about 8:00 o'clock one Monday morning.

DEALER: Wait till I get ahold o' that Phil Quota. Three weeks and still no delivery. Him and his promises! All he says is "It's on the way — it's on the way." What does he expect me to do, sell the stuff from the plant? Yeah! he's on the way out. Just wait'll I see that guy.

It appears that the dealer has the ax out for somebody today. He's just been elected to the school board. On top of this, he's head of the Red Dog Businessmen's Club this year — so he's really loaded down with plenty of headaches including those of running his feed business. The dealer figures he's the packhorse for all the troubles of his business, including all the worries he plans to blame on Phil Quota. This cloudy Monday morning, the outlook seems darker than the rat hole in the back room — and Phil is in for a stormy day when he sees his customer. There's lightning ahead and it's not coming from any rain cloud.

Phil walks in, straightens the sign card on the wall, looks over the showroom — door opens suddenly, the dealer rushes in still upset with a "chip on his shoulder" look. He spies Phil Quota, stops dead in his tracks, then points a finger, shaking it as he advances on Phil.

DEALER: I've been looking for you, Quota! How long must I sit here hoping I might see that car of feed I ordered three weeks ago? Has it been shipped from that plant yet? I'm going to take on Waco Feed. That's what I'll do.

PHIL QUOTA: (breaks into Tom's talk) Can't say I blame you, but I got a confirmation that that car was shipped last Monday. Should be in here by now. Just a minute, I'll call the freight station and check on that for you.

(Picks up phone)
Hello, freight agent? Have you got a car in from Dundee Mills for Red Dog Feed Company?

(Pauses for answer —— then turns to Dealer)
Why, the agent says the car came in last night and he forgot to call you. Say, Tom, how's business going for you these last couple of weeks? Moving much feed?

DEALER: No! Just doing average. Why, last week, I only sold a carload. If business stays like this, you know what I might have to do? I'll have to go out and do a day of resale sometime. It's that bad, Phil.

PHIL QUOTA: We'll be glad to work with you, Tom. Anything to boost your sales again — and say, that reminds me — I've just checked my records and you haven't sold much concentrate. What's wrong?

DEALER: Aw! I don't think concentrate sells around here. My boys aren't interested in selling it either.

PHIL QUOTA: Do you remember the 1-2-3 Selling Color Film I showed you about a month ago? Let's make a date for a night meeting and go over that with the boys again.

DEALER: Aw! I haven't got time, Phil. Too many evenings taken up already. No sale, Phil, no sale.

PHIL QUOTA: That's right, Tom, no sales until your boys start putting in extra time to learn how to sell and do a better job for your business.

DEALER: (looking down at floor thoughtfully) Well, I guess you're right, Phil. Next Tuesday evening seems as good a time as any.

(Film is shown and at its conclusion ———)

PHIL QUOTA: Thanks, Tom — and thanks to all of you boys for giving your time to come here tonight for more know-how on 1-2-3 Selling. I'm sure all of you are interested in making the most of your job in the feed business, or you wouldn't be here tonight. The surest way to build your job — whether it's mixing feed or driving the truck or keeping the books — is to be able to improve sales for your employer. Means more dollars in your pocket.

Questions:
1. What are the important factors in this case?
2. Did Phil Quota deal adequately with the situation?
3. How would you have dealt with it in the light of your study of this chapter?

Chapter Fifteen

Successful Suggestion Selling

'SUGGESTION DEFINED

Suggestion is a process of responding directly to a thought stimulus without the intervening thought processes which normally would occur. Salesmen interpret this definition to mean "hint, insinuate, imply, or indirectly insert into the prospective buyer's mind an uncritically accepted idea having no proof or evidence of reliability."

For a salesman, the chief difference between a reliable fact and a suggestion is that the former appeals to an individual's logic and reasoning, while the latter appeals to his emotions. In many cases, the individual's mind does not respond readily and easily to logic and reasoning even when it is overwhelmed with proof, pressure and push. Actually, too much *proof* causes many prospective buyers to become suspicious and to erect a mental and emotional barrier against the marketeer's claims. Therefore, *suggestion selling* is very effective because it makes no claims and thereby tends to disarm any suspicions and safeguards which the buyer's past experience may have caused him to retain.

THE POWER OF SUGGESTION

The following episode illustrates the power of suggestion: A professor displayed before his class an important-looking piece of apparatus, and told them that, when he opened a valve, a peculiar-smelling gas would pour into the room. He wished to see how long it would take each student, as soon as he detected it, to raise his hand. The professor then opened the valve. Hands in the front row began to go up, then those in the next row, and soon nearly all hands in the room had been raised. Then he explained to the class that there had been no gas and no odor.

The chances are that the students who were fooled by the professor would be suspicious of any later experiments he might conduct. Whether their future reactions were associated with pleasure, pain, frustration, fear, suspicion or any other attribute, would not matter, however. Their reactions under other circumstances and with other individuals would be quite different, depending on the power of new suggestions and the apperceptive base of the individuals involved. This is explained by the conditioned reflex activity.

CONDITIONED REFLEX

There is nothing mysterious about suggestion — nothing that cannot be explained by the conditioned reflex theory.

245

For example, if a child is badly frightened by a barking dog, he thereafter shows fear at the very sight of a dog. This new connection in the child's nervous system is called a conditioned reflex. Pavlov, in his classic experiments with dogs as subjects, tried to separate the conditioned reflex from all other reactions he observed under laboratory conditions. From these experiments, indoctrination and orientation procedures have been developed — particularly the brainwashing techniques employed during recent years by the Russians and Chinese.

Many professional purchasers of industrial items have learned to condition their own reflexes. Because some salesmen have deceived them, these men have learned *not* to respond to statements about a proposition's merits until they have first investigated the product for themselves.

The story of the old army veteran walking down the street with his arms full of bundles illustrates the importance of conditioned reflexes. When someone jokingly called "Attention!" he immediately dropped the bundles and assumed the proper military posture. He had responded to a stimulus. Suggestion selling has the same effect.

Suggested Response

There are marketing people who make claims about their propositions and offer little or no reliable proof or evidence of value. This does not mean that claims are of no value in selling critical thinkers, because they are effective with them, too, when suggestion is used as part of the claims. Everybody is influenced by the emotions aroused by suggestion. However, suggestion is much more effective when the prospect is a weak reasoner who wants to feel that he is not buying on impulse or on insufficient grounds. For example:

SALESMAN: The leader in any field cannot afford to produce anything but the best. We are the leader in our field and have a reputation to maintain. Therefore, you can be certain that our products are superior and that you will benefit by buying them.

Notice that the first sentence in this claim is one that is considered true by the prospective customer. Most suggestion selling begins with an assertion to which the prospective client agrees. The tendency is then for his mind to travel with the salesman without resistance to the desired conclusion.

Other examples of employing suggestion to short-cut critical reasoning are revealed in the following statements made by many marketing men:

A manufacturer cannot grow unless he has satisfied dealers. Our Company has grown every year since it was organized. Therefore, you may be confident that you will be absolutely satisfied if you join our ranks.

Everyone knows that people don't continue buying a branded article year after year in greater quantities unless that article is giving satisfaction. XYZ is selling better than ever before, therefore it is bound to give you satisfaction.

"The cheapest is the most expensive" is a common expression which could cause the buyer to challenge a reliable fact, start an argument and induce him to think critically. It is so much simpler to by-pass logic and reasoning with a suggestion such as, "You, no doubt, have often found it to be true that the cheapest item is often the most expensive."

"Ten or twelve tons should handle your requirements," is much more suggestive than the blunt statement, "You should have twelve tons to carry you."

"You want economy and low gas bills don't you, Mr. Jones? You save on these with a compact car." This, too, is much more suggestive than the flat statement, "You save money with a compact car."

Such suggestions have almost universal appeal, since they cause a positive response without mental blocks to hinder them. Universal appeals may be considered as necessary in a marketing man's repertoire as hammers and saws in a carpenter's kit.

The following caution at this point may serve a good purpose: Suggestion words should not be confused with such hackneyed generalities as best, finest, largest, safest and similar adjectives. Nor should they be confused with the half-truths implied in such superlatives as stunning, tremendous, gorgeous, fantastic, breathtaking, spectacular and other exaggerations.

PERSONALITY AND SUGGESTION

The buyer's personality and the seller's suggestion stimulus will largely determine whether the seller's remarks are accepted. The seller must be respected by the buyer, and for this reason suggestion is most successfully practiced by a person of mature years, because people will much more readily believe and trust the ethics of such a person. Suggestability is sometimes said to be "the emulation of ideas and attitudes." Buyers, therefore, are prone to think as the seller thinks, but usually only when he regards the latter with favor.

Even unsupported statements and claims are effective if the prospective buyer looks up to the seller. When the salesman's voice rings with sincerity and conviction, when his presentation is sprinkled with similes and metaphors, when he reveals confidence and enthusiasm, the buyer will usually feel that reliable proof is unnecessary. In fact, unsupported statements are even used at times with professional purchasers when the seller can suggest buying action through his personality.

Situations vary in their suggestive power, and persons vary in their suggestibility. Some suggestions will succeed with nearly everyone; others will get the suggested response from only the most suggestible and the remainder will be critical, resistant and scornful at the unsuccessful attempt to fool and deceive them.

Suggestible Conditions

Among conditions that render most persons more suggestible than usual are alcoholic intoxication, fatigue, monotonous and rhythmical stimuli and a submissive attitude toward the source of suggestion. The last three conditions offer an explanation for why youths and immature adults like Elvis Presley, the Beatles and pop music.

Submissive attitude toward the source of the suggestion deserves an explanation. Both men and women fall into this category, but there are more submissive women than men. Women lack product knowledge and are therefore forced to submit to sales presentations. It is a rare woman, for example, who understands the mechanical construction of refrigerators, automobiles, washing machines or power lawn mowers. Women probably know comparatively little about shelter items, and even less about certain economic principles such as finance. Therefore, since the intrinsic merits of these and many other items, are very difficult for women to logically evaluate, they base the bulk of their purchasing on emotion, imagination, rationalization and suggestions from the marketing men.

THE CRITICAL BUYER AND SUGGESTIBILITY

A salesperson who uses only generalities, similes, metaphors and claims without proof arouses suspicion in the mind of the analytical buyer. Imagine the intelligent, reasoning individual who goes to an automobile show room with the intent of buying a new car. After waiting several minutes for a salesman to greet him, one of them finally appeared and said, "Yes, Sir! Good car. She's a dandy, and I can give you a good price." The salesman forgot to mention benefits, hidden values, status symbol.

The car buyer asked him the size of the tires, and he had to kneel and read the figures before he could answer. He also failed to answer practically all the buyer's questions about the product he was selling.

Under the circumstances the prospective buyer could only question everything the salesman said and did. After this performance, even the most complete proof of value and the finest kind of suggestions would have failed to convince the prospective buyer.

SUGGESTIBILITY
OF QUESTIONS

Successful salespeople often use questions to suggest ideas in an indirect way. For example, they might say, "How would you like to start saving that much money each month with this product?" Or, "What color shoes do you think would look best with your new suit?" The less expert salesmen would say, "You're losing money," or "You need new shoes." These two blunt statements of fact would not arouse the desire to buy in anyone.

Questions that can be answered "yes" or "no" are not effective for suggesting ideas. They are called "closed-end" questions because, when they are answered, the topic is closed. The alert marketing man uses open-end questions to keep the prospect thinking uncritically. If the salesman had asked, "Do you want brown shoes?" he would have asked a closed-end question, and a "no" answer would have ended the transaction. On the other hand, an open-end question would have kept the prospect talking, stimulated his desire and avoided the possibility of his asking critical questions and requesting explanations.

Questions can also be used in other ways to suggest many things. The following examples illustrate how questions may be used to suggest the desired response.

To suggest friendly attitude and common interests to a prospective buyer:	You were in business with your brother for a few years, weren't you?
To suggest a person who is a satisfied user of the seller's product or service:	You know Bill Brown, the owner of Bill's Market, don't you? He's a good manager, isn't he?
To suggest the prospect's response to the seller's reply to an objection:	When you evaluate the savings this product offers, as well as the service, the price is relatively unimportant, don't you agree?
To use a "trial close" suggestion to buy:	Mr. Brown, you seem to approve of everything about this model. When would you like to have it delivered, this week, or would next week be soon enough?

To suggest that quality is more important than price:	But you realize, do you not, Mrs. Brown, that we carry only quality merchandise?
To build customer confidence:	Mrs. Jones, I'm glad you had enough confidence in our store to come in to see us. I just want to ask you one question. Did the other item have three coats of varnish?

Here are other questions which carry suggestions:

Isn't that a beautifully constructed piece of machinery?
Doesn't that sound interesting?
Does this check with your experience, Mr. Brown?
That is what you want, isn't it?
How does that look to you?
We are agreed on that, right?
How does that strike you?
Isn't that just good common sense?
You have had that experience, have you not?

SUGGESTIBILITY OF SIMILES AND METAPHORS

Similes and metaphors are vivid forms of imaginative comparison that arouse interest and furnish a certain amount of convincing evidence because the prospective buyer easily understands and believes them.

The simile is a figure of speech, introduced by "like" or "as," comparing two unlike objects. Note how the following examples of similes through their suggestiveness, offer a certain kind of proof:

This cloth will wear like iron:
. . . as hot as a two dollar pistol on the Fourth of July.
This washer is as noiseless as a church mouse.
These mutual funds are as sound as a dollar.
This motor is as quiet as a gentle summer breeze.
. . . as silent as a burning match.
. . . as solid as concrete.
. . . as soft as a rose petal.

The metaphor, in contrast, identifies one object with another and ascribes to one the qualities of the other without the use of "like" or "as." Samples of metaphors which possess rather high suggestibility and offer proof and evidence follow:

These brakes are the guardian of your safety.
This tire is a brute for punishment.
This refrigerator is a penny-pincher on electricity.
This life insurance policy is the security of your future.
This safety belt is your assurance of safety.
This lamp will add a golden glow in your home.
The interior of this car exudes a feeling of luxury and prestige.

EFFECTIVE WORD CHOICE

As stated in Chapter V, words are one of the vehicles for transmitting ideas from one mind to another. If the word-vehicle is efficient, it quickly transmits ideas from the salesman's mind to the customer's. If it is an old and worn-out word-vehicle, it breaks down and fails to convey the desired ideas. Actually, ineffective words are the reverse of suggestive, since they detract from the value of what is being said.

Since words are part of the marketing-man's tools, they should be carefully selected and properly used in order to interest, offer proof and convince the prospect through suggestion, with a minimum of effort. Shopworn words should be avoided. For example:

In a ladies' apparel store, a saleswoman used the word "smart" thirteen times. "Smart" suggests and proves nothing. And the dictionary reveals that there are many equivalent words — lovely, clever, attractive, piquant, becoming, desirable, unusual, delightful, stylish, fashionable, distinctive.

The salesperson can find effective substitutes for many shopworn words. Instead of the word "cheap," 'for example, the salesperson can use inexpensive, moderately priced, good value, reasonably priced or excellent value. Instead of referring to a ladies purse as "nice," which is an old and uninteresting expression, he could choose stronger suggestive adjectives, like attractive, pleasing, desirable, dainty, stylish and chic. Instead of saying that an automobile "sure has the looks," the professional salesperson will suggest, convince and prove more if he says, "note the sheer, sweeping, greyhound lines, the French style, the distinction, grace and charm of the interior."

It is evident that professional salesmen analyze the features of their propositions and then select words which will effectively suggest hidden values, freshness and exclusive qualities to the prospect's mind, and transmit them in an interesting, convincing manner.

SLOGANS

Slogans are short messages designed to be frequently repeated word for word. Slogans have high suggestibility and can be used in toto or adjusted to suit the salesman's personality and the situation. The following represent some of the best-known slogans. Note their high suggestibility.

You can be sure . . . if it's Westinghouse.

Cleans your breath while it cleans your teeth.
No brush, no lather, no rub in.
Reach for a treat, not a treatment.
Ask the man who owns one.
When it rains, it pours.
A woman never forgets the man who remembers.
The pause that refreshes.
The world's most honored watch.
You won't get tomorrow's jobs with yesterday's skills.
Save the surface and you save all.
Get a good education.
Avoid five o'clock shadow, use Gem.
Biblical: "The wicked flee when no man pursueth, but the righteous are as bold as a lion."
Folklore: "A stitch in time saves nine." "Marry in haste, repent at leisure." "It's a long lane that has no turning."

RATIONALIZATION

Rationalization is a plausible explanation that a person gives to himself or to others to account for his own beliefs or behavior, though these may be based on motives not apparent to the rationalizer. The salesman knows, then, that prospective buyers may pretend to act for rational and creditable motives, but do not analyze their true motives. When rationalizing, the prospect acts on the basis of wish or habit, but explains his activity in logical, reasonable terms.

Quite often people who reason about their purchases want things because of a certain urge or desire, but they do not act because their critical minds fail to find a logical reason for purchasing. When that occurs, the marketing man may want to use suggestion to help the buyer rationalize. He does this by presenting a logical reason for buying which will satisfy the reasoning part of the buyer's mind. For example:

A person may buy an expensive automobile to gratify his pride, but explains his act by saying that the impression of prosperity that it creates helps his business.

A person may want to take a trip for the pure pleasure it affords him and his family, but he justifies the expenditure on the ground that it will benefit his health.

Florida Chamber of Commerce uses this effective headline appeal: "You need a rest." The short reason-why appeal about "rest" is followed by numerous pleasure appeals which are the real basic reasons for making the trip.

Practical Examples of Rationalization

How does suggesting by rationalization apply to individual salespeople? Suppose that, by appealing to the buyer's pride, a salesperson had developed a situation where the buyer would like to do business with him. The buyer likes the salesperson and believes that his future business relations with him will be enjoyable; he is friendly, sociable and respectful. Yet his logical, reasoning mind warns against making a decision on the basis the salesman presents. The salesperson would have to satisfy his critical mind by offering him proof of benefits showing conclusively that his products are superior and why it would be to his advantage to buy them instead of similar competing products. His logical, reasoning mind now satisfied, he would approve the order. Nevertheless, the primary reason for the purchase would be the prospect's desire to do business with the salesperson because he likes him, and he likes him because the salesman has appealed to his pride.

Other examples of rationalization may be found in a great many advertisements — particularly in the slogans used. For example, a well-known insurance company makes the blunt, positive suggestion that it "has the strength of Gibraltar." Many people are convinced by the bold-ness of this suggestion and seek no proof or evidence in the form of a certified financial statement or other facts which appeal to logic or reasoning. Using the same method, a securities salesman says, "Why work hard all your life? Make your money work for you." How many people buy stocks every year because of the assurance with which a salesman makes this kind of rationalization?

Some stores sell a limited number of prominent brands of merchandise at lower prices than their competitors. The subtle but positive suggestion is thereby made that all their merchandise must be lower priced, which may be far from the truth, but the prospective customer is nevertheless given a good start toward rationalizing. The same situation is created and the same rationalization starts when a store paints DEEP DISCOUNTS on its building or repeats the words in advertising. Without a semblance of logic or reasoning, this claim causes the typical retail buyer to rationalize himself into believing that he will save money. Actually, he rarely does.

A radio salesman suggests repeatedly and effectively throughout his sales talk, "It's the tone quality you want." An automobile salesman repeats the suggestion, "Supreme comfort and safety costs no more." A real-estate salesman obtains results with the suggestion, "What good is life if you don't live?"

People also rationalize from what they have repeatedly heard suggested to them through advertising, from associates, from those whom they believe to be recognized authorities, as well as from marketing people. For example, "the flavor of Spearmint gum lasts"; "buy now and save"; "Chesterfields satisfy"; "Ivory soap · is 99-44/100 percent pure"; "This is imported and, therefore, has a certain rare quality." These suggested rationalizations may or may not be true. However, prospective buyers accept them as truths because of repetition, because people want to believe, because most people do not want to employ logic or reasoning before they commit themselves.

POWER POINTS

This chapter has emphasized that — under ordinary circumstances — additional statements of facts, even when presented logically and reasonably and accompanied by adequate proof, are ordinarily not enough to convince a prospect. The additional ingredient of suggestion selling is needed to complete the "recipe."

The power of suggestion in selling is frequently underestimated while the power of reason and logic is often overestimated. When salesmen recognize that, through suggestion, they can deflect much critical thinking as well as awaken emotional responses, they acquire a clearer concept of the possibilities of this approach. The salesman whose product or service is merely superior does not sell as much as he could if he used more suggestion.

Suggestion selling as a method may be carried to an extreme, used where logic or thought should be employed. Nevertheless, a suggestion may be the most effective means to induce action and to remove obstructions at the conclusion of a sales presentation.

Suggestion should seldom be used to the complete exclusion of reason, just as reason should probably never be used without suggestion. Ordinarily, however, the suggestion selling method could be used by many more marketing men.

DISCUSSION QUESTIONS AND PROBLEMS

1. Define, or explain the meaning of suggestion as it is used in personal salesmanship.
2. Why is suggestion selling said to be extremely effective?
3. How does the suggestion episode about the professor and his experiment apply to a personal selling situation?
4. Give a practical example of an actual selling situation and show how the conditioned reflex enters into it.
5. Explain the principle or principles of personality and apply to suggestion selling.
6. How do you account for the fact that women are more submissive than men? What effect does their submissiveness have on their buying motivations, habits and suggestibility?
7. Explain in detail the impact of suggestion selling on the critical buyer. How does he respond? How does the methodology employed with the critical buyer differ from that used with ordinary prospects?
8. Explain how questions may be used to suggest ideas and evoke appropriate responses. Make a list of questions which you would use to sell a product of your choice.
9. Assemble a list of descriptive words that would be effective in selling. Opposite each word write equivalent words which you believe would be more effective for suggesting values and advantages to a prospect.
10. What is meant by rationalization? Give several examples of how it is used by marketing men to influence people to buy.
11. Describe how you would use suggestion selling with repeat customers in the following situations. Explain exactly why you would use them.

    a. Suggestion in the greeting.

    b. Suggesting better quality.
    c. Suggesting related items.
    d. Suggesting alternate items.

12. Analyze and then explain this statement: "Suggestion selling is really the big yell with a soft voice."
13. Do you believe that suggestion selling may take unfair advantage of buyers? Why? Can suggestion selling be carried to an extreme? Why? Could suggestion selling be practiced by more salesmen? How?

PHENOMENOLOGICAL PROJECTS

A Typical Sale (Role)

The following sale is typical for a retail salesperson. It is presented in dialogue form so that you may see and analyze each step of an excellent retail selling procedure — including suggestion selling.

The salesperson notices a customer examining a feature end display of a 32-piece dinner set and approaches the customer saying, "Good morning. That is one of our featured Cambridge dinnerware patterns."

Question:

1. What kind of suggestion selling is used in the following narrative?

CUSTOMER: It really is beautiful, but I'm afraid it is too expensive for me.

SALESPERSON: Maybe not. You see, this dinnerware comes directly to us from the manufacturer, eliminating the dealer and jobber profits. Furthermore, all expensive advertising has been eliminated; therefore, we are in a position to save you from 25 to 40 percent on better dinnerware.

CUSTOMER: I often wondered how you could sell for less. I was always under the impression that your merchandise was of cheaper quality.

SALESPERSON: All of our dinnerware is of first quality. We only accept the best. To insure this high standard, our dinnerware must pass rigid inspections. Experts made sure that all pieces are shaped evenly without chips, glazed smoothly and evenly, and that patterns are uniform in both color and application.

CUSTOMER: That certainly sounds good, but tell me, is this china, or . . . how can I tell the difference?

SALESPERSON: This is "Cambridge" — a special semi-porcelain ware, 25 percent lighter in weight than ordinary semi-porcelain.

CUSTOMER: But it looks so fragile — I'd be afraid to use it.

SALESPERSON: Yes, it does look fragile, and that is one feature that makes it so appealing. However, it is actually stronger and more resistant to chipping and cracking than similar dinnerware. Cambridge contains tremolite, a mineral ingredient which gives it the lightness and strength usually associated only with expensive china.

Question:

2. What kind of suggestion selling is used in the following narration?

CUSTOMER: I really didn't know there was so much difference in dinnerware. You see, I'm planning to be married shortly and thought I'd look around today.

SALESPERSON: You are certainly more than welcome to look around in my department, but I do believe you have your heart set on this Cambridge dinnerware. Will you be using these dishes for company or were you planning to use them everyday, too?

CUSTOMER: Well, quite frankly, I'm pretty sure I am getting a luncheon set and one of those bright-colored sets as gifts. I intended to use those for everyday and buy a new set for my best dishes.

SALESPERSON: Since these are mostly for best, you'll want something nice — something you would be proud to use when entertaining your friends. (Here the salesperson goes into a little more detail about pattern and styling.)

CUSTOMER: Yes, I'm sure this is the pattern I want.

Question:

3. What kind of suggestion selling is being used in the following?

SALESPERSON: Of course, you'll want the 95-piece set with complete service of twelve.

CUSTOMER: Oh, I am sure I'd not be having more than eight guests at one time. I think the fifty-three piece set that serves eight will be all right.

SALESPERSON: The larger set is complete, including two handled soup cups and square plates. You may not use the entire service for twelve, but the extra pieces are good reserve stock — if you break a piece you'll have the replacement on hand. Considering how much more you get for your money, don't you think you should take the larger set?

CUSTOMER: I would want complete service — but I hadn't intended to spend so much for dishes. In fact, I don't have that much with me.

SALESPERSON: Perhaps you would like to use our budget payment plan. You could get the whole set now and pay for it a little at a time. You will probably want glassware too.

CUSTOMER: Well, I could do that. There are a lot of things I will need and it would be easier than paying for all of them at once.

SALESPERSON: Let me show you some of the goblets we just received. They would really look good with your dinnerware. (The salesperson brings a goblet, a sherbet, and a plate to match and arranges a single place, adding a 24 piece set of glassware to the 95-piece dinnerware order.)

Question:

4. What kind of suggestion selling is used below?

SALESPERSON: (After closing the sale) Please come in again. I will be only too glad to help you select the kitchen utensils that you will need.

CUSTOMER: Thank you, you've been very nice. I certainly will come to you for whatever I need.

SALESPERSON: You might walk through our furniture and drapery department — we have some beautiful things there, too. I am sure you will find whatever you need at our store, and I know you will be well pleased with the merchandise.

Ruby Shoe Company (Role)

A Ruby Shoe Company man checked into his hotel, arranged his samples in a showroom, and then went to Main Street to call on dealers to whom he had sold shoes on his previous visit. The first dealer on whom he called was busy, and the salesman had to wait for about thirty minutes. Finally, however, the dealer's business slowed down long enough for the salesman to invite him over to the hotel to look over the shoes he had on display.

DEALER: I really can't make it today. We're terribly busy and I'm short two shoe-fitters. I just don't see how I can leave even for a few minutes.

SALESMAN: But you should see my line, the best buys I've had for years.

DEALER: Well . . . bring your samples over here and I'll look them over. 'Bye for the moment — I've got two customers over there waiting for me.

SALESMAN: But for heaven's sake, man, you can't expect me to bring all that merchandise over here . . . trunks full of samples . . . can't you drop over after closing up?

DEALER: No, not today or tonight. I'm slated for a town meeting right after closing. The only way I could see them would be here on the selling floor, and even then it would have to be between customers. This is my busy season, you know.

SALESMAN: Sure, it's my busy season, too. I'm leaving town tomorrow, and you don't get a chance to see merchandise such as mine very often. I just can't bring all those shoes over here. If you want to buy right, you'll have to come over to the hotel.

DEALER: I told you once I couldn't come. (Getting hot under the collar.) And don't bother me about it any more. Goodby, I've got to take care of my customers.

SALESMAN: Well . . . it's your loss if you don't want to see the best merchandise that's come to this town for months.

Questions:

1. In the light of what you have learned about suggestion selling, what do you think of the behavior of this salesperson? His attitude? His perception? His sympathy?

2. How would you have handled this buyer? Why?

Chapter Sixteen

Creative Retail Selling

PRESENTING AND DEMONSTRATING

Much of a retail salesperson's success will depend on how he starts his presentation of the merchandise. In this respect, there are three broad rules to observe: *Cleanliness, promptness* and *showmanship*.

Cleanliness — This means not only personal cleanliness, but also a neat counter, neat stock and attractive displays.

Promptness — Every customer should be approached and greeted promptly as soon as she enters a store or a department. Nothing irritates a prospective customer more than to be ignored while the salespeople engage in conversation, housekeeping or bookwork.

Showmanship — This begins with a greeting which can range from "Good Morning, Mrs. Doe," to "May I help you?" or even to a pointed reference to a product that has caught the customer's eye.

After the greeting, the salesperson shows the merchandise. For example, if the salesperson happens to be selling furniture, he can sound out the customer by saying something like, "May I show you some of our new easy chairs?" If the customer does not want easy chairs, she will usually tell the salesperson why she came in. The main idea is to start the

customer talking and to get some indication of what she came in for.

If she says, "Just looking," the salesperson can say, "Fine, we are glad to have people look. I will be glad to answer any questions." The customer's attention may also be directed to a nearby display or item of merchandise.

The salesperson may ask the customer if she is interested in fine chairs and receive only a laconic 'chairs' or 'tables,' in reply. More questions will then be necessary to pin down the type of chairs or tables that the customer wants. However, the salesperson should not ask bluntly, "What kind of chairs?" Instead, he should ask, "Something for your living room?" If this draws a "yes" reply, he can then find out whether the customer wants a pull-up chair, a lounge chair, a rocker or an occasional chair.

As soon as the customer indicates the type of merchandise she wants, she should be led directly to it. The merchandise which the salesperson believes the customer may like should then be selected and the sales presentation started.

Sighting Shots

The first merchandise shown by the salesperson is usually in the nature of a "sighting shot." Few customers will have decided in advance exactly what they want. They may know only how much they can spend, but be open minded on style, design, color and utility. Or color or style may be the determining factor, and price a lesser consideration.

In any case, the salesperson will have to find out what is in the customer's mind. Probably the easiest way for the salesperson to do this is to pick one piece of merchandise he thinks the customer may want and then begin his sales talk. The salesperson can soon tell what is uppermost in the customer's mind from the customer's questions and reactions to his presentation. If no interest is shown in a particular item, it is generally advisable for the salesperson to direct the customer's attention to another piece of merchandise.

The Starting Price

Suppose a customer wants merchandise that comes in several price ranges. Which should be shown first? The safest plan is to show merchandise in the middle-price range. The salesperson can then work up or down the price scale according to the customer's preference and ability to pay.

If the salesperson begins with his lowest-priced merchandise, he may lose the chance of selling better merchandise at a higher price. It is very difficult to switch a customer from the lowest price to the very highest price. Also, a sensitive customer may be offended if the salesperson immediately shows her the lowest-priced merchandise he has in stock. Finally, the difference in price between the lowest- and the highest-priced merchandise may create an artificial barrier to a successful sale: when the spread in price is too great, some customers will walk out.

On the other hand, if the salesperson begins with his most expensive goods, he may discourage the customer, especially if the goods are out of her price range,

and lose the sale. Or he may make his "economy" line appear cheap in comparison, forcing the customer to go elsewhere.

Beginning with goods in the middle-price bracket is usually the most sensible plan. If the customer indicates an interest in something better, the salesperson can easily switch to higher-priced goods. If something less expensive is wanted, the customer will not be so hesitant about going to the next lower-price range as he would be in jumping from the highest to the lowest.

Consequently, if it develops that the customer wants something definite in color or style, it is easier to satisfy her if the salesperson can offer something that costs a few dollars more or less than the original price the salesman suggested.

THE RETAIL SALES TALK

Many businesses, such as house-to-house selling concerns, use "canned" sales talks that salesmen are required to memorize. Because a retail salesperson may sell many varied items, a canned talk may not work for him. Like the outside salesman, the retail salesperson must apply selling techniques to suit the customer and the merchandise.

It usually pays the retail salesperson, however, to develop a general pattern which can be adapted to fit the individual sale. In this way, he is sure of covering his entire selling presentation.

A good retail salesperson should make it a rule to cover all his sales points in a way that represents the viewpoint of the customer. The following sales points cover the major points of view of the customer, even though motives for buying may vary with the merchandise.

Comfort and Enjoyment — Because many items are bought chiefly for this reason, the salesperson may want to concentrate on this point if it applies to his merchandise.

Appearance — This motive is very important to the customer who is proud of her personal appearance or her home, and should be employed in the sales presentation when applicable.

Convenience — This is an important motive for many women customers and should therefore be stressed when selling merchandise such as furniture, appliances, hardware and similar items.

Quality — The salesperson may also talk about features such as strength and durability which provide benefits. Since this is an important factor with careful buyers, the salesperson should stress the manufacturer's reputation, the store's guarantee, and the wearing qualities, appearance, style and other attributes of the item. Most better grade merchandise is sold on the basis of quality.

Price — This should not be discussed until the last, unless the customer lets the salesperson know at the beginning that the price is of utmost importance. The customer's desire for the goods should be developed and if the goods are wanted badly enough, price usually is a secondary consideration. It should be recalled that price is justified only on the basis of quality. Therefore, the salesperson must be ready to show where the value lies. If the customer demands to know the price, the salesperson should tell him and not evade the issue. If she thinks the price is too high, the salesperson can say, "Yes, but let me show you why it is worth it." The customer's attention can also be directed to a lower-priced item.

A customer should be given all of the facts available on a product, with emphasis on its benefits. Usually, one of the above points will appeal to her. As soon as the salesperson notes which benefits seem to impress the customer most, he should concentrate on those particular benefits. It requires only one or two benefits of a product to obtain a favorable buying decision.

SHOWING AND DEMONSTRATING

Very few important items are sold by sight and words alone. In nine cases out of ten, showing and demonstrating influence the customer to buy. A customer will be induced to buy costume jewelry if the jewelry is demonstrated or if she tries it on and sees how much it improves her appearance. She is persuaded to buy an easy chair because it is comfortable when she sits in it. She is inclined to buy an appliance after she tries it out.

No matter what the product is it can be sold more easily when it is shown or demonstrated. A man should not only be told that he would look good in a blue suit but also that he should try it on and find out for himself. A customer should not only be told that the cutlery is handy to have in the kitchen but she should be encouraged to try it out. End tables should be placed next to sofas or chairs so that the customer can see how they would look in her home.

How to Demonstrate and Tell

While the salesperson is talking, he should let the customer share in the demonstration of a product. This will provide an opportunity for injecting many questions that bring a "yes" answer and build up to a decision to buy. Also, the customer gets a feeling of ownership from trying out the items. She sees the benefits that the merchandise will bring her.

Whenever a salesperson talks about his merchandise, he should handle it at the same time. The customer should also be encouraged to touch, feel, smell or try on the merchandise. For example, if the item has a pleasant odor, like soap or perfume, the salesperson should persuade the customer to smell it. The salesman should always handle his merchandise as appreciatively and carefully as a jeweler handles a rare stone or a high-priced watch.

When the retail salesperson is showing or demonstrating an item, he should stand behind or beside the product and talk across it. The customer can then see him and the merchandise at the same time. Also, the salesperson can see the customer's reactions to each sales point that he has proffered.

SUGGESTION SELLING

The salesperson often gains command of the sale from the start by using suggestion selling in a greeting. He may say to an approaching customer, "Good morning, this is an unusual item. You'll be interested in seeing how it works. Would you like to examine it?" In this way he can arouse the customer's interest in using the merchandise. This technique is always productive when the salesperson suggests that the customer examine the article or when he suggests that the customer watch the operation of a mechanical item. Suggestions in a greeting help make sales. Good salespeople use them constantly.

Trading-Up Through Suggestion

Customers often ask to see a low-priced item when what they really want is one of very good quality. They do this because they fear that the higher price for a quality product will be prohibitive.

Trading-up is the answer to that. The alert salesman will show an item from a better selection as soon as possible. When he has aroused the customer's interest, he will point out that the higher-priced item is usually the better buy because of its additional features.

The following example shows how this idea works when stoves are being sold. The customer appears to be interested in the least expensive model.

SALESMAN: You certainly couldn't go wrong on that stove, but I suppose your wife likes to keep her salt and pepper handy when she's cooking. This model over here has its own condiment set and a light that illuminates the entire top. Most of my customers who have bought this type say they wouldn't be without that light for anything.

Another thing, you'll notice there is a better type of regulator on this model. It provides more accurate heat control. With the less expensive kinds your regulator may say 250, for example, but your actual oven heat may vary 10 degrees either way. With the better type, 250 degrees means 250 degrees— right on the head. It means that you won't have to do any experimenting with the oven to find out how to regulate it.

Stoves, of course, are only one kind of merchandise that can be traded-up. Trading-up will work with almost any item.

Suggesting Related Items

Once the big sale has been made, there is usually opportunity to make it even bigger by suggesting other merchandise. Many experienced salesmen can take what started to be a modest sale and, by logical suggestion, triple the amount in just a few minutes. The number of items related to other items is almost unlimited. For example, a can of paint suggests a brush, turpentine, cleaner and varnish remover. Shoes suggest polish and laces. Wallpaper suggests paste or a kit of wallpaper tools. Skirts suggest blouses and jackets. In fact, nearly every item sold in a retail department suggests something else.

Suggestion selling after the close is appreciated by three out of four customers. It is actually a reminder to a customer about some thing she may have forgotten.

Suggesting Alternates

The phrase "suggesting alternates" means to mention a similar item when the exact one the customer asks for is not stocked. The word "alternate" is preferred to "substitute." Too many times retail salespeople are content to say "I'm sorry" when the customer asks them for merchandise they do not have.

But consider these points. The customer is in front of the salesperson and she has expressed a willingness to buy. In fact, she would rather buy from this particular salesperson than spend the time and energy looking elsewhere. Therefore, the alert salesperson will take advantage of the circumstances to interest the customer in something similar to the article she originally requested. For example, the salesperson might say, "I'm sorry: we're all out of that item just now, but here are some new designs that will be very popular this fall. Would you like to look them over? I'm sure you'll see something you'll like."

NARROWING THE CHOICE

When a salesperson offers the customer a large selection from which to choose, he should try to narrow the customer's choice. It is easier for a customer to make a selection between two items than to make a selection from many. The salesperson can eliminate items because of color, style or price, but he should do this without reflecting on the quality of the merchandise that has been eliminated.

Building Up to a Favorable Decision

A salesperson's entire presentation and demonstration is a buildup to have the customer say "yes" when she is asked for the order. One of the most effective ways to do this is to work the customer into a receptive frame of mind. This is done by sprinkling the showing and demonstration with questions which ask for "yes" answers. For example, "This is a beautiful color, is it not, Mrs. Wood?" Or, "This table extends very easily, doesn't it?" Or, you may simply say, "You agree, I see!"

SALES RESISTANCE

The salesperson in a store has to overcome

the same kind of sales resistance that salesmen everywhere encounter. All the methods described in the chapter entitled "Overcoming Common Sales Obstacles" can be used by the retail salesman. But when a customer comes into a store, the salesperson needs to be alert to certain obstacles that salesmen everywhere do not meet in the same form. And the good retail salesperson often turns these objections into a sale.

Excuses

Probably the most common form of resistance is when a customer says, "I am just looking." This is usually an excuse offered to prevent the salesperson from interesting her in his merchandise. But the salesperson can be assured that the customer would not be in his department if she did not have some interest. The best way to meet this type of resistance is by prevention instead of cure. The greeting, "May I help you?" asks for the excuse, "I am just looking." But when something is said about the merchandise in the salesman's opening statement, the customer's response is different.

Price Objections—The best way to handle the retail price objection is by meeting it fairly and squarely. The price may be justified, for example, in terms of service, comfort, convenience or durability. The salesperson who can convince the customer of the basic quality of the merchandise will have less trouble when it is time to talk price.

Another way to overcome price resistance is by talking about the easy payment plan, if the store has one.

CUSTOMER: But we had not planned to spend $398.00 on floor covering.

SALESMAN: That sounds like a lot, I know, but look at it this way. This is well-made, beautiful carpeting. You will be proud to have it in your home, and it will give you years of good service.

Now, on our special plan, you pay us only X dollars down and the rest in small payments every week (or month). You pay for it in a way that doesn't hurt and you have the rug right in your home where you can use it while you are paying for it.

If the store does not have a time-payment plan and the customer has a charge account, it may be possible to arrange for payment over a period of sixty or ninety days, with a portion of the sale price being billed each month.

Taking the "Ice" out of Price. A customer was looking for an item in a furniture store, where she had been a regular patron for several years. She liked the item but finally told the salesman that she would look around before she made up her mind.

She went to another store where she saw what looked like an identical item for 20 percent less. Very much annoyed, she hurried back to the first store and overwhelmed the salesman with these words:

CUSTOMER: I am astonished that a store of your reputation would attempt to rob customers who have faithfully purchased from you for years.

SALESMAN: Mrs. Jones, I am glad you had enough confidence in our store to come back and see us. I just want to ask you one question. Did the other item have three coats of varnish?

CUSTOMER (with a certain degree of indecision): I don't know about that . . .

SALESMAN: Ours has. Let me show you, and also some other important features.

The customer finally bought the item, and neither the salesman nor the customer knew whether or not the furniture at the rival store had three coats of varnish— and neither really cared.

This salesman had sense enough to

build up the value of his merchandise in the customer's mind, rather than to attempt to sell on "price" alone. The inefficient salesman always sells on price in the hope of increasing his volume, while the intelligent salesman attempts to increase the customer's appreciation of his merchandise until the customer's appraisal of its value equals or exceeds the price.

This example illustrates how the question method of closing can be used effectively to put the customer on the defensive as well as how to take the "ice" out of price.

RETAIL CUSTOMER BEHAVIOR

If a salesperson wishes to be technical, he can list almost as many kinds of sales resistance caused by customer behavior as there are customers. There is no foolproof way of dealing with the different kinds of resistance. Retail customers can be identified, however, by certain outstanding behavioral traits that can be used as guides by the retail salesperson.

The Looker — The looker is a common type of retail prospect. Perhaps she came into the store to escape from the rain, or because the store's displays are attractive or because she likes to look around. But she should not be dismissed casually. She is a potential buyer, if not an immediate buyer. She will continue to remember the merchandise that caught her attention and come back later when she needs it. Or she will tell friends that she saw "a darling hat" at Blank's and maybe the friend will buy it. The salesperson should try to sell her something, but if she is not interested she should be treated courteously and perhaps invited to browse around.

The Shopper — This type of customer usually knows what she wants and desires to make the best possible selection. Because the purchase is important to her, she will shop in two or three stores before making up her mind. She will then buy from the store she likes best, or from the one that has the most suitable merchandise.

This customer merits a salesperson's most careful attention. She is the one who tests salesmanship skills because a salesperson in one store will have to do a better job of selling than the salesperson in the store down the street to get her business. She may not buy today—but if she is sold on the merchandise, she will return.

The Bargain Hunter — Salespeople see these price-minded customers whenever a store has an advertised special, a season sale or a bargain day. She will buy almost anything if it is priced right. She should be sold a special, or if possible, she may be traded-up to a better buy. For this type of buyer, however, price is usually the only consideration and she must be handled accordingly.

The Dubious Customer — Every person who comes in the door represents a potential sale. He should not be classified at first glance by the salesperson as to whether or not it is worth while to wait on him. There is no way of determining a customer's buying power accurately. Many wealthy people dress quietly or even carelessly. Many timid-appearing people have stubborn minds. Sometimes a person who looks like a fugitive from a rag bag will buy expensive merchandise because it represents a good value. The safest plan is to treat everyone as a potential buyer of a four-figure order. It is also wise to recall that many well-dressed customers are poor credit risks.

The Irritating Customer — Often a salesperson will have customers who seem to have "chips on their shoulders." They do not like anything. They may be sarcastic in their comments. They may argue with every point the salesperson raises. They may be hypercritical of the merchandise. They may even be belligerent, overbearing or dictatorial in attitude. But whatever the provocation, the salesperson can never afford to lose his temper.

Most irritating customers are not angry with the salesperson or the store. Something else may have put them in a bad humor and they may try to take it out on the salesperson because he is the nearest at hand. But one of the penalties of serving the public is that one must be tolerant of the customer's moods. Meeting disagreeableness with courtesy and pleasantness can usually clear the atmosphere and often end in a harmonious transaction. Meeting like with like, on the other hand, will make an enemy for the salesperson and a "knocker" for the store. A salesperson cannot afford to risk such a situation.

Instead, the irritable customers should be met with good humor and understanding. They need something or they would not have come in. If the salesperson refuses to be upset by comments or attitudes, he may obtain a sale. And instead of making an enemy, the salesperson may make a friend and a permanent customer.

The Complainer—A customer with grievances, whether real or fancied, is seldom tactful. He may burst into the store airing a complaint in a loud voice and create a lot of damage to the store's prestige. The best way to handle a complainer is—first —to calm the customer. The salesperson should talk in a low voice, be courteous and show a readiness to listen. If necessary, the customer should be eased off the sales floor and into a private office where other customers cannot eavesdrop. Then the salesperson should learn what the trouble is and adjust the matter if it is at all possible. Otherwise, the salesperson should call someone who will be able to make the proper adjustment.

USE OF ORAL TESTIMONY

Most salespeople are familiar with the use of testimonials in newspapers and magazines, and on radio and television. This form of advertising must be very effective in influencing people or large corporations would not spend so much money on it.

Testimonials can also be used to combat retail sales resistance. A casual mention that "Mr. Gotrocks has purchased a television set (a rug, a living room suite or any other product) just like this one" can be the statement that clinches the deal for the salesperson. Most customers have confidence in what Mr. Gotrocks or other well-known, prominent local persons buy and use. Names of a customer's friends and neighbors who have bought similar merchandise from a salesperson may also break down certain types of resistance. A woman, however, may not care to buy a hat or dress like Mrs. Astorbilt's, but she will buy the same type of furniture, car or house in the belief that Mrs. Astorbilt's judgment in buying is sound.

Another type of advertising by testimonial covers style merchandise. Many people will buy style merchandise such as household appliances, wearing apparel and furniture if the salesperson produces proof of its popularity at the moment. "It's very chic and very popular now," is an example of this type of sales talk.

Endorsements of nationally known bureaus, seals of approval and underwriters' laboratory tags on electrical merchandise, as well as other informative labels, are all testimonials of quality that are used by successful salespeople.

SUCCESSFUL CLOSINGS

A decision to buy may start with the buyer's original idea of making a purchase or with the salesperson convincing a customer to buy. Thus, the decision making process could have begun when a salesperson checked his appearance, speech and attitudes before approaching a customer, and continued as the salesperson presented and demonstrated the merchandise, successfully countered sales resistance, won customer confidence and obtained a commitment to buy.

The time a salesperson should attempt to work toward obtaining the commitment to buy can be determined from the buying signals displayed by the customer.

Buying Signals

If the customer has looked at several articles and returns to one which she has already inspected, this usually indicates a genuine interest in the article. It shows that she has compared values, and assured herself that the article is what she wants. This is a buying signal that should not be ignored.

If the customer holds a garment in front of a mirror or tries it on, this action may indicate that she is interested enough to buy. If a customer manipulates an appliance or tries it out, this may also be a buying signal.

When a person asks about the wearing qualities of a dress, whether or not it will shrink or fade, how to clean it, whether it is guaranteed, or whether she may return it, these questions are definite buying signals. They prove that the customer is thinking of the merchandise in terms of her own needs and is probably ready to buy.

When a customer is accompanied by a friend or a relative, the customer will turn to the friend or relative and say, "How do you like this?" The salesperson should listen carefully for a buying signal from the other person's reply. If the reply is favorable, he should ask for the order. If the reply is unfavorable, he should bring out more merchandise and direct his attention to winning the friend's or relative's approval. Although retail salespeople can become very discouraged with friends or relatives who interfere with sales, it is a mistake to disregard them.

When buying signals are not in evidence, the salesperson has to help the customer decide. He probes for buying cues by asking questions; he finds out why the customer hesitates. Then he explains why the purchase will satisfy the customer's motives behind his interest in the merchandise.

Attention-Focusing

The salesperson should concentrate on the items that interest the customer. After the customer has narrowed her choice to a few articles, he should take away the merchandise that does not appeal to her. This focuses the customer's attention on the favored merchandise and helps her reach a decision more quickly. It also allows the salesperson a better opportunity to concentrate his selling points on fewer items. The salesperson must be sure, however, that the items he removes are definitely not wanted by the customer and must employ tact to avoid creating an impression of being impatient or rushing her.

Minor Points

The salesperson leads the customer to make a number of minor decisions that result in a sale. He does this by asking questions and listening to the answers. He tries to obtain "yes" replies from the customer at frequent intervals. For example:

SALESPERSON: First of all, Mr. Black, you want an appliance that will last, don't you?

CUSTOMER: That's right.

SALESPERSON: Then, you want a device that will not require constant attention — something that will work easily for you?

CUSTOMER: That would certainly be an advantage.

SALESPERSON: And on top of that, you want an appliance that has beauty and style, comfort and usefulness.

CUSTOMER: Naturally.

SALESPERSON: Then this is the appliance you want. It's made of the finest-quality chromium-plated steel, and has given hundreds of our customers long and satisfactory wear. Furthermore, it is automatic; you don't need to watch it. You press down this knob, and the appliance does the rest: less waste and easier operation. And notice the design and beautiful shiny appearance. You certainly would enjoy this in your home, wouldn't you?

Obtaining a number of favorable minor decisions goes hand-in-hand with putting the customer in the "yes" frame of mind. For example:

"Do you prefer the large or the small model?"
"Would you prefer the deluxe model or the standard model?"
"When you consider all these features, don't you think this is the model that best suits your needs?"
"The use that you will get from this appliance will save you money in the long run. That is important, isn't it?"

These minor agreements—when taken together — are definite indications of a desire to buy. When the customer has responded favorably to several statements involving a minor decision, it is easier to persuade him to make a major decision to buy.

Summarizing

Agreement to buy may often be obtained by reviewing the main selling points at the end of the presentation. For example: "Now, let's get back over these points, Mrs. Customer. Here's what you get. First . . ."

If agreement is not obtained by this technique, the salesperson can at least determine the customer's objections and then try to overcome them by using new and different appeals. Agreement is often brought about by impressing the customer with the feeling of ownership. For example: "Think of the beauty and comfort that will be obtained from having this furniture in your home. Just watch the family go for this when you bring it home."

When a salesperson is ready to close the sale, he should stop talking, showing and demonstrating. Many sales have been lost because the salesperson simply talked himself out of them. The successful salesperson knows exactly when to stop talking and reach for his sales book. At the same time, he can ask for the order through a direct or double question.

Questions to Close

Following are some of the direct questions which can be used to clinch the sale:

"Which do you prefer?"
"When could we start?"
"Would you prefer to pay cash, or open an account?"
"Shall we deliver it?"
"When would you like to have it delivered?"

The customer may also be induced to buy by the salesperson asking double questions, both favorable to the sale. For example:

"Do you prefer this one or that one?"
"Do you wish to open an account or pay cash?"
"Shall I have it shipped express or parcel post?"
"Do you want one black and one red?"
"Will a dozen be enough?"
"How many do you wish?"

While the closing questions are being asked, the salesperson can assume that the customer has reached a decision and have the salesbook ready and pencil poised to write the customer's name. Here again, tact and judgment must be exercised to avoid the impression of high pressure. For example:

SALESPERSON (writing out order): I'm sure that you get a lot of satisfaction in using this appliance.

The salesperson, using this "assumption method," must be doubly certain that the customer's objections have been removed and that she is convinced of the desirability of the article.

SPECIAL INDUCEMENTS
Price

The salesperson may tell the customer that the article is a special and will not be available later at the same reasonable price. A special discount for quantity purchases may also be offered as a buying stimulus where company policy authorizes it. However, price inducements should be used only where other methods have failed. Special price inducements should be handled with extreme tact to prevent the feeling that high-pressure selling is being used.

Terms and Special Services

The use of terms and special services to help retail decision making are shown in the following example:

SALESPERSON: If you don't wish to make a cash payment at this time, may I suggest that you open an account? I am sure that our credit deaprtment will welcome your order.

SALESPERSON: With this beautiful appliance, you get lifetime service. If you ever get even a little scratch on it, just call us up and we'll have our service man come out to give you free repairs.

Guarantee or Refund Policy

How to use the guarantee or refund policy

to obtain a decision to buy is shown by the following example:

SALESPERSON: Why not let us deliver this desk, Mrs. Snodgrass? After using it a few days, I'm sure that you will come to like it. If I'm wrong, then you can give the factory a ring and we'll come out and pick it up. Your complete purchase price will be refunded.

This method is particularly effective with prospects who cannot make up their minds as to whether the merchandise is of the quality or kind they want. This can be a dangerous method to use, however, since it might encourage the salesman to rely upon the guarantee or the company's refund policy, rather than on his sales ability.

POWER POINTS

When attempting to obtain a decision, the salesperson should not rush the customer. No attempt should be made to obtain a decision before all sales resistance has been overcome. It will always lead to suspicion on the part of the customer. "Rushing the customer" is often said to be high-pressure selling. The decision to buy should be allowed to ripen in the customer's mind in a natural manner.

Salespeople must not stand around with an indifferent look on their faces when decision making time has arrived. A sales talk must not be weakened with words such as "if" and "provided." Successful salespeople assume that the customer will buy and they convey to the customer their confidence in the merchandise. They use a positive approach, saying something like this:

"I know you will enjoy having this, Mrs. Jones, because . . . . When you get this in your home, you will always enjoy its beauty."

Salespeople should avoid just hoping for the sale. For example, they should avoid saying: "I wish you would give this a try, Mrs. Jones," or "I was hoping you would let me give you a demonstration, Mrs. Black."

Customer sales resistance is a natural part of any sale. It is usually the customer's way of obtaining more information, or of reassuring herself about the quality, quantity or price of the merchandise. She may speculate that a color will fade when in reality she wants to be shown or to be reassured that it will not fade.

A customer must never be left in a state of indecision. Customers must be helped in their decision making. Salespeople should not say, "It's up to you, sir"; or "Well, I think all three of these are desirable." If the customer lacks decision, the salesperson should supply reasons that will help the customer reach a decision. For example: "You can't go wrong on either of these, but I feel that this would be more suitable because . . . ."

Salespeople should not review the wrong selling points. Early in the discussion they should discover just what the customer's needs are and then fit their sales presentation to those needs. They should pick out the selling points that answer the customer's needs or those in which the customer has shown a strong interest, and keep stressing them throughout the sale.

It rarely pays to try to force the customer to buy. It is always better in the long run to retain the customer's confidence and goodwill rather than to make an unsatisfactory sale.

Good salespeople do not continue talking about the sale after the customer is ready to buy, because the customer is already sold. The salesperson can, however, talk about the terms and the care of the merchandise or suggest additional merchandise and make other pertinent remarks to tidy up the transaction.

Good salespeople do not show dissatisfaction if the customer does not buy. They let a customer know that they are ready to help her whenever she comes back to them. They hide their disappointment and are courteous. They leave their customers in a pleasant frame of mind. A customer should never have reason to say, "I dislike trading at Blank's because they look so angry if you do not buy." It is good business to say, "It has been a pleasure to show you our merchandise. Come in again, please."

When the customer is ready to buy, the salesperson should stop presenting and demonstrating a product. Many sales have been lost because a salesperson liter-ally talked himself out of them. The experienced salesperson usually senses when the sale can be made and starts reaching for his order pad and pencil while he asks a single or a double question.

There are intangibles in salesmanship which go far deeper than glibness, knowing the right answers, persuasiveness and the technique of asking for the order. These things may be subtle and difficult for many salesmen to apply. They have the magic, however, not only to make the individual grow in sales ability and personal depth but also to make his customer like him, trust him and cling to him.

DISCUSSION QUESTIONS AND PROBLEMS

1. What are the three rules to observe when showing merchandise?
2. Explain what you would *say* and *do* to discover what merchandise is of interest to a customer.
3. Why are questions by the salesperson important at the start of a retail sale?
4. What would you say to place sales *suggestions* in your greeting?
5. Why should a salesperson begin with medium-price goods?
6. What is the purpose of a "sighting shot"?
7. How would you proceed to *trade-up* your merchandise through suggestion?
8. Exactly how would you handle *price* in a retail sale?
9. Why are *hidden values* important? Give several examples of how to *sell hidden values.*
10. Why is it important to *show* and *demonstrate* merchandise?
11. Why should the salesperson get the customer to demonstrate, test or use the product?
12. Select an item which you believe you would like to sell. Then, show how you would present and demonstrate the item according to the instructions in this chapter.
13. What is meant by suggesting *alternates*? What would you say and do to suggest alternates?
14. When should a salesperson stop talking and reach for the sales book?
15. How would you deal with the following kinds of customers:

the looker?	the dubious customer?
the shopper?	the irritating customer?
the bargain hunter?	the complainer?

16. What are the chief causes of complaints and how can they be settled?
17. How may oral testimony be used to combat retail sales resistance? Give several examples.
18. How would you handle the excuse, "I want to look around"? Use the exact words you would employ with an actual customer.

19. What is the best way to meet the price objection? Use the words you would employ with a retail customer.
20. How would you handle objections to special features? What would you say and do?
21. What is the opinion-asking method and how would you use it with the opinionated type of customer?
22. What is the *anticipation* method of answering objections? How would you use it?

PHENOMENOLOGICAL PROJECTS

Stuffy Duffy Store

Not long ago there was an advertisement which described bedspreads for sale in one of Chicago's large department stores. I went to the store.

Piled on several tables were hundreds of spreads. A salesgirl was nearby. I approached her, described the color of the rug and walls in my room, and asked if she had something suitable in a bedspread. She sweetly said, "All we have are on the tables. You may find something there." I looked and found something I liked. Triumphantly I handed two spreads to the salesgirl saying, "Here's a sale for you." She smiled and said, "These are not returnable. Are you sure you want them? Chartreuse doesn't blend with everything." I hesitated and then said, "Perhaps you're right. Although these spreads appear to be unusual bargains, they aren't bargains if I can't use them in my home."

Analyze the conduct of this salesperson. What should you do to improve this salesperson's selling technique?

Chapter Seventeen

Advertising, Promotion and Credits

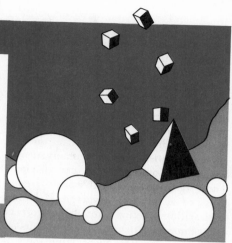

The development of advertising over the past fifty years has been related to the general improvement in the skills, understanding and knowledge of salespeople. Actually, they are so closely related that advertising has been described as "written salesmanship" and salesmanship as "oral advertising." Although these descriptions are not entirely accurate, salesmanship and advertising have the same basic *objective:* to obtain buying decisions from prospective purchasers. Advertising is said to condition and pull the customer toward the proposition, while salesmanship is said to push the proposition to the prospective buyer. This "push-pull" action, when effectively employed, has often proved to be an unbeatable combination.

BENEFITS OF ADVERTISING FOR SALESPEOPLE

Advertising means different things to different people, but it is most easily understood by reference to the media in which it is displayed. Advertising is carried in different forms in such media as national magazines, newspapers and brochures and booklets, on television, radio and billboards, through car cards and direct mail, and in window or interior displays.

In any of these forms, advertising benefits both "inside" and "outside" salespeople by building trade acceptance for company reliability or product or service quality. Advertising is a goodwill builder in the sense that it actually carries acceptance and confidence in a name to the consumer.

Advertising can become the advance agent for the sales force. Company advertising of almost any kind offers the salesman new talking points. In the introduction of new products, advertising "conditions" or presells the prospect before the salesman arrives. It thereby reduces sales resistance and enables the salesman to obtain a quicker decision to buy. Alert salespeople usually study their company's advertising carefully to locate the dominant points which they can use in their daily work.

USE OF ADVERTISING WITH DEALERS

Presentation to Dealers

A salesperson's biggest opportunity to use advertising in a presentation arrives when he shows his prospective dealer how it extends his reputation and brings him faster turnover and increased sales volume and profits.

Radio and television advertising and billboard and car card displays are equally effective for gaining consumer acceptance, even though the salesman cannot carry them with him. Nevertheless, they are worth talking about, particularly if the salesman takes the trouble to gain information from his company's advertising department, a broadcasting company's report on the listening audience for his radio program or an outdoor agency's statistics on how many people see its billboards or car car displays. These figures are obtainable and are good proof of advertising coverage. It is also good selling practice to invite the prospect or customer to listen to advertisements on radio and television, mentioning the station, the time, the nature of the program and the headliners to be presented.

Portfolio Materials

Many companies provide their men with portfolios of advertising and promotion materials. Where a company does not furnish a portfolio, professional salesmen build their own. They carefully study tear sheets, reprints or samples of promotion materials and then place them in their advertising portfolio. Acetate or cellophane covers enhance the materials by adding glamor, cleanliness and orderliness.

When the advertising portfolio is used as a sales aid, such a salesperson is said to obtain two to five times the results of those salesmen who disregard their company advertising. Advertising is used by salesmen because personal salesmanship in itself cannot perform the whole selling job. Advertising provides sales power and makes it possible for salespeople to increase their effectiveness.

Company Advertising

Salespeople seem to have a tendency to overlook other sales promotion material provided by their companies. Samples, catalogs, direct-mail circulars, stuffers, publicity stories and visual aid manuals can all be important selling aids. For example, catalogues and manuals prepared by many companies give the salesman complete technical facts about his line of products. Many salesmen consider their catalogs and manuals as their "bible," and familiarize themselves with every page, so that they are ready to turn to the information required at the proper moment.

Circulars related to specific products can be advantageously introduced during the presentation, left with the prospect as a summary, or even enclosed in courtesy letters to work for the salesman between calls. Many circulars are designed for dealers to use in their own advertising efforts. When space is provided in a circular for the dealer's imprint, the salesperson calls attention to this feature, knowing that people generally like to see their names in print. He makes it his business to know where such imprinting can be done and what it costs, if the imprint service is not provided by his home office.

Company Promotion Materials

Many companies provide promotional materials such as window and counter cards, streamers, posters and banners. These materials are costly to produce and it is difficult to induce people to use them. Further, the dealers sometimes have to pay for the materials. This places an extra burden on the person who must induce dealers to accept the materials, but means greater returns for the dealers if the materials are used. By relating their successful use by other dealers, the salesman will make the dealer want them and ask for them. When advantages are emphasized, dealers usually regard such materials as opportunities to increase profits. Whether a charge is made for this promotional material or it is provided free, it is the salesperson's responsibility to be sure that it is used.

Local Advertising

The salesman helps dealers sell his goods

to consumers as a means of assuring orders, for the dealer will not need stock again until he has sold his supply.

The knowledgeable, alert salesman can help his dealers plan their local newspaper advertising, window and interior displays, promotions, demonstrations and such promotions as style shows and other special events.

Gaining Dealer Buying

Dealer buying decisions arise in the following manner. The ultimate consumer or user sees or hears the advertising message and it interests him. He then inquires or searches for the source of the product. When the dealer or other source discovers that advertising has caused the buying interest, he will want to stock the product for which advertising has created a demand. He will normally be eager to keep stock in good supply so that he can capitalize on the profit possibilities of the product that advertising has popularized.

The salesman should call his prospects' and customers' attention to the fact that his company's advertising builds acceptance of a product name. He then opens his portfolio and shows the buyer the product features he is emphasizing. Some salesmen read the important statements aloud to the buyer, although this procedure depends on the nature of the material as well as on the salesman's ability to read effectively. Effective reading requires much practice and only short informative sentences should be read by the salesman. The salesman should also avoid giving the impression that he believes the prospect to be incapable of reading for himself.

Mañana Disease

Many distributors and dealers are afflicted with "mañana disease." They prefer to put up displays or conduct promotions "tomorrow" and push expensive material into a corner to collect dust or dirt. Even when they have to do the job themselves,

many salesmen place this material where it will invite the dealer's customers to buy.

In addition, the salesman usually has to sell the dealer on local advertising by showing him the advantage to be gained through a tie-up with a national program. Many salespeople overlook this opportunity to help the dealer move goods. Their excuse is that they are not advertising experts, and cannot do layouts or write copy. The alert salesman makes an effort to obtain as much information as possible on advertising to do the job. He analyzes current advertising; he reads books on advertising; he discusses advertising with those who have a knowledge of it. Finally, he helps the customer with his local advertising by offering him ideas, layouts, mats, printed materials and other miscellaneous services.

PERSONAL ADVERTISING

Personal letters and cards are, in effect, a means of personal advertising for the salesman. He may add to their effectiveness by including a reprint of the latest company advertising or a copy of a circular. He may also find it profitable to discuss an advertising enclosure by mentioning its good points, the introduction of new product features and other details. In this way, he has his company's advertising work for him.

Publicity Material

Another type of effective enclosure in a letter is a publicity item clipped from a newspaper or trade publication. This may relate to the salesman's product, company, personalities, product usage or new inventions that will affect the industry—in fact, anything that the prospect or customer is interested in. When the salesman culls the newspapers for such material, he will not be forgotten by the prospect to whom such advertising is sent.

Following Leads from Advertising

Many advertisements carry offers of free

information, booklets or coupons for samples to be sent on request. Such offers, in addition to educating new users for a product or service, may obtain leads for the salesman. When action is postponed on these leads, however, the prospect may feel that his inquiry was not valued by the company. Thus, the salesman may not only lose an opportunity for an easy sale but also risk the danger of building resistance to his presentation.

The alert salesman always follows leads from his company's advertising immediately. He considers them as goodwill builders with an opportunity for new sales. The creative person is not content to accept what his company provides. He is constantly seeking new ideas and new ways to use advertising and sales promotion materials so that he can earn more money for his company and for himself.

CREDITS AND COLLECTIONS

Few salespeople like to concern themselves with credit and collection duties. Nearly all are inclined to remark, "This is not for me. It's my job to sell. It's up to the credit department to establish credits and to collect money for goods sold."

It is true that nearly all companies give the bulk of this responsibility to a credit manager. It is also true that the majority of business enterprises do not expect their salespeople to pass on credit references or to make collections. Nevertheless, the credit department cannot do all the work and the competent salesperson knows that when he makes a sale, he should at least be aware of the importance of credits and collection and be willing to assist in dealing with them.

While many salespeople do not at first understand and appreciate the importance of credit and collection activities, they do so when the facts are explained to them and they then fully agree:
—That no order can be profitable until it has been paid for in full by the purchaser.

—That a good reason exists for company credit and collection policies.
—That there is a need for cooperation in this field between salesmen and management, with the salesman collecting credit data and reporting them to the credit manager.

Credit Responsibilities of the Salesman

A salesman should acquire a perfect understanding of his company's credit policies. His best source of information on this topic is the company credit manager. The credit manager will probably be delighted to outline the assistance the salesperson can furnish which will be helpful in determining the credit to be allowed the prospects in the salesman's territory. The reason that the credit manager will be delighted is that the salesman has the opportunity to observe conditions at first hand. He can see and hear many things which have a bearing on the character, capacity and capital of the prospect or customer, things that ordinarily do not appear in credit ratings supplied by such organizations as Dun and Bradstreet. The salesperson can make a personal appraisal of the prospect's properties, plant and equipment. If the prospect handles merchandise for resale, the salesman can gain much information from observing the stock and its condition. He can tell whether it is fresh or shopworn; whether the dealer is overstocked or in short supply and whether the stock is of good quality or not. He can also see whether the store is in a good location for attracting trade.

Appraising a prospect or customer in this way requires diligence, care and keen judgment. To obtain valid facts and make reliable judgments, the salesman should question the local banker, insurance man, the prospect's competitors and other miscellaneous sources before he formulates a report to be passed on to his credit manager. Such intelligent and conscientious reportings on the things he sees and hears —things which affect a customer's ability to pay — will benefit the salesperson in many ways.

Benefits to the Salesman

That the salesman profits when his company profits should need no further clarification. However, an intelligent understanding of the relationship that exists between sales and credits may prove beneficial to a salesman in these ways: (a) his ability to intelligently discuss and interpret credits and collections will gain him the goodwill of his customers and thereby assure him future business; (b) it brings to him the realization that he should spend his time only on those prospects who can pay for his products or service easily and quickly. The competitive salesman educates his customers to pay promptly. The salesman should be alert to any signs of financial deterioration in an account. In a frank discussion with the customer, the salesman can obtain the true economic status of the account. He can sustain a weakened account or help make special arrangements for payment to tide a customer over hard times. This can save his company from a loss and gain the goodwill of a customer. A customer whose accounts are in arrears may well begin looking elsewhere for his stock and become "open territory" for competition. The account may then be lost and the company invoices remain unpaid; both the company and the salesperson will lose out. But when a credit reputation is not damaged during a hazardous period, everybody gains.

A salesperson who understands his customer's financial situation is in a position to know how much debt the customer can handle. The amount a prospect could safely buy may differ from month to month or from year to year, depending on such factors as increasing competition, economic competition and customer selectivity.

New Accounts

When competitive selling is in full force, salespeople in all fields are asked to locate new customers for a wider distribution of the products they sell. The new outlets, however, must be good credit risks or the new sales will never be consummated. More than 300,000 new businesses are established each year in the United States, and many of these new businesses are not given credit ratings by reporting agencies. The salesperson, in his search for new customers, trains himself to observe "credit signals" so that he can judge whether it is wise for him to spend much time with a prospective account or to move along to more profitable customers.

Reviving Accounts

Good credit judgment will prompt the alert salesman to revive customer accounts that have been rejected because of poor credit ratings or slow collections. These companies may have made bad starts or encountered lean years and yet have overcome their difficulties through capable management and become good credit risks. Bringing old accounts back into the fold may be difficult, and require tactful handling, but it can be an effort well spent.

Special Terms

A good company representative always adheres to the credit policy of his house. There are occasions which may justify special arrangements and concessions, but such action should be undertaken only with the understanding and approval of the credit manager. Under ordinary circumstances, special credit terms are regarded as an indication of poor personal marketing that frequently leads to difficulties.

Credit Terminology

For the man in business, legal knowledge is a valuable asset. Although no one expects a salesperson to be able to pass a bar examination, the salesperson stands to gain if he knows how to analyze financial statements, understands the meaning of current assets and current liabilities, can recognize a valid contract and is aware of the legal aspects of credit and collections. The effort to acquire such facts will be amply rewarded.

If the salesman feels that giving so much time to observing credits and collections in his territory is limiting his selling time, he is regarding the situation from the wrong angle. What he is actually doing in this effort is laying the foundation for *selective selling*.

By reviewing the prospective customer's credit position through a careful study of the general market, through business reports and news items and an intelligent estimate of local conditions, it is possible to judge accurately how much a customer can buy and how rapidly he can turn over his stock. Such analyses make it possible to have maximum sales with profit; a decrease in losses due to poor credit and additional profits for all.

Collections

In most businesses, salesman are not required to make collections. However, those who acquire basic knowledge of credits and collections can be of great assistance to their credit managers.

Whenever a company has to "push" a customer for payment, it nullifies the goodwill which has been so carefully built. Also, it becomes difficult to obtain a friendly acceptance on later calls. On the other hand, tactfully following an account on collections will often enable a salesperson to obtain additional business.

Irritations can be forestalled by planting the importance of prompt payments in each customer's mind. As each customer is presented with sales aids, materials, ideas and suggestions that will help him turn his stock more quickly, the salesman contributes to a more satisfactory credit and collection situation. This kind of selling is one of the best aids to prompt collections.

Frequent conferences with the credit manager can help to solve collection problems. The credit manager can restate the company policies and methods, so that even if he has had no part in actually collecting, the salesperson can serve as a "business counselor" to his customers, and in this way avoid misunderstandings and ill will. The credit manager can also explain the conditions under which longer credit terms are permissible.

The good representative never overlooks his part in the company profit factor, for that is where his income and success begin. This was well expressed in the following ditty:

A MORAL IN RHYME
Count that day lost
Whose low descending sun
Finds profits shot to glory
And business done for fun.

POWER POINTS

Advertising — A close parallel exists between the preparation and placing of advertising and the work of salespeople. It follows that the two should work hand-in-hand, each complementing the other.

The salesperson who dislikes, distrusts or ignores advertising when it is available suffers from a self-imposed handicap. Salespeople are to be found who still harbor a negative attitude toward advertising; they regard it as a usurper, a poacher on their preserves — a parasite that consumes a lot of money which could be better spent in giving salespersons higher commission or a few more bonuses.

On the other hand there are far more salespeople — generally the professional and successful men — who refuse to sell a product or service that is not advertised in the trade or national press or by direct mail. They believe that advertising is very helpful, preparing the ground for their presentations and in backing up their efforts.

If a prospect has seen the salesperson's company and products featured in advertising, his sales resistance is softened considerably. In such cases, the salesperson takes only a minimum of time to tell who he is, *whom* he represents and what he is selling. His available time for actual face-to-face selling is increased and successful closings are more frequent.

Credits — There should be complete harmony between salespeople and the credit department. Few businesses grow large or attain national significance without a progressive credit policy. That is the chief reason why a credit man should sit in on matters that affect sales planning.

Sales and credit are like Siamese twins. A complete divorcement of them is foolish and could be fatal. Cooperation and mutual understanding are necessary to remove the antagonisms which often creep in between the two departments.

Many leading businesses give rank to their credit managers and include them in the higher echelons of company officials. Some do not and they are the losers. Where the credit men have an opportunity to display their rich resources of experience and information to the salespeople, the whole organization benefits from the teamwork.

Credit and sales are not in competition. Credit's value begins with a preview of the risk, and is not a post-mortem. The credit man would rather be a pioneer at the birth of a sales opportunity than a coroner at the autopsy of a risk.

DISCUSSION QUESTIONS AND PROBLEMS

1. Give a full explanation of this statement: "Advertising and sales promotion condition the market."
2. Name, describe and explain eight forms of advertising which might be of use to a manufacturer's salesman. What services would advertising offer him?
3. What advertising might a salesman place in his briefcase or portfolio to be used in his calls on prospects and customers?
4. How would a salesman find and use facts in his company's advertising? Which media would possibly be of most value to him?
5. How may a manufacturer's salesman help his wholesale and retail distributors with their local advertising?
6. What are "promotional materials?" How can salesmen induce their customers to use such materials? Is the "mañana disease" prevalent among wholesalers and retailers? Why?
7. What kind of personal advertising and publicity material can be used by a salesman? Where would he find it? How would he use it?
8. In what practical ways can a salesman use the leads that often result from his company advertising?
9. Explain this statement: "No order is profitable until it has been paid for by the buyer."
10. Name five contributions a salesman can make to cooperate with his company credit manager. Is it correct to state that the salesman is the credit manager's representative in the field?
11. What factors should be considered in a personal credit appraisal made by a salesperson? To whom would he go for such information?

12. What information would a salesperson, because of his familiarity with local conditions, be able to give his credit department that would (a) justify the acceptance of an order; and (b) grant credit that otherwise would have been refused? Which factors should he observe that may indicate a good credit risk?

13. Write a credit policy which a company might use. State the exact words you would use to explain the credit policy to a new customer.

14. Over and above the routine credit reports, what other credit information can a salesman uncover about his prospects and customers which might interest his credit department?

15. State in detail *how* and *why* the salesman profits from his credit and collections activities with both old and new accounts.

PHENOMENOLOGICAL PROJECTS

Don Ramsey (Case)

Don Ramsey has been selling industrial chemicals for many years. He has dealt with many small manufacturers whose credit often becomes important in doing business. Don learned a long time ago how to separate the sheep from the goats in the matter of finding prospects whose credit standing was questionable. Don would watch these people and if their credit improved, he would try to sell them. Otherwise, he would pass them by.

Sometimes he would encounter a prospect who used Don's credit policy as an excuse for not buying. They would say that Don's employer's terms were "too tough." Then Don would say, "Mr. Prospect, our terms are standard in the industry. However, if you will tell me just what terms you feel would be satisfactory to you, I'm sure I can prevail upon my company to accept any reasonable proposition."

Questions:
1. Do you believe that Don's policy of refusing to sell dubious credit risks is a good one? Why?
2. What is your opinion of the way Don handles the prospects who use their credit standing as an excuse for not buying?

Dick Dyke (Case)

Dick Dyke is a salesman for a firm which manufactures and sells automatic control systems. His income is good, but not what he wants it to be. He knows how to analyze a situation and suggest improvements. For example, he showed a prospect how four costly jobs could be eliminated and their operation speeded up more than ten times. He knew how the prospect could gain greater efficiency and further cost reductions by the installation of system control.

Dyke was able to tell a good story — good enough to arouse great curiosity and a want-to-buy feeling on the part of the prospect. But how was the prospect to know that the equipment could perform as promised? At this point, Dyke would reach into his brief case and pull out four tear-sheets of his company's advertising. Each ad described the case history of a specific firm to which the business system had previously been sold and stressed the benefits that the firm had enjoyed through the installation.

So far, so good! But Dick Dyke did not close as many deals as he should. His company had many different kinds of advertising which Dyke did not use. What other advertising did the company provide which Dyke might have used to increase his sales?

Part Four

Improving Your Sales Performance

Chapter Eighteen

Building a Clientele

FINDING CUSTOMERS

Much of a salesman's success in his clientele-building efforts depends on his own attitude toward his business. If he is enthusiastic about his company policies and services and if he believes in what he is selling, his confidence will be contagious and will carry over to his customers. The salesman who really believes in his proposition simply cannot prevent others from believing in him.

Clientele-building is an individualized activity and when and how it is done depends largely on the salesman himself. All over the nation, creative salespeople are out in their communities and trade areas digging for business. Rather than loafing around on slack days of the week or month, these salespeople are scouring their communities for hidden business.

Cold Canvass

Quite often the only effective way to build a clientele is to use the "cold-canvass" method. This method is rugged: the salesperson has to arm himself with his sales kit and "hit the road," making house-to-house or person-to-person calls to secure prospective clients. This kind of clientele-building calls for much ambition, initiative and selling skill, but it can be effective for those who understand its use.

Referrals

A most important source of new business, and a source which is usually ignored, is the customer who knows a salesman and his product and is often pleased to supply the names of friends and acquaintances who would buy what the salesman has to sell. The salesman should not be restrained by timid feelings from asking his customers for the names of possible new buyers. It has always been true that nothing gives a person greater pleasure than doing a favor for a friend. These are the important ways in which satisfied customers can help to build a bigger clientele:

They can pave the way for an interview with friends, acquaintances or relatives by phoning them, writing a letter of introduction or by personal introduction.

They can write testimonials giving proof of satisfaction with the product or service.

They can give names of their acquaintances and important information about them.

They can provide experiences that point out how badly they needed the product or service and the benefits they received since buying it.

It has been said that a salesperson's *users*, or his customers, are the lifeblood of his business. In a sense they sign his paycheck! A continual job of prospecting among satisfied users and customers is a vital part of a salesperson's job. In other words, sell them but never forget them!

Goodwill

A clientele is built slowly through the years and is based on the customer's understanding, sentiments and beliefs about the salesman and his company, in other words, on goodwill.

Goodwill is the advantage in trade which a business has acquired beyond the mere value of what it sells. It can also mean friendly or kindly feeling.

If goodwill exists, it is not always necessary to have a better product or service for the price than a competitor. It is not even necessary that a product or service be as good as a competitor's if goodwill makes up for the difference in value between the two propositions.

In this book, emphasis has been placed on what is believed to be superior sales skills and procedures. However, there is no denying the fact that superior products, services, skills and procedures are usually not enough. To build a faithful clientele, it is necessary to have the plus value of goodwill as well as superior products and superior sales methods.

There are generally three ways to build plus values and a faithful clientele: through company effort; through the product and service; through the personal efforts of the salesman.

Using the Company Effort

Reliable companies continuously build plus values and faithful clientele through the following activities:

Years of satisfactory service, resulting in recognition of dependability and ethical principles.

Advertising — educational in character and building buyer acceptance through consumer appeals and repetition.

Quality of products or services.

Fair dealing with customers.

The company's quality standards in making the product, in servicing accounts, in policy making, in advertising and other managerial functions are beyond the salesman's control. A Professional salesman knows, however, that these elements make up the goodwill of his company and that it is one of his most valuable assets. He makes the most of his company goodwill by constantly explaining his company's policies, objectives and services to his customers. He realizes that the continuing goodwill his customers hold for his company depends very largely upon himself, for to customers the salesman is the company.

A salesman, for example, can build goodwill by showing tear sheets, reprints, or photographs of his company's merchandise to his prospects, together with facts about how many consumers they reach and the potential sales increase which may follow. He should be prepared to indicate the increased number of readers who will be influenced in favor of his merchandise. He should try to expand the interest produced by the advertising into desire and action, or its effect will be nil. He must use his advertising to the fullest extent or it ceases to be an advantage. When good advertising and good selling are teamed together, they may form an unbeatable combination.

Without these assets, a salesman cannot continue to sell his merchandise profitably. Mere statements designed to sell his company's record, experience, and prestige are not sufficient.

The Salesman's Personal Efforts

The alert salesman realizes that his clientele-building depends in a large measure on himself. He knows that to his customers and prospects, he is his company. When they think of his company, prospects do not think of the sales manager or the president; they think of their direct personal contact, the salesman. They think of his appearance, speech, and manner, his knowledge of his products and how they may help solve their problems; they think of his knowledge of modern marketing services. All of these have a bearing on clientele building. When cordial relations are established with prospects, salesmen can cement goodwill and make themselves sure, profitable clienteles.

Many companies are constantly improving their products through experiments, tests, and research. They also create and develop industrial and efficiency reports, merchandising plans, cost control systems, and many other services for customers. These goodwill-building devices may not be appreciated, however, unless the salesman tells his prospects about them and motivates them to buy.

On the other hand, when the salesman misrepresents, ridicules complaints, resorts to unfair practices, and fails to provide service and aids, the goodwill which the company has built up over many years at great expense is destroyed or lost.

Little interest is aroused, for example, when a prospect is told that the salesman's company has been in business for twenty years. However, success stories from satisfied users over the years will influence their buying decisions. Company "exclusives" and "firsts" are also impressive, as well as written testimonials and other tangible evidence. Tear sheets of company advertisements and references to radio and television shows sponsored by the salesman's company are also impressive to customers and prospects.

In addition, the salesman's personality is quite important. The people he is trying to sell have natural human attitudes, reactions, prejudices, and individual behavior traits. When the buyer likes and respects the salesman, a fine start has been made toward building acceptance and goodwill.

Empathy

Since friendship and goodwill are so closely related, clientele-building is aided when a salesman likes his customers. Each individual has good and bad points and the good traits almost always outweigh by far the bad ones. The salesman should look for the good traits in a prospect and remind himself to like everyone. Everybody will like him in return. A friendly, cordial attitude can work wonders in clientele-building.

Presentation Manner — The manner in which a presentation is made can affect clientele-building. A supercilious, know-it-all, unenthusiastic manner can never build a clientele. These things will never convey the idea of benefits to prospective customers.

The benefit story may become "old stuff" to a salesperson, but it is always fresh and interesting to his listeners. Repetition of the benefits of products or service is nearly always worthwhile and will usually serve to counteract the impressions other salespeople may have made between his calls.

Courtesy With Objectors — When handling objections, it is quite easy to incur a prospect's displeasure, particularly if his views are slighted or an argument is permitted to arise. On the other hand, clientele-building is most easily accomplished by handling objections with tact.

Follow-Through — After each sales effort, whether successful or unsuccessful, the prospect should be left with the idea that the salesman will be back again for an order. He should leave the prospect with the happy feeling that it will be a pleasure to call on him again, that the prospect will look forward to future calls because of his personality, thoughtfulness, and fairness.

Goodwill is also built when a sale is followed up to determine if a product or service is living up to promises or to offer the buyer advice and help in using or caring for it. Thus, a salesman can create much goodwill in the buyer's mind, whether he needs help or not. Buyers like repeat calls provided they are offered helpful suggestions, advice, and assistance.

Customers are pleased when they are not forgotten or overlooked. The alert salesman tries to keep in touch with them through telephone calls, courtesy letters, remembrance cards on birthdays and anniversaries, and congratulatory cards for special occasions.

When call-backs are made to build a clientele, they should be kept on a strictly business basis. They are not social visits; they are business calls, and something worthwhile should be done at each call. This often requires considerable advance thinking to find helpful suggestions for the prospect.

Services
The salesman who hopes to enjoy the benefits that come from a faithful clientele must be willing to put something extra into his relationships. He must prepare himself to help his customers. He must give them new ideas about how to increase their business, suggest different ways for moving their merchandise, inform them about new products and new uses for old products, mention new promotional methods and profit-wise applications of new ideas.

An alert salesman will be able to estimate the local market, to secure facts about it, evaluate them and report to his customers. He should be able to report those facts in an inspirational, yet logical, manner. If he sells to dealers, he should

be able to advise them about every phase of their business: finance, record-keeping, departmentalization, displays, training, sales techniques, and many other things that will help him to build a strong clientele.

Other services that can be offered as a part of clientele-building may include such things as expediting deliveries, notifying customers when they may expect deliveries, checking on delivery dates, and being on hand at delivery time to help install or operate the product or service. These services not only build goodwill; they also enable the salesman to correct errors and complaints which may destroy goodwill.

Company services may also be used to build goodwill — services such as laboratory tests, engineering assistance, and the solution of a prospect's production or distribution problems. In brief, an alert salesman knows the buyer's problems and helps to solve them.

Many salesmen hesitate to offer company services because they are looking for something big — something outstanding that will enhance their personal importance. Although an accumulation of small services over a period of time may be less evident, it generally will produce better results than a single "big" service.

As part of his preparation for personal service, a successful salesman frequently asks himself, "What will my proposition do for the prospect and what can I do to help my customers?"

To answer this question in part, a salesman who sells to retailers has a photographic collection of window and counter displays that have been unusually successful in stores of other cities. These visual aids arouse considerable interest on the part of customers.

An office equipment salesman who subscribes to several business magazines and trade journals may lend them to his customers. He also keeps up with the new books that are written on salesmanship, merchandising, and advertising, and should be glad to lend these to customers.

Some salesmen carry newspaper clippings, bank bulletins and charts, and analyses of business conditions which are effectively used with certain prospects who would probably not see such materials because their entire time is given to their businesses.

These are all potential methods of producing goodwill. A salesman who uses these methods makes himself and his company distinctive because the average salesman will not go to the bother of helping the customer by bringing him new and profitable ideas.

The word "service" is somewhat shopworn, but the willingness to serve in order to give complete satisfaction helps build a clientele. Service can be expressed only in deeds, not in words. Successful salesmen build up a reputation for *giving* service, not merely for just talking about it.

Learning from Errors

Another part of clientele-building is an analysis of the results of every call, whether it led to a sale or not. It is important for the salesperson to discover the reason behind every "yes" and "no." The clientele-builder will never overlook the value of analyzing his major mistakes and of developing an attitude of self-evaluation. The following listing may be of assistance to the clientele-conscious salesperson in his efforts to discover why his efforts were sometimes negative:

Went into the interview without necessary information and the prospect did not buy.

Was worried by competitor's advertising and started a comparison of the two products instead of discussing the merits of his own merchandise.

Failed to have reserve selling points and additional information to gain a favorable buying decision.

Engaged in an argument and lost the goodwill of the prospect.

Neglected the prospect, who was sold by a competitor.

Did not present and demonstrate properly, and the prospect lost interest.

CUSTOMER BEHAVIOR

When a customer complains, it should be realized that the customer really wants to buy from the salesman or he would not ordinarily take the trouble of making a complaint, but instead simply sever his relationship with the company. Therefore, the salesman should be a good listener and allow the complaining customer to do most of the talking. By asking a few pertinent questions, he can usually guide the customer toward the realization that perhaps he was a bit hasty and that he was not as badly treated as he at first thought.

Salesmen who are unusually successful in obtaining large orders from chronic complainers, say: "Be polite, calm, and cheerful!" Some people enjoy ill health and some enjoy fault-finding, but they always respond to personal interest and good service. The professional salesman has learned not only to anticipate complaints and gripes but to prepare himself to take advantage of them to build his clientele.

Customers' goodwill can rarely be regained by avoiding them. Instead, the salesman meets the complainers with courage and has face-to-face visits and heart-to-heart talks. Perhaps he now has some new items to introduce or a new sales program that will make money for the disgruntled customers. An attitude of friendly helpfulness will usually win them over and in this way the salesman adds to his clientele.

Marshall Field and Company, of Chicago, spends thousands of dollars each year to prove their slogan, "The customer is always right." But this slogan has earned the company millions of dollars.

A good salesperson emulates Marshall Field's slogan and does not believe that a customer's complaint is a reflection on him or his company. He sees in a complaint an opportunity to be of service by handling it promptly and cheerfully. He regards a complaint as a challenge and another opportunity to add to his clientele.

Prevent Misunderstandings

Many misunderstandings arise simply because some salesmen do not thoroughly explain certain details such as exact quality, delivery dates, prices and terms when they are closing their deals.

For example, if terms are not mentioned when the order is taken, the customer may not be ready or willing to pay when the seller returns in thirty days and tries to collect. The customer may stall and say he expected sixty or ninety days.

Clearly, the time to talk terms is when the order is given. The customer is then friendly. Furthermore, he is satisfied. He does not owe the salesperson anything at this time. The big decision to buy has been made and the minor decision as to terms is only natural and logical.

When an order is received, the customer's goodwill can be preserved by giving him all of the details, not only those related to price and terms, but also how to use the product or service. When customer acceptance has been won, he is likely to tell others about it and this kind of recommendation is the most effective way to build a clientele.

POWER POINTS

Built slowly through the years, a clientele is based on the customer's knowledge and sentiments about the salesperson's company — its traditions, policies, services, and products — and the customer's sentiments and beliefs about the salesperson — his personality, traits, honesty, ethics and his ability to inspire confidence and belief.

Personal information offered by salespeople builds confidence and friendship. Personal friendships are the basis for nearly all of the clientele built by a salesman. And pleasant personalities build friendships. The salesman who desires to build a clientele must be willing to put something into his work if he hopes to get anything from it. He must equip himself to help his customers and prospects. He must give them new ideas about how to increase their businesses, unique devices about how to sell more merchandise, suggestions about new applications of new ideas. A clientele means *repeaters* and *resales*. Therefore, the value of having friendly, loyal, prosperous, and well-informed customers is apparent.

Clientele-building means work — leg work, planning, telephone calls, letters — and more work, as well as unlimited imagination. A salesperson builds his clientele not only through work but also through building loyalty to his house and himself, through advising his prospects and customers and by developing a friendly, helpful, inspiring personality.

DISCUSSION QUESTIONS AND PROBLEMS

1. What is meant by goodwill? What is the relationship between goodwill and clientele-building?
2. Give the meaning of this statement: "It's not always necessary to have a better product than a competitor when goodwill exists."
3. What are three ways to build goodwill?
4. How can advertising be used to build a clientele?
5. How can product and service help to build a clientele?
6. How can personal service help to build a clientele?

7. How can a salesman turn complainers into boosters and thereby build his clientele?

8. Why does prompt, cheerful handling of complaints tend to build clientele?

9. Why does follow-up after a sale help to build clientele?

10. If you were asked to devise a plan for clientele-building for a specific company, what would you suggest? How would you do it?

11. What services can you suggest which a salesman might use to help build a strong clientele?

12. What quality of personality do you believe may be most useful in building a faithful clientele?

PHENOMENOLOGICAL PROJECTS

Lester B. Colby (Case)

"We want you to go out," said the memorandum from headquarters, "and ask a group of management men what they think of gift-giving, wine-tossing, and double-sirloining as part of routine sales operation.

"Let names be off the record. We want honest opinion. We want to know if common sense is coming back in style after the expense account jag so many firms indulged in during the war.

"We realize that most company policies probably will be found to lie in some middle ground between no entertainment at all and free spending at the salesman's discretion. So we're trying to distinguish between the kind of entertainment (or the sort of gift) that is a casual courtesy and the kind that is too lavish, in questionable taste, and of highly debatable business value."

After a couple of weeks of prying and talking to executives and to buyers in a variety of industries, a fistful of findings rose floating to the top for skimming. This is the drift of opinion:

"Expense accounts got as loose as a Mother Hubbard during the wartime cost-plus hubbub and immediately thereafter, when spending for selling's sake was a farce anyway, inasmuch as you could move anything you had or might hope to have at almost any price any time." (The boys then contended they were building goodwill for the future.)

Question:

1. Do you believe that entertaining customers and prospects helps to build a clientele?

"If you are going to court the friendship of anyone, go after the solid buyer. He's the man who is more anxious for goods that will turn over fast or ideas that will speed the turnover.

"Out of our experience we have developed a 'no-entertaining' policy. Instead of entertaining, we tell them to take sales ideas to our customers and their buyers.

"Under our marketing system, the dealers belong to the distributors, so any expense in dealing with the dealers is supported by the distributors.

"The company allows a reasonable latitude for factory specialists and district salesmen to do moderate entertaining, like buying luncheons or refreshments for dealers when the factory man goes with the distributors' men to make a call or discuss a project."

Question:

2. When does a friendly gesture become a danger to building a clientele?

"We manufacture parts for other manufacturers, largely for the automotive industry.

IMPROVING YOUR SALES PERFORMANCE

I became a buyer of steel and other metals a couple of years ago. I hadn't more than settled myself in the chair than gifts began to come in. At first I accepted some with grace, not knowing what to do. They began to get bigger and more valuable and I saw that what constituted bribery was in the air."

Questions:

3. Do you believe that "bribery was in the air?" Why?
4. How would you deal with this situation? As the buyer? As the salesman?

The Maytag Company (Case)

Boy, was he proud! My next-door neighbor recently drove his new car home, beautiful and shiny. The entire family piled in and drove around for the neighbors and friends to see.

Was the salesman happy? I'll say he was, just as much as the owner. There is no greater fulfillment in selling than to sell a product that the owners want to show to all the world.

And that's why this salesman took a little extra time and effort to turn the car over to his customer bright and spotless. He was not only proud of it, but realized the value of first impressions.

But a few weeks later, friend neighbor returned the car to the garage for some slight adjustments. This time though, a mechanic got some grease smears on the upholstery and apparently made little or no attempt to remove them.

Questions:

1. Which part of this transaction would build a clientele?
2. Which part would tend to destroy a clientele? Why?

Unimportant? Well, perhaps so, but I've heard this new owner remark, "I wish those guys would give their customers the same treatment after they buy as *before* they buy."

The customer not only bought a car but also service for it. True, he got the car, which he is immensely proud and pleased to drive, and he got the service he bought but not the friendly, accurate service he expected.

At first glance this may seem trivial, yet it meant an owner satisfied with the product but dissatisfied with the dealer's service.

Question:

3. How would you feel if you received this treatment?

What customers think of you is based almost entirely upon the treatment they receive from you, even long after the sale has been made. Customers rightly expect the prompt installation and demonstration of their new purchase. They expect prompt and courteous service, should the purchase require adjustment.

Question:

4. Do you agree or disagree with these statements? Why?

Chapter Nineteen

Managing Selling Time

Sir Isaac Pitman aptly said, "Well-arranged time is the surest mark of a well-arranged man."

Well-arranged time is one of the salesperson's greatest assets, since it helps him to organize his thinking and planning. It helps him conserve not only valuable working hours but also his effort and expenses as well as the time of his busy prospects and customers.

PLANNING TIME FOR SELLING

Suppose a stranger bound from Manhattan to Newark, N.J., found himself stranded on a Jersey City pier. He would see nothing but a maze of buildings, twisted streets, and confusion. If he were driving, he might ask directions of eight or nine people before reaching his destination, get misdirected half the time and finally arrive in Newark three hours later, when the main highway might have been only three blocks away. This is a simple example of what can happen when a salesman is so buried in problems and so far behind on his original plans that he can't see for the life of him how he will ever finish his work. It may require three days to accomplish what could have been done in one day, with planning.

If the same salesman could, on the other hand, ride in an airplane over the Hudson River for five minutes, he would see Newark just across the Jersey Meadows, he would see the main highway across the Pulaski Bridge and he would see that the highway was just near his starting point. That airplane view, that vision from a few thousand feet up, represents the essence of maximum use of time for selling.

When a salesman obtains a birds-eye view of his job, assembles the problems and clusters the various tasks, he will not be confused and he can proceed directly to his destination. In his daily work the salesman can choose the most important duties, line them up in order of importance, work at one duty at a time and end the day without night work or a feeling of pressure, because he will be getting maximum use of his selling time.

PREPARATION FOR SELLING

In any discussion of the effective use of time by salesmen, it has been traditional to emphasize the few hours of each working day that the average salesperson spends in the presence of customers and prospects. The professional salesperson thinks of every hour of his working day as "action time." He is definitely time-

289

conscious and spends a great many hours in preparing to sell in addition to working his regular hours. From this person's viewpoint, even the time spent in getting a good night's sleep and in seeking recreation and social activity are considered to be preparation for his hours of action.

Getting Ready for Next Day

The most important item in "preparatory time" may be the time the salesman spends each evening in getting ready for the next day's work. In these hours he brings to a focus all of his territory and individual accounts, preparing his task assignment for the "action hours" of the next day. Each evening he sets the pace he must maintain if his weekly, monthly, and annual personal sales quota is to be realized. Successful salesmen find it highly profitable to plot their time in advance, and to know every night before they go to bed where they are going the next day, what routes they will follow and whom they are going to see. A half-hour each day spent on planning the route will often save one day each week. And the person who plans his route will usually sell more quantity to more quality buyers and do both in less time.

Time Spent with Buyers

One investigation has indicated that the average salesman spends approximately three hours each day in the presence of prospective buyers. Another investigation of an industrial specialty business revealed that their salesmen spent approximately two hours and thirty minutes each day in the presence of buyers. The exact figures may not apply in all cases, but they do indicate the limited action time available to salesmen. For example, the salesmen for National Cylinder Gas Corporation are reported to have spent their working hours like this:

Travel	30 percent
Waiting	25 percent
Reports, etc.	20 percent
Shooting the breeze	5 percent
Action time	20 percent
	100 percent

According to these figures, this company's salespeople spent only 20 percent of their work time in the presence of prospective buyers. Much of the 80 percent was wasted because of poor planning, according to the sales trainer of this company. Many sales managers believe that approximately 50 percent of a salesman's time could be spent in the presence of prospects if he really tried to increase his action time through just a little planning, analysis and self-organization.

Time and Duty Study

Another picture of how time is broken down was revealed by a time and duty study[1] made by Salesweek. This was a study of 255 salesmen in nineteen different fields of work. Their average 9.3-hour working day broke down in the following way: getting ready to sell (including planning work, gathering information, and prospecting) — 19 percent of time; activities between interview (including travel, waiting, and lunch) — 45 percent; actual selling — 36 percent.

In a time and duty study made by Atlantic Refining Company, the average salesman's day was divided this way:

Selling to customer	17 percent
Selling new business	1 percent
Related sales activities	27 percent
Waiting for customers	5 percent
Non-direct selling talk	11 percent
Travel between calls	37 percent
Time unaccounted for	2 percent
	100 percent

1. Special Management Report, "Cure For High Sales Cost: Better Time Usage," Salesweek, December 12, 1960, p. 13.

As a result of this time and duty survey, Atlantic Refining Company corrected certain poor practices and achieved a reduction in base selling cost of 38 percent in one area, with an increase in new business of more than 15 percent — all in a period of six months.

Daily and Monthly Plans

Assuming that sales volume and personal income are roughly in proportion to the time spent in the presence of prospects, salesmen who plan on adding one or two hours each day to their action time will attain a proportionate increase in their sales total and personal income.

Route cards should be inspected every month to note the gaps in service and the customers who should receive calls. Those who are most important should be identified and listed for an early call. Prospects may also be listed who should be called on at some time during the month.

When all of the above calls are added up the salesman has an "airplane view" of the number of calls to be made in a month of planned effort. The difference between this total and the total number of calls he can make represents the number of calls the individual should consider and organize.

However, no monthly plan is worth much without daily work plans to supplement it. Each night, the salesman should plan for the next selling day, telling himself not only where to make his first call of the day but also where to go every minute during his working hours.

When his daily schedule is brief, he can memorize it. If many calls are to be made, however, the schedule should be written down with adequate regard to balance between active accounts and desirable prospective accounts. A salesperson has the right to decide whether he will increase his efficiency or ignore it altogether. He alone is the one who can increase his income and personal satisfac-

tion. Actually very few people will ignore the idea of increasing their efficiency, but many unconsciously dislike the idea of planning and therefore, avoid it.

Suppose, for example, that an individual encounters an unexpectedly big job at 8:00 A.M. This job involves several details and if he has no daily plan, his mind quickly slides over the consequences to the rest of the day and he starts to do the job immediately. He reasons (falsely, of course) that the job has to be done, will require a certain amount of time and might as well be concluded that day. So he starts the unexpected job and probably destroys the balance of the day's efforts, when an organized day's plan might have brought him success.

There may be times when a daily plan should be abandoned, but when the salesman has a carefully developed daily plan that directs him to be at the best places at the best time, he is in a position to make a decision based on the facts and not on wishful thinking. A particularly shaky account or one in which a particularly serious situation exists and cannot be solved at a later time might call for a decision to abandon the day's plan. However, this decision is then based on facts and considered judgment, not on guesses.

A *clean-up day* might be set for the middle of the week in certain kinds of selling. Emergency phone calls, requests from the office to make a collection, miscellaneous requests for advice or assistance, follow-up promises and similar matters should all be cared for on this day. This could be a "helter-skelter day" and even include jumps from one side of the town to the other. In this way he can scatter his shots on only one day of the week and plan for the other five workdays. In this connection, the salesman should not treat calls from customers for immediate service as emergencies that require him to stop everything else and make a headlong rush to the customer's door. When a call comes in for fast service or a prospect demands that the salesman "drive over here right away," it should be remembered that the customer has probably known of his difficulties for quite a while but just "got around" to telephoning.

Clustered Calls

If a salesman has averaged too few calls in past months, he can be sure that it was caused by a lack of personal management and most of his working days were a mixture of prospecting, service, and miscellaneous calls. Most salesmen could probably plan for clustering their shots and raising their call average each month.

In planning a day's work, the calls should be clustered so that the minute the salesman finds the buyer is out, he can slip almost next door and find one who is in, and then come back again. He should not just route calls but should also include in the plan the time he expects to be at each call. When he runs into longer calls, he should schedule them ahead for the less important hours, and then plan to "work his plan."

Advance Appointments

If the nature of the salesperson's business and daily routine permits, he should not overlook the importance of making advance appointments with potential buyers. This will, in many cases, eliminate time wasted in reception rooms as well as time spent in fruitless travel. While advance appointments may not always be possible, the opportunity should not be overlooked to add another 25 or 30 minutes each day in the presence of buyers.

Seeing the Right Buyer

Whether you are selling to a regular customer or to a prospect, be sure to see the man who has the authority to say "yes." It may require some Scotland Yard sleuthing to discover who the man is with the

final say about buying. It will also help if you can discover whether he makes his own decisions or relies on the opinions of others, perhaps a shop foreman or another executive. Do not waste five minutes on the man who has no authority to buy or who has no influence on the person who can say "yes" to your sales proposal. Even the courteous attention of the wrong man will not help you make a sale.

Spending More Time With the Best

Another time-waster is the failure of many individuals to apportion their time according to a buyer's potential purchasing power. It simply does not make sense for a person to spend an exorbitant amount of time with nickel-and-dime buyers, if it forces him to spend only a few minutes later in the day with a buyer of substantial amounts. Time-saving means more than spending time face-to-face with prospects; it also means spending more time with the best.

The big account is a challenge to the professional person, because it is usually more difficult to sell. To the person who is well prepared, however, the challenge is welcomed with confidence.

The average salesperson is often afraid of big-volume buyers, although they are often easier to sell than small-volume buyers. Big buyers are usually "big men" and they are therefore, seldom gruff and discourteous. They welcome well-informed people. Some individuals may not be adept enough to land the biggest accounts, but they can close larger accounts than they have had before if they are not afraid of the big-volume buyer.

Oral Presentation

A good oral presentation will assist in providing more action time because nothing will speed up communication faster than to be quickly and favorably understood. Perhaps salespeople would improve their presentations if they would:

1. Analyze their sales talks and learn to use a better word-choice

2. Practice answering common objections before they are asked

3. Learn to "think on their feet"

4. Learn to use visual sales aids and devices

5. Learn sure-fire closing techniques

Observance of these fundamentals would:

1. Help to decrease lost motion in the salesman's daily procedure

2. Increase his ability to react more promptly

3. Help him keep his presentation to the point and thereby eliminate extraneous matters and time-involving discussions

4. Help reduce complaints and callbacks and thereby save the time of the salesman and the customer

An excellent method for adding to selling time is to have the sales talk so well in mind that the presentation can be made with dispatch. Skilled salespeople cover the essentials but do not linger. They terminate the interview themselves, feeling it to be a psychological advantage over the prospect. Buyers like planned presentations because streamlined sales talks with accurate facts and a comprehensive review of benefits to be gained by the buyer are welcomed as time-savers by purchasers.

Visual Sales Aids

Action time itself can often be cut in half when visual sales aids are used. What buyers see attracts their attention almost nine times more than what they feel, touch, smell, and hear combined. Visual sales aids also help buyers remember a product or service about 65 percent longer. A recent survey revealed that 82 percent of the purchasing agents like salespeople to use visual sales aids. Sales managers also like salespeople to use visual sales aids because they are known to have increased sales 15 percent the first month

they were used. Sales aids, therefore, enable salesmen to decrease wasted time and to increase selling time.

The Right Start

Getting started right is believed to be half the battle and the first call of the day is therefore the most important. For this first call a prospect should be chosen who will be available. A nearby alternative call may also be listed in case the first choice is not in, so little time will be lost.

Salesmen cannot even approach the professional level if they do not plan for personal management. A plan gives a salesman the "prodding" or "bossing" he needs to start a successful day.

In many businesses the successful salesmen are usually those who are "over the hill by noon." One of the secrets of the professionals is to plan and finish a definite number of calls by noon. This type of planning leaves the afternoon wide open and tailor-made for several service, emergency, or prospecting calls.

Early Morning and Saturday Calls

Professional salespeople are careful not to make their early morning calls on prospects who insist on going through the morning's mail and planning their daily routine before talking to salesmen. These salesmen know which companies and prospects restrict salesmen's interviews to certain hours of the day or even certain days of the week. Early morning calls are possible, however, in practically every community, if the salesman restricts them to buyers whose daily schedule makes such interviews possible.

The point is that salesmen should not assume that all prospects are tied up at the start of a business day and on Saturday. They can always start the day with a call on a customer or prospect they are reasonably sure they can see or with whom they have made a definite appointment. There are likewise many buyers who have no objections to interviewing salesmen on Saturdays and the salesman should welcome the opportunity because the buyer will probably be able to give him more time, be more relaxed, and be in a more favorable mood. Also, successful salespeople do not mind working overtime because they know that no one has ever been successful who worked a straight forty-hour week.

Off-Time Calls

Some buyers must see as many as twenty or thirty salespeople a day during certain days of the week. They cannot possibly give each salesperson more than a limited amount of time. Many sales are lost because the salesperson is pressed for time in his presentation. By observation, inquiry, prearranged appointments, or casual approach, the *un*approachable can sometimes be reached at off-times and sold. The salesperson is then able to obtain undivided attention and successfully hold the prospect's interest until he wants to buy.

Ending the Interview

Started on their action hours with an early morning call, good salespeople do not spoil their daily schedule by not knowing when to say "good-bye." They do not drag out interviews or talk themselves out of sales just because they have mislaid their "terminal facilities." They do not yield to the temptation of letting hard-hitting presentations degenerate into mere social hours. They know that minutes can be saved daily, and hours saved every week by reaching for their hats when the reason for their calls has been accomplished. They not only save profitable time, but their buyers do not have the chance to change their minds.

Return Calls

When he enters an area he has not visited for several weeks, the professional salesman carefully reads the local newspaper to acquaint himself with events of interest to local buyers. As he plans his calls for the following day, he reviews for each customer or prospect such basic data as:

The problem or problems which the salesman's products or services will solve.

The importance of potential buyers, so that small-fry accounts will not be cultivated at the expense of other accounts representing higher value.

The buyer's personnel set-up, so that the salesperson's time will be spent with the individual who is authorized to buy or order what he sells.

EXCEPTION TO PLANNING RULE

Although the necessity of a carefully worked-out daily plan has been stressed, there are times when it should be laid aside. This is because every salesman has moments when he hits the crest of a selling wave. These times are apt to occur when the salesman unexpectedly obtains a big order from a particularly rugged buyer. At that particular time the salesman often reaches his selling peak and believes that *all* prospects are easy to sell.

Therefore, he wants to do something about it. He wants to quickly see the biggest and toughest buyer in the city and make his presentation while he is "hot." He does not want to cool down and he cannot afford to do so. He should abandon the plans he has made for the day and call on the big, and tough buyers just as fast as he can get to them. At this time, the salesman's best is far above his worst *and* he would be quite foolish if he did not temporarily abandon his plan.

Turning Social Time Into Sales Time

It is usually proper to take a good prospect or customer to lunch. When kept on a business basis, luncheons can accomplish much that might be impossible on a regular call. Likewise, by taking a buyer to dinner after business hours, a salesperson can frequently accomplish the same objective as he could on a call during the day. This is one more way to add that profitable extra hour each day.

Much time can be saved by avoiding long lunch hours and an irresistible urge to sneak in a little nap, a recess for golf, a ball game, or a movie in the name of good-will. A salesman is his own boss when he is out selling and sometimes stern self-discipline is necessary to resist the siren call of these distractions.

Car Curse

A salesman is sometimes fortunate if he does not use an automobile. The trouble with a car is that it is an easy means of running from one part of town to the other. But the man who must carry a brief-case, exhibits, or a product on the bus will plan his days so that his calls are clustered. He will take a downtown section between 25th and 32nd streets for a day's prospecting and will call on every prospect in the area that day, thereby finding prospects he never knew existed. On down-town calls, it rarely pays to use a car. When calls are made in rural areas or in other hard-to-reach places, a car is obviously necessary.

Out Tuesday, Back Friday Complex

The "out Tuesday, back Friday" complex unfortunately affects many salesmen who cover a territory outside a metropolitan city. These people offer many reasons why they must work at home or in the office on Monday and Saturday. However, the bee that gets the honey doesn't hang around the hive, and those salesmen who have an "out Tuesday, back Friday" complex are simply deluding themselves. They are trying to rationalize their laziness by claiming the need for paperwork or for plant contacts or other excuses. A great part of these two days can usually be turned into action time for the salesman.

Personal Records

A successful salesperson keeps records on himself to assist him in his planning. They indicate his past performance and enable him to plan for better future performance. They enable him to establish a goal.

He keeps actual time sheets or records of his calls, travel time in between, waiting time, even planning and record-keeping time as well as time for correspondence and seeking new prospects.

In addition, at each day's close, many individuals find it advantageous to compare the planned-in-advance schedule with the day's actual accomplishment. This gives them a means of discovering short-comings, of figuring out where time is being lost, and provides a basis for de-termining how such losses can be elimi-nated in the days ahead.

Records may be compared to a mirror showing what a person is accomplishing. Many people do not keep records for the same reason that many people are averse to looking into a mirror — they are afraid of what they will see there. Nevertheless, records provide a valuable method for turning wasted time into action time.

POWER POINTS

The following are some of the time wasters which would not be practiced by profes-sional salespeople:

Late starts from the office.

Neglecting those customers who are in their offices before nine, after five, and on Saturdays, Sundays, and holidays.

Calls on friendly accounts that do little but bolster a salesman's ego.

Excessive trips back to sales head-quarters.

Repeated call-backs on buyers who have little business potential to offer.

Poor routing of sales calls, resulting in jumps from one side of town to the other.

Failure to make appointments with prospects, resulting in excessive wait-ing time.

Inadequate sales presentation, few sales aids, and poor planning.

Little or no planning or organizing of selling time.

Too much time spent on socializing with prospects and customers.

Little or no idea of the supreme importance of time.

Failure to plan for more and better calls each day.

Failure to exercise self-discipline.

Failure to realize that time is a salesman's most important asset.

Failure to properly qualify prospects and therefore calling on too many "suspects."

Failure to properly locate prospects.

Poor use of basic selling methods.

Failure to keep personal records for purposes of periodic evaluation.

DISCUSSION QUESTIONS AND PROBLEMS

1. Why is personal management particularly important for a salesman?

2. What is meant by "action time?"

3. In relation to personal management, what basic elements should be included in planning?

4. How much more "action time" could be spent with prospects and customers if the salesmen planned and organized their work?

5. What are the advantages of a "daily and monthly plan?" Should a plan ever be abandoned? Why?

6. How may sales aids increase action time?

7. Would qualifying prospects increase action time? Why?

8. Would knowing where and how to locate prospects help increase action time? Why?

9. It has been said that greater knowledge and use of basic selling methods will provide more action time. Discuss and explain.

10. a. Do you believe a "route review" at frequent intervals is necessary? Why?
    b. Do you believe a salesman should be expected to plan his own route? Why?
    c. Should the salesmanager analyze the route and compel the salesman to follow it rigidly? Why?

11. Read each of the following questions carefully before answering them. Your text and the selected references will provide the answers.
    a. What values can you name for a "planning hour?"
    b. What will a well-spent "planning hour" do for a salesman?
    c. What makes a successful "planning hour?"
    d. What should the salesman do during the "planning hour?"

12. What method do you believe would be most effective for "organizing" your own file of written materials, sales aids, or evidence supporting your product or service so that the file would be easily accessible during your presentations?

13. Make an "action time" plan for yourself as a salesman of a product or service of your choice. Include the following in your plan: (a) a time schedule showing the apportionment of your day; (b) a set of rules or guides that would give you the most direct and thorough coverage of your territory; (c) a series of record forms that you feel would provide the necessary information on your prospects and selling activities.

14. Assume that you are selling burglary alarm systems to commercial and business firms and that you want to make an appointment with Mr. Miller, vice-president and general manager of the Howard Grocery company. Prepare, in written dialogue form, a telephone presentation that you feel will secure the appointment for you.

PHENOMENOLOGICAL PROJECTS

Victor Adding Machine Company (Case)

When a Victor salesman walks and talks his line of products, he does just that. He covers his territory block by block. He goes into every store, office, and plant (even homes) in the search for prospects who can and will buy. And having found them, he talks with them, educates them on the value of a Victor, and persuades them to own one.

Question:

1. Would you describe this kind of selling as peddler's work—beneath the dignity of a real salesman?

Canvassing done by the productive salesman requires intelligent planning. It also calls for ability to stick by the plan, no small matter.

Question:

2. Why is the ability to "stick by the plan" an important part of selling?

Sometimes PLANS DON'T ALWAYS WORK — but try to

It is one thing to say that the successful salesman locates his prospects by systematic round-the-clock canvassing. It is quite another task to do this. Perhaps the very ease with which it is described on paper makes it deceptive to the beginner, for the inexperienced salesman is quite apt to canvass in a new section of his territory each time he takes up the task.

Question:

3. Why is a new salesman apt to canvass in a new section of his territory?

Or perhaps he will kill a few hours (and "killing" is just as brutal as it sounds) canvassing in the vicinity of a red-hot lead that he got from the office.

Question:

4. What is wrong with following up a "red-hot lead?"

Even more foolish is the hit-and-miss canvasser. Despite every word to the contrary, this "wise" individual insists on qualifying potential prospects according to the appearance of their stores and office (outside view). If they are not up to his standards, he bypasses them without even a look-see inside.

Question:

5. Why is the hit-and-miss canvasser foolish?

Question:

6. What are some of the factors which create a good impression in addition to the sales talk?

Pretzel Routing: C.·H. Bietlerfield Case

The words *pretzel routing* simply means that some salesmen cover their territories by doubling back and forth pretzel fashion. Other, better salesmen make their daily calls with a minimum amount of lost time and mileage between each call. The figure below shows the pretzel routing used by a salesman to make nine calls.

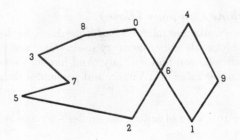

Question:

1. How would you plan these nine calls to save selling time and gasoline?

Recent surveys have revealed that lost selling time was due to poor route planning.

Question:

2. Do you believe a "route review" at frequent intervals is necessary?

You know your territory and the location of each prospect in it in relation to other prospects better than anyone else. When you lay out your next day's work schedule, do you make it a practice not only to list the nine calls that you expect to make but also to indicate the order in which you expect to call on them?

Questions:

3. Do you believe a salesman should be expected to plan his own route?
4. Would it be advisable for the sales manager to make a "job breakdown" and compel the salesmen to follow his routings?

Many times the difference between a high-paid salesman and an average salesman is merely the ever-lasting attention that the topnotcher gives to small details.

Question:

5. Do you agree with this statement? Why?

Chapter Twenty

Building Personal Worth

The master keys to building personal worth, the purpose and basis of our personalities, are *attitude* and *perceptual awareness*.

Attitude is a learned emotion, mental state, or a mood. It is a manner of feeling, thinking, or acting that show's one's disposition, opinion, bias, frame of mind, or temperament.

Perceptual awareness is the ability to see, to identify, and to understand the thinking, motives, interests, and expectations of people.

It is important to note that both attitude and perceptual awareness are learned, not inherited. We create them ourselves. Furthermore, attitude and perceptual awareness are consistent and predictable and therefore enable us to know with considerable accuracy how people will react in certain situations.

ATTITUDE DEVELOPMENT

Do you have a goal or a wish you hope to achieve? If you can steer yourself toward it, you can attain it. The trick is to plant a clearcut and sharply visualized goal in your brain and nervous system and then your automatic guidance system will take you to that goal. We are all born with an automatic servomechanism which helps us to achieve certain goals.

A servomechanism operates somewhat like a dispensing machine for candy, cigarettes and other standardized items. Imagine a serviceman opening the machine and filling it with his merchandise. You want what it dispenses and you insert a coin, pull the proper knob, and the wanted item emerges.[1] Our human servomechanism receives, stores and dispenses attitudes in much the same way, although it is more complicated.

The only information available to our servomechanism is that which we permit ourselves to feed into it. We can feed into it all of our past successes and failures and our memory will keep it in our storehouse of knowledge. Further, the mechanism cannot detect the difference between actual and imagined experiences. For example, if we think of success factors in vivid detail, they will be fed into our servomechanism as real images and the mechanism will automatically respond

1. A detailed explanation of servomechanism may be found in Maxwell Maltz, *Psycho-Cybernetics* (Englewood Cliffs, N.J.: Prentice-Hall, Inc., 1960).

with success-type emotions and reactions. When we feed failure factors into the mechanism the feedback will be failure-type reaction. The process of concentrating on success factors has been named *positive self-imagery*.

Postive Self-Imagery

Positive self-imagery (autosuggestion) may be the key to the success of a salesperson's attitude. If his normal image is inadequate—and most people are said to underrate themselves — then the person corrects it by systematically imagining that he already has the kind of personality he wants. To develop an attitude and attain self-realization, an acceptable self-image must be fed into the mechanism. Then, when the appropriate stimulus is applied, an appropriate attitude response, or feedback, will occur.

The concept of positive self-imagery and servomechanism is not new. The Bible states it in these words: "As a man thinketh, that he is."

When we feed success concepts into our servomechanism, we will be able to exceed ourselves; we will be able to achieve things others cannot. The procedure is to have a positive self-image of success, to think success, to never cease trying to be successful; to feed success formulas into the servomechanism. To start planting a positive self-image in our mechanisms, we might try saying Emile Coue's words to ourselves morning, noon, and night: "Every day in every way, I am growing better and better."

WINNING FAVORABLE BUYER ATTITUDE

One of the most difficult aspects of selling is being able to discern when the other person has a positive attitude toward the salesman and his proposition. Even those who have had long experience are not always able to determine when this quality has entered into the interview. All too

often the buyer will sit and look at a salesman with an apparent attitude of approval, but actually he may be thinking of something far away.

When the buyer sits with his arms folded or his legs crossed, he is displaying a poor attitude toward the salesman and is not particularly interested. His attention is probably divided between what is being said and some other matter that is on his mind. This clue is not always recognized and the mistake is made of thinking that the buyer has a favorable attitude when the opposite may be true.

The prospect's attitude and his environment should be observed very closely. Involuntary attitudes of interest should be detected and used as guides to steer the presentation. The prospect's eyes, in particular, as well as facial expressions and other body movements reveal much to the skilled observer. These signals are watched for and the salesperson acts accordingly because he knows that he cannot begin to motivate until he has a positive attitude and attention from his prospect.

It is generally agreed that winning favorable attitude and attention and thereby making a favorable impression is the result of three factors: (1) attitude and appearance; (2) opening statements; (3) enthusiasm throughout the presentation.

Attitude and Appearance

We know that people respond with favorable attitudes toward the person who knows how to make a good entrance. A professional salesman, like a professional actor, walks into an office or onto a stage with vigor and a dramatic flair. He always brings the impression that he has something worthwhile to do, that life is short, and that there is much to accomplish before his time expires.

Even the mood music that precedes a radio program is planned to indicate the nature of the program and to set the attitude for the listening audience. In much the same way, a salesman sets the stage, creates the mood, and builds the attitude for a sales presentation. A poor start hurts. When a salesman slouches in with his shoulders sagging, his chin down, his mouth and eyes at half-mast and his clothing wrinkled, it is easy for his prospects to assume negative attitudes.

When a salesman walks with a spring in his step, his eyes alert, his clothing neat and attractive and his speech cheerful and enthusiastic, his prospects respond to his good entrance by adopting a positive attitude. The success of any salesman largely depends on how well he can sustain the enthusiastic attitudes of his prospects for his proposition. A cheerful greeting, a word of praise, and an inviting appearance all serve to create the atmosphere and the attitudes that help to make buying easy for the prospect.

Opening Statements to Create Attitude

The first words a salesman utters must influence the prospective buyer to like him as a person, and at the same time stir his curiosity enough to make him want to hear more. Many successful salespeople spend hours over opening statements. When a buyer says, "Sit down, I'd like to hear your story," the salesperson has reached his objective in creating a positive, favorable attitude.

It is practically impossible to outline definite forms of address that will serve to create the right attitude for all interviews. It is always advisable, however, to avoid commonplace openers and stereotyped phrases such as: "I thought I'd drop in and see if I can interest you in . . ." "My name is Jones, representing the Blank Company. We make a very good product and I'd like to tell you about it."

Every succesful salesperson avoids such beginning remarks because they do not create a positive attitude. A professional

opening to a successful sale may require only sixty seconds if a salesman has properly prepared himself. How to prepare and how to deliver opening remarks are fully discussed in Chapter VII.

Enthusiasm Throughout the Presentation

Is it possible for an enthusiastic attitude to be spontaneous with some people and not with others? Can an attitude of enthusiasm be developed by a person for whom it is not natural? The answer to both questions is "yes."

There is no doubt that an enthusiastic attitude is a powerful force in human relations and it can be developed by most people. However, whenever it is unnatural with a person, he should be careful to remain sincere. If he puts on an act and is insincere about his feelings, if his attitude of enthusiasm does not arise from a firmly held belief, then it can do him more harm than good. But when one's attitude is honest and sincere, it can be a powerful tool.

Enthusiasm is usually the result of a person being "sold" on his ability, and the more a person knows about himself and other people, his product or service, his customers or prospects and his selling skills, the more enthusiastic he becomes.

What does an attitude of *contagious* enthusiasm mean to people who sell? Does it mean that a salesman sounds as if he believes what he is saying, that his smile is contagious, that he holds our attention, that he always says the right thing, and that his enthusiasm is catching? This is all true but there is a more basic meaning for the salesman: Enthusiasm is an attitude and any attitude is likely to be contagious.

If we have an enthusiastic attitude, we may expect an enthusiastic reaction from the person with whom we are talking. Crissey and Cash have named this phenomenon "recipathy," a combination of reciprocity and empathy.[2] On the other hand, if we show an unfriendly attitude, an unsure attitude or no particular attitude, it will rub off onto the person with whom we are conversing and he will respond in the same way. For enthusiasm is an attitude easily recognized by the person with whom we do business.

Misinterpreting Attitudes

Are all attitudes recognized as easily, quickly or accurately as enthusiasm? Is there any danger of a person misinterpreting what we do and mentally labelling us with an attitude that is not real? Do prospects sometimes misinterpret our attitudes? Yes, this can frequently occur.

There was an ambitious salesman who felt people were not receptive to his personality, ideas, or suggestions. It was later discovered that one of the reasons people were not too fond of him was because he used the wrong words when he tried to put over an idea. Instead of saying, "Here's an idea you might want to consider" or "Here's a suggestion which might have possibilities," he'd go in and say, "Here's what you ought to do . . ."

Naturally, this approach was resented. While the salesman's real attitude was that of making suggestions for the betterment of the prospect, it appeared that he had an attitude of telling the person what to buy or how to respond. He used commands rather than suggestions and did not realize the attitude he was revealing.

Probably the greatest advantage of enthusiasm as an attitude is that it leaves very little room for misunderstanding or for misinterpretation.

Empathy

The salesman with empathy finds it easy

2. Harold C. Cash and W. J. E. Crissey, "Personality and Sales Strategy," *The Psychology of Selling*, Vol. 4 (New York: Personnel Development, Inc. 1957), pp. 12-14.

to appreciate the emotions and attitudes of his prospects. He believes that they are his friends and not his enemies. It is effortless for him to match his presentation to the attitudes of the people on whom he calls. He does not need to use force or pressure because he understands and appreciates the other person's problems, conflicts, emotions, and attitudes. When buyers identify their attitudes and interests with those expressed by the salesman, an excellent relationship is established.

A salesperson with too much empathy, however, can find himself in trouble, for he may find it difficult to control the interview so that he can ask for the order. Instead, he may identify himself too closely with the buyer's problems and emotions. Or a buyer who is not empathic may regard the salesperson as an intruder.

Sympathy

The person who possesses a sympathic temperament and a warm personality can quickly establish a friendly atmosphere in harmony with the other person's temperament. This is very important to a salesperson who is trying to persuade and motivate a prospective buyer. Obviously, one has an easy task when trying to interest a sympathetic person and a difficult task when trying to interest an unsympathetic person.

A sympathetic salesperson can break down the emotional barrier between himself and the prospect. The salesperson, however, must usually manifest his sympathy first if he expects the prospective buyer to reciprocate. Sympathy, however, should not be confused with pity in a business transaction.

Recipathy

Recipathy is a coined word which means "a feeling created by interaction with another person." The person who says and does the right thing at the right time is recipathic. He exudes understanding, sympathy, and empathy, and these elements are reciprocated by the other person. When the person smiles, for example, the other person invariably returns the smile. The recipathic salesman adjusts easily to a buyer because he watches for and identifies feelings or emotional clues. Having identified the extent of the buyer's recipathy, the salesman is cued not only on what to say and do but also on the factors of why, how, when, and where to conduct himself.

ATTITUDES TO AVOID
Fixation
Fixation is a term used to indicate "an arrest at one of the levels of personality development." Fixation has also been defined as "an unreasonable conviction which persistently dominates and hampers a person's thinking, even when the conviction is incorrect."

It has been said that the unconscious harboring of fixed ideas, opinions, and attitudes is the prime source of a salesman's failures. For example, a salesman may have a fixation on the notion that prospects can be typed and that each type will respond to only one kind of appeal. His fixation may cause him to avoid the use of other appeals when all objective facts show that the prospects may be entirely different.

Every possibility of winning favorable attitudes, even the most remote, should be entertained. We should resist the temptation to excuse ourselves in advance by classifying the person as "impossible" or "just not my kind."

We can also fixate on positive goals. A strong wish actually develops a new goal. When a positive wish becomes permanently fixed on one worthwhile goal to the exclusion of others, we can attain the goal because we are fixated on it.

A humorous example of the fixation attitude is revealed in the story about the man who thought he was dead. No amount

of persuasion could convince him otherwise. Finally, a psychiatrist asked him if dead men bleed. The man said, "No, dead men don't bleed." The psychiatrist stuck him with a pin and the man bled. "I was wrong," the man said, "Dead men do bleed."

Likewise, some of us will have a fixation regarding some of the concepts we shall examine and suggest in this chapter. Salesmen should preserve an open mind, clear of pseudo-thinking. They should be willing to examine all facets of a principle before arriving at a conclusion.

The Seven Devils
The following expressions reveal negative attitudes. They are included for the purpose of ridiculing the persons who express them and to emphasize the need for positive attitudes.

The Seven Devils
1. But we've always done it this way!
2. We tried it once and it didn't work!
3. They didn't do it that way where I come from!
4. Let's try it later in the year.
5. What's the use of saving half a day?
6. It's O.K. but they'd never let us do it!
7. It's not in the budget!

BUILDING GOOD ATTITUDES
Attitude Restraint
Our attitudes are often a reflection of our emotions. If someone criticizes us, we may resent it. Our extra effort to do a better job may be ignored. In either case, our attitude becomes resentful and we have to restrain our emotions to keep them from showing.

Perhaps a customer we had considered 100 percent loyal suddenly announces he is checking out and intends to buy from a strong competitor. We mull it over, brood about it, worry it around and start building up a head of steam. We become angry, and finally our attitude shows in front of the wrong person. We are "dead ducks" because of our lack of restraint.

All of us have had reverses of one kind or another; we have had annoyances that pile up until they become too heavy to bear. We may suffer from misplaced aggression. What can we do to prevent our emotion from gaining the upper hand and causing us to take it out on an innocent person?

Attitude Control

How can we keep our attitudes from showing? How can we control our emotions? This is an area of behavior in which we all can improve. Several suggestions are:

> Refuse to permit emotions to control us.
> Discuss the situation with another person.
> Regard problems intelligently, not emotionally.

We learn to realize that an individual who rants and raves under adversity is usually one who fails to recognize that there are two points of view — or if he does, he reacts this way:

> In controversial situations,
> My perception's rather fine.
> I always see both points of view,
> The one that's wrong, and mine.

We have all seen people who "blow their stacks," while others rarely seem to become angry or reveal negative attitudes. Everyone becomes angry at times. The difference is that one person gets angry and makes little attempt to control his emotions while the other individual has reached a level of maturity that permits him to control his attitudes and keep them from showing.

One definition of maturity is "the power of meeting any situation, especially a difficult situation successfully by proper adjustments." In Webster's dictionary this is the definition for intelligence! Perhaps

a less emotional and a more intelligent examination of the upsetting situations we all encounter would help us to develop more mature attitudes when calling on our prospective customers.

Antidote for Negativism

"Don't be a part of the problem" is a good antidote for negativism. Another good guideline, used to excellent effect in the Army is "Never mind what won't work— plan an attack that will work!"

These guidelines apply equally well with the prospective buyer, customer, boss, friends, or family.

Harmful Attitudes

All sales executives seem to agree that a salesman's attitude is a tremendous factor affecting his success. We can all think of an instance when our attitude might have affected our success.

Harmful attitudes are what we want to avoid, for a person is criticized not so much for what he has done or not done, but for the attitude he displays. All of us can probably recall cases which show that the severity of the punishment depended more on the attitude about a mistake than on the offense itself.

Many of us can recall specific instances in our work experience in which attitude has been involved. All of us still undoubtedly agree that our attitudes are often responsible for getting us into trouble or at least causing criticism.

The following attitude examples are based on actual selling situations. They illustrate at least two kinds of attitudes.

A district sales manager for the Chili Charlie Chili Company has Jim Jiminez come into the office. The manager explains to Jim that he is checking with all men below 85 percent of their quota to see what can be done to alleviate the situation. He then asks Jim why he has sold only 65 percent of his quota. Jim's answer is this:

"Well, in the first place, I've got a heck

of a heavy quota for my territory. Whoever set this quota certainly didn't know the conditions. The fact that I ended up last year with 65 percent of quota should prove that it was wrong to give me the same quota this year.

"I don't know what more I can do. I'm working as hard as I can now. Why, it's a job just keeping the buyers we have. I'm lucky I haven't lost more business than I have, with my competition throwing their weight around. Most of my time is spent putting out fires and keeping buyers happy.

"My buyers all feel there isn't any money to be made in selling some of our items — and they just aren't interested in building their sales. Any good prospects I do find in my territory are all tied up with competitors. This is their territory, you know, with lots of promotion, big deals and three — three, mind you — salesmen covering the same territory I do. Besides, with that aviation plant closing up and people moving to Georgia, business is just folding up and disappearing. The business just isn't here — not for us, anyway."

What kind of attitude is that? It is clearly a defeatist, negative, and defiant attitude. In his answer, Jim criticized others, shifted the blame. revealed a closed mind, tried to justify himself, and gave excuses. Think about these attitudes for a moment!

The sales manager of Wyandot Products Company[3] is holding a staff meeting.

He states that too much business is being lost to competitors because of price and that he would like a discussion of the problem to see what the solution might be.

The comments of the staff members are as follows:

(a) "I'd like to know the answers to that one. I've got a lot of it going on in my territory."

(b) "Me too."

3. The Wyandot Products Company and the Charlie Chili attitude examples are used with the special permission of Mr. D. C. Legault, Dayton Industrial Products Company, Division of Dayco Corporation.

(c) "This isn't a new problem. We've had it for years. Maybe it's getting worse, but I don't see how you are going to whip it. We'll just have to live with it like we always have."

(d) "What are we going to do if there's an 'under-the-table' payoff?"

(e) "What about legal violations? Couldn't you get in trouble if you got the business on a low bid?"

(f) "If you come up with a solution, competition will do you one better and we'll be back in the same old rut. There just isn't any answer to the problem."

In addition to the negative comments of the salesmen, the advertising manager demonstrated a bad attitude by leafing through his notes, since the subject didn't concern him. His attitude could be considered boredom, dislike, disinterest, disdain, disrespect, or disgust. These are all bad attitudes as well as bad manners.

What is the attitude problem in this case? Did these men offer good suggestions? Were their opinions of any value? If they were of little value, try to explain why.

This case reveals a completely negative response. Instead of trying to help solve a problem, each person brought up an obstacle and added to the problem. This is a very common failing and everyone is apt to do it at some time or other. Salesmen should watch for it in the next meeting they attend—it will be there, but it should not be permitted to become a negative attitude of the whole group.

Negative Attitudes of Prospect
Some people may resist buying because they dislike the seller. Their dislike may be caused by his manner of talking, his behavior, his mood, or his manner, or he may remind them of someone whom they do not like. For any number of reasons, their attitudes may not be in rapport with the salesman. A brief analysis of the buyer's attitude will usually reveal the cause of the fault. If caused by the salesman, he

should attempt to correct it. If caused by the buyer, the salesman should be prepared to deal with it.

Prejudicial Buying Attitudes

A prospect may have the attitude that a certain price is right or a preference for a certain brand or quality of product or a particular style or color. Many prospects do not like to change their attitudes and thus it is part of a salesperson's job to jolt such prospects out of their complacency and self-satisfaction. They can do it through relaxed expanation, interesting presentations, and through the application of their motivation techniques.

Negative attitudes may also be based on bias, misinformation, or misjudgment of the salesperson, his proposition, and his company. From the moment the salesperson starts his presentation, he may need to work toward eliminating a certain prejudicial attitude which the prospective buyer may have.

Contradictory Attitudes

Attitudes persist as tendencies to action, ready to assert themselves once contradictory restraining tendencies are no longer aroused.

Suppose a salesperson has carefully planned his entire procedure to suit a particular buyer. Will the buyer conform exactly to the salesman's preconceived ideas about him? Probably not. The salesman must be prepared for the unexpected and be ready to deal with the prospect as he finds him. At the start of the interview, it is the salesman's job to try to discover the buyer's feelings, attitudes and general state of mind, in addition to making his sales presentation. The salesman may have to modify his plans when certain conditions are found to exist.

If the buyer is in a bad mood or if he is emotionally upset, he may have a negative attitude toward the salesman. Obviously, a planned, standard presentation will come to naught if applied to this kind of buyer.

Some salesmen under these circumstances proceed with their planned presentations, hoping that the buyer's attitude will change as the presentation progresses. This rarely occurs, however, because the business-like behavior of the salesman usually tends to irritate the prospect.

Displaced Aggression

The salesperson, his company or his product may not cause the buyer's emotional upset, but they may be blamed by the buyer for his irritated, negative attitude. Actually, the buyer may be employing displaced aggression, and he can be expected to exaggerate and distort the facts whether or not the salesperson, his company or his product is really to blame.

If the fault lies with the company, the salesperson will want to make an adjustment, but he should do so only after he has allowed the buyer talk out his anger. For the adjustment of a compaint before the buyer's feelings have been soothed will not be appreciated. The best approach when confronted with a negative attitude is to be a pleasant and interested listener, and to encourage the buyer to talk so that his mind will be freed of whatever is bothering him. The salesperson can then handle the adjustment.

Buyer Preoccupation

Another contradictory attitude problem is encountered when the buyer is preoccupied and resents being interrupted. The cue at this point is to discover whether the buyer is beginning his task or is nearing its completion. If he is just starting the job, he will be more likely to adjust positively and listen to the proposal. If the buyer is near the end of his job, on the other hand, he will be reluctant to stop. If his predicament is ignored by the salesperson, the buyer may refuse to pay attention or become irritated and resentful. What should be done?

There are several alternatives available, each of which is better than trying to sell an individual whose attention is divided. First, the salesperson can offer to wait until the buyer's task is completed. He could also take the opportunity to do some creeping-vine selling; that is, to see other people who may be the prospect's subordinates, associates or superiors who might influence the buyer's decision or who can furnish important facts.

The salesperson can also offer to come back at a later time. While this is not always the best procedure, it may sometimes be necessary. The less favorable the buyer's attitude, the more difficult it will be to see him later. If the salesman offers to come back later, it is important that he make a definite appointment with the buyer for the return visit. After he leaves, the salesperson should confirm the new appointment by letter or by telephone, so that he will not make another unprofitable call.

PERCEPTUAL AWARENESS

A salesperson's attitude depends largely upon his perception, for perception is the ability to see, identify and understand the thinking, and motives of people. Perception includes an awareness of objects and situations.

Perceptual awareness is very important, but the average salesperson is aware of very few of the objects and situations around him. Unless he has more than average perceptual power, however, he will be unable to rise above the status of an average salesperson, or one who is as close to the bottom as he is to the top. Salespeople are especially concerned with perceptive factors such as motives, interests, and expectations.

Perception Through Motivation

When a salesperson presents the right motives or reasons for buying, the benefits will be perceived by the prospect as a means of filling his needs or solving his problem. The prospective customer's desire for gain is probably the most powerful motive that can be used. Even the dullest person will have perceptual awareness of statements which suggest profit, mark-up, volume, turnover, savings, loss prevention or other specific benefits that imply or state that he will gain if he buys. How to motivate people was thoroughly discussed in Chapter IX.

Perception Through Interests

People tend to pay greater attention to those things which interest them and much less or none at all to those which do not interest them. The list of interests at various ages shown in the following tabulation probably dominate the attitude, attention and perception of almost all people at these age levels. A salesperson who can perceive the appropriate age of his prospective customers can plan to influence his decision through emphasizing the interests that dominate people in his age group.

Chief Interest of People at Various Ages

Age	Interest
18	Ideals and social growth
20	Appearance
23	Morality
26	Good impression
30	Income and living costs
31	Success
33	Security
38	Health
over 45	Health

Perception Through Expectancy

Perception through expectancy means that we often have a mental image of situations to come and muscular readiness for actions which have been satisfactory in the past. Such anticipation leads us to be more clearly aware of certain situations than of others and to react to them promptly and vigoously with prepared useful reactions.

Expectancy plays a major role in selecting what we will perceive. When the salesperson has had four successful days he will not perceive the possibility of a failure on the fifth. The figure below illustrates expectancy. When viewing a series of two-digit numbers, many people will report that they have seen the number 13. Another group of individuals who have been exposed to letters of the alphabet will see the letter B. In the one case, the subject has acquired an expectancy for numbers while the other has been exposed to the letters of the alphabet.

In most situations, the old adage "we see what we want to see" applies, for we often perceive what we expect to perceive and therefore many of our perceptions are false.

Expectancy is probably the most important factor that determines attention and thus perception for our expectancies largely direct and order whatever we see, smell, taste, or feel. Without them, our perceiving would be largely at the mercy of random fluctuations in the environmental stimuli.

The price-value illusion also illustrates the principle of expectancy. When one card is placed over the other, the two cards are exactly the same size. When they are placed side by side, the one at the right will appear to be larger. In this way, the price-conscious buyer has his perception directed toward value and drawn away from price. The importance of price is diminished and the concept of value is enhanced. This attracts the buyer because his mind is expecting more value than he wants to pay for in price.

Principle of Direction

The psychological principal of direction should be understood by salespeople for it can govern thinking. When we get the wrong mental direction, we are in trouble. When we get the right direction, we have a great advantage in solving problems and in thinking straight through a selling situation.

Research has revealed the advantages and disadvantages of obtaining the right direction in problem solving. How the wrong direction can interfere with a solution is illustrated by the nine dot problem. The problem is to connect the nine dots by drawing four straight lines without taking the pencil off the paper and without retracing. Allow five minutes to solve this direction problem.

In attempting to solve this problem, the average person makes one inference after another and all are relevant because they concern the nine dots. They fail to conform with the instructions and are rejected almost as soon as suggested. The person has a *set*, in other words, that is related to the dots and to the instructions. The *set* makes him keep all lines within the limits of the area bordered by the dots. As long as his thinking follows this direction,

he cannot solve the problem. Every inference will prove inadequate, but when the person thinks of the possibility that lines may go outside of the area within the dots, he has the right direction. The solution may not be found immediately, but at least he will have made inferences more closely related to the methods of solution. Many situations will arise in a salesperson's activities when he will need to be perceptually aware of the right *direction*.

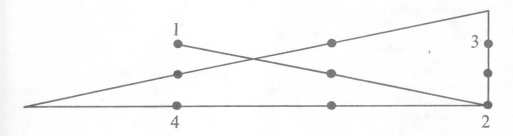

Answer to Direction Problem: The creative person is sufficiently flexible to look for solutions beyond the limitations that he believes to exist. So his lines do not stay within the box since that requirement was not specified.

DEVELOPMENT OF PERCEPTUAL POWERS

Perception is one of the chief elements in persuading and motivating people to buy. What can we do to develop and strengthen our perceptual power? We can develop our awareness, learning how to become more vigilant in observing or in drawing inferences from what we see, hear, smell, taste, or touch.

An increase in awareness should make salespeople become more alive, awake, alert, aware, cognizant, and conscious of the behaviour of the people with whom they transact business. It should also stimulate sensitivity so that one may become more susceptible to excitement and more responsive to stimulation in selling situa-

tions. These results should improve self-control. The development of perceptive power may be started with an analysis of perception, sensitivity, and awareness.

If the reader had the mental flexibility, sensitivity, awareness, and perception to solve the nine dot problem before he read the solution, he is far above the average person in perceptual power.

Analytical Capability

The simple analyses of perceptual power which follow reveal if a person is fairly perceptive. Accurate measurement of mental ability to confirm the existence or absence of these talents would necessarily be made by a reliable psychologist.

1. How imaginative are you?
   Using a separate sheet of paper, list all the possible uses you can think of for a red brick. Time limit is four minutes.
2. How aware and analytical are you?
   A five-car train leaves New York at 7:29 A.M. heading for Washington, D.C. some 225 miles away. It travels at sixty miles

an hour and makes no stops. At 8:31 A.M. a five-car train leaves from Washington for New York, traveling at forty miles an hour and making no stops. When the two trains pass, which will be closer to New York?

3. How well do you think?
Three men, asking to share a hotel room, are told by the bellboy that the rate of $30 is payable in advance since they are without luggage. Each gives him a $10 bill. When the boy goes to the desk, he is told the room costs only $25, and the cashier gives him five one-dollar bills in change. The bellhop, knowing the guests were willing to pay $30, keeps $2 for himself and refunds $1 to each man. Each of the three had paid out $9, which amounts to $27, and the boy has retained $2, for a total of $29. What has become of the other dollar?

4. How creative are you?
a. If it takes three and one-half minutes to boil one egg, how long does it take to boil six?
b. How many cubic inches of dirt are there in a hole that is one foot deep, two feet wide and eight feet long?

Answers to Problems:
1. All the possible answers are impossible to count. But if we find only construction

uses, the number is small. Other answers: paperweight, doorstop, weapon, hammer, bookends.

2. An important element in perception is the ability to recognize the basic elements of a problem. In this one the figures are irrelevant. When the two trains pass, they will be equidistant from New York.

3. The problem is deceptively stated. The $27 paid by the three men included the $2 kept by the dishonest bellboy plus the $3 refund: $30.

4. a. Three and one-half minutes if boiled in the same pot.
b. No cubic feet of dirt in a hole of any size.

Awareness Development

The following awareness tests will further enhance understanding of perceptual awareness.

Triangle

Can you read correctly the simple, well-known phrases printed in the triangle below? Take as much time as you like, but do it before you read the comment that follows. Look at each triangle and repeat aloud or write down on paper what you think it says.

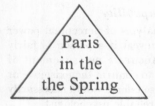

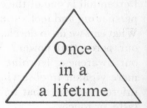

Comment: Unless you are unusually perceptive, you repeated or wrote, "Paris in the spring." But the triangle reads "Paris in the the spring." Likewise, in the second and third triangles the words "the" and "a" are repeated. Extensive research

has shown that only one of forty persons can read these triangles correctly.
Circle
Which circle is bigger? They are actually the same size, although a casual glance suggests that the circle on the left is larger.

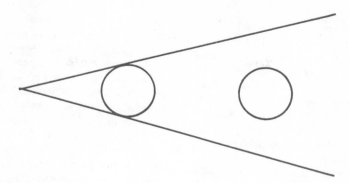

Hidden Word
The word *nationality* hidden in the figure sometimes takes students several minutes to find even after they have been told that the word is in the figure.

These awareness tests should have made the reader more conscious of the state of his awareness, sensitivity and perception. Awareness can be developed and it is important, Albert Einstein said: "Awareness is more important than knowledge. Knowledge is limited, but perceptive awareness embraces the whole world, stimulating and creating progress."

BUYER PERCEPTION
The Way They Buy

How the prospect sees the product service is another facet of perception which the salesman should understand. Does the proposition appear the same to the prospect as it does to the salesman? The answer is no, unless the salesman understands the prospect's mind and emotions and uses this knowledge as part of his selling process.

Psychologists have pointed out that present needs and past experiences influence a person's perception of objects and situations. If the needs and experience of the prospect and salesman differ, their understanding of the proposition will differ. Only naive persons believe that the thinking of a prospect is swayed entirely by objective sales talk. The prospect is also influenced by his perception and his need. Therefore, the first step in selling is to discover the buyer's needs. Then, when those are known, the salesman can present his proposition in the proper frame of reference and in a manner which will be perceived by the prospect as a means of filling his needs.

Prospect's Past Experience

A prospect's experience affects his perception probably somewhat less than his needs affect it. Nevertheless, the basic reason why a salesperson learns all he can about a prospect, including his occupations, is so that he can use the information to help attain favorable prospect perception. Whatever experience the prospect has had will cause him to perceive and appreciate certain specific product or service features, and the salesman should stress those points whenever he deals with individual prospects.

If, for example, a plumber is buying a house, any special aspects of heating and pipefitting would guide his perception and such items should be emphasized in the sales talk. If a printer were buying a house, such features as durability, careful workmanship and beauty might be emphasized in the sales presentation. An artist might be interested in unique features of design and landscaping and these should be stressed when selling a house to him.

Prospect's Self-Perception

Knowing how the prospect perceives himself is as important as knowing how he perceives the product or service. In this respect, there are three aspects of the prospect's perception to be studied by the salesman:

1. The way the prospect appears to himself.
2. The way the prospect would like to appear to others.
3. The way the prospect actually appears to others.

The way the prospect appears to himself is important in this way: If the salesman does not know or appreciate how the prospect appears to himself, but treats him from the salesman's viewpoint, he may offend the prospect or at least reduce his own effectiveness in dealing with the prospect. An appreciation of this view will cause the salesman to modify his approach and proceed with some knowledge of how the prospect may react.

The way the prospect would like to appear to others is likewise important. Suppose the prospect was a "nobody" in his community, but wanted to become a "somebody." The salesman could then make the presentation in a way that would make the prospect feel more important to his acquaintances and neighbors. In other words, if the salesman senses that the prospect has a blank between what he is and what he wants to be, he should present the benefits of his merchandise so that the buyer sees it as a way of meeting his goals.

How the prospect appears to the salesman may be important because it determines the tenor, emphasis, direction or dynamics of the presentation and the salesman may thus be able to control the interview.

PERCEPTUAL ROADBLOCKS

How many of us have perceptual roadblocks? We probably have access to full cerebral storehouses of perceptive abilities, but we are doing nothing about them. How many of us have ever asked ourselves if we are using all of our perceptual power or what roadblocks are preventing the use of all we possess?

Psychologists say there are four reasons and they can all be corrected just as soon as they are dredged up and recognized.

1. Many people believe they are not idea men. They cannot generate sensitivity or awareness.
2. Many people have a *suggestion block* caused by their management's refusal to experiment or to welcome new ideas.
3. Others have a *neurotic block* which smothers awareness and imagination for

murky reasons, hidden in their subconscious mind.

4. Most people do not know how to tap those tremendous assets of awareness, imagination, and perception.

What can be done about it? Here are some good suggestions for tapping perceptive power.

1. Make yourself dissatisfied.
2. Imagine what would make your job ideal.
3. Find out what is preventing the job from being ideal.
4. Devise ways to overcome the obstacles.
5. Force yourself to be more perceptive.
6. Never suppress an idea. Ideas and perception are closely related. Stimulate yourself to be curious and to welcome new ideas. Do not bury your curiosity.
7. Set aside a definite time for exercising perceptive powers.
8. Practice in a quiet place: train, plane, bus, bathtub, den or parlor — any place where you can concentrate.

POWER POINTS

Attitude is the master key to our personal worth.

Our appearance, knowledge, appreciations, ethical standards, and selling skills reflect our attitudes toward ourselves, our prospective buyers, our product or service, our associates, and our management.

Competition is forever present and good attitude will produce more results than words alone or lucky breaks.

A positive attitude is the equalizer that results in recognition, accomplishment, and success.

Both attitude and perceptual awareness are learned, not inherited. They are consistent and predictable and therefore enable us to know with considerable accuracy how people will react in certain situations.

We are all born with an automatic servomechanism which helps us to achieve certain goals.

Unless we have more than average perceptual power, we will be unable to rise above the status of an average salesperson, and remain one who is as close to the bottom as he is to the top.

Obtain a small rubber ball — the kind children use to play a game of jacks is best. Place the ball in the palm of your hand and squeeze it. Notice that when you squeezed the ball, the effect on your muscles was so slight that it was not even measurable.

If the rubber ball were carried constantly, however, and if we kept on squeezing it regularly, as wrestlers and boxers do, our muscles in that hand would develop so much power that even the strongest man would gasp during a handshake.

The same principle of practice applies to the job of selling. There is no other way to increase selling power! If we want muscles in our arms, we must keep squeezing the rubber ball. If we want muscles in our selling, we must keep on practicing.

The suggestions offered should help you toward much greater perceptiveness and those dormant difficulties in your mind can rise to challenge and generate their own challenges. It has been found profitable to ask ourselves, "What can I do to become a better salesperson?" We should think about that question, day in and day out, until good answers emerge. It is known that when salesmen become that alert, they soon seek new ways of doing things and new sources of business without even being aware of it.

No one is ever too old to acquire better attitudes and greater perceptual awareness. Both increase with age. But both combined amount to little unless another ingredient is added: practice. Application and practice may not be easy, but anything easy does not have much value.

DISCUSSION QUESTIONS AND PROBLEMS

1. Why are attitudes and wishes said to be the master keys to successful behavior?
2. Why is a knowledge of contradictory attitudes and displaced aggression important to the success of the individual who engages in any kind of selling?
3. Explain the impact of an attentive attitude on personal success. What attitude was displayed in the cases?
4. Explain the antidote for negativism suggested in this chapter.
5. Assume your attitude could be improved. What would you do to improve it?
6. What does an attitude of contagious enthusiasm mean to people who sell?
7. Is there any danger of a person misinterpreting our attitude and labelling us incorrectly?
8. What are the meanings of the following words? Explain their relationship to salesmanship. Empathy. Sympathy. Recipathy.
9. What is the relationship between servomechanism and attitude? Explain in detail.
10. What is positive self-imagery and how can it help you in your personal relationships?
11. What is an attitude of fixation? What can be done to avoid it?
12. How can our servomechanism be used for the development of an attitude of success?
13. Explain how greater perceptional awareness through an understanding of motives, interests, and expectancy can help in dealing with people.
14. What are perceptual illusions? Why should salespeople study the topic of illusions? Do you have any personal perceptual illusions?
15. What can be done to strengthen and develop perceptual power?
16. What the salesperson sees is important, but what the prospective customer sees is equally important. How will an understanding of buyer perception help the salesperson?
17. "Knowing how the prospective customer perceives himself is as important as knowing how he perceives the salesperson and the product or service." Explain the three aspects of the prospect's perception.
18. What perceptual roadblocks may be preventing the use of our perceptual powers? What can be done to banish them?
19. What is the learning principle behind the rubber ball exercise?

PHENOMENOLOGICAL PROJECTS

The Fuzz Chudapoff Company (Case)

The sales manager once said, "Over 50 percent of our salesmen's success stems from a sales-winning attitude. Customers forgive honest mistakes or lack of knowledge, but they always remember a salesman's attitude. Personality traits for salesmen mean the ability to get along with people and to be effective in dealing with them. A sales-winning attitude means a desirable physical appearance, desirable character traits, desirable social traits, and desirable mental traits. Atttiude is the mirror in which we see ourselves; it is a reflection of our living, it is us as others see us. Attitude is like a foundation on which we erect our lives, a good foundation furnishes strength for the building on it.

Creative salesmen are those who develop the right attitudes and learn how to influence people. To develop a winning attitude, one must realize the need for improvement and have a strong desire to improve. Then he must make a survey of his attitudes based on a self-analysis, a rating of oneself as others see him, and a comparison of one's ratings with the ratings of others. Finally, one must form a systematic plan for development. He must work on the attitudes that he wants to develop and decide on new habits that will improve certain attitudes to get desirable attitudes established.

Question:

You have studied the chapter. You know something about attitudes. Do you "buy" the statements in this case study? Why?

James T. Mangan (Case)

The buyer is a bigger liar than any salesman ever hoped to be.

You call on him and what's the first thing he does? Freezes up on you! Pretends you are about as welcome as roaches in the pantry. Because you are out to sell, you push on in spite of the frigid atmosphere and goad yourself to make him listen to your description of your plant, your service, your product, and your ideals.

Then, what does he say? "Not interested!"

That's a lie. The buyer is a liar. He is interested. Mildly, perhaps, for your exposition of your own merits may have been poor, but he is interested just the same, just as any human being is interested in another human being and his work. Yet, the buyer says he is not interested. The buyer is therefore a liar.

You shoot at something definite. You ask him if there is anything coming up on which you may figure. He says "No!" That's another lie. The buyer knows very well that there's something about to break.

But suppose you have even gotten so far as to be allowed to figure on the work. Your bid is in, and you drop around to find out what happened.

What saith the liar—I mean, the buyer?

"The order is already let. You were too high!"

The liar! The double liar! He has told you two lies, not just one. The order hasn't been let, and furthermore, you weren't too high, you were low!

The buyer is a liar! Every word, every statement that issues from his mouth is a lie. You—poor, trustful salesman that you are—have been conducting your own activities according to the code of all good salesmen. You tell the truth, you avoid misrepresentation, you play fair with the buyer.

You have gone so far as to believe what he told you. How sad! Don't do it any more. The buyer is a liar and if you believed what he told you and were a consistent man, you would have to quit selling and go out of business at once.

The only time the buyer tells the truth, as far as you're concerned, is when he says, "Here's the order!" When he signs his name or hands over his money. Then he's sincere. Then he's honest! Then he's playing fair!

Buying everywhere has taken a great advantage of selling. It has forced the salesman to tell the truth, while reserving the right for the buyer to lie his head off without violating the "ethics" of business.

So your only chance to even the score is to take this somewhat radical attitude: "The buyer is a liar! Nothing he tells me is right or honest until he wants to buy."

Questions:
1. Do you believe that this attitude is the correct one for a successful individual?
2. If we agree that the statement, "the buyer is a liar," is true, should it be regarded as important?
3. What would happen to sales volume if this attitude were adopted toward all buyers?

Index

Successful Industrial Selling, 149 (n. 1)
Suggestibility of buyers, 247-248
Suggestion selling
    and buyer's personality, 247-248
    conditioned reflex, 245-246
    importance of, 245, 252
    through language, 249-250
    through questions, 248-249
    retail, 260-261
    through similes and metaphors, 249
    slogans, 250
Surveys, sales, 65-66

T

Tangibles, selling of, 20-22
Telephone usage, 80
Telepurchasing, 25-26, 35 (n. 2)
Testimonials, 68, 98, 107-108, 129,
    151-152, 159-160, 281
Time, use of
    planning, 289, 291-295
    records, 295
    scheduling, 289-291
Today's Living, 96
Toledo Scale Company, 62 (and n. 1)
"Too busy" problem, 68, 176, 184
Trailers, 164
"Transforming Idea," the, 3-4

Transparencies, 164
Transviewer, 163

V

Victor Adding Machine Company, 57
Visual aids
    advantages, 152-153, 156-157, 293
    described, 162-165
    use in presentations, 157-165, 284
Vocabulary
    building, 73-76
    kinetic and latent, 74
    role in selling, 74-75
Voice, in selling, 78-80

W

Walk and Talk Magazine, 57
Wanamaker, John, 20
WAVE-TV, word tips, 79
Weiner, Norbert, 137 (n. 3)
Wholesaler's representative, 26-27
Williams and Myers, 157
Wittich, Walter Arno, 161 (n. 2)
Wyandot Products Company, attitude
    example, 305 (and n. 3)

Y

Yankee peddler, 19